# Contents

# Illustrations and Maps

# DECEMBER 1941

## Twelve Days that Began a World War

Evan Mawdsley

YALE UNIVERSITY PRESS
NEW HAVEN AND LONDON

First published in paperback in 2012



For information about this and other Yale University Press publications, please contact:

US Office: sales.press@yale.edu yalebooks.com
Europe Office: sales@yaleup.co.uk www.yalebooks.co.uk

Set in Minion by IDSUK (DataConnection) Ltd
Printed in Great Britain by TJ International Ltd, Padstow, Cornwall

Library of Congress Cataloging-in-Publication Data

Mawdsley, Evan, 1945–
December 1941 / Evan Mawdsley.
p. cm.
Includes bibliographical references and index.
ISBN 978-0-300-15445-0
1. World War, 1939–1945. 2. World War, 1939–1945–United States. I. Title.
D743.M365 2011
940.53–dc23

2011021435

ISBN 978-0-300-18787-8 (pbk)

10 9 8 7 6 5 4 3 2 1

**Maps**

# Terms and Abbreviations

ABC: American-British (military staff) Conversations, January–March 1941
AG: Army Group (*Front*)
B-17: Boeing 'Flying Fortress' four-engined bomber
BatDiv: Battleship Division (US)
BJ: British designation for decrypted diplomatic correspondence
CAST (Cavite): US Navy communications unit in Manila
CIGS: Chief of the Imperial General Staff (Britain)
C-in-C: Commander-in-Chief
CINCAF: C-in-C, Asiatic Fleet (US)
CINCPAC: C-in-C, Pacific Fleet (US)
CNO: Chief of Naval Operations (US)
COS: Chiefs of Staff Committee (Britain)
DF: (radio) direction finding
FEAF: Far East Air Force (US)
FECB: Far East Combined Bureau (Britain)
*FHO*: *Fremde Heere Ost* (Foreign Armies East) (Germany)
*Gaimushō*: Foreign Ministry (Japan)
GHQ Far East: General Headquarters, Far East (Britain)
HYPO (Hawaii): US Navy communications unit at Pearl Harbor
IGHQ: Imperial General Headquarters (Japan)
JIC: Joint Intelligence Committee (Britain)
KROHCOL: Kroh Column (Britain)
MAGIC: information from intercepted communications (US)
MAUERWALD: HQ of German Army, East Prussia
NCO: non-commissioned officer
*OKH*: *Oberkommando des Heeres* (Army High Command) (Germany)

*OKW*: *Oberkommando der Wehrmacht* (Armed Forces High Command) (Germany)
OPNAV: Office of Chief of Naval Operations (US)
ORANGE: codename for Japan (US)
PatWing: Patrol Wing (US)
PBY: Consolidated 'Catalina' flying boat
POW: Prisoner of War
PURPLE: codename for Japanese Foreign Ministry Type 'B' Cipher Machine (US)
RAF: Royal Air Force
*RAM*: *Reichsaussenminister* (Reich Foreign Minister)
RN: Royal Navy
SPENAVO: Special Naval Observer (US)
*Stavka*: Supreme Headquarters (Russia)
ULTRA: information from intercepted communications (Britain)
USAAF: US Army Air Force
USAFFE: US Army Forces in Far East
USN: US Navy
WOLFSSCHANZE: HQ of German Armed Forces (East Prussia)

# Introduction

'This is a new war, with Russia victorious, Japan in and America in up to the neck.'[1] Winston Churchill was speaking with his personal doctor, Sir Charles Wilson. The two men stood on the open deck of a British battleship, ploughing through a heavy Atlantic swell. The date was 16 December 1941, and the Prime Minister and his party of statesmen and soldiers were three days into their voyage across the Atlantic. Their destination was Chesapeake Bay, from where they would travel on to Washington for momentous meetings.

Some moments in history are pivotal, but very few are pivotal on a global scale. The first days of December 1941 can truly be called 'world-shaking'. Two weeks earlier, on 1 December, the 'Allies' had amounted to the British Empire and Soviet Russia. In reality these old enemies were more companions in misfortune than allies, and their situation was grim. For two years Hitler's Wehrmacht had won victory after victory in Europe; for five months his troops had hacked out unbroken success in Russia. German armies had now reached the outskirts of Moscow and Leningrad, and seemed set to plunge into the Caucasus. Pessimists thought the Red Army had suffered total defeat; optimists saw it as a spent force, able to undertake only desperate defence. Britain was besieged and bankrupt, its oceanic trade threatened by the U-boats and some of its vital Middle Eastern possessions under threat. France and much of Europe were occupied. Italy and some smaller states had thrown in their lot with Nazi Germany. There seemed no conceivable way for British forces to set foot on the Continent again, let alone shake Hitler's hold there.

In Asia, meanwhile, an aggressive, militarist Japan seemed poised to pick off Britain's Asian colonies. Indeed it was on this first day of December that the Imperial Conference in Tokyo approved for the final time the decision for war and the deployment of attack forces.

The United States was still not directly involved in hostilities in either hemisphere. Many Americans opposed fighting a foreign war, even against Hitler. President Franklin D. Roosevelt could have no confidence that Congress would vote to declare war on the aggressor states, and he had no wish to take a divided nation into battle.

This book is about Monday, 1 December, and the eleven days that followed it. By Friday, 12 December, Churchill's 'new war' had taken shape. By then it was clear to the more far-sighted leaders on both sides of the conflict that Nazi Germany's first campaign against Russia, Operation BARBAROSSA, had failed. The Soviet Union had not been overthrown in a few months – as Hitler and his generals had expected. From 6 December onwards the Red Army had mounted sudden and successful counterattacks in front of Moscow. Hitler's grey legions proved not to be, after all, invincible. The new British Army gained its first full-scale victory against the Panzers in North Africa, overwhelming Rommel and driving his German and Italian forces back from Tobruk and the Egyptian frontier. In these same days, too, America was plunged into the 'European War'.

Above all, on 11 December Nazi Germany declared war on the United States – not the other way around. Hitler made his declaration, furthermore, after Japan had delivered surprise attacks against American (and British) territory. The people of the United States were suddenly committed – 'up to the neck' – to a global war effort. Winston Churchill famously recalled the night he heard the news of the Japanese attack: 'I went to bed and slept the sleep of the saved and thankful.'[2] Events both in the Pacific and in Russia would indeed transform Britain's chances of surviving and even of overcoming Hitler and the Third Reich. By 12 December the outlines of a 'grand alliance' were becoming visible. On that day Foreign Secretary Anthony Eden arrived in Russia for the first high-level political talks with Stalin, and Churchill departed London for Scotland and the battleship that would take him to consult with President Roosevelt.

The 'new war', however, also had a dark side. Victories in Russia were matched by defeats in Southeast Asia and the Pacific. For all Churchill's relief on the night of 7–8 December, Japan began the war with a series of stunning victories. The Army and Navy of Imperial Japan proved to be far more powerful than most outsiders imagined, and the forces of the British Empire and the United States far weaker. The Japanese achieved strategic and tactical surprise, despite the impossibility of concealing the preparations for their broad-ranging offensive operations, and despite their opponents' extraordinary knowledge – thanks to codebreaking – of some of their innermost secrets. Why this happened is one of the main themes of my book.

Another adverse aspect – for the Allies – of the 'new war' was the fruitless shift of resources to Asia to deal with this new threat. This would undo, for a time, the military success of the British in their main combat theatre, North Africa. More broadly, it would take over a year for the new 'Grand Alliance' of Britain, Russia and the United States to transform its strength on paper into military power. Desperate defensive battles would be fought up until the last months of 1942.

Most sinisterly of all, it was in these days of December 1941, when the Russians halted the Blitzkrieg and the Americans entered the war, that the Nazi leadership secretly committed itself to the deportation and destruction of Europe's Jews.

* * *

The story of these twelve days unfolds chronologically. Most chapters in this book cover just one day in time. The order of events was often critical, but global history raises global complexities. Some readers may be aware that Japan's war with Britain and the United States began on Sunday, 7 December, in London and Washington, but on Monday, 8 December, in Tokyo. This book is not written from the point of view of one particular place. In actual fact the calendar day begins in the Central Pacific, on the International Date Line, and so each chapter's description begins with locations nearest that line and then progresses westward. From the Pacific and the Far East the story moves on to Europe, and finally across the Atlantic to America.[3] The following list sets out local time relative to Greenwich Mean Time (GMT).[4]

| | |
|---|---|
| Wake Atoll | +11 hours |
| Japan | +9 hours |
| Hong Kong | +8 hours |
| Philippines | +8 hours |
| Malaya | +7 hours 30 mins |
| Moscow | +3 hours |
| Libya | +2 hours |
| Germany | +2 hours |
| London | +1 hours |
| GMT | 0 |
| Washington | –5 hours |
| Hawaii | –10 hours 30 mins |
| Wake Atoll | –13 hours |

'International History', of which this book is an example, has attractions and challenges, both having to do with travel and research. The British Academy, the Carnegie Trust for the Universities of Scotland, and the late-lamented Faculty of Arts at the University of Glasgow all provided very generous financial help with research trips. Without this assistance the work for this book would not have been possible.

My 'home' libraries at the University of Glasgow and at the National Library of Scotland in Edinburgh provided an ideal base and boast rich collections. For access to the latter, I am especially grateful to Tania Konn-Roberts (at Glasgow) and to the late John Erickson (for his bequests to the NLS).

While writing this book I have had the good fortune to spend time in libraries and archives that are both well-organised and welcoming. I must give my thanks to the staff of the following institutions, who were unfailingly helpful and courteous, both in email correspondence and during my visits: the National Archives at Kew in London; the British Library at St Pancras and at Colindale; the University Library at Cambridge; the Liddell Hart Centre for Military Archives at King's College London; the Imperial War Museum in London and at Duxford (where Stephen Walton was of especial help); the Churchill Archive Centre in Cambridge (special thanks to Allen Packwood and Andrew Riley); the Borthwick Institute for Archives at the University of York; and Special Collections at the Cadbury Research Library of the University of Birmingham. (For material at Birmingham I am indebted to Lady Avon for permission to quote from the papers of Anthony Eden.)

In the US I received courteous help from staff at a number of places: the National Archives at College Park, Maryland; the Operational Archive Section of the Naval Historical and Heritage Command, at the Washington Navy Yard; the Library of Congress; and the Franklin D. Roosevelt Presidential Library in Hyde Park, New York. In Germany I greatly benefited from the help of staff at the Bundesarchiv-Militärarchiv; for facilitating my work at the BA-MA I am grateful to Jana Brabant.

Personal hospitality was especially important for long-range research. Dick and Pat Parker encouraged my trip to Japan and organised me once I arrived there. Although my visit to the Far East did not relate directly to the current project in terms of paper sources, I was able to go to the Japanese Naval Academy at Eta Jima, and to Yokosuka; above all, I developed a stronger 'feel' for that extraordinary country and its remarkable people. Jürgen Förster did much to make my visit to Freiburg im Breisgau enjoyable. A long expedition to America would have been much more difficult, and certainly much less pleasant, had it not been for the hospitality of my old friends Bill Schauman and Marta Brenden of Silver Spring, Maryland.

Historians and other individuals with an interest in my topic have been unfailingly generous with their help, and with their painstaking responses to my questions. In many cases this has led to long-term friendship. I would mention Simon Ball, Anthony Best, Robert Citino, John Ferris, Jürgen Förster, Gabriel Gorodetsky, Alexander Hill, Steve Kepher, Craig Luther, Joe Maiolo, Alexander Marshall, Philips O'Brien, Geoff Roberts, Ben Shepherd and Thomas Titura. Duncan Campbell provided advice – genuinely invaluable – on web searches for primary sources.

My editor at Yale, Heather McCallum, went to great effort to coax out of me what I hope has ended up as a readable book, Rachael Lonsdale patiently saw it through production, and my copy editor made invaluable contributions. I am grateful also for the suggestions of the two anonymous readers.

My patient family – Gillian, Michael and Robyn – put up with unsociable hours, frequent trips away from home, and occasional preoccupation. They were throughout 2008–11 an essential counterbalance to 288 hours in December 1941. This book is dedicated, with love and gratitude, to them.

CHAPTER 1

# MONDAY, 1 DECEMBER
# Japan, Germany and the Coming World War

*At the moment our Empire stands at the threshold of glory or oblivion.*

General Tōjō Hideki

*It is extremely unfortunate that Chancellor Hitler is not in the city, which makes it impossible to contact him. . . . As far as the German authorities are concerned, we understand Japan's desire for haste. Therefore I will do my best to secure as early an interview as possible.*

Joachim von Ribbentrop to Ambassador Ōshima

## Tokyo

The Imperial Conference of 1 December was a starting point, not a turning point. The nineteen solemn men who gathered in the Imperial Palace in central Tokyo for two hours on that Monday afternoon met to ratify decisions made weeks and months earlier – and to light a very short fuse. Their empire was already at war; the Japanese Army had been fighting a full-scale conflict in China for four years. The leaders of Japan now planned another campaign, covering a vast new territory, and taking on stronger and more fearsome enemies from Europe and America. They had made all but the final preparations. Ambassadors abroad had been put on alert. Ships and troops had been readied and on the move for weeks. The Imperial Japanese Army and the Imperial Japanese Navy were set to take up their final attack positions, and to strike.

The statesmen and generals faced one another behind two long tables. The Emperor sat, silent throughout, on a raised seat before a gold screen. Tōjō

Hideki, whom the Emperor had accepted as Prime Minister six weeks earlier, opened the solemn event. He was an efficient, incisive, 'political' general who did not suffer fools gladly; his army nickname was *kamisori* ('the razor'). The future subject of a thousand grotesque caricatures, Tōjō was a man of mild appearance despite the military man's shaved scalp; he wore horn-rimmed spectacles and had a generous moustache. He reminded his listeners that on 5 November the previous Imperial Conference had resolved to follow a 'two-track' policy. Japan would prepare for war, but continue talks with the Americans in Washington. These negotiations, he noted – not without some inner satisfaction – had failed to bring the desired results: 'Under the circumstances, our empire has no alternative but to begin war against the United States, Great Britain, and the Netherlands in order to resolve the present crisis and assure survival.'

Five officials then reported on the Empire's readiness. Foreign Minister Tōgō Shigenori will feature more than once in our story, because of his correspondence with Japan's embassies. Tōgō was a grey-haired, distinguished, professional diplomat. A German speaker with a German wife, he had been Ambassador in Berlin in 1937–38. At the meeting on 1 December he outlined in more detail the course of the talks with the Americans. He repeated Tōjō's judgement that the final response of US Secretary of State Cordell Hull, made five days earlier, had been unacceptable. Admiral Nagano Osami, the Chief of the Naval General Staff, spoke for both the Army and Navy. He reported that Japan's forces had carried through the required preparations for offensive war: 'We are now in a position to begin these operations, according to predetermined plans, as soon as we receive the Imperial command to resort to force.' America, Britain and the Netherlands had improved their defences in recent months, Nagano explained. 'However, we judge that their present state of preparedness is not greatly different from what we had anticipated; and hence we are convinced that it will present no hindrance to our launching military and naval operations'. Tōjō himself then described Japanese public opinion, which he deemed ready to accept the challenge of extended war – extended beyond the four-year conflict with China – and he reported that preparations had been made to deal with any dissidents. The Finance Minister stated that the fiscal capacity of the empire was sufficient to support a war against Britain and the United States 'for any number of years', despite challenges. Finally, the Minister of Agriculture gave similar assurances about food supply.

The five presentations were followed by some questions by Hara Yoshimichi, the President of the Privy Council. Hara listened and spoke on behalf of the

Emperor. The responses given to him were reassuring, and Hara declared his conviction that war was unavoidable.

General Tōjō brought the Conference to a conclusion:

> At the moment our Empire stands at the threshold of glory or oblivion. We tremble with fear in the presence of His Majesty. We subjects are keenly aware of the great responsibility we must assume from this point on. Once His Majesty reaches a decision to commence hostilities, we will all strive to repay our obligations to him, bring the Government and the military ever closer together, resolved that the nation united will go on to victory, make an all-out effort to achieve our war aims, and [set] His Majesty's mind at ease.

The man who sat before the gilded screen remained silent but content. The Chief of the Army General Staff, General Sugiyama Hajime, made a note in his diary: 'The Emperor nodded in agreement to each explanation that was made and displayed not the slightest anxiety. He seemed to be in a good mood. We were filled with awe.'[1]

* * *

What had led Japan to the brink of war with Britain and America? Underlying causes were the excessive role of the Japanese military and radical nationalists, and the dominance, even in mainstream civilian political life, of authoritarian nationalism. Looming in the background was the costly four-year war in China, begun in 1937 and still nowhere near a satisfactory end. In Tokyo's view the conflict's resolution was blocked by the unreasonable support of America and Britain for the government of Chiang Kai-shek.

Then Hitler's victories in Europe, during the summer of 1940, created a radically changed, and unexpected, state of affairs. The German Wehrmacht had defeated and occupied France and the Netherlands, a stunning victory with reverberations in Southeast Asia; French Indochina and the resource-rich Dutch East Indies were now cut off and defenceless. Even Britain was in no position to protect its faraway possessions; the United Kingdom was under threat of invasion, and Italy had opened a new Mediterranean front. Japanese nationalists and militarists now believed that they lived in a changing world where the old European imperialist powers were being replaced by a 'New Order' (a term widely used in Japan). Japan would secure its own place as a great world power by securing control – directly or indirectly – over the economic wealth of Southeast Asia.

Japan's relations with America were more complex. Unlike Britain or the Netherlands, the presence of the United States in the Far East was limited. The main US possessions were the Philippine Islands, which Washington had announced would be made independent in the late 1940s, and which in any event were of no great economic interest to Japan. The United States, however, possessed global economic power; its powerful Navy had rivalled that of Japan throughout the 1920s and 1930s; and it served, especially after the summer of 1940, as the backstop of the British Empire.

A spiralling series of actions transformed tensions and expectations into direct confrontation and then war. The Japanese government chose sides in September 1940, when it signed the Tripartite Pact with Nazi Germany and Fascist Italy. The three states declared that they would work together for the New Order in Europe and Asia. More specifically, they aimed to deter the neutral United States from intervening in either arena. Under the terms of the Tripartite Pact if Washington were to make war on any of the signatories, then the others would provide full political, economic and military assistance.[2] The Tripartite Pact was a document of the greatest importance. It led, ultimately, to the declaration of war by Germany and Italy against the United States on 11 December 1941.

President Roosevelt's government opposed many of Japan's policies. It objected to the war in China, it feared an encroachment on the European colonies, it disliked Tokyo's open orientation towards Nazi Germany and Fascist Italy, and it understood that the United States was the target of the Tripartite Pact. The Japanese government of Prince Konoe (Tōjō's predecessor), however, and not without some inconsistency, thought that it might be possible to lessen the tension between the two countries. In April 1941 the Japanese Ambassador in Washington, Nomura Kichisaburō, began secret talks with Secretary of State Hull. Indeed, Hull now became the main spokesman for the Western powers in Asia; the embattled British were very eager to obtain American support and the London-based Dutch government in exile followed the British lead. However, the gulf between the Japanese and US positions proved too wide to be bridged.

The final slide into war began at the start of July 1941, when an Imperial Conference in Tokyo confirmed that the main thrust of Japanese policy would be 'taking steps to advance south'. Thailand and French Indochina were identified as the first areas required for an advance into what the Japanese called the 'Southern Area' (*Nan'yō*). No measure was excluded in carrying out these plans: 'our empire will not be deterred by the possibility of being involved in a war with Great Britain and the United States.'[3] Later that month Japanese forces moved into southern Indochina, and began preparing air, land and sea bases for further movement (Japanese troops had been present in northern Indochina since

September 1940). To the surprise of the Japanese, the Roosevelt Administration retaliated immediately with very strong economic countermeasures, imposing an embargo on the shipment of oil and other raw materials, and freezing Japanese assets in the US. These American measures were also taken up by the British and the Dutch.

The trade embargo was a powerful diplomatic weapon, but it was based on Washington's calculation that Japan was weak and could be forced to make concessions. In reality the embargo created the most dangerous of situations. Tokyo could see that the empire would, month by month, become weaker relative to its enemies, as its economy wilted under the embargo and America built up its own armed forces. Tokyo now came to believe that a gamble on war was better than national destruction and humiliation. In early September the Japanese government under Prince Konoe resolved to follow the 'twin-track' policy, one being diplomacy, the other, war. A choice between the two would be made in the last days of October 1941.

As the moment of decision approached, Prince Konoe lost his nerve and resigned. In the middle of October the Emperor appointed General Tōjō to form a new government in his place, and with this act it is clear – from hindsight – that the Imperial Palace had concluded war was unavoidable. The Imperial Conference held on 5 November was the first presided over by Tōjō. It resolved to continue the twin-track policy, but with more resolute preparation for war: 'The time for resorting to force is set at the beginning of December, and the Army and Navy will complete preparations for operations.' Midnight on 1 December was designated as the final point by which a diplomatic breakthrough could be achieved.[4]

This was the background for the last stages of the Hull-Nomura talks in mid-November in Washington. Neither side made concessions. The American government did contemplate a temporary easing of the tension with a 'live and let live' arrangement – the so-called *modus vivendi*. This would have gained time to strengthen the US military presence in the Far East. But President Roosevelt – aware of Japan's fundamental inflexibility – decided against it. The Japanese, for their part, were keenly aware that delay would only make them weaker. On 26 November the Secretary of State presented to the Japanese representatives a memorandum setting out the final US position.

The famous 'Hull Note' began with a statement of idealistic principles of international relations. It then went on to state that there could be no general normalisation of Japanese-American relations or any slackening of the economic embargo until Japan agreed to withdraw its troops from China and French Indochina and until it rejected the Tripartite Pact. The Hull Note was in no sense an 'ultimatum', but the Japanese government found its terms intolerable. As Prime Minister Tōjō told the Imperial Conference on 1 December, 'This not only belittled the dignity of our empire and made it impossible to harvest the fruits of the China Incident, but also threatened the very existence of our empire.'[5] Nor was this outcome unexpected by the majority of the Japanese leadership, especially the Army and Navy. Over recent months the Japanese military had made extensive preparation for full-scale war in the Pacific and the Far East.

On Monday, 1 December, as the statesmen met in Tokyo, the generals and admirals of Japan were busily undertaking their final practical measures. At 0000 hours, the Imperial Navy changed the radio call signs of all its ships and sea-going commands. Foreign monitoring stations eavesdropped on Japanese radio traffic; the adjustment blocked their attempts to pinpoint individual vessels and to untangle the Imperial Navy's chain of command.

After the Imperial Conference meeting on 1 December the Army section of Imperial General Headquarters (IGHQ) despatched orders to General Count Terauchi Hisaichi: 'The Commander-in-Chief, Southern Army [Terauchi], will begin invasion operations on 8 December.'[6] The Imperial Navy would send out its own, later more famous, executive order on the following day.

* * *

The Japanese armed forces had towards the end of 1940 begun long-term preparations for a possible move into the Southern Area. In October of that year the Army's 5th Division – a formation which will play a major part in our story, with its landing in the Kra Isthmus of Thailand – began training in amphibious operations near Shanghai. Similar training for three more divisions commenced in South China before the end of 1940. In January 1941 the Japanese Army set up a special institute on Formosa (now Taiwan) to study warfare in the tropics. From July these measures suddenly took on a greater urgency.

The Army had to balance the concentration of its divisions between Manchuria, China and Southeast Asia. The Navy had to decide whether its main fleets would operate in the Central Pacific or the South China Sea. The planners of both services needed to take account of the seasons, and with them the changing weather. Offensive operations across the South China Sea, the approach route to Thailand and Malaya, had to be started by December; after that, the full-strength northeast monsoon of January and February made movement too risky. Meanwhile, major operations in Southeast Asia, including the Dutch East Indies, needed to be completed before March 1942 and the end of winter, because at that time conditions would make operations by the Soviet Army – or against it – possible. The Japanese planners estimated that three months were required for the 'Southern Operation', so December 1941 had been fixed as the latest starting date.[7]

In the middle of August 1941 the Army and Navy had agreed on the basic strategic shape which an advance to the south, if it occurred, might take. The programme was ambitious in the extreme. Potential objectives were Thailand, the Dutch East Indies, the American possessions of the Philippines and Guam, and the British colonies of Malaya, Burma and North Borneo. The challenge to the Empire of Japan was immense, but its forces were limited. The Army already had huge commitments on the Asian mainland, fighting a war in China and facing down the Red Army in Manchuria. The pool of available merchant shipping was not unlimited. The Imperial Navy, as a battle force, would have to both support invasions in Southeast Asia and deal with the American fleet in the Central Pacific.

The plan was much more ambitious than the governments of Britain and the United States imagined possible. The Japanese military had decided that it would not simply take cautious steps against weak and neutral Thailand or the orphaned European (French and Dutch) colonies. Japan would not even only attack one great power. It would make war on both Britain and the United States.

There was a logic to this audacious plan: the logic of geography. The British and Dutch colonies contained the rich economic resources that Japan coveted, while those of the US did not. However, the planners in Tokyo could not rely on America remaining neutral if Japan invaded the British and the Dutch territories, and above all they could not accept the risk that the Philippine Islands might become a base for enemy forces. The north-south shipping channel between the Philippines and the Chinese mainland was about to become a vital artery. Japan was preparing to send invasion fleets across the South China Sea against Thailand and the British and Dutch colonies. The wealth of the newly-captured regions of Southeast Asia would need to be sent back by sea to Japan. Shipping in either direction could be choked off by enemy warships and aircraft based in the Philippines. In addition, Luzon Island in the Philippines, although 1,150 miles from the southern Japanese mainland, was also the closest place from which American (and British) operations could be mounted against the home islands. Luzon might provide a forward base for the American and British fleets, or even – with rapidly advancing aviation technology – for air raids against Japan. So the invasion of the Southern Area and the total security of the empire required Japanese control of the Philippines; and control of the Philippines required war with America.

The planning staff debated whether it would be better to start with the British forces in Malaya and Burma, and then attack the Americans, or whether they should finish off the Philippines first and then move on the British and Dutch further south. In a piece of further strategic audacity they decided to take on operations in two directions *at the same time*.[8]

The outline of the Southern Operation fell into two major parts, with each part further broken down into phases. The very first phase of Part One comprised the simultaneous operations carried out on or just after *X-nichi* ('X-Day'), the first day of war: these included the occupation of neutral Thailand, landings in northern Malaya, and air attacks on the island of Luzon in the Philippines. This phase also took in the capture of American possessions of Wake and Guam in the Central Pacific – islands on the supply route to the Philippines. The Japanese Army in China would meanwhile begin an attack on the valuable British enclave at Hong Kong.

The next phase included the landing of small detachments of the Japanese Army on Luzon, in order to secure air fields. This would take place during the week after *X-nichi*, once American air power there had been neutralised. The full-scale invasion of Luzon – in division strength and from several directions – was set for two weeks after *X-nichi*. During this phase other Japanese forces would drive south through Malaya to the British 'fortress' at Singapore.

Part Two of the Southern Operation comprised the invasion of southern Burma and the Dutch East Indies.

The general strategy was confirmed by the armed forces on 20 October (shortly after the creation of the Tōjō government). Final approval of the military plan was delivered by the Imperial Conference on 5 November.

Plan began to become reality in November. The day after the meeting of the Imperial Conference, an order was issued for the Army branch of IGHQ to create its command structure for the attack on the 'Southern Area'. The Southern Army of General Terauchi would have its headquarters at Saigon in French Indochina. Terauchi was to concentrate his main forces in Indochina, South China, Formosa and the Ryukyu Islands and await orders to move.[9] Under him would be four Army-level commands, and four lieutenant generals – Yamashita, Homma, Iida and Imamura. Each of the Japanese field 'armies' consisted of two or three divisions, making them comparable to little more than a corps in the military establishments of most other countries. In view of the distances involved and the limited amount of shipping available, even these small forces could only be brought into combat piecemeal, and they would have to be used over and over again.

General Yamashita was to make the first advance, targeted against Malaya, but with his main initial landings in Thailand. The bulk of his 25th Army would assemble in the weeks before the outbreak of war on Hainan Island (an occupied territory off the coast of Southeast China) and in Indochina. Transport ships would carry elements of 5th and 18th Divisions across the South China Sea to the Kra Isthmus in the extreme south of Thailand; the Imperial Guards Division would meanwhile march overland across Thailand from southern Indochina, taking control of the political centres of that country en route. Yamashita's 56th Division was to be held in reserve in Japan. The planners in Tokyo carefully took into account the new factor of air power, and the Army and Navy despatched large numbers of fighters and bombers to southern Indochina to provide support for Yamashita. The objective of General Homma's 14th Army was Luzon in the Philippines. On the eve of the war his two divisions were to assemble on Formosa and the Ryukyu Islands. Army and Navy aircraft would provide long-range support from Formosa.

Terauchi's two other armies would commence major operations after the initial objectives in Thailand, Malaya and Luzon had been secured. General Iida's 15th Army (two divisions) would undertake the invasion of Burma. General Imamura's 18th Army would invade and capture the Dutch East Indies, using divisions that had completed their tasks elsewhere.

The Imperial Japanese Navy, meanwhile, was also readying itself for action. Preparations brought to a head the uneasy relations between the Chief of the Naval General Staff (NGS) and the C-in-C of the main sea-going force, the Combined Fleet. Admiral Nagano Osami at the NGS was in charge of drafting the annual war plan for the Navy, but it was Admiral Yamamoto Isoroku who would have wartime command of the ships and aircraft of Combined Fleet.[10] Admiral Nagano was based ashore in Tokyo. Admiral Yamamoto flew his flag aboard the battleship *Nagato*; the big warship was usually anchored in Saeki Bay, near the entrance to the Inland Sea and around 475 miles west of Tokyo.

In 1941, before the Pacific War had started, Combined Fleet was organised into six numbered fleets of warships, and two 'air fleets'.[11] Operation Order No. 1, of 5 November 1941, assigned elements of these fleets to specific tasks in the projected grand campaign.[12] The geographical objectives of the Southern Operation were under British and Dutch control, but the main immediate naval threat – at least at the planning stage – was American. For operations against the US Navy in the Pacific the six aircraft carriers of the 1st Air Fleet of Admiral Nagumo Chūichi were transformed into the Mobile Force, with the addition of two fast battleships and three cruisers. The small 4th Fleet, operating as the South Seas Force, would deal with the central Pacific. The Advanced Force, with most of the 6th Fleet submarines, was assigned to the eastern Pacific.

A second crucial task for Combined Fleet was to support the amphibious operations of the Japanese Army in Thailand, Malaya, the Philippines and the Dutch East Indies, by covering them against the Royal Navy in Singapore and the small US Asiatic Fleet in Manila. To accomplish this, a Southern Force command was set up under Admiral Kondō Nobutake.[13] Southern Force was assigned powerful surface, submarine and air forces. The warship core comprised most of the heavy cruisers of 2nd Fleet (Kondō's pre-war command), reinforced by two fast battleships, some submarines and other vessels. Vital air support was provided by several hundred land-based bombers and fighters of the Navy's 11th Air Fleet, deployed to Formosa and Indochina.

On 7 November 1941 the senior commanders of the Japanese Army and Navy had been given a warning that the start of war against Britain and America was provisionally set for 8 December (Japanese time). Three days later General Terauchi and Admiral Yamamoto met in Tokyo to agree on the co-ordination of joint Army-Navy operations. On 15 November the Emperor was shown the completed general war plan. On the same day Terauchi issued his main directive. The commanders of the four invasion armies gave out their own orders a week later.[14]

The first transport ship, the 8,400 ton *Kashii Maru*, steamed into the port of Samah (now Sanya) on Hainan Island, off southeastern China, on 25 November. Sixteen more big transports would arrive, one by one, at Samah over the next week. Other groups of warships and transports intended for the invasions in Southeast Asia and the Pacific assembled at ports and anchorages: Saigon and Camranh Bay in Indochina, Mako in the Pescadores Islands, Hahajima in the Bonins, Amami Ōshima in the Ryukyus, and Truk and Palau in the Carolines. Surprise was a crucial element of the plan. Deployment of ships and planes to the final attacking positions was to come as late as possible.

* * *

On 1 December, the same day that the Imperial Conference ratified the decision for war, and the Army and Navy began their sprint to offensive deployments, the Japanese Foreign Ministry – the *Gaimushō* – pushed ahead with its own covert diplomatic preparations. The embassy in London and consulates in Hong Kong, Singapore, Manila and Batavia,[15] were instructed to destroy some or all of their cipher machines and code material.[16]

In the month preceding 1 December the Foreign Ministry had taken steps to deal with the complex and dangerous situation in which Japan found itself. On the one hand, Foreign Minister Tōgō attempted to supervise negotiations in Washington in order to achieve a favourable outcome on the diplomatic 'track'. On the other, the *Gaimushō* had to make technical steps to prepare at least for a major break in relations with Western powers and possibly for general war.

The Japanese Foreign Ministry kept in close contact with its representatives abroad using communications facilities which it assumed to be completely secure. Tōgō attempted to put pressure on Nomura to achieve results by making clear to him, in a number of encrypted messages, how close Japan was to war. He sent the Ambassador the details of the current Japanese negotiating position on 4 November, and on the following day informed him that the deadline for achieving diplomatic results was the 25th. (The government had in fact designated midnight on 1 December as the deadline, but Tōgō perceived the elderly Nomura to be slow-moving.) On 22 November Tokyo extended the deadline available to its Washington representatives – Nomura having been joined by Special Envoy Kurusu Saburō – to the 29th. But Tōgō explained that this was the final deadline and he added, ominously, 'After that things are automatically going to happen'. On the 28th Tokyo informed Nomura and Kurusu that negotiations were over, but told them that they should try for the next few days to give the impression that this was not the case.[17]

Meanwhile technical preparations relating to the whole network of Japanese diplomatic posts abroad had proceeded apace. It was vital that new enemies not lay their hands on secret correspondence nor have the opportunity to examine Japanese cipher machines and codebooks. The Foreign Ministry also had to make provision for sending secret instructions to its overseas representatives once normal channels had been blocked, either by the action of foreign powers or as a result of the self-destruction of code materials. On 19 November, the *Gaimushō* sent out, in encrypted form, two messages which set up a new alarm system. The first message explained that a warning would be provided if diplomatic relations with certain foreign countries were near the point of being broken off, or if access to normal communication channels was about to be lost. Coded messages would be sent via the usual daily short-wave Japanese-language news broadcast. The phrase 'east wind rain' would mean relations with the US were in danger, 'north wind cloudy' applied the same warning to the USSR, and 'west wind clear' referred to relations with the British Empire. If these messages were heard, all cryptographic material and secret documents were to be destroyed. The second circular specified that shorter coded versions, 'east', 'north', or 'west', would be repeated five times at the beginning and end of information broadcasts should a warning be necessary.

On 27 November, a little more than week after the 'winds' set-up messages, the *Gaimushō* sent another encrypted message to a number of its overseas embassies and consulates, which laid out an additional emergency communications system. Ostensibly normal messages, sent by commercial radio or telegraph links, would include a selection of code words. To differentiate these messages from others, they would end with the English word 'stop'; later on this system would be known as the 'stop' code or 'hidden word' code.[18]

Ironically, all these Japanese efforts to control diplomatic activity and secure communications facilites were potentially counterproductive. The Tokyo government had prided itself on its advanced communications facilities, with systems of encryption which it believed to be 'unbreakable' (hence, in part, the need to protect them in the event of conflict). The most important device used by the Foreign Ministry to exchange highly confidential messages with its major representatives abroad was the Type 'B' Cipher Machine, introduced in 1939. But as it turned out, US Army code experts had in 1940 developed the ability to decrypt messages produced by that machine, which they codenamed PURPLE. (Decrypted messages, distributed only to the most senior US government and military leaders, were known by the codename MAGIC.) The Americans shared their codebreaking methods with the British from the beginning of 1941.

As a result of this extraordinary intelligence coup the British and Americans had read the encrypted Japanese diplomatic messages sent in November, usually within a few days of transmission. They knew about Tokyo's limited timetable of negotiations. They were aware of Japanese communications contingency planning (the 'winds' and 'stop' codes, the destruction of code machines and cryptographic material). It was clear from these revelations that Tokyo anticipated a major confrontation or even war occurring in the very near future.[19] Even more extraordinary information would become available in the next few days, as the codebreakers began to intercept messages exchanged between individuals at the highest levels of the Japanese, German and Italian governments.

## Berlin

On the evening of 1 December, the Japanese Ambassador to Berlin, Ōshima Hiroshi, drove to the offices of the Reich Foreign Minister at Wilhelmstrasse,

74–76. The square-jawed little Ambassador was a general in the Japanese Army. The son of another general who had studied the German military tradition and lived in Germany, Ōshima was an enthusiastic supporter of close links with the Third Reich. He spoke German, and had served as military attaché in Berlin from 1934 to 1939, before returning to head the embassy in early 1941. Over the next four years General Ōshima would be the unwitting source, through his intercepted reports home, of some of the most important intelligence received by the Allies about Nazi military preparations.[20]

Then there was Foreign Minister Joachim von Ribbentrop. The *RAM* (*Reichsaussenminister*) cut a handsome figure, but was notable for a personality that was, even by Nazi standards, arrogant and overbearing (although he seems, nonetheless, to have got on well enough with Ōshima). Ribbentrop was a former champagne salesman who had become a foreign policy adviser to Hitler, and then Ambassador to Britain and (from 1938) Foreign Minister. At the core of Ribbentrop's foreign policy was an abiding contempt for, and detestation of, the British, against whose empire he tried to unite as many enemies as possible, from the Russians in 1939 to the Japanese in 1941.

This Monday evening Ōshima brought to Ribbentrop momentous news and an urgent request. There was a strong possibility, he announced, that war would break out in the very near future between Japan, Britain and the United States. His government requested that Germany and Italy join Japan in this war, in accordance with their commitments under the Tripartite Pact, and that they agree not to sign an armistice or a peace treaty with Britain or the US without mutual consent. The Tripartite Pact was a very brief document, and it did not necessarily encompass Japan's current intentions. The key clause (in Article 3) was the following: '[Germany, Italy and Japan] undertake to assist one another with all political, economic and military means, in the event one of the three contracting powers *is attacked* by a power at present not involved in the European war or in the Chinese-Japanese conflict.'[21]

Ribbentrop assured his visitor that he understood the desire for haste but said that the Reich government could not immediately fulfil the Japanese request: 'It is extremely unfortunate that Chancellor Hitler is not in the city, which makes it impossible to contact him.' The Foreign Minister explained that he hoped to confer with the Führer on the following Thursday (4 December), but warned that he might not have the opportunity to do so until Friday. Ribbentrop spoke positively about extending German and Italian support to Japan, but he asked Ambassador Ōshima not to communicate this to his government until Hitler's decision was known. The Ambassador dutifully sent off a report of this meeting to Tokyo.[22]

When Ambassador Ōshima visited Ribbentrop that Monday evening he was acting on urgent instructions sent from Japan. These instructions, in turn, were based on proposals made by Foreign Minister Tōgō at the 'Liaison Conference' held in Tokyo late on Saturday afternoon, 29 November.[23] The conference approved the proposed measures, and on Sunday, Tōgō sent a message to Ōshima in Berlin confirming that the Washington talks had failed, and requesting that he arrange an interview with Hitler and Ribbentrop. The German leaders were to be told that Britain and the US were planning military moves in East Asia. 'To meet this,' Tōgō explained, 'we too have been compelled to move troops, and it is greatly to be feared that an armed collision will occur and we shall find ourselves in a state of war with BRITAIN and AMERICA. You should add that this may happen sooner than is expected.'[24] Germany was to be asked to join the war against America, and not to make a separate peace. Tōgō instructed Ōshima to forward essentially the same message to Ambassador Horikiri Zenbei, in Rome; Horikiri was to consult Mussolini and Foreign Minister Ciano.

* * *

Forty-eight hours can be a long time, on the brink of a war. Two days earlier, on Friday evening, 28 November, Ōshima had had a quite different conversation with Ribbentrop about the international situation. At this Friday meeting the Ambassador informed the Reich Foreign Minister – not for the last time – that the Hull-Nomura talks in Washington had broken down. Ribbentrop responded with probing questions about what Japan's next concrete steps would be. Ōshima was, in fact, not yet fully informed; he did not know that on Sunday Tokyo would tell him that war with Britain and America might happen 'sooner than is expected'. He speculated – and it should be remembered that he was both an ambassador and a senior general in the Japanese Army – that the most likely military developments would be of a preliminary nature, beginning with the Japanese occupation of Thailand and Dutch Borneo, to secure oil and forward bases. Britain was more likely to make a military response to these steps than was the United States, Ōshima thought. The Ambassador's suggestions were in line with the opinion of foreign diplomats in Britain, the US and Germany: 'Policy changes,' the Germans concluded, 'could be effected in Japan only step by step.'[25]

The remarkable thing about this Friday meeting, on the 28th, was not General Ōshima's flawed prediction about future military operations. What was really interesting and important was Ribbentrop's response. The Reich Foreign Minister expressed strong hostility to the Americans, and said that he believed they were weak. In the course of the conversation Ribbentrop twice urged a Japanese 'showdown' with America: 'the situation,' he said, 'can never be more favourable to Japan than it was now.' Towards the end of the conversation with Ōshima, Ribbentrop made a commitment: 'Should Japan become engaged in a war against the United States, Germany of course would join the war immediately. There is absolutely no possibility of Germany's entering into a separate peace with the United States under such circumstances. The Führer is determined on that point.' Ribbentrop's loose reading of the Tripartite Pact of September 1940 showed a shift in German policy, which previously had been to keep the US out of the war. Ōshima had dutifully forwarded the substance of the new German commitment to Tokyo in a message dated 29 November.[26]

* * *

No one can ever say with certainty what Adolf Hitler thought or knew, at any given time. But it may be that there is something to be learned from what he said and did not say on the eve of these great events. At the end of November 1941, a number of Axis representatives met in Berlin for a conference organised by von Ribbentrop. On 27–29 November Hitler and his Foreign Minister had a battery of meetings with allies and potential allies. The most important of these was on the 29th, when Hitler spoke at length with Count Galeazzo Ciano, the young Italian Foreign Minister, married to Mussolini's daughter Edda. The Führer's words to Ciano were designed to reassure, but they were probably close to his own real assessment of the situation.[27]

'On the whole,' Hitler told Ciano, 'the war was already won.' He spoke at some length about the situation in Russia, which he thought was progressing favourably.[28] What is surprising – from hindsight – is how little Japan, the Far East or America figured in Hitler's survey of the war situation. Ciano it was, rather than the German dictator, who referred in passing to Japan. Serrano Suñer, the Foreign Minister of Franco's Spain – neutral but pro-Axis – later arrived to join the discussion. At that point the Führer did raise the topic of America; he expressed concern about the security of Spain's Atlantic islands in the event of action by the US Navy. But Hitler's emphasis was on President Roosevelt and America making war on Germany, with a *subsequent* involvement in the war by the Japanese, whose 'situation was not dissimilar to that of Germany'. Hitler did not raise the possibility of Japan attacking Britain or America. To Suñer he also dismissed the war potential of the United States, 'which did not possess the inner power of resistance [*Widerstandskraft*] which characterised some European countries'.[29] This underestimation of America was not just rhetoric to pull the Spain into the Axis; it was a frank expression of one of the German dictator's core beliefs.

The global view and global expectations of Hitler and the German high command in November and December 1941 were complex. Understanding them requires disentangling four different possibilities relating to the two great neutrals – America and Japan – and their entry into the war. The first possibility was war between Germany and the United States, brought about by American support for Britain and especially by the US Navy's involvement in the Atlantic convoy battles. This war might or might not involve Japan, depending on whether or not Tokyo honoured the Tripartite Pact – a decision which could not be predicted with certainty. The second case involved Japanese entry into the war against the USSR, alongside Germany. This development, too, would not necessarily bring the United States into the war, and it might not even lead to an active British-Japanese war. The third possibility was war between Japan and Britain, with a Japanese offensive aimed at Singapore and the resources of the British Empire in Southeast Asia. America might well not go to war even in this event. The final possibility was that Japan would initiate war simultaneously against Britain and the United States.[30]

The first possibility seemed most likely to the Germans. For over a year the words and actions of the American President had been pro-British and anti-German. Beyond some anti-Roosevelt rhetoric, Berlin had not retaliated. An 'undeclared' naval war of sorts had developed as the US Navy began to escort transatlantic convoys in the autumn of 1941. In the last months of the year the German Navy High Command, at least, would argue that it would be better to accept an open war with the Americans than to require the commanders of German submarines and surface raiders to fight the convoy war with one hand tied behind their backs. Ribbentrop's biographer maintains that by October the Reich Foreign Minister and the German admirals had convinced Hitler that, from this point of view, war with the US was inevitable. On the other hand, Ernst von Weizsäcker, who was the most senior career diplomat in Ribbentrop's Foreign Office, thought that the US was in no hurry to get directly involved in Britain's war. He claimed – in his memoirs – that the Foreign Office was a major source of German restraint towards America. According to Propaganda Minister Joseph Goebbels, who had a long talk with Hitler on 21 November, the Führer was himself overconcerned: 'He doesn't underestimate the United States, but neither does he see the entry of the USA into the war as an acute danger. It can't change the situation on the Continent. We sit securely in Europe, and we won't let things slip through our fingers here.'[31]

The second hypothetical case involved Japan entering a war against the USSR. After the surprise invasion of Russia on 22 June 1941, Hitler from time to time expressed a belief that Japan might take part. There was, however, German ambivalence on this matter, on the part of Hitler and of his generals. The initial hope – and expectation – was that Stalin's Russia would collapse in a matter of months. In that eventuality, therefore – as it was put, in the hearing of General Warlimont at the Wehrmacht HQ – 'We don't need grave robbers'.[32]

On balance the leadership in Berlin thought that the most useful target for the Japanese would be not Russia but Germany's long-term enemy, Britain – and this was was the third possibility. If Goebbels' account of his meeting of 21 November is correct, Hitler still believed Japan would enter the war: 'The Führer puts great hopes on Japan. He thinks that perhaps it will enter the war in the foreseeable future [*in absehbarer Zeit*].' Presumably this meant entering the war with Britain, not necessarily war with America. Goebbels provided no further information about Hitler's thoughts, but Ribbentrop's behaviour at the meeting with Ōshima on 28 November strongly suggests that he had reliable sense of Hitler's actual attitude, as a result of conversations with him. Ribbentrop must have been confident that the German dictator was prepared to encourage the Tokyo government to strike against Britain, even if this involved the risk of pulling both Japan and Germany into a war with the United States. The Reich Foreign Minister would hardly have taken this initiative on his own.[33]

As for the fourth possibility, a Japanese war with the United States (as well as with Britain), this would have the advantage, for Germany, of compelling Washington to send ships, planes, troops and supplies to the Pacific. America would be less able to deploy forces in the Atlantic and to send war supplies (as Lend-Lease) to Britain and Russia. But the recollection of Weizsäcker at the Foreign Ministry was that the German leadership did not expect a Japanese attack on the US.[34] Despite what President Roosevelt would say in his condemnations of Hitler after 7 December, the Germans never pressed Tokyo for a direct attack on America. The ideal for the Third Reich – at least in the short term – was a Cold War in the Pacific. A Japanese *threat* of war with the US would keep the Americans from transferring their forces and their war production to Europe; this, indeed, had been the logic behind the Tripartite Pact of September 1940. The danger was that a full-scale Japanese attack might provide President Roosevelt with a 'back door' into open war against Germany.

Whether it fought Russia, Britain or America, Tokyo was for the leaders of the Third Reich still an unknown quantity. Fundamentally, the Nazis regarded the Japanese as racial inferiors. There was, moreover, little evidence as yet that the Japanese armed forces would be any more useful than those of Italy in a modern global war. As late as the end of October 1941, at a naval conference, Hitler had described even the new Tōjō government as 'still too indecisive and reluctant to take action [*noch zu laurig und wenig aktionsfreudig*].'[35]

Hitler, the Reich Foreign Ministry and the Wehrmacht High Command should have had a clearer notion in these last weeks of what was coming. The German embassy in Tokyo had excellent connections with the Japanese armed forces. By October 1941 it had come to the (correct) conclusion that Japan was *not* going to move north against Russia. On 6 November – significantly, the day after the penultimate Imperial Conference – Naval Attaché Admiral Paul Wennecker had accurately reported that Japanese operations in the south would probably begin in the current year.[36] Two weeks later, on 18 November, Ambassador Eugen Ott, himself a military man, told Berlin that he did not think the conflict between Japan and the United States could be resolved peacefully. In view of the fact that a Japanese attack on America would fall outside the defensive terms of the Tripartite Pact, he requested instructions. Information from the Tokyo embassy may have been the source of Hitler's remark to Goebbels on 21 November about Japan entering the war in the 'foreseeable future'. (This might, of course, have meant that Japan intended to go to war with the British Empire alone, rather than Britain and the US.)

On the 22nd, Ott and Military Attaché Colonel Alfred Kretschmer reported – again, accurately – that the Japanese forces would concentrate their strength in Southeast Asia for a simultaneous attack on Thailand, and on British and Dutch Borneo. Furthermore, they claimed that if there were no changes in Washington's negotiating position in the Hull-Nomura talks, the Japanese would also attack the United States in the Philippines. Ott and Kretschmer provided Berlin with the name of the overall commander for the Southern Operation, General Terauchi, and with the identities of his main subordinates. The two Germans, like British and American intelligence officers, had some doubts about what was possible for Tokyo, in view of the limited Japanese ground forces available. A 'quick and decisive Japanese victory' could be expected 'only if there is complete surprise and a sharp concentration of forces on the main targets.'[37]

In this swirl of information and expectation a number of things stand out. Japan had decided on war against both Britain and the United States, and was making thorough political, military and diplomatic preparations. Britain and the United States, as of 1 December, had just had their first warnings that Japan was actively preparing for some kind of drastic action. Germany and Italy did not know about Japan's decision to attack the United States, and were not even clearly informed about the timing of Tokyo's action against Britain. That the Japanese government delayed until the very eve of the war before approaching Berlin and Rome suggests that European partners were less important to Tokyo than the achievement of strategic surprise. There is no evidence that the leaders of the Third Reich thought through – or cared – how the United States might respond to a British-Japanese conflict. They also gave little thought to the possibility of a direct Japanese attack on American territory.

Partly this was because Hitler was, at heart, a rather parochial central European, and because most of his military advisers thought in European terms. For them, East Asia and the Pacific were abstractions. The United States and Japan were only hypothetical participants in the war, and participants whose capabilities could not be clearly assessed. Partly it was because in these days – as we will see in the following chapter – the Germans were preoccupied with two other strategic crises, one in Africa, and one, potentially far more important, in Russia.

CHAPTER 2

## MONDAY, 1 DECEMBER

# The Fight to the Death in Russia

*[T]he expenditure of strength worries us too. But one must summon one's last strength to bring the enemy down.*

General Franz Halder

*Comrade commander, have you heard about the events at Rostov? Breaking up the German offensive against Moscow means more than saving Moscow, but it is only possible to begin a serious defeat of the enemy by active operations, with objectives that are decisive. If we do not do this in the next few days it will be too late.*

General Vasilevskii to General Konev

### East Prussia, Poltava, Rostov

When Adolf Hitler met, one by one, the representatives of his Axis 'partners' in Berlin on 27–29 November he repeatedly stressed that the war was as good as won. 'The resistance that was still being offered in Russia,' he told Count Ciano on the 29th, 'did not come from man but from nature, that is, the weather and the character of the terrain.' On the parts of the front where snow was falling the troops would go into winter quarters. As operations were dependent on supply lines and road and rail communications, further advance would be towards the southeast, into the Caucasus.[1] It is most likely that at this moment, and for a few hours more, the Führer actually believed in this comfortable picture.

But by the beginning of Monday, 1 December, the Russian front and the German high command were in crisis. For the Chief of the German Army General Staff, General Franz Halder, it was to prove a most difficult day, and he recorded the events in his personal war diary. At 4.00 a.m. on Monday morning teleprinter messages had clattered through to the German Army HQ compound (codenamed MAUERWALD) near Angerburg in East Prussia. The messages came from Hitler's own Wehrmacht headquarters (WOLFSSCHANZE), situated around ten miles to the southwest, in woods near Rastenburg. The Führer ordered high-level command changes. He dismissed the veteran C-in-C of Army Group South in Russia, Field Marshal Gerd von Rundstedt, after only the briefest consultation with the C-in-C of the German Army, Field Marshal Walther von Brauchitsch. At the same time he ordered tank reinforcements to be rushed to three front-line Panzer divisions, nearest the Russian city of Rostov.[2]

The crisis had blown up at about the time the German dictator was speaking to Count Ciano, on the 29th. During the morning of that day the 1st SS Division *Leibstandarte Adolf Hitler* – formed from Hitler's bodyguard – had to pull out of Rostov in the face of counterattacks by greater numbers of Soviet troops. The Red Army had achieved its first significant success of the terrible five-month campaign. Rostov had been taken by the *Leibstandarte* on 20 November. Now, after little more than a week, they had been forced to abandon it. Here was something new in the European war: Hitler's armies had not been able to hold a major prize that they had seized.

The confrontation reached the highest echelons of the German leadership, pitting Hitler against von Rundstedt and his subordinate, General Ewald von Kleist, who commanded 1st Panzer Army in front of Rostov. Rundstedt had opposed the risky November dash to Rostov, and now he wanted to establish a solid defensive line well to the west of the city. Kleist, for his part, after giving up Rostov on the 29th, had twice issued orders to withdraw about sixty miles west to the Mius and Sambek Rivers. Hitler – not used to giving up territory in battle – wanted to hold a line halfway between Rostov and the Mius. For him this would be less embarrassing than a deep retreat, and the so-called 'intermediate position' would encourage a renewed attack on Rostov. Hitler put pressure on Field Marshal von Brauchitsch to order Rundstedt to countermand the withdrawal command.

Not realising that the message to cancel Kleist's order effectively came direct from the Führer, Rundstedt replied that he would resign his post if he was not given freedom of action. Hitler took this as direct disobedience by the elderly field marshal, and dismissed him. Just as Rostov was the first German defeat, so the dismissal of Rundstedt was the first time that Hitler had – in wartime – sacked a senior commander. And Rundstedt was very senior and very successful. More than any other German commander he could claim credit for the decisive victory in France in 1940. His removal was, in itself, an admission of the serious faults in the military machine of the Third Reich. (Indeed, news of Rundstedt's replacement was not allowed to leak out in the German press until towards the end of December.)

There was an element of misunderstanding in this exchange – aside from Rundstedt's ignorance of just whom he was dealing with. Despite access to teleprinters, telephones and radio, the parties to the discussion were still separated by a distance of a thousand miles. Hitler had been in Berlin, away from Wehrmacht headquarters, from 27 November until the 29th. During those three critical days he had had no chance to confer directly with Halder or Brauchitsch (both of whom remained in East Prussia). There was confusion about the geography of the area around Rostov, and about the state of the German troops fighting there. The strength of the local Red Army forces was also not clearly understood. The professionals of the German Army High Command were preoccupied with battles in distant parts of Russia to the north, especially around Moscow and Leningrad. More fundamentally, however, there lay in the background Hitler's growing loss of faith in Brauchitsch and other senior Army officers.

As Chief of the Army General Staff, Halder had not opposed the withdrawal to the Mius-Sambek line, partly because he was much more interested in Moscow than Rostov. He tried during the afternoon of the 1st to intervene with Hitler's headquarters. But his advice proved unnecessary. That afternoon Field Marshal von Reichenau – the new C-in-C of Army Group South – reported that the Russians had broken through Hitler's proposed 'intermediate position' between Rostov and the Mius. Reichenau, like Rundstedt before him, now asked to be allowed to pull back. This time permission was granted. 'So it is,' grumbled Halder, 'that we are now where we could have been yesterday evening. We have sacrificed strength and time, and we have lost von Rundstedt.'[3]

* * *

Only a small part of the German *Ostheer* (eastern army) was actually fighting around Rostov. The formation that was directly involved, General von Mackensen's III Panzer Corps (part of Kleist's 1st Panzer Army), consisted of two Panzer divisions, a motorised infantry division, and the SS *Leibstandarte* division. In contrast the army group in front of Moscow consisted of fourteen Panzer divisions and sixty-one infantry divisions. Nor could it be said that the battles around Rostov caused the German command serious worry. The retreat to the Mius line did not involve heavy losses in men or matériel, and once the line was reached the German position was not under serious threat.

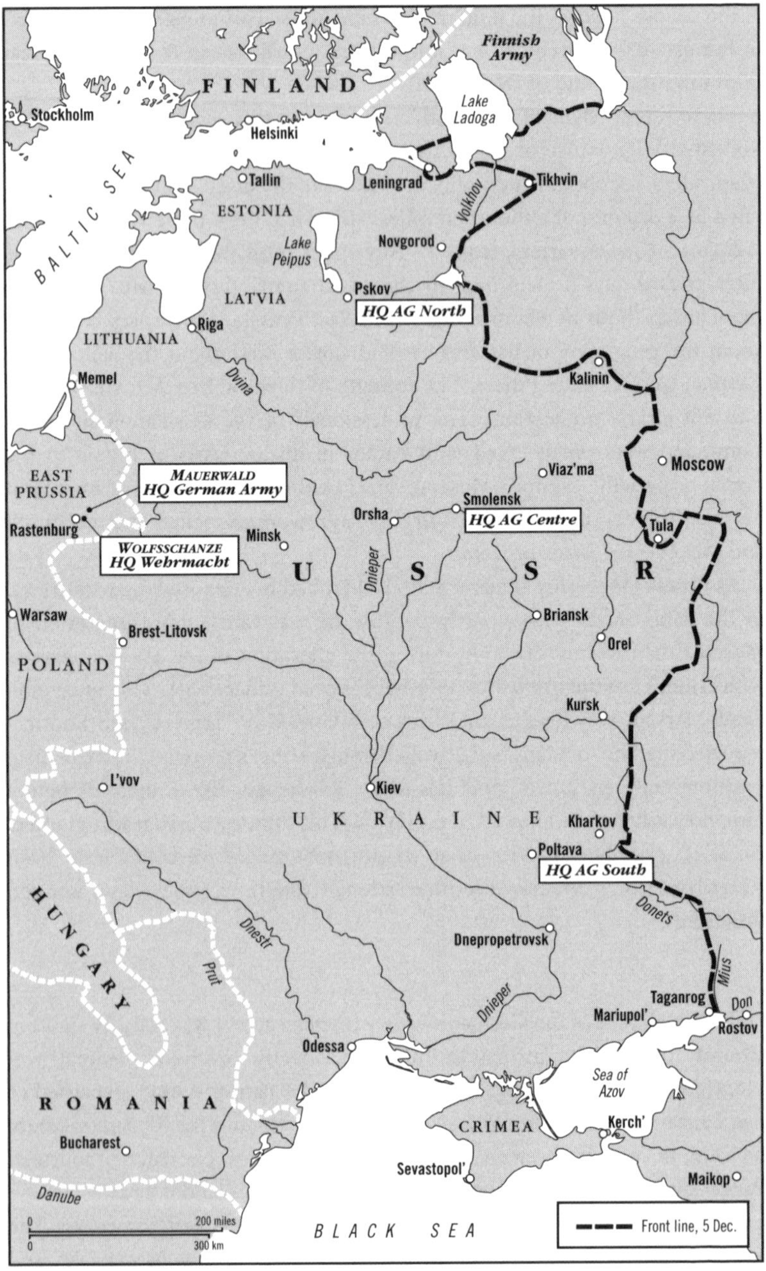


**Map 1.** The Russian-German Front.

Rostov, however, was not just anywhere. It was one of the largest cities in the USSR, and strategically vital. Situated around twenty-five miles up the Don river from the Sea of Azov, Rostov controlled the bridges over the lower part of the river and was the outer gateway to the resources of the Caucasus region. Some 170 miles to the south of Rostov was the first of the Russian oil centres, at Maikop. For Hitler – if not for Brauchitsch and Halder – Rostov had become the 'centre of gravity' (*Schwerpunkt*) of the Russian campaign.

There was a deeper reason why the late-November setback at Rostov caused such severe ructions in the German high command. The essential feature of the strategy of the Third Reich was speed. This had been set out in the December 1940 planning directive for Operation BARBAROSSA, the invasion of Russia: 'The German Wehrmacht must be prepared, even before the conclusion of the war against England, *to overthrow [niederzuwerfen] Soviet Russia in a rapid campaign*'.[4] From the time it began planning the Russian campaign the German Army High Command had thought in terms of a full-scale campaign lasting only a couple of months. During this period the main field armies of the USSR would be destroyed, and there would then follow a pursuit of the remnants of the Red Army deep across European Russia.

The high command had realised by October that the Russian war would not be over in 1941. This dilemma was masked by the unbroken run of 'operational' military triumphs won by the Wehrmacht, as late as October and November 1941. Hitler could not have sounded more confident in his annual speech on 8 November to the Nazi Party faithful in Munich's Löwenbräukeller. He spoke of an estimated Soviet loss of 8–10 million soldiers – killed, seriously wounded, or captured – in the war so far. 'My party comrades, no army in the world can recover from this, not even the Russian one.' And looking back over the last four and a half months, Hitler told his listeners that the original strategy of Operation BARBAROSSA had been sound: 'I have never used the word *Blitzkrieg* because it is a really idiotic word. If it can be applied to any campaign at all, however, then to this one! Never before has a gigantic empire been shattered and defeated in a shorter time than the Soviet Union has been this time.'[5]

But the Red Army was still fighting. The best chance of taking Leningrad by quick assault had ended during September. The drive on Moscow in October had been stalled by the autumn mud. And now, three weeks after Hitler spoke in Munich, the German armies had been stopped and thrown back at Rostov. If the situation for the Wehrmacht in Russia was not yet a strategic crisis, it was certainly less good than it had appeared a month before, and the onset of the Russian winter was approaching. Hitler was angry enough to sack von

Rundstedt, without worrying overly about the consequences. He was within hours of taking the equally drastic step of flying out to the battle front itself, to determine by personal inspection the causes of failure.

## East Prussia, Smolensk, Moscow

At his headquarters in Smolensk, 225 miles west of Moscow, Field Marshal Fedor von Bock, C-in-C of German Army Group Centre, made a note in his own war diary about the situation in the south: 'The setback at Rostov is stupid. A deep withdrawal by 1st Panzer Army seems to be necessary there.'[6] But Bock had enough problems of his own to worry about on 1 December.

Bock was a tall officer, his face austere and thin, with prominent cheekbones. At sixty he was a year older than von Brauchitsch and five years older than Halder. Like them he was the son of a general; his mother was the sister of Erich von Falkenhayn, Chief of the German General Staff from 1914–16. In 1939–40 Bock distinguished himself in the Polish and French campaigns, and he led the victory parade through Paris as C-in-C of an army group.

Army Group Centre was by far the largest single force in the Army of the Third Reich, with seventy-five divisions. (It dwarfed the army of six divisions with which General Terauchi was about to begin his operations in Southeast Asia, not to mention Rommel's tiny force of three German divisions in Libya.) Bock's army group was deployed along a front of 650 miles – a staggering distance considering that the entire Western Front in 1914–18 had extended only 450 miles from the English Channel to Switzerland. It consisted of six powerful formations. The 9th Army, Panzer Group 3, and Panzer Group 4 were on the left (northern) flank. The 4th Army, large but mostly marching (unmotorised) infantry, was in the centre, deployed along the Nara River. The 2nd Panzer Army, and 2nd Army, were on the right (southern) flank.

The ambitious von Bock had been an enthusiastic supporter of the renewed offensive to envelop Moscow, which began on 15 November. But now, with his forces ground down by two weeks of heavy fighting, and with the weather changing for the worse, even the Field Marshal believed it was time to call a halt. In a teleprinter message of 1 December to German Army headquarters at MAUERWALD, von Bock complained that his exhausted troops were being asked to make impossible frontal attacks. 'The battles of the past 14 days have shown that the idea that the enemy in front of the army group has "collapsed" was a fantasy.' The enemy had superior numbers and could use the railway system, centred on Moscow. 'The forces of the army group [AG Centre] are no longer

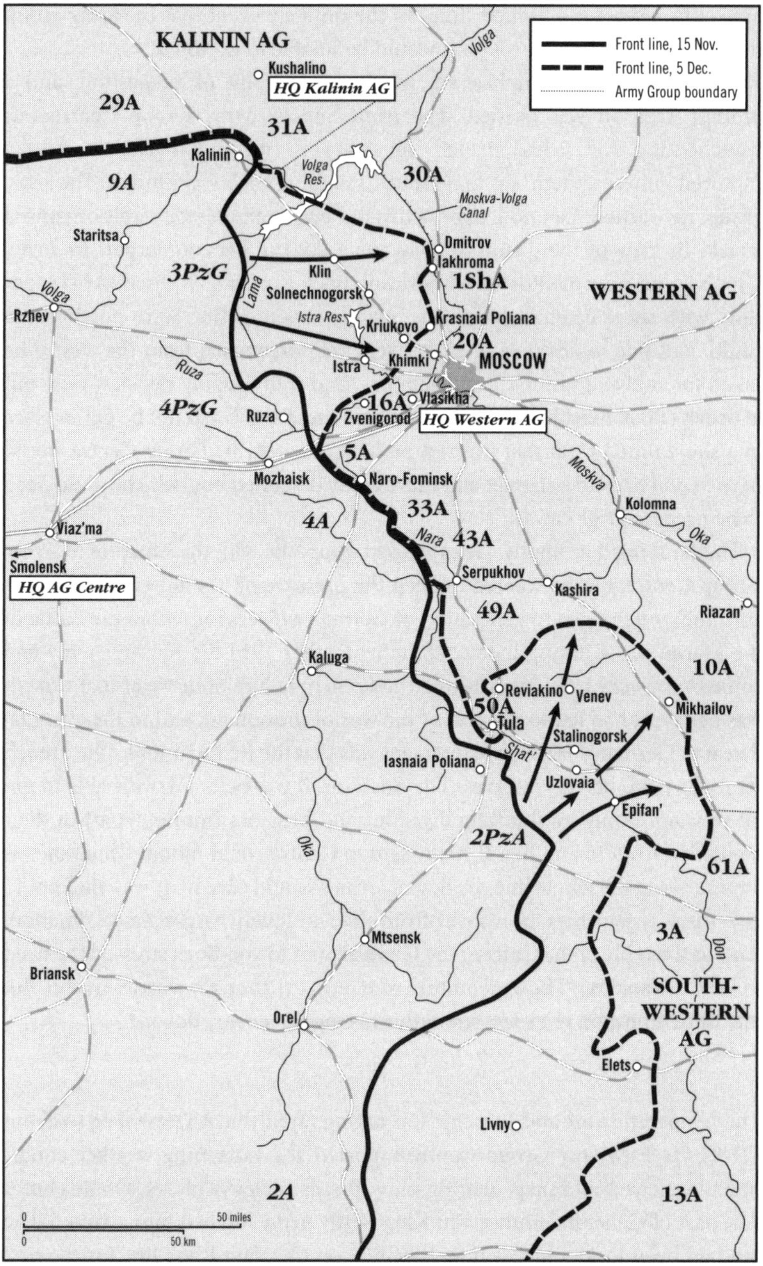


**Map 2.** Battle of Moscow: Last Phase of Operation TAIFUN.

up to this, even for a limited time.' In the unlikely event that the army group should achieve a breakthrough it would be unable to exploit it.

The troops, Bock emphasised, were on the point of exhaustion, and a prompt decision was needed. The front line of Army Group Centre was stretched too thin, it had virtually no reserves – just one division – and the captured railway system was in no state to support his hungry forces. The army group, he warned, 'can no longer withstand even a moderately well-organised attack'. In view of the dismissal (that same day) of his counterpart in Army Group South over the Rostov withdrawal, Bock expressed himself to his superiors with some care. As he put it, two courses of action were possible. He could continue to advance if he was sent reinforcements from the west – he asked for twelve divisions – and supplies, and if the supply railways were put in order. (Bock must have known that these measures could not be put in place in a short time.) Or if that was not possible, then Army Group Centre would have to pull back to a shorter and more easily defended line, which would need to be prepared right away.[7]

Halder replied promptly. He expressed sympathy with the situation of Army Group Centre, but he wanted to keep the pressure on the Russians. Halder – and Bock – belonged to generation of German officers for whom the Battle of the Marne was a lasting memory.[8] In September 1914 the Kaiser's Army had come to the very brink of crushing the French; failure of nerve at that time, it was believed, had led to the end of the war of movement, and to the eventual defeat of Germany. Halder's assessment was that the Red Army, like the French Army in 1914, had no reserves. The Russians, it was believed, were able to put up resistance only by shuffling divisions and brigades from one part of their embattled front to another. If Army Group Centre could mount simultaneous attacks along the whole line the Soviet armies would cave in. It was vital not to give the Russians time to recover from their uniquely hard-pressed situation. And so the reply of the Chief of the General Staff to von Bock stressed the need to keep advancing: 'The expenditure of [German] strength worries us too. But one must summon one's last strength to bring the enemy down.'[9]

* * *

The temperature around Moscow was falling rapidly on 1 December, to about −10°C (14°F). Army Group Centre reported the worsening weather conditions: 'Renewed cold snap, drifting snow. Roads are icy in places.' On this bitter day, part of General Günther von Kluge's 4th Army lurched into action.[10] The 4th had been locked in positional combat on the Nara River line for the first two weeks of the latest offensive. In their dugouts, the German troops could see the searchlights and the exploding anti-aircraft shells over Moscow, but they were still forty-five miles away from the centre of the city. In a pre-dawn attack, two divisions were able to break through the Soviet positions south of the Minsk-Moscow highway. German troops captured the town of Naro-Fominsk and established bridgeheads on the opposite side of the Nara.

On the flanks of Army Group Centre, north and south of 4th Army and of Moscow, the situation on 1 December was both more dramatic and more difficult. On these two wings were concentrated most of von Bock's armour and motorised infantry divisions, including nine of his fourteen Panzer divisions. These were elite troops, but they were exhausted and their supplies were running low. On the northern wing, Panzer Groups 3 and 4 – commanded by Generals Reinhardt and Hoepner – had on 1 December just completed two weeks of fairly steady forward movement, covering some seventy miles. They had carved out a large salient or 'bulge' northwest of Moscow and including the towns of Klin and Istra. Some German divisions of General Reinhardt's Panzer Group 3 had reached the important (north-south) line of the Moskva-Volga Canal. In General Hoepner's Panzer Group 4 sector, nearer Moscow, the spearhead 2nd Panzer Division had broken through on the previous day, 30 November, to Krasnaia Poliana. This village lay just beyond the city limits of Moscow and around twenty miles north of the Kremlin.

On the southern side of the Soviet capital, General Guderian's 2nd Panzer Army had pushed a similar distance forward from a position south of Tula.[11] Heinz Guderian was the father of the German Panzer force, and the operational hero of the battles in France in 1940 and in western Russia in 1941. Over the next twelve days the forces of 2nd Panzer Army advanced east and north, capturing Stalinogorsk and then moving north in the direction of the Soviet capital. On 1 December Guderian turned the main weight of his attack against the besieged city of Tula, west of the Stalinogorsk bulge. Four days earlier his 17th Panzer Division had been threatening the Oka River crossing at Kashira, around seventy miles southeast of the Kremlin, but it had been stopped by local Soviet cavalry and armour counterattacks. (In his war diary Bock – possibly from hindsight – described 27 November as a 'black day' for Guderian and his Panzer group.)[12] But even on 1 December other elements of 2nd Panzer Army, on the far, eastern, side of the Stalinogorsk bulge, still threatened the vital strategic Soviet railway running southeast from Moscow into the Russian hinterland.

* * *

The story of the Battle of Moscow went back to July 1941. At that time there had been a prickly debate in the German high command about how to exploit the stunning initial victories in the Soviet borderlands. Many of the generals, and Halder in particular, had urged an immediate thrust towards Moscow, using von Bock's Army Group Centre. Such a threat to Stalin's capital would compel the main force of the Red Army to enter battle and allow for its defeat in a classic 'battle of annihilation'.[13] Adolf Hitler had in the end taken a different view, deciding in July on a concentration of his vital Panzer forces on the strategic flanks of the great attack, in Army Group North against Leningrad, and in Army Group South against Kiev and Ukraine. This decision resulted in spectacular successes, but forces were diverted away from Army Group Centre.

In early September 1941, when Army Groups North and South seemed to have destroyed the main enemy strength facing them – Leningrad had been closely invested and Kiev was in grave danger – Hitler finally gave in to the wishes of the Army High Command, and granted permission to prepare an advance towards Moscow. This offensive was assigned the codename Operation TAIFUN (typhoon). For the first time in the Russian war the invaders directed their main strength in one direction – the Moscow axis – and concentrated three of the four Panzer groups here, as well as the bulk of the Luftwaffe in Russia.[14] The stated objective of TAIFUN was not the Soviet capital itself, but rather the forces that were defending it. '*Heeresgruppe* [Army Group] *Timoschenko*' – as the Germans called it – was believed to be the last serious fighting force in the Red Army.[15]

For the first time, also, it was becoming uncomfortably clear to the Germans that the sand in the hourglass was running out. The task set out in the Operation TAIFUN directive ran as follows: 'This [defending Soviet] army group must be defeated and annihilated in the limited time which remains *before the winter weather breaks* [my italics].' In his proclamation to the troops, issued at the start of TAIFUN on 2 October and released to the world seven days later, Hitler summed up the overall strategic situation. Months of repeated victories had created 'the preconditions . . . for the last great blow, which will crush this enemy before the winter weather breaks.' 'Today,' he declared, 'the last great decisive battle [*Entscheidungsschlacht*] of this year begins. It will have a crushing effect on this enemy and, at the same time, on the instigator of this war itself, England. By beating this opponent, we will eliminate England's last ally on the continent.'[16]

In battles fought in early October around the towns of Viaz'ma and Briansk, west of Moscow, the Soviet defenders suffered devastating losses. They were caught by surprise, and their high command in Moscow delayed giving the order to retreat. German Army Group Centre carried out two huge encirclements, one south of Briansk and the other west of Viaz'ma. The headquarters of seven of the fifteen Soviet field armies that took part in the battle were caught in the German trap, along with sixty-four divisions out of ninety-five, eleven tank brigades out of thirteen, and fifty artillery regiments out of sixty-two. According to the most recent Russian official history, up to a million Soviet troops were lost, two-thirds of whom were taken prisoner rather than killed in action; in addition to the human cost the defenders lost 830 tanks and 6,000 guns and mortars.[17]

The Germans, with good reason, believed that the Viaz'ma-Briansk victory had achieved all the goals set out in Hitler's proclamation of 2 October. At a news conference on 9 October Reich Press Chief Otto Dietrich went so far as to announce victory in the Russian war: 'The campaign in the East has been decided by the smashing of *Heeresgruppe Timoschenko*'. The Nazi Party newspaper carried the banner headline: 'The Great Hour had Arrived: The Campaign in the East has been Decided!' A smaller headline on page one announced: '*Das militärische Ende des Bolschewismus*' ['The Military End of Bolshevism'].[18]

Nothing that happened in the next few weeks shook this confidence. The German motorised troops quickly broke east into undefended country. Very few combat-ready Red Army forces now stood between the old Viaz'ma-Briansk defensive line and Moscow. To the south, a German spearhead raced ahead to the city of Orel (taking it on 7 October). To the north, Field Marshal von Bock pushed one Panzer column far forward to seize on 14 October the strategic town of Kalinin (Tver'), northwest of Moscow on the railway line to Leningrad. The local trams were still running when the first tanks burst into Kalinin. Panic reigned for a few days in the Soviet capital, where on 15 October Stalin ordered a large-scale evacuation. Government ministries and foreign embassies were sent 650 miles east to Kuibyshev (Samara) on the Volga.

It was against this backdrop that, at the end of October and at the height of the 'decisive' Moscow campaign, the Wehrmacht HQ made the decision to halve the air strength supporting Army Group Centre. Most of the strength of the entire Air Corps (*Fliegerkorps*) – several hundred aircraft – and Field Marshal Kesselring's Air Fleet 2 headquarters were to be moved from in front of Moscow to the Mediterranean.[19]

Unfortunately for Hitler and his generals, the Battle of Viaz'ma-Briansk proved to be a victory, but not a 'decisive victory'. And the foolhardy German strategic decisions in late November and early December make sense only against the background of this misjudged Wehrmacht triumph in early October.

* * *

The German drive on the Moscow front and elsewhere slowed in the second half of October. There were several reasons for this. One was the need to deal with the encircled Russians at Viaz'ma and Briansk, rounding up vast numbers of prisoners of war (hundreds of thousands of whom would starve or freeze to death in the next few months). Another was the growing supply problem, as Army Group Centre moved further and further away from its railheads. Most of all, there was the onset of the *rasputitsa*, European Russia's autumn mud season, which turned the roads into quagmires. The Russians had time to bring up reserves by rail and to regain their nerve. And in some places Soviet units put up desperate resistance to the Panzer spearheads. A critical German setback would turn out to be the failure of 4th Panzer Division in Guderian's Panzer army, racing forward from Orel and Mtsensk, to take the strategic town of Tula 'off the march' on 30 October. When the second phase of the Battle of Moscow began in mid-November Tula would be a vital corner post, protecting the southwestern approaches to the capital and threatening the flank and rear of Guderian's Panzer group.

For the German leaders a nagging worry began to take hold: five weeks after the great victory at Viaz'ma-Briansk, the Wehrmacht had still not taken Leningrad or Moscow. When Hitler spoke on 8 November in Munich he replied (rhetorically) to those who asked why the Wehrmacht appeared to have lost momentum: 'Because it is raining or snowing at the moment, or because the railway is not yet completely repaired. The tempo of this advance is . . . exclusively determined by us.' Hitler was more frank when he secretly briefed a small group of Nazi party leaders the following day. Propaganda Minister Goebbels recalled his words: 'In four weeks he hopes to reach the objectives that have to be reached before the beginning of winter, and then the troops should go into winter quarters. In the event that the weather god [*Wettergott*] is not completely against us and gives us another ten or fourteen days of favourable weather, i.e. frost without snow, he thinks that the Caucasus can be cut off, Moscow enveloped, and the Volga reached at many places.'[20] The *Wettergott* would, in the event, prove to be less than amenable to the German invaders.

In hindsight the final deciding point for the German Moscow campaign was a staff conference held in the occupied Russian town of Orsha, seventy miles west of Smolensk, on 13 November. General Halder had travelled out by special train from MAUERWALD with a large number of his officers from the General Staff. The front-line Army-level commands were represented by their Chiefs of Staff. Most – but not all – of the front-line representatives urged a consolidation of the German position on existing lines. Their armies were beset by serious supply problems, they had few reserves, and they feared the onset of winter. Halder, however, prevailed and set the *Ostheer* on a continuing advance. Army Group Centre, the most important part of the attack as far as the German Army High Command was concerned, would embark on a second phase of Operation TAIFUN, another lunge toward the Soviet capital. In hindsight the front-line representatives were right and Halder was wrong. But the Chief of the Army General Staff saw a grand-strategic imperative: the need to knock out Soviet Russia before the danger from the British and the Americans became too great. And he saw an opportunity: the *rasputitsa* was coming to an end, and with the cold weather – 'frost without snow' – the ground would be harder and suitable again for tanks and trucks.[21]

For his part, Field Marshal von Bock had been eager in mid-November to pursue the campaign. He agreed with Halder that the Russians had been so weakened that the task could be accomplished. Of the senior staff officers who met at Orsha it was Bock's Chief of Staff, General von Greiffenberg, who was closest to Halder's position. Bock seemed optimistic that – in the face of a weakened Soviet Army, and given a certain amount of good luck with the weather – he could take Moscow itself that December.[22] In any event Halder returned to his MAUERWALD headquarters, and Operation TAIFUN was resumed on 15 November.

* * *

The Nazi leadership and the German armed forces faced two interconnected challenges in the last weeks of 1941. First of all, there was the frustration that they had not achieved the decisive victory expected in June 1941 (and again in October 1941). They were still locked into an uncompleted campaign in the East and – in global terms – a two-front war against Britain and Russia. Meanwhile the front-line crisis at Rostov and Moscow had brought to the boil a crisis in the German high command. The command structure of the Third Reich could cope with victory, but not with setbacks. The final resolution and a momentous development would come within three weeks. On 19 December Adolf Hitler personally took over command of the German Army, alongside command of the Wehrmacht. He would then truly dominate – for better or worse – the war effort of the Third Reich until 1945 and his last days in his Berlin bunker. Field Marshal von Brauchitsch, while not openly disgraced, was unceremoniously dismissed and shuffled into retirement.

The high command was indeed in a muddle in the late autumn of 1941, with the overlapping authorities of the Wehrmacht (armed forces) High Command (*OKW, Oberkommando der Wehrmacht*) and the Army High Command

(*OKH, Oberkommando des Heeres*). Confusion and conflict existed despite, and partly because of, the fact that the professional heads of both headquarters were all products of the Imperial German Army. The problem was partly structural. The campaign in Russia was by far the largest undertaking of the German armed forces, and the *OKW* was the supreme command – presided over by the German dictator – with authority over all three armed services. The *OKW*, however, did not have the trained personnel on hand that were required for planning large-scale land campaigns. Operation BARBAROSSA had, as a result, been largely organised by the *OKH*.

Of course, it mattered a great deal that Adolf Hitler was head of the Wehrmacht High Command.[23] He was, moreover, a civilian dictator who claimed both extraordinary rights and extraordinary gifts when it came to dealing with all aspects of national life, especially the conduct of military affairs. His position and authority as supreme war leader had been vastly strengthened by the triumphs of the Wehrmacht in Poland, Norway, France, the Low Countries and the Balkans. He was 'advised' within the Wehrmacht High Command by senior but compliant generals, Field Marshal Wilhelm Keitel and General Alfred Jodl.

The Nazi Party and the German Army had a close but ultimately strained relationship. Between Hitler and 'his' generals there was an underlying political and even cultural tension. Hitler was an Austrian of humble origins and limited education. He was the leader of a radical populist political movement. The generals were an elite, often from the service or land-owning nobility, often from Prussia. The better part of a generation separated the Nazi party leaders from the older army commanders. Hitler and Goebbels – respectively a decade and two decades younger than the senior generals – later joked about the 'old gentlemen' and their inability to cope with the physical demands of their posts.[24] And although the Nazis and the generals certainly shared similar strategic goals, they each wanted to be the force to lead Germany towards their realisation.

Field Marshal Walther von Brauchitsch had become C-in-C of the German Army in 1938. He was a handsome and charming man, although many of his contemporaries found him lacking in forcefulness. He was personally obliged to Hitler, who had smoothed divorce proceedings from his wealthy first wife. But he found it increasingly hard to deal with the dictator's demands. Hitler was never an easy person to work with, and his intrusions into the planning and conduct of the war had become more evident since the quick and successful campaigns of 1939–40. One important witness to the relationships within the high command of the Third Reich was General Walter Warlimont, a Wehrmacht High Command staff officer. He recalled in his memoirs that meetings with Hitler had a physical effect on Brauchitsch. After the Army and Wehrmacht headquarters both moved to East Prussia in June 1941 the Field Marshal had to make the ten-mile rail trip to WOLFSSCHANZE several times a week to brief Hitler. Otherwise a self-assured and able man, Brauchitsch seemed almost paralysed at these meetings and certainly found it difficult to speak.[25]

Although Brauchitsch had been identified with some of the greatest ever triumphs of German arms, especially in Poland, France, and in Russia during the first months of the BARBAROSSA campaign, his relations with his Führer were increasingly strained. Hitler, for his part, believed the C-in-C was not at all assertive enough in dealing with his colleagues who were in command of the various army groups. Brauchitsch turned sixty in October 1941, by which time he had been in post for three and a half years; early in the following month he suffered a heart attack. Most important, Hitler was dissatisfied with the Army's failure to bring the Russian campaign to a successful conclusion.

Whatever the situation – even taking into account Brauchitsch's genuinely poor health – Hitler could not dismiss him without tacitly admitting that the German Army was less than the infallible monolith depicted in the propaganda of the Third Reich. In addition Hitler could not, for all his political power, afford to ignore the collective opinion of the Army's senior officer corps. The German dictator was also looking for a replacement for Brauchitsch who was militarily gifted, but at the same time compliant and not politically ambitious. Such a paragon was not easy to find. For the moment Brauchitsch was left in his post, but this shaky arrangement could surely not go on for many more days, and it could certainly not survive a military defeat.

Franz Halder was a more complicated and paradoxical figure than Brauchitsch. The bespeckled general had a homely, clean-shaven face, with a prominent cleft chin. He was an articulate speaker, and unlike Brauchitsch was not tongue-tied in Hitler's presence. Although Halder had something of the schoolmaster about him, he was a master of detail, a cunning bureaucratic infighter, and ambitious. He has even been accused of believing that a greater role for Hitler in the Army High Command would strengthen his own position. Halder had the benefit of the vast prestige, long tradition and overbearing self-confidence of the *Generalstab*. In the end, however, he was a staff officer rather than a combat general, and some colleagues felt he was out of touch with the realities of the front line.

Unlike von Brauchitsch, Halder would not be accused of war crimes. (Brauchitsch died of a heart attack in 1948 before he could be prosecuted.)

Halder had the strange good fortune to end the war in the Dachau concentration camp. He had links with anti-Hitler conspirators in 1938–39, was sacked by Hitler after strategic disagreements in September 1942, and arrested in 1944 in the aftermath of the 20 July assassination attempt. Indeed Halder became an influential adviser to Allied occupation governments. His subordinate and protégé, Adolf Heusinger, became a senior leader of the West German Army. Halder's diaries are a remarkable historical source. However, there can be no doubt that in October and November 1941 the Chief of the General Staff was an enthusiastic supporter of the war in Russia, and of the deep advance towards Moscow which eventually led to military disaster that winter.

* * *

There was one other significant Germany military development on 1 December. *Kriegswehrmacht der UdSSR* [Armed Forces of the USSR], a classified handbook on the Soviet armed forces, was issued.[26] The handbook was an impressive piece of work. It outlined the leadership, tactics and training of the Red Army, as well as of the various branches of service within it, and provided a detailed, structurally accurate order of battle.

The overall picture presented was one of shattered Soviet forces, poorly led, and gravely weakened by a series of defeats. The Red Army might be rebuilt to regain some initiative, but this would not happen until the spring of 1942. Even then, efforts to reconstruct Soviet tank forces and air squadrons would be crippled by the loss of major production facilities.

The assessment of Soviet strength on 1 December – to which we will return in Chapter 9 – was significant. The Red Army as a whole was reckoned to have the equivalent of 265 rifle (infantry) divisions (with independent brigades added together as fractions of divisions), 40 cavalry divisions, and 50 tank brigades. Of these, 200 rifle divisions, 35 cavalry divisions, and 40 tank brigades were believed to be facing the German Army.[27]

The handbook made a crucial assumption about the availability of Soviet reserves:

> The *combat strength* of the majority of Soviet Russian formations is at the present time quite limited, they have not been replenished with heavy [infantry] weapons and artillery. In recent days newly-formed units have been met only in isolated cases. The Red high command is now continually forced, as an emergency measure, to pull individual units out of sectors of the front which are not under attack and to use them to deal with nearby crisis points. All this suggests that *combat-ready units at present are no longer available to*

> *any extent as reserves and that the replacement system is in a state of crisis* – at least for the moment. *The reason for this, alongside shortages of officers and NCOs, trained manpower, and equipment, lies mainly in organisational and transport difficulties (the evacuation of the population and of industry).*[28]

A detailed breakdown of Soviet strength was attempted. The seven armies of the Western Army Group, whose commander was listed as one General 'Shukov' (for Zhukov), were estimated to have a nominal strength of 50 rifle divisions and 19 tank brigades, with an effective strength (*Kampfwert*) of only 23⅔ rifle divisions and 11 tank brigades. The three Soviet armies around Rostov were given an effective strength of 8 rifle and 4 cavalry divisions, with 2⅔ tank brigades.[29] On neither front should the level of enemy strength amount to a serious danger to the forward movement of the German armies. The air strength of the Red Army Air Force in Europe was given as only 900 combat planes.

The German report did not totally dismiss enemy potential. In the longer run, by the spring of 1942, the intact railways and relatively short supply lines might enable the Red Army to regroup and to bring up some fresh forces. The informed estimate was that the Russians had enough equipment to create by the spring thirty-five new rifle divisions and twenty tank brigades. Russian soldiers were capable of stubborn defence of their homeland. As for the higher-level Army leadership (*die oberen Führer*), the handbook concluded, it 'has strengths which usually lie more in the realm of will than of ability, and its command structure is poorly developed. It will continue frequently to make mistakes both at an operational and a tactical level, but it will act with great ruthlessness and severity.'[30]

In some respects the estimate of Soviet strength by German Army intelligence was remarkably accurate, and a lucid and professional piece of work. In others it was deeply flawed. How serious the mistakes were would become clear, for the first time, in the battles over the next two or three weeks.

## Moscow

Over the front line, on the Russian side, the situation had finally begun to improve in the last days of November. The four armies under General Cherevichenko's Southern Army Group had forced the advancing III Panzer Corps to give up Rostov. On 30 November Stalin publicly praised the Rostov victors on the front page of *Pravda*, and a large photograph of Cherevichenko was printed there.

The Germans did not yet know it, but the enemy forces defending Moscow were, on 1 December, also preparing large-scale counterattacks. As part of this preparation a preliminary order was issued at 3.30 a.m. to Kalinin Army Group in the name of the *Stavka VGK* (Headquarters of the Supreme C-in-C). The 'Stavka' essentially meant Joseph Stalin, the Supreme Commander-in-Chief. Stalin operated from a new command post that had been set up for him in the Kremlin only a few weeks before.[31] The practical machinery of strategic command was the Red Army General Staff, in particular its Operations Directorate, located in nearby Kirovskaia Street. The order sent out early on the 1st was signed by Stalin and the Deputy Chief of the General Staff, General Aleksandr Vasilevskii. The hour of transmission was not unusual; Stalin worked late at night, and his advisers had to follow the same regime.

Kalinin Army Group was commanded by General Ivan Konev. A grim-looking man of forty-three, high cheek-boned and with the shaven head favoured by Soviet officers, Konev was destined to be one of Stalin's three or four great marshals. He was a poorly-educated peasant boy who had shown his abilities as a Red Army political commissar in the civil war. When the German invasion began in 1941 Konev was a general in command of a field army, and he had acquitted himself well enough in the early months. In late 1941, however, his career – and perhaps his life – hung by a thread, because it was he who had been in command of Western Army Group during the disastrous Viaz'ma-Briansk battle. Experienced Army-level leaders, however, were few in number, and Konev was given a new command.

The Stavka order noted that the attacks mounted in the last few days by Konev's army group had been ineffective. Now, over the next two or three days, he was to assemble a 'small shock group' of five or six divisions. Supported by whatever heavy artillery, rocket launchers and tanks Konev could muster, the shock group was to attack south from near the German-occupied town of Kalinin into the deep rear of the enemy's 'Klin group'. Together with Western Army Group it would destroy the enemy concentration.[32] The 'Klin group' was Reinhardt's Panzer Group 3.

Konev's headquarters was sited in the village of Kushalino, around 110 miles northwest of the Kremlin. Little more than an hour after 3.30 a.m. Konev was called to the *Bodo* (Baudôt) teleprinter by Vasilevskii to discuss the situation and to confirm he would make the required attack. The task was really the responsibility of the Chief of the General Staff, rather than his deputy, but Marshal Boris Shaposhnikov was ill, and Vasilevskii had taken his place. Konev grumbled that he had no tanks and his forces were too weak, with divisions of 2,500–3,000 men. Vasilevskii insisted on serious action:

> Comrade commander, have you heard about the events at Rostov? Breaking up the German offensive against Moscow means more than saving Moscow, but it is only possible to begin a serious defeat of the enemy by active operations, with objectives that are decisive. If we do not do this in the next few days it will be too late.[33]

* * *

Stalin's relationship with his generals – like Hitler's – was complex. The Soviet dictator had, after all, presided over a massacre of the top leadership of the Red Army in the purges of 1937–38. But this had at least created a rejuvenated corps of senior commanders (*die oberen Führer*, in the German view) who were a decade or two younger than their opposite numbers in the German Army; Ivan Konev was one example. In contrast, Marshal Shaposhnikov, the Chief of the Red Army General Staff, was one of the very few Soviet officers who had held mid-level rank in the Imperial Army. He had attended the Nikolai General Staff Academy and had attained the rank of colonel by 1917. Shaposhnikov was fifty-nine years old in 1941, a contemporary of Brauchitsch and Halder. He was treated with an unusual degree of respect by Stalin, who addressed him using his name and patronymic (Boris Mikhailovich), but like his German contemporaries he was not in good health. Shaposhnikov was ably assisted by General Vasilevskii – aged only forty-six – who as the son of an Orthodox priest had his own politically dangerous links to old Russia.

Shaposhnikov, Vasilevskii and Konev play important roles in this story, but of the Soviet military leaders the most important was the C-in-C of Western Army Group. General Georgii Zhukov had, like Konev, risen from the rank and file of the wartime Tsarist Army, and he had survived the 1937–38 purge. He was sixteen years junior to his opponent on the other side of the Moscow front line, Field Marshal von Bock; 1 December 1941 happened to be Zhukov's birthday, when he would turn forty-five. He was intelligent, energetic and ruthless. Civil war cavalry veterans dominated the Red Army leadership in the late 1930s, and Zhukov was an offensively-minded cavalryman. He had made his name – and won Stalin's confidence – fighting the Japanese in the 1939 border clash at Khalkin Gol in Mongolia. Zhukov had repeated Hannibal's Cannae strategy and encircled and destroyed a whole Japanese division, using tanks, artillery and aircraft. From then until June 1941 Zhukov was the Red Army's leading expert on offensive warfare.

In the desperate autumn months of 1941 Stalin had turned to Zhukov, not as a master of the offensive, but as a tenacious defender. Zhukov had held the line, first at Leningrad in late September, and then on the Moscow front, to which Stalin recalled him in early October after the collapse of the Red Army defensive line there. In the first weeks after his arrival – Zhukov took over command of Western Army Group on 10 October – he could do little but try to stiffen the resistance of the defence and plug gaps. His raw material was the survivors of the Battle of Viaz'ma-Briansk and scraps of units assembled in Moscow. Zhukov had shown the required ruthlessness; in at least two cases, division commanders accused of panicking were executed.

* * *

The Moscow counterattack was concocted by these men and by Stalin, in haste and in a state of real desperation; the critical decisions had to be made in the last ten days of November. In this respect it was quite different from the Japanese Southern Operation or the Wehrmacht's Operation TAIFUN or even the British Operation CRUSADER in Libya (a subject of the following chapter). Improvisation did not, however, make Soviet plans any less important.

Although Stalin and the General Staff had been thinking since the beginning of November about how to take the initiative, it was the launching by the Germans of the final lunge of Operation TAIFUN, north of Moscow on 15 November, and south of the city three days later, that set in train the events that eventually led to Zhukov's victory. After military catastrophes in the summer and autumn of 1941, Stalin and the General Staff had begun to assemble fresh – if poorly trained and equipped – divisions in the Stavka Reserve (*Rezerv VGK*), and to man a new defensive line *behind* Moscow on the central Volga River.

The first big decision was whether to risk these forces in what might be an unsuccessful defence of the Soviet capital. In his memoirs Zhukov recalled a telephone conversation with Stalin about this. The general did not recall the exact date, but he thought it occurred shortly after the initial German breakthrough on 15 November. He was at Western Army Group headquarters in the village of Vlasikha, about eighteen miles west of the Kremlin.[34] 'Are you sure that we can hold Moscow?' Stalin said. 'I ask you this with pain in my soul [*s bol'iu v dushe*]. Speak honestly, like a Communist.'

'We can certainly hold Moscow,' Zhukov replied. 'But at least two more armies will be needed, and if possible 200 tanks.'

According to Zhukov Stalin was reassured. 'Contact the General Staff,' he said, 'and work out with them where the two armies you have asked for will be concentrated. They will be ready at the end of November. *We have no tanks*.'

Within half an hour – in Zhukov's version – Vasilevskii had agreed to transfer 1st Shock Army and 10th Army to Zhukov's control from the Stavka

Reserve, as well as formations from the Moscow Defence Zone that would later make up part of 20th Army.[35]

The documents tell a somewhat different story. According to them it was not until the 29th, two weeks after the start of the German offensive, that the Stavka released 1st Shock Army and 20th Army to Zhukov; 10th Army was released only on 1 December.[36] The General Staff's secret history of the Battle of Moscow, written in 1943 under Marshal Shaposhnikov's supervision, did, however, mark out an earlier date, 20 November, to have been highly important. According to this account it was then that Stalin and his General Staff advisers made a preliminary decision to move troops up towards Moscow from the defensive line covering the central Volga, enabling the Red Army to undertake more than a passive defence of the capital.[37] The Stavka ordered the formation and concentration of new 19th and 20th Armies, which were to be under its direct control.[38]

The deployment of the new 19th and 20th Armies (proposed on 20 November) must have been related to the breakthrough of the two Panzer groups north of Moscow. Probably the Russian high command saw the two new Soviet armies playing a defensive, rather than a counter-offensive, role. They would have been a backstop (a 'second echelon') for 30th and 16th Armies. The 19th Army was to assemble north and northeast of Moscow; it was soon given the name 1st Shock Army.[39] Movement of its troops was ordered to begin on the 25th. Meanwhile 20th Army was to assemble southeast of Moscow and then to move into position (again, by the 27th) at Khimki, north of Moscow, between 1st Shock Army and the city.[40]

Whatever these early discussions and decisions, the situation for the Russians rapidly worsened. They had expected the strike south of Moscow to come through Serpukhov. In fact when the German General Guderian moved on 18 November he swung the armoured spearhead of 2nd Panzer Army through a point sixty-five miles further south, and headed towards the small towns of Uzlovaia and Stalinogorsk. (The name of the second town – 'Stalin Hills' – was not without political significance in 1941; it is now called Novomoskovsk.) The Panzers achieved tactical surprise, taking the two places on 21 November.

Zhukov ordered the commander of 50th Army, General A.N. Ermakov, to counterattack. When divisions of 50th Army withdrew against orders, Zhukov dismissed Ermakov; he even sent an angry teleprinter message to Stalin late on the 22nd accusing Ermakov of being 'guilty of the surrender' of Stalinogorsk.[41] Zhukov had to rapidly shift his local reserves back from Serpukhov to Kashira to prevent Guderian pushing north into Moscow across the bridges over the Oka River. On 27 November – Guderian's 'black day' – these reserves blocked the immediate threat to Moscow south of the Oka. The city of Tula, however, further to the south, remained exposed and under attack.

North of Moscow the fighting continued to go badly. The important town of Klin on the Moscow-Leningrad railway fell to mobile troops from Panzer Group 3 on 23 November. The enemy had blown a hole between General Dmitrii Leliushenko's 30th Army and General Konstantin Rokossovskii's 16th, with the former withdrawing to the north and the latter south towards Moscow. In his memoirs Zhukov recalled that the withdrawal on 25 November of 16th Army from the small town of Solnechnogorsk (between Klin and Moscow, and at the northern end of the Istra Reservoir) created a 'catastrophic situation'. After overrunning the town German troops were able to get across the Moskva-Volga Canal at Iakhroma and, further south, to reach the villages of Krasnaia Poliana and Kriukovo, just outside the Moscow city boundary.

Nearer Moscow, in the sector threatened by Panzer Group 4, the Russians were also hard pressed. Zhukov had a violent argument with the commander of 16th Army, General Rokossovskii, who wanted to fall back behind the natural defence line of the Istra Reservoir, rather than to 'fight to the death' – Zhukov's instructions – further to the west against superior enemy forces. When Rokossovskii ordered a retreat Zhukov became even more angry. 'It is I who command the Army Group!' he told Rokossovskii. 'I am changing the orders to withdraw behind the Istra Reservoir. I order the holding of the present line and that not one step back be taken.'[42] The directive proved impossible to fulfil, and Rokossovskii had to fall back, giving up Istra on Wednesday, 27 November. As an emergency measure, Zhukov had to shift units from other parts of his army group, including anti-aircraft battalions from the Moscow air defences, with their weapons to be used as anti-tank guns.

The 26th and 27th – Wednesday and Thursday – were the worst days for the Russians; after that their enemy appeared to run out of steam. Guderian's withdrawal south from Kashira was the first hopeful sign. Zhukov recalled that on Saturday, 29 November, he telephoned Stalin and asked for permission to launch a counterattack. 'And you are sure,' Stalin enquired, 'that the enemy has reached a crisis and will not be able to bring up any major new forces?'

'The enemy is exhausted,' Zhukov replied. 'But if we do not liquidate the dangerous enemy penetrations now, the Germans will be able to reinforce their forces in the Moscow region.'[43]

That Saturday an order from Stalin and Vasilevskii released to Western Army Group the two armies created on 20 November, now designated 1st Shock (formerly 19th) Army and 20th Army. The order assigned as commander of the 20th Army General Andrei Vlasov, a man who would later become one of the most controversial figures in Russia's Second World War history. (Captured by the Germans in 1942, he would agree to lead an anti-Soviet 'Russian Liberation Army'. For many years Vlasov would be 'erased' from Soviet histories of the Battle of Moscow.)[44] Two days later, on Monday afternoon, Zhukov was also given control of General Fedor Golikov's 10th Army, forming southeast of Moscow.[45]

On Sunday morning, 30 November, Zhukov sent a brief handwritten outline of his plans to Vasilevskii, details of which were given on an attached map. Zhukov asked the Deputy Chief of the General Staff to show it to Stalin immediately. The outline was co-signed by Zhukov's commissar Nikolai Bulganin – a member of the Stalin's Politburo – and by Zhukov's Chief of Staff, General Sokolovskii.[46] Zhukov identified what he regarded as the immediate tasks: 'To defeat the core grouping of the enemy on the right flank of the armies of Western Army Group by attacks towards Klin, Solnechnogorsk, and on the Istra axis, and to defeat the enemy on the left flank with attacks on Uzlovaia and Bogoroditsk on the flank and in the rear of Guderian's group.'[47] The 'core grouping' on the Soviet right flank was Panzer Groups 3 and 4; 'Guderian's group' on the Soviet left flank was 2nd Panzer Army.

Zhukov proposed that the attack begin on 3 or 4 December. Golikov's new 10th Army would strike the southern wing. The other two new armies (1st Shock and 20th), along with General Rokossovskii's 16th Army, would move against the northern wing on 5 or 6 December. Their attack would be joined by a new assault from the north, delivered by Leliushenko's 30th Army. All the air strength of Western Army Group would be thrown into the attack, three-quarters in the north, and a quarter supporting 10th Army in the south.

The response was scrawled in crayon over the first page of Zhukov's outline: '*Soglasen*, *I. Stalin*' – 'Agreed, J. Stalin.'[48]

CHAPTER 3

## MONDAY, 1 DECEMBER

# London, Libya and the Dangers of the Far East

*Nothing will make me unduly optimistic but I am absolutely confident. Ritchie has grasped battle completely and is thinking far ahead.*

General Auchinleck

*He (the Prime Minister) had explained that, in his view, we should not resist or attempt to forestall a Japanese attack on the Kra Isthmus unless we had a satisfactory assurance from the United States that they would join us should our action cause us to become involved in war with Japan.*

War Cabinet Minutes

### Libya

The new editor of *The Times* met the British Prime Minister on Monday evening, 1 December. 'Then Winston from the War Cabinet, looking (at 67) very fresh and young and spry. He is a different man altogether from the rather bloated individual whom I last saw (close to) before the war. His cheerful, challenging – not to say truculent – look is good to see just now; but it covers up a great deal of caution, even vacillation at times.'[1] Winston Churchill had turned sixty-seven on the previous Friday.

Monday had been a long and taxing day for Churchill and the men around him. They had a great deal on their minds. Unlike their enemies – or potential enemies – in Berlin, Rome and Tokyo, they faced challenges that were truly global. The most immediate military crisis for the British high command at the very start of December was not in Southeast Asia or in Russia (although

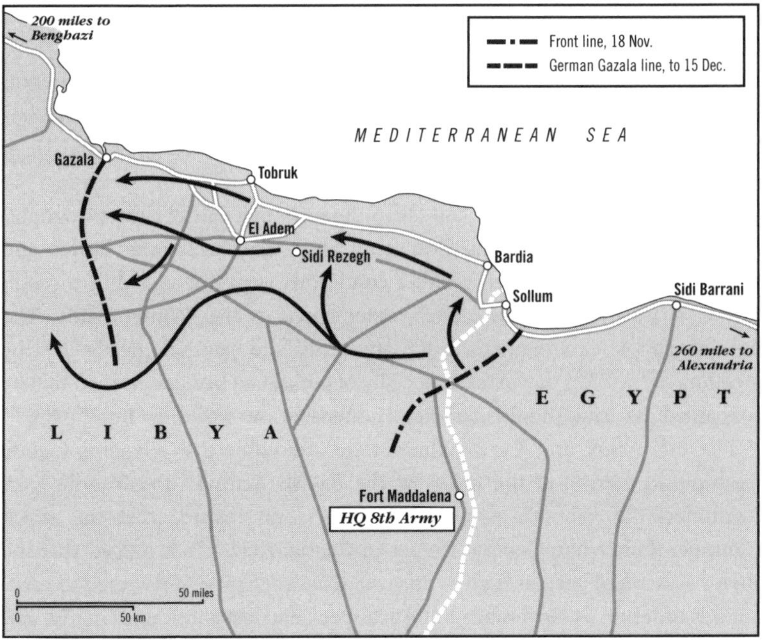


**Map 3.** Libya: Operation CRUSADER.

both those places were regarded as important) but in Libya. In the middle of the previous week the British forces there had seemed on the very edge of military catastrophe, and the commander on the spot, General Sir Alan Cunningham, was secretly dismissed.[2]

Operation CRUSADER was launched into north-eastern Libya, close to the Egyptian border, on 19 November, four days after the Germans began their final drive on Moscow. For the first time in the whole war the British Army, supported by the RAF, had undertaken a general offensive against German forces. For the first time, too, the British outnumbered the enemy, on the battlefield, in tanks and aircraft. The immediate plan for Cunningham's 8th Army had been a quick and decisive defeat of Axis armoured forces in Libya and the simultaneous relief – hopefully within a week – of the besieged port of Tobruk. Instead, on 1 December CRUSADER had entered its fourteenth exhausting day, and even the fate of Tobruk was far from clear. Cunningham had previously won a famous victory against the Italians in East Africa, but he was no armour specialist. While he had achieved complete surprise at the outset of CRUSADER, he failed to concentrate his tanks. The talented General Rommel had counterattacked vigorously with *Panzergruppe Afrika*, a formation comparable to the four Panzer forces in Russia, but comprised of a mix of German and Italian divisions.

Cunningham and Rommel had fought the Battle of Sidi Rezegh from 21–23 November. Sidi Rezegh lay twenty miles southeast of Tobruk and was the site of an important air strip. The battle had been the biggest clash of armoured forces in the Second World War so far, outside the summer 1941 battles in western Ukraine. It had taken the form of a classic desert 'dogfight', with rapid movement and no clear front lines. The terrain was barren and largely featureless. Although weather conditions were not as bad as those in Russia, it was cold; this was later remembered as the 'Winter Battle'. The fighting shook Cunningham, both physically and psychologically. By the morning of the 23rd the losses, especially of tanks, had become so high that he concluded his army should abandon its offensive and withdraw into Egypt.

The 8th Army and Cunningham were subordinate to General Claude Auchinleck, C-in-C of the forces of the British Army in the Middle East. Auchinleck flew to 8th Army headquarters and insisted that the attack continue. Rather like General Halder in Russia, Auchinleck judged that the enemy losses had been as high as his own. Cunningham endeavoured to carry out this order on 24 November, but Auchinleck had lost confidence in him and appointed an officer from his own staff, General Neil Ritchie, in his place. Meanwhile, in the afternoon of the 24th Rommel set out at the head of his two Panzer divisions on a raid towards the Egyptian frontier, later known as the 'dash to the wire'. Auchinleck's steadiness and Rommel's foolhardy dash determined the battle's outcome. Rommel was usually a master of the manoeuvre but (again like Halder in Russia) he had overestimated enemy losses. The 'Desert Fox' expected that his sudden move would stampede the survivors of the British force. This time, despite much confusion, the enemy kept their nerve. On 27 and 28 November, after a few days of aimless manoeuvres on the frontier, Rommel had to return to his starting point.

Three days later, on Monday, 1 December, our story really begins. The epicentre of the fighting had now shifted off to the west and north of the Sidi Rezegh battlefield, to the eastern approaches of Tobruk. The little Libyan port town was garrisoned by a reinforced division. In British hands, it blocked the Libyan coast road and hung over the flank of any Axis army advancing around it towards Cairo and the Suez Canal. Should it fall into Axis hands, Tobruk would provide a vital forward supply port for a further advance into Egypt. Securing it had been one of Cunningham's main objectives. When CRUSADER began he had sent two infantry divisions marching along the coast towards Tobruk, and ordered the garrison to break out to meet them; the link-up had been achieved on 28 November. On 1 December Rommel broke the link again, but during the fighting the Tobruk defenders extended their perimeter, throwing back the Italian troops besieging them.

Most important, CRUSADER had become a battle of attrition, and by 1 December the strength of Rommel and his Italian allies – in terms of tanks, aircraft, ammunition and fuel – was waning. Like the Germans in Russia they had no reserves, and they were very far from their supply bases. Furthermore, the convoy routes across the Mediterranean to those bases were blocked by the Royal Navy. The motley British Empire forces, although less well-led on the battlefield than the Germans, were being reinforced and re-supplied. On this same day, 1 December, General Ritchie ordered preparations for a new drive forward to seize the Panzer-group base at El Adem, west of Sidi Rezegh. Auchinleck joined Ritchie at his headquarters, and stayed for ten days, providing moral support and looking after Ritchie's newly-arrived reinforcements. He sent a positive report to the Prime Minister that Monday: 'Nothing will make me unduly optimistic but I am absolutely confident. Ritchie has grasped battle completely and is thinking far ahead.'[3]

* * *

The Mediterranean and North Africa had been at the heart of Winston Churchill's grand strategy throughout the summer of 1941. The main strength of the German Army and the Luftwaffe was from June tied up in the Russian campaign, and supply problems made it hard to reinforce Rommel. Repeatedly, Churchill urged the British command in the Middle East to go over to the offensive, and he had sent Auchinleck to Egypt in July to prod 8th Army into action; the 'Auk' however, was insistent that his troops be fully equipped and trained before they saw battle.

The British Prime Minister – simultaneously the Minister of Defence – was both aggressive and ambitious. On the eve of CRUSADER Churchill drafted for Auchinleck an extraordinary message to the 8th Army: 'For the first time, British and Empire troops will meet the Germans with an ample equipment in modern weapons of all kinds. The battle itself will affect the whole course of the war. . . . The Desert Army may add a page to history which will rank with Blenheim and Waterloo.'[4]

Churchill had a vision of how the next phase of the war should go, and he outlined this strategy, building hope upon hope, in a letter to President Roosevelt in late October. Auchinleck, he told the President, would use his superior forces to destroy the German and Italian armies and then advance to Benghazi and perhaps even Tripoli, completing the conquest of Libya. With

Tripoli taken, the Vichy French forces in the western part of North Africa, under General Weygand, might be 'stirred into joining the war' on the British side. Spain would then resist German efforts to lure it into the conflict; Turkey, too, would stand up to German pressure; and a profound effect might be produced upon 'an already demoralised Italy'. Churchill hoped that the United States would be able to send troops to support this grand enterprise, even without a declaration of war. American soldiers might garrison Northern Ireland, to free up British troops for an invasion of French North Africa (Operation GYMNAST), or they might take part in the expedition themselves. Churchill also saw the political importance of Africa with respect to Russia. As he told the War Cabinet on the day before CRUSADER was launched, if the operations in eastern Libya were successful 'they would have a profound effect on our relationship with other countries. In regard to Russia, we should no longer be in the position that they were fighting and we were not, except in the air.'[5]

The demands of the Libyan campaign had a global significance. The British Empire was certainly not without military forces, but what was available was limited – particularly in comparison with the huge task at hand. Britain could not readily fight simultaneous campaigns. What military resources Churchill could afford to send abroad – after the demands of home defence – went to the Middle East, where Britain had active enemies, rather than to East Asia, where it did not – yet. Troops from Australia, New Zealand and India (as well as South Africa) had been sent to Egypt, not kept back to defend the Far East. The best British equipment to be sent overseas went to the Middle East. At the end of November 1941, 8th Army had some 750 tanks, the equivalent of two armoured divisions, in Libya; two more armoured formations were available in Syria and Egypt. The total was probably more than the number of operational tanks available to either side in the Battle of Moscow.[6] There were no tanks at all in Malaya. Operation CRUSADER was supported by over 700 aircraft, a force three times that available to the RAF in Malaya and Burma.

## The Kra Isthmus

During the past few days, Southeast Asia had suddenly developed as a pressing priority for Churchill and his generals, ranked just below that of the CRUSADER battle in Libya. The decision-makers in Whitehall could not know, on 1 December, that Tokyo's Imperial Conference had finally put the wheels of aggression in motion. But they had a stream of fresh information telling them that some Japanese action was likely, and they did not know how to deal with it.

Southeast Asia, with the rubber and tin of British Malaya, the oil of British Borneo and the resources of the Dutch East Indies, was vital. British strategy in the region was centred on the naval base and fortress of Singapore, located on an island at the southern tip of Malaya. Singapore controlled the Straits of Malacca between the South China Sea and the Indian Ocean and was the key position in the so-called 'Malay Barrier', blocking Japanese access to the south. Naval dockyards, coastal fortifications, and RAF airfields had been established at Singapore in the 1920s and 1930s, in the face of growing Japanese power. The essence of the British 'Singapore strategy' in the event of a confrontation with Japan had been to hold the fortress long enough for a major fleet to arrive from Europe; Singapore would then provide a base from which that fleet could operate against Japan. Until 1940 Singapore was remote from any Japanese bases, and the expectation was that coastal artillery and an army garrison would prevent any attempt at a *coup de main* before the Navy arrived.

Unfortunately for the planners in Whitehall, world events put paid to this plan. The commitments of the Royal Navy in the Atlantic and the Mediterranean meant there was now no reinforcement fleet to send to Singapore. Meanwhile, the Japanese advance into Indochina put potentially hostile forces within 700 miles of the Singapore bastion – uncomfortably close. There was a belated attempt to develop 'aerodromes' for the RAF on the northern border of Malaya – 400 miles north of Singapore – but only limited air and ground forces could be deployed there.

By the autumn of 1941, Thailand, situated on the other side of that border, had become another source of worry for the British. As Siam, Thailand had been one of the few territories in the Far East to avoid European colonialism. But despite a military build up in the 1930s and a population of some 14 million, the country still lacked the ability to defend itself against one of the major powers. A Japanese presence in Thailand, however achieved, would present an immediate threat to northern Malaya (and British Burma) and in the longer term a danger to Singapore. This favourable military position would, at the very least, increase the diplomatic pressure which Tokyo could put on the British and the Dutch.

On 1 December, if there was one particular place in Thailand, and in the Far East as a whole, that caused the British concern, it was the Kra Isthmus. This remote region was the southernmost panhandle of Thailand (and Burma), and a long land bridge to Malaya. It was around thirty miles wide at its narrowest part, with the Indian Ocean to the west and the South China Sea to the east, and it stretched south from the town of Kra Buri to the Malayan border, a distance of some 250 miles.

The Kra Isthmus mattered in 1941 for two reasons. First of all, it could – and would – provide a landing place and advance base for an enemy force preparing to attack Malaya and then Singapore. Here the invader's air forces and supplies could be consolidated. Most important strategically were the small Thai ports at the far end of the isthmus, Singora (Songkhla) and Patani; around fifty miles from the Malayan border, they faced the South China Sea. Because Singora and Patani were in neutral Thailand they could not (unlike ports in northern Malaya) be fortified or defended by British forces. Secondly, the isthmus (on the Burmese side) was a vital stop-over on the only route by which RAF fighters and light bombers could be flown to Malaya from India.

The specific question confronting the British War Cabinet and the Chiefs of Staff that Monday (1 December) was this: should their forces try to prevent a Japanese occupation of neutral Thailand, and especially of the Kra Isthmus, by invading and occupying southern Thailand themselves? British intelligence predicted that a move into Thailand was Japan's most likely action. The British C-in-C in the Far East, Air Marshal Robert Brooke-Popham, had asked permission, most recently on 28 November, to occupy the ports on the Kra Isthmus if Japanese naval convoys should be seen approaching the area. The plan for the pre-emptive occupation of the Kra Isthmus, especially Singora and Patani, was called Operation MATADOR.[7]

Any decision involved risk. If Britain allowed Japan to occupy Thailand without a fight, the threat to Malaya and Burma would, in a few weeks or months, be much increased. If British forces only entered the Kra Isthmus after a Japanese incursion in the north from Indochina they would probably set off a war with Japan. If the British moved into the isthmus *before* the Japanese entered Thailand, or if the RAF attacked Japanese ships at sea, Tokyo could use this as a pretext for its own invasion, or for attacks on the Dutch East Indies or vulnerable parts of the British Empire, like North Borneo or Hong Kong. Whitehall had been told, possibly accurately, that the Japanese might even attempt to trick Britain into taking the first step into Thailand. The British Ambassador to Bangkok, Sir Josiah Crosby, certainly opposed a military incursion.[8] Worst of all, if MATADOR set off a war with Japan over Thailand, Britain might not have the support of the United States.

The Prime Minister, accompanied by Foreign Secretary Anthony Eden, Viscount Cranborne (the Dominions Secretary) and the Chiefs of Staff, had met two senior Australian representatives, Sir Earle Page and Stanley Bruce, in Downing Street on 1 December. Churchill explained that, in his view, 'we should not resist or attempt to forestall a Japanese attack on the Kra Isthmus unless we had a satisfactory assurance from the United States that they would join us should our action cause us to be involved in a war with Japan'; the same would apply if Japan attacked either Russia or the Dutch East Indies. When the British Chiefs of Staff Committee (COS) met at midday, they too could not recommend execution of MATADOR. That evening Churchill reported to the War Cabinet that the view of the COS should be accepted. Until assured of American support, Britain should take no steps. Even the beginning of a Japanese occupation of the Kra Isthmus, it was decided, would not automatically lead to war with Japan if American support was not certain. Oliver Harvey, Private Secretary (PPS) to the more uncompromising Eden, discussed these events with his chief, and concluded, 'PM is defeatist and appeasing where Far East is concerned and so, as usual, are the Chiefs of Staff'.[9]

So important and difficult an issue was Operation MATADOR becoming that, on 30 November, Churchill had turned for advice both to the Dominion governments and to Washington. He did not get a clear or consistent response from either direction. The Dominions – with the exception of Australia and South Africa – thought Whitehall should ensure the support of the United States before taking action.[10] Washington, for its part, was not prepared to make an open commitment, or even to send an immediate warning to Japan.

* * *

Readers of history armed with hindsight are fond of the 'might have been'. Operation MATADOR, however, was not such a missed opportunity. London's decision before (and after) 1 December to hold back MATADOR was not a fatal mistake that doomed Malaya. The operation was almost certainly not a practical proposition, if the Japanese planned – as they did – to mount strong simultaneous operations, overland in northern Thailand and by sea against the Kra Isthmus. The warning time for the defenders was simply not long enough. The relative quality and strength of the opposing forces was also wholly in Japan's favour, as would be demonstrated tragically in a week's time, on the ground in northern Malaya and in the air above it. A pre-emptive strike would only have led to an even earlier crumbling of the British defences. MATADOR was, however, important for what it revealed about British perceptions and plans, and about relations with the United States.

Anyone who read the newspapers was aware of the worsening state of Japanese relations with the United States, and to a lesser extent with Britain, over the past weeks and months. The economic embargo of Japan continued. A military-dominated government had been formed in Tokyo in October. But a small inner circle of leaders in both London and Washington had a unique insight into Tokyo's intentions, through their ability to read intercepted Japanese diplomatic messages.

When US Army code experts had in 1940 developed the ability to decrypt messages produced using the Japanese Foreign Ministry's Type 'B' Cipher Machine (the PURPLE machine), they had also built a small number of analogs (functional replicas) of the machine to aid rapid decryption of Japanese messages. In 1941, in an exchange of technical information, the American government gave the British two of these machines, one of which was installed at the super-secret codebreaking centre at Bletchley Park.[11] Decrypts relating to the Far East (and other places) were sent to Whitehall and circulated to a very select few in the form of carbon copies known as 'BJs' and in the frequent Admiralty 'Special Intelligence' bulletins.[12]

The Americans themselves intercepted a number of important Japanese diplomatic messages in November, and it is very likely that London was made aware of these. Foreign Minister Tōgō outlined the current negotiating position to Ambassador Nomura in Washington on 4 November, and on 5 November he informed him that the deadline for arranging an agreement with the United States was the 25th; the Americans decrypted these messages almost immediately. On 22 November Tokyo extended Nomura's deadline to the 29th, making clear that after this 'things are automatically going to happen'; Washington read this signal on the date after it was sent. On 28 November, Tōgō informed Nomura and Kurusu that negotiations were over, but that they should now try to stall for time; the Americans decrypted this message on the same date it was sent.[13] The British themselves decrypted Tōgō's circular of 20 November, in which he informed Japanese foreign missions that no further concessions would be made.[14] By 25 November the codebreakers at Bletchley Park had also made available to the British government the *Gaimushō* circular of 19 November setting up the 'winds' codes, intended to warn Japanese diplomatic representatives abroad of the imminent breakdown of diplomatic relations with Britain, America or the USSR.[15]

These intercepted messages may well have influenced Churchill's advice to President Roosevelt, sent early on 26 November, opposing even a short-term compromise with Japan. The Prime Minister's message is sometimes seen as the reason why the Americans opted to give the Japanese the inflexible Hull Note rather than an alternative, and more conciliatory, document known as the *modus vivendi*.[16]

The diplomatic decrypts were not the only source of intelligence. Other information that was becoming available to Churchill and his colleagues in London in the last week of November suggested an imminent military danger in Southeast Asia. British and American consular officials stationed at points on the Asian coast – Shanghai, Hong Kong, Hanoi, Saigon and Bangkok – pooled their information, and could discern very threatening shipping movements. On 25 November, Reed, the US consul in Hanoi, reported information from a French source to the effect that the Japanese would attack the Kra Isthmus 'on or about December 1', and would simultaneously advance by land into northern Thailand. This message was relayed to London by a British diplomat (Meiklereid) in Saigon, along with details of Japanese troop build-ups and airfield construction; it was considered serious enough to be circulated to the British War Cabinet on the 26th. On that day the US consul (Browne) in Saigon reported that since 21 November a number of troopships and supply ships had arrived in the Indochinese port, landing some 20,000 men; another 10,000 had come by rail from the north, bringing the total in southern Indochina to 70,000: 'it would appear,' Browne suggested, 'that operations against Thailand may soon begin.'[17]

Meanwhile, listening posts in Manila, Singapore, Borneo, Penang, Batavia (in the Dutch East Indies) and elsewhere monitored Japanese military radio traffic. The vital British intelligence organisation was the Far East Combined Bureau (FECB), based at Kranji near the Singapore naval base and including personnel from the three armed services. This was linked both to Bletchley Park and to similar secret American organisations in Washington, Manila and Hawaii, with which it exchanged radio direction finding (DF) and decryption information. The codebreakers in Singapore, even after sharing information with the Americans, could read only fragments of high-level Japanese military messages, in contrast to the extensive access to high-level diplomatic correspondence enjoyed in London and Washington. Nevertheless, the listening posts were able to use even their limited knowledge – especially of the radio call signs of various vessels – to track the movement and organisation of Japanese warships. DF allowed monitoring stations to locate the position of Japanese transmitters by triangulation, and traffic analysis gave considerable information about who was talking to whom – if not what they were talking about.

The British, both in London and Singapore, received some or all of the reports produced by the US Navy radio monitoring stations in the Pacific. These were Station HYPO in Hawaii and Station CAST in Manila, and they sent important reports on 26 November based on radio traffic analysis. This was the period in which a number of Japanese warships had begun to surge into forward positions in preparation for the invasion of Southeast Asia, and many of the reports were quite accurate. Hawaii reported that a large operational command ('task force') had been set up under the C-in-C of the Japanese 2nd Fleet. A strong force from this command was preparing to operate in Southeast Asia, while smaller components might operate in the Central Pacific. In fact the Americans had detected the movement of Admiral Kondō's 'Southern Force', set up to cover the invasions. Manila generally supported the assessment from Hawaii. Neither report suggested a location for the main force of Japanese battleships (the 1st Fleet), but the Manila paper located the aircraft carriers in the Sasebo-Kure area in southern Japan. In any event these reports confirmed major Japanese naval movements.[18] From the point of view of the British what was really important was that a large number of powerful ships were heading in their direction.

An American report from Station CAST in the Philippines and dated 1 December, described another significant development, and one that was almost certainly known to the British: 'All Orange service calls for units afloat were changed at 0000, December 1, 1941.'[19] (The Japanese were usually designated by the codeword ORANGE.) The Japanese Navy had suddenly changed all their radio call signs – for the second time in a month – and that was itself a warning of a highly abnormal situation.

The British were also made aware of serious alerts issued to American forces. Admiral Harold Stark, the US Chief of Naval Operations, had on 24 November warned 'that a surprise aggressive action in any direction including attack on Philippines or Guam is a possibility'.[20] (The original Japanese cut-off date for negotiations, as set out in the intercepted Tōgō-Nomura telegram of 5 November, was 25 November, which may well have been a factor behind the warning.) One of the addressees of Stark's message was the American Special Naval Observer (SPENAVO) in London, and his warning was presumably passed to the British. The British Admiralty was certainly informed by the office of the SPENAVO on 28 November about a second US Navy 'war warning' that had been sent by Admiral Stark on the previous day. Negotiations with Japan had ceased, the CNO announced, and 'an aggressive move by Japan is expected in the next few days'. He mentioned threats to both British and American territory, as well as to Thailand: 'The number and equipment of Japanese troops and the organization of naval task forces indicates an amphibious expedition against either the Philippines Thai [sic] or Kra Peninsula or possibly Borneo.'[21]

Air Marshal Brooke-Popham in Singapore collated various pieces of military intelligence when he despatched an important and urgent warning to London on 28 November. Brooke-Popham specifically referred to the same squadron of large Japanese cruisers mentioned in the American intelligence reports of the 26th (from Hawaii and Manila), and he said that these vessels could reach the Kra Isthmus on 30 November (which date, it will be recalled, was known to be the Japanese diplomatic deadline).[22] Brooke-Popham added that the number of Japanese aircraft in French Indochina had risen from 74 to 245 in the past month; that the Chinese General Staff had reported the arrival in the region of the Japanese 5th Division, highly trained in landing operations; and that no fewer than 330 motorised landing craft had been moved from central China since October.[23]

* * *

Although incorrect in some details, Brooke-Popham's message of 28 November was a remarkably accurate statement of Japanese strength. The problem was that the assessment misunderstood the *intentions* of the adversary. Brooke-Popham judged that the Japanese would attack (or occupy) neutral Thailand and not British, Dutch or American territory. Moreover, a landing in the Kra Isthmus in Thailand was not seen as an immediate danger to Malaya ('attack on Kra Isthmus if carried out at all at this time of year when it is largely waterlogged is not likely to be an immediate prelude to an attack on Malaya').[24]

This fatal miscalculation of Japanese intentions and potential was shared by Whitehall. The Joint Intelligence Committee (JIC) was a sub-committee of the Chiefs of Staff Committee; it was chaired by a relatively junior Foreign Office official, an aristocrat and career diplomat named Sir Victor Cavendish-Bentinck. 'Bill' Bentinck's committee included representatives from the Foreign Office and the three armed services, and coordinated the expertise of those bodies alongside that of the Secret Intelligence Service (SIS). It had two years' wartime experience and enjoyed extraordinary sources of information, especially signals intelligence. As an organisation for co-ordinating intelligence, the JIC was superior to that which existed in other countries at the time, including the United States. And it was nearly right about the very first Japanese step. On 18 November the military experts on the committee had concluded that if the Washington talks failed and if Japan 'decided to proceed irrespective of the risk of war with Britain, America and the Netherlands', it was more likely to attack neutral Thailand than Malaya, the Dutch East Indies or Russian Siberia. This JIC assessment was shared with the White House; on 21 November the gist of it was communicated to Harry Hopkins, President Roosevelt's influential adviser.[25]

One week later, on 28 November, the JIC still took the view that a Japanese *land* advance from Indochina into Thailand was the most likely event, and might 'follow closely' the breakdown of the Washington talks (that event had effectively occurred two days previously). The 'estimate' played down the immediate danger to Southeast Asia more generally. A major Japanese *naval* expedition against the Dutch East Indies, Malaya, or even Thailand was not likely, let alone simultaneous strikes against all three. (The estimate made no comment about US territories such as the Philippines.) The Americans had a powerful naval force able to threaten Japanese territories in the the central Pacific, and the British fleet in Singapore was being strengthened with capital ships. (The new battleship *Prince of Wales* and the battlecruiser *Repulse* were shortly to arrive there.) Southern Thailand lay 2,000 miles away from the Imperial Navy's main bases in the Japanese home islands. In view of the 'characteristic caution' of the Japanese, the JIC felt it was 'questionable' whether they would split their fleet and send a major force, including capital ships, into southern waters to attack Malaya or the Dutch East Indies. A less ambitious Japanese seaborne expedition against the Kra Isthmus was, however, conceivable. Such an operation could be screened by Japanese submarines and coupled with a land advance from Indochina into northern Thailand.

Aside from this basic underestimation of the ability of Imperial Japan to mount simultaneous attacks in different directions, the JIC report of 28 November exaggerated the technical difficulties that would hold Japan back from mounting extensive operations south of Thailand. First of all, the British were ignorant of the relative capabilities of the air forces on either side, especially Japanese land-based aircraft. Any hostile fleet movement to the south, the JIC forecast, would be threatened with an air attack by defending bombers, 'against which they [the Japanese] could only employ ship-borne aircraft'. In reality British and American bombers would prove almost useless over the next two months, while Japanese *land-based* bombers would sortie from Indochina and Formosa and sweep the South China Sea clear of British and American ships.

A second error concerned the effect of weather conditions on Japanese operations in December. Although not ruling out the possibility of a seaborne landing, the JIC also stated that weather conditions for a seaborne landing in the Kra Isthmus would be 'at their worst' from November to January. Finally, another fundamental miscalculation by the JIC – like that of Brooke-Popham in his message of 28 November – was the anticipated timescale for operations. The JIC report suggested that even if the Japanese occupied the Kra Isthmus in Thailand, and even if they intended further operations against British Malaya, their forces would not represent an immediate danger. This was partly because the British expected a ponderous Japanese logistical build-up of the kind their own forces would have required. The Japanese, they thought, would need two or three months, and possibly longer, to develop their supply lines and construct air bases in southern Thailand. The climate was also a factor, as movement in the rainy season – up to March 1942 – in southern Thailand and northern Malaya would be very difficult: 'good roads are liable to flooding, bad roads liable to disintegrate, and movement off the roads out of the question'. The overview was as follows: 'If the Japanese are prepared to risk war with ourselves, there are sound strategical reasons why they might attempt to occupy Thailand at the very beginning of 1942 so as to be able to go forward in strength against Malaya about March or April.'[26]

In reality the Japanese armada that carried out the landings in the Kra Isthmus and northeast Malaya would lose only one transport ship to British action on the night of 7–8 December. The stormy weather had little effect, except to hide Japanese ships from British scout planes. And less than thirty-six hours after the first landing in Thailand the vanguard of General Yamashita's army would cross from the Kra Isthmus into Malaya, where it advanced rapidly, on and off the roads, to the south.

The assessment of commanders in the field or of the middle-ranking intelligence officers on the Joint Intelligence Committee was not necessarily that of Churchill, the British Chiefs of Staff, or the Foreign Office. Nevertheless, as of 1 December all these authorities were in agreement. The consensus was that Japan might take some kind of initiative, but it was not likely to make war against the British Empire, let alone against Britain and the United States together.[27] The more fundamental arguments Churchill had made three weeks earlier in his Lord Mayor's Day speech at Mansion House still seemed relevant. 'Viewing the vast sombre scene as dispassionately as possible,' the Prime Minister had said on 10 November, 'it would seem a very hazardous adventure for the Japanese people to plunge quite needlessly into a struggle in which they might find themselves opposed in the Pacific by States whose populations comprise nearly three-quarters of the human race.' Japan was economically weak: 'steel is the basic foundation of modern war', and Japan's annual production was only 7 million tons, compared to the United States' 90 million, plus the 'powerful contribution which the British Empire can make'.[28]

Although the Prime Minister's words could be seen as a public warning to Japan – rather than a wholly objective assessment – and although more danger signs about Japanese intentions became apparent in the second half of November, the speech did represent the Prime Minister's basic view on 1 December: Japanese behaviour would be step-by-step and cautious.

From Churchill's point of view, Japan would never in the long term be able to prevail against the combined strength of the British Empire and United States.

In the short term a combination of a reinforced British Eastern Fleet at Singapore and the powerful US battle fleet threatening Japanese possessions in the mid-Pacific would make a broader Japanese attack risky to the point of national suicide. The de facto economic blockade by America, Britain and the Netherlands was having its desired effect. When he wrote to President Roosevelt on 26 November, arguing against even a short-term *modus vivendi* with Japan, Churchill's calculation was that Tokyo would back down. '[W]e certainly do not want an additional war,' he told the President, but Tokyo was in a difficult position. 'We feel,' Churchill concluded, 'that the Japanese are most unsure of themselves.'[29]

Foreign Secretary Eden was at least as sure as the Prime Minister about the value of taking a hard line with the Japanese.[30] There was, however, one dissenting voice: the British Ambassador to Japan. Although not an East Asian specialist, Sir Robert Craigie had very wide experience and had served in Japan since 1937; he had also dealt with the Japanese as chief negotiator in the naval disarmament talks of the 1930s. He believed both that there was good reason to negotiate with the Tokyo government, and that the Japanese were capable of going to war. Sir Robert was certainly aware of the diplomatic importance of the United States; his wife was American, he had served in Washington and later headed the American desk in the Foreign Office. Nevertheless, he felt it had been a mistake to let Washington take the lead in negotiations with Japan. America's interests, he argued, were different from those of the British Empire, and the diplomatic position of President Roosevelt and Secretary Hull seemed to him to be both inflexible and unrealistic.

Looking at events with the benefit of hindsight, it is clear that Craigie, both in November 1941 and in later writings, placed unrealistic hopes in the possibility of negotiating with Japan. Unlike Churchill and Eden (and unlike Roosevelt and Hull), he did not have access to the decrypts of diplomatic messages, which showed how intransigent and two-faced Tokyo's policy was. He also dealt mainly with politicians and diplomats and underestimated the influence of the military elite in Japan's decision-making. But Craigie had a better understanding of Japanese psychology than did Churchill and Eden. He was right about the flaws of American foreign policy, and above all he was right about the dangers to Britain.

In his last major despatch to the Foreign Office, on 1 November 1941, Craigie stressed the threat of general war in the Far East. In view of deteriorating relations between Japan and the US, he complained, 'an explosion could now occur at any time'. The British Empire might be the first victim of such an explosion, because Japan's initial action might take the form of a direct attack on British territory 'from which Japan might hope to achieve the first results before the ponderous machinery of the United States Government had had time to project the United States into active participation in the war'. '[A]bout the worst mistake that we and the Americans can make at this juncture,' Sir Robert astutely warned, 'is to under-estimate the strength and resolution of this country [i.e. Japan] and its armed forces, in the event – perhaps now not far distant – that it may feel itself driven to desperation.'

Sir Robert was also right about the implications of a new conflict in the Far East on the course of the Second World War as a whole. Nazi Germany was the real danger to Britain, he argued. American power should be devoted to the war against Germany, not a sideshow in the Pacific. 'What we presumably want is the United States in the war on our side, and Japan *really* neutral . . . If Hitler's motto is "One by one," the motto of those who take too lightly the prospect of Japan's entry into the war appears to be "The more the merrier"'.[31]

Much of what Craigie said was true, although his advice really applied more to the situation in the summer of 1941, rather than that of late autumn. The Japanese decided to go to war on 5 November, and conflict was inevitable at least from the time of the formation of the Tōjō government in October. No last-minute diplomatic effort would have made a difference. Craigie also did not fully grasp the extent to which Britain was now – and would be in the future – dependent on developments in Washington.

CHAPTER 4

MONDAY, 1 DECEMBER

# Washington, MAGIC and the Japanese Peril

*[The United States] felt much interest in and were very much encouraged about the news from Libya and Russia, and it looked as though we might be turning the corner into a more favourable situation.*

Cordell Hull

*At one point he [President Roosevelt] threw in as an aside that in the event of any direct attack on ourselves or the Dutch, we should obviously all be together, but he wished to clear up the matters which were less plain.*

Lord Halifax

## The Atlantic Ocean

On 1 December the United States was already taking part in the global struggle against Nazi Germany. The country was perhaps not yet involved – to use Churchill's later words – 'up to the neck', but the policy of its government was far from neutral. On this day convoy WS.124 was deep in the South Atlantic, approaching the Cape of Good Hope, having left Halifax, Nova Scotia, on 8 November, sailing via Port of Spain, Trinidad. The US Navy called the convoy 'William Sail', using its phonetic alphabet, but 'WS' was a British abbreviation meaning 'Winston Special', after the Prime Minister. The designation was applied to a series of 'fast' British troop convoys which, since August 1940, had been running men and equipment from Britain to the Middle Eastern battle front, around the Cape of Good Hope. But this WS convoy was different. WS.124 comprised the three biggest and fastest ocean liners flying the

American flag, SS *Washington*, *Manhattan* and *America* (now in naval service as USS *Mount Vernon*, *Wakefield* and *West Point*), as well as three other large American transports. On board the American ships were no fewer than 22,000 British troops – mainly from the new 18th Division – intended to fight the Germans and Italians in the Middle East. The escort was made up exclusively of American warships, two heavy cruisers and six destroyers, as well as a naval oiler. Until four days previously, when well into the South Atlantic, the convoy escorts had included the big aircraft carrier USS *Ranger* – flying the flag of an American Rear Admiral – and two more destroyers. WS.124 would reach Durban, South Africa, on 9 December.[1]

As it happened, neither U-boats nor German surface raiders attacked the heavily-escorted convoy. (The British 18th Division would suffer a tragic fate, but not in a form anyone expected. Diverted to India and then the Far East, it was landed in Singapore just weeks before the Japanese took the fortress.) Neither the German naval high command nor the American public knew of the convoy's existence. But WS.124 was an example of the participation, growing in scale and intensity, of America and its armed forces in the war against Germany.

Other ships of the US Navy were on combat duty in the North Atlantic on 1 December. HX.161, a convoy of fifty-two merchant ships, was in mid-ocean, having left Halifax nine days earlier. Its escorts against German U-boat attack consisted of six US Navy destroyers, which would accompany the convoy to the 'MOMP' (Mid-Ocean Meeting Point) some 500 miles west of Ireland, where a British Escort Group would take over, covering the final stage of the voyage to Liverpool.[2] Like other ships in the US Atlantic Fleet the six destroyers escorting HX.161 had orders to 'shoot on sight'. Due to successful British convoy routing and the limited number of U-boats available, the Americans would not have an opportunity to try out these simple rules of engagement. The main enemy would be the harsh mid-winter weather of the North Atlantic. Since mid-September, destroyers of the neutral United States had routinely escorted convoys two-thirds of the way across the North Atlantic. Meanwhile American battleships and cruisers were based on the edge of European waters at Hvalfjord in Iceland, with orders to intercept German surface raiders attempting to break through the Greenland-Iceland gap.

* * *

President Franklin Delano Roosevelt was a Democrat in the tradition of Woodrow Wilson. He wanted the United States to play an active, and indeed central, role in world politics. He had surrounded himself with like-minded men: Cordell Hull and Sumner Welles from the State Department, Secretary of War Henry Stimson, Secretary of the Navy Frank Knox, and Secretary of the Treasury Henry Morgenthau. From the late 1930s Roosevelt had been a vociferous opponent of the Nazi regime in Germany. Hitler was for him the greatest danger to world peace and to American interests. Once the fighting in Europe started he committed the United States, as far as he could, to aid those countries that were at war with Nazi Germany, in the first instance the British Empire and France, and from June 1941 the USSR.

The President faced two great problems. The first was that the United States of America was a divided democracy. A considerable share of public opinion was 'isolationist'. Roosevelt ran for office in 1940, for an unprecedented and controversial third four-year term, and he did so on a platform of keeping the country out of war. Under the American Constitution it was Congress that could declare war, not the President. Although the November 1940 election was a victory for 'FDR' the electorate was deeply divided: some 27 million Americans cast their votes for Roosevelt, but 22 million voted for the Republican Wendell Wilkie. The division was hardly surprising; after a decade of the Great Depression and Roosevelt's 'New Deal', opinion was polarised about economic policy, and many voters were concerned about the growth of presidential power. The Democrats kept control of over two-thirds of the Senate, and 60 per cent of the House of Representatives, but the party was an amalgamation of divergent interests. Congress could not be relied upon to approve all initiatives from the White House; the most remarkable wobble came in August 1941 when the House passed by only one vote the renewal of the one-year 'Selective Service' conscription system; 203 Representatives voted in favour, 202 against.

Roosevelt's second problem was the state of the US Army and the US Navy. They were unready for war, and certainly unready for a global war in both Europe and in Asia. Such a multi-front conflict had become more likely with the September 1940 Tripartite Pact (which meant, as we have seen, that American intervention against Germany and Italy in Europe could lead to Japan taking arms against America in the Pacific). Although the American fleet was strong on paper, it was still far from being the projected 'Two-Ocean' Navy. The condition of the US Army – little more than skeletal in 1941 – was much worse. Although American armament production had increased rapidly, much of the equipment – especially aircraft – was sent to countries that were already involved in the fighting, particularly to the British Empire. The leaders of both the American armed services secretly pleaded for a delay before entering hostilities. There was no immediate threat to US territory by German or Italian forces, but American possessions in the Far East and the Pacific, especially Guam and the Philippines, were vulnerable to a Japanese attack. On 5 November the Joint Board – the nearest thing America had to a military supreme command – had argued strongly to the President for caution in the Far East, in view of both the need for time to build up American forces there, and the greater importance attached to a war with Germany.[3]

The result of these two problems facing Roosevelt was a strange inconsistency between the rhetoric of the President and the action taken. Roosevelt might describe Nazi Germany as the greatest enemy the United States had ever faced, yet he was unwilling to lead his country directly into war against it. What the President could do was use his executive powers to take steps legally 'short of war'. The American government could aid those countries fighting Hitler, it could plan for entry into war with Germany (alongside potential 'associates'), it could build up the air, land and sea forces of the US, and it could make the posture of those forces more 'warlike'. There were, in all this, undoubtedly elements of both calculation and provocation, as well as the memory of what had happened in 1915–17. The President hoped that his actions would goad Hitler's Germany into a belligerent response that would increase interventionist sentiment in America.

In September 1940, after the fall of France and at a critical point in the Battle of Britain, the President agreed to give the Royal Navy fifty old destroyers. In exchange the US received bases at eight locations on British territory in the Western hemisphere. In December 1940, Roosevelt explained his foreign policy to the American people in a radio address. 'Never before since Jamestown and Plymouth Rock,' he declared, 'has our American civilisation been in such danger as now.' The Tripartite Pact proved this: 'The Nazi masters of Germany have made it clear that they intend not only to dominate all life and thought in their own country, but also to enslave the whole of Europe, and then to use the resources of Europe to dominate the rest of the world.' Roosevelt assured his listeners – not altogether logically – that the issue was one not of war but of 'national security'. The solution he proposed was to make America the 'great arsenal of democracy', providing weapons for Britain and other states fighting the Axis.[4] When the British ran out of foreign exchange to pay for munitions the President committed America to 'loan' equipment under the Lend-Lease program; this would be approved by Congress in March 1941.

With Roosevelt's approval the American military also began to plan for direct participation in the war alongside the British. Between January and March 1941 secret high-level staff talks were held in Washington, the 'American-British Conversations', or ABC-1. A grand-strategic British-American war plan, also called ABC-1, was drawn up in its final form at the end of March. It stressed one potential enemy in particular: 'Since Germany is the predominant member of the Axis powers, the Atlantic and the European area is considered to be the decisive theatre. The principal United States Military effort will be exerted in that theatre, and operations of United States forces in other theatres will be conducted in such a manner as to facilitate that effort.'[5] In April 1941, shortly after the Washington talks ended, the planners of the American Army and Navy drew up a new national war plan, following the lines of ABC-1 and known as RAINBOW FIVE.

Roosevelt and Churchill staged an extraordinary public demonstration of the strengthening links between their two countries – and an open provocation to Nazi Germany – when in August 1941 they held a widely-publicised meeting at Argentia Bay in Newfoundland (Argentia was a location where the US had gained base rights in September 1940). This was the first proper face-to-face meeting of the two leaders (although they had briefly encountered one another in 1918). Roosevelt arrived on a cruiser from New England; Churchill arrived from Britain aboard *Prince of Wales*, the new battleship that would be sunk four months later by the Japanese. Aside from putting together a declaration of joint 'war aims' – the Atlantic Charter – which was explicitly anti-German, the senior American and British military advisers also secretly confirmed the ABC-1 strategy.

* * *

Alongside the high politics of the blossoming 'special relationship' between Britain and the United States, the two countries in 1940–41 took practical steps to confront the German Navy in the Atlantic. This threat had been a major theme of Churchill's appeals for help. In his important letter of 7 December 1940 he had proposed various actions to the American President. He stressed the 'mortal danger' of both U-boat and surface raiders like the new ocean-going battleships, *Bismarck* and *Tirpitz*. He suggested that the US should assert the doctrine of 'freedom of the seas' and that US forces – battleships, cruisers, destroyers, aircraft – should escort convoys. The British Prime Minister argued in his letter that such involvement in the Atlantic would not necessarily lead America into war (although, truth be told, nothing would have pleased him more). Hitler would try to avoid the Kaiser's mistake of 1915–17; he would not go to war with the US until he had 'gravely undermined' British power. 'His maxim is "one at a time".'[6]

Churchill was knocking at an open door. Franklin Roosevelt was perhaps the most naval-minded of all American presidents, and his Chief of Naval

Operations (CNO), Admiral Harold R. Stark, advocated using the powerful fleet against Germany. For the last two decades the United States Navy had been concentrated in the Pacific Ocean. Now, in February 1941, a US Atlantic Fleet was created. In early April the President approved the transfer of three battleships from the Pacific Fleet, *Idaho*, *Mississippi* and *New Mexico*, to join three older dreadnoughts in the Atlantic. Also sent east through the Panama Canal were the new carrier *Yorktown*, five new light cruisers and some destroyers; the transfer was completed by the end of May 1941. At first the most likely action for this American force was the occupation of Portugal's Atlantic islands, especially the Azores, to prevent a German landing. By the end of May, however, it had been decided that the United States would take over the occupation of Iceland from the British. An expeditionary convoy, carrying a brigade of US Marines, arrived in July 1941, and thereafter Hvalfjord (outside Reykjavik), 2,000 miles from mainland America, became an advanced base for the Atlantic Fleet.

In 1915–17, U-boat attacks on merchant ships had been a continuing source of friction between Germany and the United States. By contrast, in 1940–41 the number of incidents involving American vessels was small, due to a combination of US 'neutrality' legislation and German caution – the latter especially after the beginning of war in Russia. Nevertheless, on 21 May 1941 a U-boat torpedoed the US merchant ship *Robin Moor* off West Africa, despite ascertaining the vessel's neutral status. Although the submarine commander gave the American crew time to take to their lifeboats, the sinking was a major diplomatic incident, and in reprisal Washington closed all German consulates.

On 4 September, *U 652* fired a torpedo at the destroyer USS *Greer* off Iceland. (*Greer* had been actively co-operating with British forces which were attacking the U-boat.) A week later President Roosevelt made a radio address in which he condemned Nazi Germany for the *Greer* attack, as well as for the sinking of *Robin Moor* and certain other incidents. The U-boats and surface raiders, FDR declared, were the 'rattlesnakes of the Atlantic'. 'From now on', he publicly warned, 'if German or Italian vessels of war enter the waters, the protection of which is necessary for American defence, they do so at their own peril.'[7] Those waters – necessary for defence – comprised the extended Western hemisphere.

As we have seen, in August, even before the *Greer* incident, the United States had agreed to escort convoys to Britain across the western and central North Atlantic. On 17 October, a U-boat torpedo damaged USS *Kearny*, part of an Escort Group of five American destroyers accompanying a British convoy. In late October a U-boat sank destroyer *Reuben James*, from another US Navy

Escort Group. Remarkably, the attack on USS *Reuben James* did not lead to a dramatic worsening of US-German relations. In any event U-boat activity in the North Atlantic was being reduced, partly because of the winter conditions, partly due to the success of routing convoys around the submarines (thanks to electronic intelligence, including the decryption of radio messages between the U-boats and their headquarters), and partly because of the deployment of so many U-boats in the Mediterranean or the area west of Gibraltar. There were no further attacks near American ships in the North Atlantic in November, and American warships would not sink a U-boat until April 1942.

Meanwhile, however, ships of the US Navy cruised the North and South Atlantic to prevent the operations of German raiders and blockade runners. On 6 November the cruiser *Omaha*, patrolling off the coast of Brazil, seized the German blockade runner *Odenswald*.

The undeclared US-German naval war in the Atlantic was no obscure footnote to history. Berlin came to assume that the United States Navy was already heavily committed to the convoy battle, and that formal American entry into the war would scarcely deepen the country's involvement. According to one account, this was the view of Hitler himself by November 1941: 'The Americans are already shooting at us, so we are already at war with them.'[8] When Germany *did* declare war on the United States, on 11 December 1941, these incidents served as the *casus belli*. The brief German declaration of war cited President Roosevelt's speech of 11 September 1941, proclaiming that 'vessels of the American Navy, since early September 1941, have systematically attacked German naval forces'; it also complained that American naval forces had 'seized German merchant vessels on the high seas'. When Hitler spoke – at much greater length – to the Reichstag on the 11th he would recite a string of American provocations, including the attack by the US destroyer *Greer* on *U 652*, and the capture of *Odenswald*.

At the beginning of November, decrypted German radio messages revealed that one of Germany's heavy ships – possibly the new battleship *Tirpitz* – might be preparing to mount a raid into the Atlantic. The American battleships *Idaho* and *Mississippi*, two heavy cruisers and three destroyers – organised as Task Group 1.3 – were sent to patrol the strait between Iceland and Greenland; British ships patrolled south of Iceland. In reality the 'pocket battleship' *Admiral Scheer*, rather than the much more formidable *Tirpitz*, was the German ship that was supposed to sortie, but as a result of engine trouble her operation was postponed.[9] Had the Task Group intercepted the pocket battleship, America's entry into the Second World War might have been very different.

## The Far East

The crews of American warships braved the storm-tossed Atlantic winter. Washington, DC, in contrast, enjoyed summer temperatures well into November, somehow emphasising the city's status as a peacetime capital. On 1 December Secretary of State Cordell Hull had another meeting with the Japanese Ambassador Nomura and Special Envoy Kurusu. The three men talked in Hull's office in the five-storey Old Executive Office Building, located across the street from the White House. They had last assembled on the previous Thursday afternoon (27 November); Hull had been holding talks about normalising American-Japanese relations with Nomura since April. Hull was a crusty Tennessee lawyer who served as Secretary of State through most of Roosevelt's term of office, from 1933–44; he was imbued with the idealistic tradition of Woodrow Wilson. Hull's advancing years – he was now sixty-nine – had not made him any more flexible. Nomura Kichisaburō was a retired Admiral of the Japanese Navy, but well-liked in Washington. On 15 November Kurusu Saburō, a more uncompromising career diplomat, though married to an American, had arrived as an additional special envoy.

There was little to talk about, and everyone in the room was painfully aware of it. None of the participants knew about the secret Imperial Conference which had been held in Tokyo half a day earlier. Kurusu, however, had left Japan just as the 'twin-track' decision of 5 November was approved. He and Nomura understood that the train on the diplomatic track had hit the buffers on the 26th, and that the other track led to war. They were aware that the Imperial Conference's deadline of 29 November had come and gone. Hull knew most of what the two Japanese knew, having read their intercepted instructions from Tokyo.

The Secretary of State complained about 'loud talk' by Prime Minister Tōjō, referring to press reports of a speech supposedly made in Tokyo the previous afternoon. Tōjō was said to have robustly defended the Tripartite Pact and Japan's 'Greater East Asia Co-prosperity Sphere' – a scheme designed to spread Japanese power over Asia – and to have denounced American meddling in the region. Hull also asked, pointedly, if the Japanese were following the news about the successes of the British and Russian armies. The United States, he commented, 'felt much interest in and were very much encouraged about the news from Libya and Russia, and it looked as though we might be turning the corner into a more favourable situation'. He did refer in passing to the accumulation of Japanese troops in Indochina, 'digging in' and posing a threat to neighbouring territories ('we do not know where the Japanese Army intends to land its forces').[10]

Across the street, in the White House, a sense of crisis was building on 1 December. President Roosevelt arrived back in the nation's capital at 11.30 a.m. He had left Washington on Friday, for a post-Thanksgiving holiday in a favoured resort (and polio clinic) at Warm Springs, Georgia, where he expected to stay until Thursday, 4 December. On Sunday morning Secretary Hull telephoned the President, and urged him to return to the capital, in view of the growing crisis with Japan. Now, back in Washington, the President summoned Lord Halifax, the British Ambassador. The President, Halifax, and Harry Hopkins had a ninety-minute talk after lunch. Secretary Hull was not present; at the top level FDR often preferred unfettered personal diplomacy.

The three men presented a study in contrasts. E.F.L. Wood, Lord Halifax, was a a tall, rather cadaverous, balding Catholic aristocrat. Halifax was no mere diplomatic messenger boy. He was viceroy of India in the late 1920s, and then held a range of powerful political posts before serving, from 1938, as Foreign Secretary under Neville Chamberlain and then Churchill. A powerful Tory politician, Halifax was Churchill's main rival to succeed Chamberlain in April 1940, and he had a stronger following among Conservative MPs than the maverick Churchill. Since the fall of France the embassy at 3100 Massachusetts Avenue had been by far Britain's most important diplomatic post, but it was also a place of political exile; Halifax was less dangerous to Churchill there than in London. The fox-hunting Halifax had not been altogether the right man to woo the American public, and he had some difficulties with Roosevelt's overly-familiar personal style. (Roosevelt wanted to call him 'Edward'; Halifax confided ironically to his diary that he wished he could call the President 'Frankie'.)[11]

Harry Hopkins was quite different: a Midwesterner, and an able and energetic social work administrator who had become the organiser of the vast New Deal relief programmes. He was a close personal friend of the President, and when war came to Europe Roosevelt despatched him on important foreign missions as his eyes and ears. His visit to London in January 1941 had marked the real start of the 'Special Relationship'.

President Roosevelt, a wily politician, very rarely kept formal records of meetings, but Halifax provided a report to his Foreign Office about this one. As had been the case in London earlier in the day – the British capital was six hours ahead of Washington – Southeast Asia was the main topic under discussion.[12] Churchill had written another of his personal letters to the President on the previous afternoon (30 November), ending it with his habitual *nom de guerre*, 'Former Naval Person'. In the letter the Prime Minister suggested that the only way to avert war with Japan was 'a plain declaration, secret or private' to the government in Tokyo. Churchill was not shy of giving the President detailed counsel: 'I beg you to consider whether, at the moment which you judge right which may be very near, you should not say that "any further Japanese aggression would compel you to place the gravest issue before Congress" or words to that effect.' Britain would follow suit, and in any event it was synchronising its actions with those of the US. 'Forgive me, my dear friend,' Churchill concluded, 'for presuming to press such a course upon you, but I am convinced that it might make all the difference and prevent a melancholy extension of the war.'[13]

At their meeting on the 1st, so Halifax reported, the President agreed that if the Japanese were sending reinforcements to Indochina 'they were not going there for their health'. But the indecisive and cautious Roosevelt was minded to tackle this challenge step by step. He proposed to begin by formally asking Tokyo what was going on. Halifax thought that any Japanese reply could only be 'mendacious or evasive'. Hopkins supported Halifax, arguing that something more than a succession of diplomatic notes was required; 'the impression [was] being created that the Japanese acted while we only sent notes and talked'. The President, unconvinced, asked Halifax to find out how his government would respond if it did not get an acceptable answer from the Japanese regarding their intentions, or if the Japanese attacked northern Thailand.

'I think,' Halifax reported to London, 'that whatever action . . . His Majesty's Government would be prepared to take, he [Roosevelt] would be disposed to support.' (The British, as we have seen, were considering putting into effect Operation MATADOR and occupying southern Thailand before the Japanese could establish advance bases there.) The President's idea of potential military support at this time, according to Halifax, involved air operations mounted from the Philippines and 'long distance naval blockade "which of course means shooting"'. These were, to be sure, Halifax's thoughts rather than presidential promises. The Ambassador also reported that the President said, 'as an aside', that in the event of a *direct* attack on British territory or the Dutch East Indies 'we should obviously all be together'. This hinted at a grey area *in advance* of a direct attack where the US and Britain would not be together – for example, the pre-emptive strike of Operation MATADOR.

President Roosevelt had spoken words of support for Britain in this crisis, but in vague terms. Under the American Constitution he could not, as head of the Executive Branch, make any binding promise to fight alongside Britain. As for Churchill's request for some kind of joint ultimatum to Japan, Roosevelt was also unwilling to move quickly. The President said that the British and Dutch could count on his support, but he would need a few days 'to get things into political shape here'.[14]

Although privately the British Ambassador thought his meeting had gone well, he was left without a firm decision from the Americans. The position of Lord Halifax in Washington was not so very different from that of General Ōshima in Berlin. Both men were supplicants; their countries were both seeking strong allies. For different reasons their prospective partners were not willing to commit themselves. Tokyo had decided on war in any event, with or without German participation, although there were concerns among some Japanese leaders about consequences in the long term. London was much less certain about whether to take pre-emptive action without a clearer commitment from the White House, and from the US Congress.

* * *

Despite Roosevelt's caution, the American government, like the British government, had many reasons to think that Japan was developing into a clear danger, not least with the formation of the Tōjō government. In early November the American Ambassador Joseph Grew – as perceptive an observer of the Japanese scene as was his British colleague, Craigie – sent a warning to Hull, which was also read by the President. Grew's advice was that the trade embargo, and even blockade, would not deter Japan, which had a state-controlled economy. While stressing that he was in no sense an appeaser, Grew questioned whether his government grasped the risks involved. 'My purpose,' he explained, 'is only to ensure against my country's getting into war with Japan through any possible misconception of the capacity of Japan to rush headlong into a suicidal conflict with the United States. National sanity would dictate against such an event, but Japanese sanity cannot be measured by our own standards of logic.' The government in Tokyo was not simply rattling sabres, he warned: 'Japan's resort to measures which might [sic] war with the United States, may come with dramatic and dangerous suddenness.'[15]

Two weeks later Grew emphasised this point in another telegram to Hull, stressing that Japan might strike suddenly and that the Tokyo embassy should not be relied upon to provide a warning.[16] In fact, as we know, the President had other, 'special' sources of information in the form of MAGIC. The intercepted messages from Tokyo, dated 5 and 22 November, showed that the Japanese government was limiting the time of negotiation with the US to the end of the month, and the message of 28 November informed the Washington embassy that negotiations were effectively over.[17] Like the British, the American codebreakers had by 25 November read the Japanese Foreign Ministry circular of the 19th setting up the 'winds' code, with one formulation to signal that Japanese and American relations were in danger of being broken off. This accumulation of damning intelligence surely contributed to Roosevelt's decision, during the night of 25–26 November, to end negotiations and abandon attempts at a short-term *modus vivendi* with Japan.[18]

On Monday, 1 December, MAGIC provided the US government with four further pieces of vital intelligence. These intercepted signals were probably not available to Secretary Hull when he met the Japanese in mid-morning, nor to President Roosevelt when he lunched with Halifax. By the end of the day, however, Washington had certainly obtained a decrypt of Ambassador Ōshima's account of his meeting with Ribbentrop on the evening of 28 November. The content of Ōshima's message did not give the purpose of his meeting, which had been to inform the German Foreign Minister that the Washington talks had broken down. It also did not provide the Ambassador's own assessment of the situation, given to Ribbentrop, which was that Japanese military actions might be cautious. The decrypt did, however, reveal that Ribbentrop had urged the Japanese to take action against Britain, that he had told Ōshima not to worry about US intervention, and that he had promised German support if Japan and America went to war. ('Germany, of course, would join the war immediately'.)[19]

That same day the Americans translated an even more sensational message, sent from Foreign Minister Tōgō to Ōshima on 30 November. This confirmed that the Washington talks had failed, and stated that there was a grave danger of war with Britain *and America*, which might occur 'sooner than is expected'.[20] A third intercepted telegram, sent from Tokyo on 1 December, informed the Washington embassy that Japanese diplomatic posts in London, Hong Kong, Singapore, Manila and Batavia had been instructed to stop using their code machines and to dispose of them.[21] Finally, there was an instruction from Tokyo to Nomura and Kurusu in Washington, with information that was so secret that it was not even to be shared with other embassy staff: Japan's final deadline for negotiation – 29 November – had come and gone, and the situation was 'increasingly critical'. 'However,' the Foreign Ministry explained, 'to prevent the United States from becoming unduly suspicious we have been advising the press and others that though there are some wide differences between Japan and the United States, the negotiations are continuing.'[22] These would not be the last revelations from MAGIC.

* * *

As well as vital diplomatic information, the leaders of the United States needed to know about the preparations of the Japanese armed forces. The Americans, like the British, monitored Japanese naval radio communication (there was little success against the Japanese Army). The US Navy codebreaking unit was located in Washington, DC, and designated OP-20-G. It was, based on the top 'deck' of one of the wings of the Main Navy Building in Washington, an ugly concrete complex erected on the north side of the Mall in 1918. The codebreakers of OP-20-G, even in collaboration with their colleagues in Hawaii and the Philippines, and with the British, could not readily break Japanese naval messages encrypted in what the Americans called at that time the 'AN-Code'. This was partly because of a lack of resources; much of the effort of OP-20-G was focused – not very successfully – on German naval Enigma ciphers. In addition, there were few Japanese messages to use as a basis for systematic decryption.[23]

The US Navy's Pacific monitoring stations, HYPO in Hawaii and CAST in the Philippines, had revealed information about the Japanese southern 'task force' on 26 November,[24] and then the changes of Japanese Navy radio call signs. The last development received special attention, as call-sign changes usually came every six months, and one had come into effect only on 1 November. The communications summary of Station HYPO noted the significance of what had happened: 'The fact that service calls last only one month indicate [sic] an additional progressive step in preparing for active operations on a large scale'. The monitoring stations also commented on a sudden reduction in the amount of signals traffic; this suggested that Japanese ships, moving into an operational state, were observing radio silence.[25]

Intelligence gathered from American and British sources was laid out in the 'Summary' of the Office of Naval Intelligence (ONI) on 1 December. Japanese troops, supplies and equipment had been 'pouring' into Indochina during the past fifteen days. There were now 25,000 troops in the north, and between 70,000 and 100,000 in the south. Some 200 planes were based in Indochina, and as many again on Hainan Island. The position of the Imperial Navy was threatening, with a new command ('task force') under the C-in-C of 2nd Fleet (Admiral Kondō), which was concentrating ships and land-based aircraft on 'the Southeast Asiatic coast' and in the islands of the Central Pacific ('the Mandates').[26] In many respects the Summary was highly accurate, and it clearly identified the general and immediate Japanese threat to Southeast Asia. What was now lacking was the precise objective, and when the Japanese forces would move towards it. But one statement would prove to be fatally incorrect: 'Although one division of battleships also may be assigned, the major capital ship strength remains in home waters, as well as the greatest portion of the carriers.'[27] The carriers were actually on the move, and they were not heading south.

Prior knowledge of Japanese movements down the China coast was crucial. President Roosevelt intervened on 1 December to improve the local intelligence picture by more traditional means. That evening, Admiral Stark, the Chief of Naval Operations, sent a message to the C-in-C of the US Asiatic Fleet (CINCAF), Admiral Hart, which began with the phrase: 'President directs that the following be done'. CINCAF was instructed, within forty-eight hours, to set up a 'defensive information patrol'. He was to charter three small vessels and send them to patrol off the coast of Indochina to determine what was happening in the South China Sea and the Gulf of Siam. The identity of the ships was to be established as US men-of-war, and they were to be commanded by a US officer, but should have the smallest possible crew.[28]

The President's initiative was later described as an 'incitement to war'; if the Japanese had attacked one of these 'warships,' Congress might have been convinced to open hostilities.[29] On the other hand, Roosevelt's initiative made a good deal of sense, because the stakes were so high. The three vessels were intended to serve as 'picket ships' in three critical patrol areas along the Japanese route. The first was between Hainan Island and Hue (in northern Indochina), the second between Camranh Bay and Cape St Jacques (near Saigon), and the third off Cape Cambodia (the southern tip of Indochina, and the entrance to the Gulf of Siam). American or British reconnaissance planes could reach these distant places only with great difficulty. The vessels of the 'defensive information patrol' were not anonymous and easily-sacrificed, as has sometimes been suggested. The only ship mentioned by name in Stark's message, the USS *Isabel*, had served as Admiral Hart's yacht. The 'defensive information patrol' did not achieve its objectives, because only *Isabel* reached her station on the 5th, and she was almost immediately recalled. For want of information there would be a critical gap between the departure of the main Japanese invasion convoy from Hainan on the morning of 4 December and its sighting by a British search plane off Cape Cambodia over two days later – and 875 miles further south.

* * *

The impasse in the Washington talks and the evidence of a growing concentration of Japanese strength prompted the leaders of the American armed forces to send out extreme warnings to their overseas forces. On the afternoon of Monday, 24 November, Admiral Stark in Washington had sent an urgent message to his admirals in the Pacific, the commanders of the Asiatic Fleet (Admiral Hart) and the Pacific Fleet (Admiral Kimmel), warning of possible attacks on the Philippines or Guam. The Asiatic Fleet, based in Manila, was a token force intended to 'show the flag' in the Far East; its main surface forces were two cruisers and some destroyers. The Pacific Fleet, based in Hawaii and the West Coast, was much larger, and comprised the main naval strength of the United States. On the 27th Stark sent out a message that was even more dramatic: a 'war warning' which mentioned the imminent possibility of a Japanese landing in the Philippines, Thailand or Borneo. The commanders of the Asiatic and Pacific Fleet were ordered to '[e]xecute an appropriate defensive deployment preparatory to carrying out the tasks assigned in WPL 46'.[30] WPL 46 was the Navy's part of the overall American war plan, RAINBOW FIVE.

General George C. Marshall, effectively the C-in-C of the US Army, but bearing the title 'Chief of Staff',[31] sent out similar warnings on 27 November to several overseas Army commands, the most threatened of which were in the Philippines and the Hawaiian Islands: 'Negotiations with Japan appear to be terminated to all practical purposes with only the barest possibilities that the Japanese Government might come back and offer to continue. Japanese future action unpredictable but hostile action possible at any moment.' The overseas commands were to undertake reconnaissance and any other measures deemed necessary. But it was a peculiar warning: the precautionary steps were to be taken in a way that did not alarm the civilian population or 'disclose intent'. Marshall added an important political rider: 'If hostilities cannot repeat not be avoided the United States desires that Japan commit the first overt act.'[32]

The professional heads of the two American armed services were still not at all eager to go to war in Asia or the Pacific at this time. On 27 November, Marshall and Stark had sent another joint memorandum to the President. 'The most important thing now', they argued, 'is to gain time.' 'Precipitance [sic] of military action on our part should be avoided'. What was especially important was to build up American forces in the Philippines. The two commanders agreed that any Japanese action against British or Dutch territory should not be tolerated by the United States. However, a continued Japanese action in China or even a Japanese entry into northwestern Thailand should *not* be countered by military means. If the Japanese invaded Thailand they should be warned against any *further* advance into the southern or western part of the country.[33]

This reluctance to take military action in the Far East stemmed from an awareness of how unready the American forces there still were. It was also due to what would now be called a 'mindset'. Roosevelt and his closest advisers, both civilian and military (and including Marshall and Stark), were preoccupied with a forthcoming war against Nazi Germany. This was the main focus of America's global war plans. These plans had been created in the spring of

1941 in a rather different climate – before the German invasion of Russia (which removed the northern threat to Japan), before the Japanese entry into southern Indochina, before the American oil embargo, and before the beginnings of the American reinforcement of the Philippines. But the plan had not changed in its essentials. RAINBOW FIVE put the task as follows: 'If Japan does enter the war, the Military strategy in the Far East will be defensive. The United States does not intend to add to its present Military strength in the Far East but will employ the United States Pacific Fleet offensively in the manner best calculated to weaken Japanese economic power, and to support the defense of the Malay barrier by diverting Japanese strength away from Malaysia.'[34]

Unfortunately for the United States the Empire of Japan had its own plans for bringing America into the war. Moreover, the Japanese military was much more capable than the Americans expected, and the armed forces of their prospective British partners much weaker. The next few days would show that limited war in the Pacific was not going to be an option for Washington.

CHAPTER 5

## TUESDAY, 2 DECEMBER

# Two Doomed Battleships in Singapore

*Climb Mt. Niitaka 1208*

Combined Fleet Executive Order

*The President is still deliberating the possibility of a message to the Emperor, although all the rest of us are rather against it, but in addition to that he is quite settled, I think, that he will make a Message to the Congress and will perhaps back that up with a speech to the country.*

Henry L. Stimson

### Singapore and Tokyo

Watchers on the waterfront in Singapore could see the distant shapes of the two great ships, conspicuous against a background of blue sky and green islands, as they made their stately way past the city. It was midday on Tuesday, 2 December. HMS *Prince of Wales* and *Repulse*, with four escorting destroyers, disappeared to the east, bearing around Singapore Island. They would proceed up the Johore Strait and into the big Naval Base on the north side of the island.

*Prince of Wales* had come all the way from Scotland. She was the second ship of the 'King George V' class, the most modern battleships in the Royal Navy. Although in commission for less than a year, the ship had already fought a famous gunnery duel with the German battleship *Bismarck*. The battlecruiser *Repulse* was an older ship, dating back to the final years of the First World War, but she was powerfully armed and her crew had seen much action since

September 1939. Both vessels were capable of the high speed of nearly thirty knots.

* * *

A week later, on 8 December, the British Prime Minister would report with enthusiasm to Parliament that 'some of the finest ships of the Royal Navy have reached their stations in the Far East at a very convenient moment'.[1] Churchill spoke just after the news reached London that Japan had gone to war with Britain and America, and that the Imperial Navy had landed troops in southern Thailand and northern Malaya.

But in truth Whitehall had decided to send capital ships to the Far East for other reasons and in different circumstances. The critical moment was the middle of October, with first thoughts dating back to August. In the late summer of 1941 the Royal Navy's presence in the Far East had been limited to a handful of cruisers and destroyers, but the situation there was growing increasingly complex and threatening. Japanese forces had been sent into southern French Indochina; Washington imposed economic sanctions, and Britain and the Netherlands followed suit. War with Japan had become a distinct possibility. The Admiralty's solution, put forward when Churchill was still on his way back from the Newfoundland conference with President Roosevelt, was gradually to build up battleship strength in Singapore and the Indian Ocean, using six or seven of the older and slower ships.[2] The Admiralty envisaged a limited naval war, in which the big ships would prevent raids by Japanese cruisers on British supply lines (on the model of the raids the Germans were already carrying out in the Atlantic).

Winston Churchill, as was often the case, had differing ideas from those of his advisers. In a minute of 25 August he called for the sending of a 'deterrent squadron' to the Indian Ocean. This was to happen in the 'near future'.[3] The force, in the opinion of the Prime Minister, should consist of 'the smallest number of the best ships'. Churchill specifically mentioned the inclusion of one of the new 'King George V'-class battleships, as well as a battlecruiser and a new aircraft carrier; he had just sailed to Newfoundland and back aboard *Prince of Wales*. For Churchill and Foreign Secretary Eden, this proposal had a significant political dimension, which included reassuring the Australian and New Zealand governments, maintaining credibility with the Americans, and deterring Tokyo. The Japanese, for all their aggressive behaviour, were believed to be in a weak position economically, and susceptible to bluff.

Churchill added a personal twist, in what a later generation would call 'mirror-imaging'. The threat of the fast German battleship *Tirpitz* (and before her the *Bismarck*) dominated British Atlantic strategy in 1941. Thus, the Prime Minister argued, the threat of a small but powerful capital-ship raiding force in the Pacific would force the already overstretched Japanese to think twice about further mischief. The Admiralty's plan for a slow defensive squadron of older battleships would not accomplish this.

There then ensued a pause of two months, partly because *Prince of Wales* was escorting a crucial convoy to Malta in the last week of September: Operation HALBERD. Two developments then pushed planning forward. One was the crisis on the Russian front in the first weeks of October, when it appeared that Moscow might fall and the Japanese might join the attack on the USSR. The other was the resignation of the Konoe government in Tokyo on 16 October; Prince Konoe would be replaced two days later by the even more difficult General Tōjō.

Meetings of the War Cabinet's Defence Committee were held on 17 and 20 October. Churchill, Eden and others argued for the immediate despatch of *Prince of Wales* to the Far East, while the Admiralty argued for keeping her, with the two other new battleships, in European waters and sticking to the plan of gradually accruing a force of older ships. The meeting on the 20th reached a compromise. Admiral Dudley Pound, the First Sea Lord, agreed to send *Prince of Wales* to Cape Town, and to postpone a decision as to whether the big ship should proceed on to the Far East. (The battlecruiser *Repulse* was already on convoy duty in the Indian Ocean.) The final decision to move *Prince of Wales* on across the Indian Ocean to Singapore, was settled informally, it would seem, between Admiral Pound and the Prime Minister at some point over the following two weeks.

The Royal Navy's reinforcement of the Far East was not intended to be kept secret. Indeed, it was extensively publicised, and for Churchill publicity was the main point of the exercise. Churchill used his Lord Mayor's Day speech of 10 November to announce the movement of his ships. Owing to the improved naval situation in the Atlantic and the Mediterranean, and

> owing to the completion of our splendid new battleships and aircraft carriers of the largest size, . . . we now feel ourselves strong enough to provide a powerful naval force of heavy ships, with its necessary ancillary vessels, for service if needed in the Indian and Pacific Oceans. . . . [T]his movement of our naval forces, in conjunction with the United States Main fleet, may give a practical proof to all who have eyes to see that the forces of freedom and democracy have by no means reached the limits of their power.[4]

*Prince of Wales* had slipped away from the naval base at Scapa Flow in the Orkneys on 23 October, three days after the decision of the Defence Committee; she was escorted by destroyers *Electra* and *Express*. On the following day the ships, designated as Force 'G', made a secret stop at the Clyde estuary to embark Admiral Tom Phillips and his staff. Phillips was to take command of the new fleet in the Far East. After a stop in Freetown (Sierra Leone), *Prince of Wales* continued to Cape Town, where she spent two days. The Japanese Consul-General in Cape Town informed Japan about her departure; later, at Tokyo's request, he relayed details of the battleships current camouflage scheme.[5] Force 'G' arrived at Colombo in Ceylon on 28 November; the following day it was joined by *Repulse* and by two more destroyers.

The tragic Tom Phillips – on 2 December he had just a week to live – was a remarkable officer. Aged only fifty-three in 1941, he had enjoyed a rapid promotion, first from Captain to Rear Admiral (in 1939), and then to Vice Admiral (in 1940); in December 1941 he held the 'acting' rank of full Admiral. Phillips had been a leading war planner at the Admiralty in the 1930s. He was a protégé of Admiral Dudley Pound, having served directly under him in the Mediterranean fleet in the late 1920s. When Pound became First Lord (and Chief of Naval Staff) in 1939, Phillips became Deputy Chief of Naval Staff and then Vice Chief.

Phillips had known Churchill well, as First Lord of the Admiralty and then as Prime Minister. With his energy and direct approach Phillips was, for a time, something of a favourite of Churchill's, spending weekends at Chequers (the Prime Minister's country residence). The Admiral seems to have fallen out with the Prime Minister in mid-1941, with his forthright views on Mediterranean strategy – which now differed from Churchill's. He was not, however, as is sometimes suggested, 'exiled' to the Far East that October. Able flag officers could be expected to be rotated from staff posts in Whitehall to major sea-going commands, and Phillips went to the Eastern Fleet because he was the First Sea Lord's choice.

Only 5 feet 2 inches tall, pale-faced and weighing 126 pounds, Phillips was nicknamed 'Tom Thumb' or 'Tich' by his sailors.[6] Churchill, when Phillips was in his good books, called him 'the Cocksparrow'. Some senior naval colleagues regarded him as a 'Pocket Napoleon', and he was certainly a difficult character who did not suffer fools gladly. His experience near the centre of power was important, as well as his diplomatic work before the war in disarmament talks. One of the requirements of his new post would be the ability to deal with American, Dutch, Australian and New Zealand commanders and politicians. The Admiral was, however, a staff officer with little direct experience of modern naval warfare, and eyebrows were raised when he was given a new battleship and a difficult operational task in the Far East. 'What on earth is Phillips going to the Far Eastern squadron for,' grumbled Admiral Cunningham in the Mediterranean. 'He hardly knows one end of a ship from the other.'[7] Whatever his operational abilities, Phillips had in fact opposed Churchill's plan to send *Prince of Wales* to the Far East in October when he was still working at the Admiralty. Now he had to make the Prime Minister's plan work.

* * *

In Japan, diplomatic and military preparations proceeded apace on Tuesday, 2 December. The Emperor granted an audience to the leaders of the Army and Navy, General Sugiyama and Admiral Nagano. He was briefed on the detailed preparations for X-Day.[8]

That evening, Combined Fleet headquarters aboard battleship *Nagato* despatched a coded warning to all its major commands: '*Niitakayama nobore* 1208' ('Climb Mount Niitaka 1208').[9] The message would become one of the most famous in naval history. '1208', the following Monday, 8 December, had been confirmed as 'X-Day' – the opening of hostilities against Britain and America. The coded message alerted various elements of Combined Fleet which were pre-positioned at a dozen points around the Pacific Ocean. But the chosen coded phrase also suggested the size of the task that had to be scaled. Formosa's Mount Niitaka was the highest peak in the Japanese Empire; with a summit of nearly 13,000 feet, it rose higher even than Mount Fuji. (Mount Niitaka is known today as Yushan.)

On 2 December *Sakura Maru*, the last of seventeen big transport ships, arrived at the Hainan rendezvous. During the day the expedition carried out a full-scale training manoeuvre for the landings at the Kra Isthmus and Malaya.[10]

After the final decision has been made on Monday to go to war, further measures were taken to prepare Japanese embassies and consulates around the world for the outbreak of hostilities. Preliminary warnings in the form of the 'winds' and 'stop' codes had been sent out in previous weeks. Now the Foreign Ministry passed from contingency plans to concrete steps. Encrypted circulars were sent out ordering Japanese diplomatic posts to destroy their codes (except for one copy of certain codes); they were to confirm destruction by sending the codeword 'HARUNA' back to Japan. All secret papers were to be destroyed.[11] The crucial Washington embassy, for its part, was told to take drastic security steps: 'Please destroy by burning all of the codes you have in your office, with the exception of one copy each of the codes being used in conjunction with the [cipher] machine.' In addition, one of the cipher machines was to be destroyed. Staff were, at their discretion, to dispose of correspondence and other secret papers.[12] These instructions were of the highest secrecy; should future enemies learn of the steps being taken they would surely know that war was imminent.

## Rostov, Moscow, Berlin

The city of Rostov and the approaches to the Caucasus still occupied the centre of Adolf Hitler's attention on 2 December – far more so than Moscow. Hitler had sacked Field Marshal von Rundstedt, C-in-C of Army Group South, on Monday. Now, early on Tuesday morning, Hitler himself set off on an audacious secret trip to inspect the scene of battle. He was bypassing the formal command structure of the German Army. He flew from the airfield at WOLFSSCHANZE in East Prussia, via Kiev, to the forward Luftwaffe airfield at Mariupol' on the Sea of Azov, across nearly a thousand miles of occupied Russia. The aircraft, part of Hitler's special flight, was a Heinkel He 111, a twin-engined medium bomber, modified to carry six passengers. It was flown by the Führer's personal pilot, the veteran Nazi Hans Baur. Hitler was accompanied by Colonel Rudolf Schmundt, Dr Theodor Morell and Heinz Linge (respectively his chief Wehrmacht adjutant, his physician and his orderly). It was very cold, and the Heinkel's heating system was rudimentary. Hitler had not come well prepared. 'Baur,' he complained, 'it's shockingly cold in your plane. My feet are like lumps of ice.'[13]

The weather on the ground was also severe. German Army weather reports indicated a continuous frost across the whole area of Army Group South, with temperatures as low as −17°C (1.4°F) and occasional snowfall. Mariupol' was about sixty miles west of the front line. Hitler was met by Field Marshal von Kleist, C-in-C of 1st Panzer Army, and SS-*Obergruppenführer* Josef Dietrich, commander of the *Leibstandarte* division. Hitler was immediately motored to the headquarters of the Panzer Army at Taganrog, which was directly behind the fighting front. 'Sepp' Dietrich was a close comrade of Hitler – a personal friend, as far as this was possible – and he had acted as head of his bodyguard from the late 1920s onward. Dietrich confirmed to Hitler that the situation was very difficult, supplies were scarce, and that – even with the strongest will – the line east of the Mius River could not be held.

Evidently satisfied with what he had seen, the Führer and his party took the return flight the following morning. This time Hitler was equipped with fur-lined flying boots, for which he wrote out a receipt to the Luftwaffe quartermaster at Mariupol'. The weather was poor, so Hitler had to spend the nights of 3–4 and 4–5 December in Poltava, about 200 miles north of Mariupol', where the headquarters of Army Group South and of 6th Army were located. During his stay he discussed, late into the night, the situation at the front with a number of German senior officers, including General Walter Reichenau, the new C-in-C of Army Group South, and Hitler's Wehrmacht adjutant, Schmundt. General von Sodenstern, Chief of Staff of Army Group South, recounted details of misunderstandings that had arisen in communications with Keitel and Jodl at WOLFSCHANZE. According to Sodenstern, his tale reduced the group to shocked silence, and Hitler declared his anger at no one having told him about all this. The dismissed von Rundstedt was summoned to talk to the Führer, and a reconciliation of sorts took place.[14]

As his luggage had gone ahead in another aircraft, Hitler had to make do with the spartan offerings of Reichenau's lice-ridden HQ, which reminded him of his experience in the trenches of the last war.

* * *

As Hitler was making his way down to the Rostov front on Tuesday morning, the German advance on Moscow, 600 miles to the north, was reaching its culmination point. Here too the weather was severe, and getting colder. The sky was clear and the sun shone all day, but there was a severe frost with the temperature dropping to –20°C (–4°F) in places. In the evening the skies became increasingly cloudy, and there was scattered snowfall. The roads were now mostly icy, with some snow drifts.

From Smolensk, Field Marshal von Bock instructed his commanders to take advantage of what was evidently, for the Russian defenders, a moment of grave crisis. He confided in his diary, however, that he was not sure the exhausted German troops were still capable of continued action.[15]

Following the retreat of General Rokossovskii's 16th Army from Istra on 27 November, the front had remained fluid. A German motorised reconnaissance detachment from Panzer Group 4 – half a dozen motorcyclists and a couple of light trucks – had probed its way through the foggy morning twilight to the Khimki railway station on the Moscow-Leningrad line. In Khimki the German scouts were only eleven miles from the centre of Moscow; the small town was also the location of the headquarters of Vlasov's new 20th Army (and the HQ of Rokossovskii's 16th Army was only five miles to the west, at Korostovo). Fortunately for the defenders the patrol quickly withdrew, and the Germans did not return.[16]

On the Russian side, General Zhukov's plan of 30 November, such as it was, had specified a co-ordinated counterattack by his Western Army Group beginning on 3 or 4 December. German pressure, however, kept the Russians off balance. In the small hours of the night of 1–2 December, at 1.30 a.m., General Sokolovskii, Zhukov's Chief of Staff, had issued orders for General Kuznetsov's 1st Shock Army to go over to a 'decisive offensive', from the morning of 2 December. The starting line was the Mosvka-Volga Canal, and the general direction was toward Klin. This was probably an attempt to break a local German encirclement around the 'group of forces' of General Georgii Zakharov, about ten miles west of the canal.[17] Although the fighting was heavy the Russians made no significant progress to the west.

Some forty-five miles to the southwest, the left wing of General Kluge's 4th Army had finally begun an advance across the Nara River – due west of Moscow – on Monday. For several days this operation enjoyed some success. The HQ of Soviet 5th Army at Pokrovskoe was put in direct danger for a time. One spearhead force – Zhukov recalled it was a German regiment or reinforced regiment – actually threatened the headquarters of Western Army Group at Vlasikha. The Germans were engaged in a small birch forest by the security regiment of the HQ, with some of the members of Zhukov's staff also participating. Although Zhukov now realised that his HQ compound was sited too far forward – and was now within range of enemy artillery – he was reluctant to withdraw, for fear of setting off a general panic. The situation was not, Zhukov recalled, 'conducive to the calm work of the staff', but ultimately the crisis was overcome. An account of the battle edited by Zhukov's Chief of Staff recalled that the forward siting of the Western Army Group HQ did give the staff a good sense of the 'pulse' of the battle. On the following day the Germans pulled back behind the Nara; their expedition had involved them in heavy fighting and cost many casualties.[18]

On the southern wing of the Moscow front, 120 miles away, General Heinz Guderian had set up his own forward headquarters (of 2nd Panzer Army) at the historic site of Leo Tolstoi's country estate at Iasnaia Poliana, preserved as a museum, about nine miles south of Tula. Later, the Russians maintained that the German barbarians had wrecked the home of the master of world literature, burning books and furniture and desecrating his grave; the incident was even mentioned at the Nuremberg Trial. Guderian vigorously denied all this in his memoirs.[19]

In November 1941, however, '*der schnelle Heinz*' ('fast Heinz') had concentrated his thoughts on the town of Tula, which was now an embattled outpost south of Moscow, held by some divisions of the Soviet 50th Army and connected to the core defenders in the capital by a narrow corridor. With the direct push north to Moscow quashed on the approaches to Kashira on 27 November, Guderian had shifted his priority to finishing off the siege. On 2 December, 2nd Panzer Army succeeded in temporarily cutting communications to the town. A Panzer force drove across the north-to-south corridor, reaching the railway line by the evening; the following day it pushed on to the Moscow-Tula highway. Tula's last link to the north had been severed, and its fate hung by a thread.

* * *

*Fremde Heere Ost* (Foreign Armies East), or *FHO*, was the section of German Army intelligence which dealt with the Red Army; it was headed by Colonel Eberhard Kinzel. *FHO* continued to play down any sense of potential danger. 'The pulling of [Soviet] forces out of the defensive front and their direct employment in particularly endangered places again confirms that the enemy has at present no accessible reserves available and that he is trying, by last-ditch employment of all forces, with help of particularly strong minefields and by constant counterattacks, to bring the German attack to a halt in various sectors of the front.' This opinion was accepted at the very pinnacle of the General Staff. In his war diary, after describing Guderian's action, General Halder noted: 'The attacking wing of Army Group [Centre] pushes forwards amidst heavy fighting. Overall impression: Enemy's defence has reached its height. No new forces available [i.e. to the Russians].'[20] This would turn out to be a fatal underestimation of the potential of Zhukov's Western Army Group.

The British, too, were thinking about the situation in Russia on 2 December. Bentinck's Joint Intelligence Committee produced an assessment of the overall picture. Most concerning was the position in the south, which carried a long-term threat to the Middle East. In the eyes of the British (and probably, in reality, those of Hitler), the German strategic imperative had to be to secure the oil resources. In a worst case scenario, the Germans might counterattack at Rostov and perhaps get to the oil centre of Groznyi in the Caucasus by mid-February 1942.

As regards central Russia, however, the JIC thought the Germans were probably stalled. Moscow was seen as being important 'both for prestige, and for winter quarters.' 'The cold weather and the lack of reserve formations,' Bentinck's committee concluded, 'are likely to cause the Germans to close down their attacks by about the middle of December, and . . . to accept the fact that the city cannot be captured this winter.' The British report stressed 'stabilisation.' As the JIC saw it, the Wehrmacht High Command would not need to commit all its vast forces to control the situation. The German Army would require fifteen to twenty divisions for offensive operations in the Crimea and the Caucasus; they could hold the central part of the front line, before Moscow, with a hundred divisions ('in the outpost line and on occupation duties'). This would leave them with considerable reserves; they would be able to move fifty to sixty divisions back to Germany to refit them and to prepare for operations, anywhere in Europe, in the spring.[21] The British had at least one thing in common with their German enemies: both were seriously underestimating the weakness of the Wehrmacht's position in Russia.

The Battle of Moscow featured in a telegram received in Berlin on the afternoon of 2 December. Ambassador Ott reported from Tokyo that he had met the Japanese Foreign Minister two days earlier (30 November) and, with the help of some maps, outlined to him the military situation in Russia and North Africa. Ott's assessment was, as might be expected, an optimistic one, and Tōgō replied that he looked forward to a re-opening of the Trans-Siberian Railway 'after the fall of Moscow and the disappearance of the Stalin regime'.

The meeting had a more significant aspect. The Foreign Minister had explained to Ott 'in strict confidence' the developments in the Washington negotiations. The Japanese negotiators had taken a firmer line since the arrival of Special Envoy Kurusu, but so had the Americans. Differences ran very deep, particularly regarding China, and Japan's commitment to the Tripartite Pact. While Tōgō did not go so far as to say that the talks had been broken off, he noted that Japan did not fear this, and he trusted that if the occasion arose Germany and Italy would stand by Japan. Ott responded positively; Tōgō said this meant that 'Germany would . . . regard her relationship with Japan as a bond of common destiny.' When Ott stated that Germany would be prepared to enter a mutual agreement to this effect, the Foreign Minister replied that he might return to the question of this agreement before long.[22]

## London and Washington

Winston Churchill read Ambassador Halifax's report of his Monday lunchtime talks with Roosevelt and Hopkins, at which the suddenly looming Japanese threat in Southeast Asia had been discussed. In response, the Prime Minister wrote a minute to Foreign Secretary Eden explaining how he saw the current overall situation, and laying out the best options presently. The President's vague words were not a basis for British action, he thought. The country's 'settled policy' was that it would not take forward action in advance of the United States. Churchill still did not consider a Japanese attack on southern

Thailand very likely; he repeated professional advice given him by the military in London and Singapore that 'an attack on the Kra isthmus would not be helpful to Japan for several months'. But in any event he did not want to take 'forestalling action without a definite guarantee of United States support'. The main danger, as the Prime Minister saw it, was now to the Dutch East Indies, and he questioned how far Britain should go to defend that strategic region if America did not act.[23]

By the afternoon of 2 December the codebreakers at Bletchley Park had decrypted and distributed a translation of Sunday's warning message from Foreign Minister Tōgō to the embassy in Berlin. Japanese troops were on the move; the Germans were to be told that 'it is greatly to be feared that an armed collision will occur and we shall find ourselves in a state of war with Britain and America', and that this may happen 'sooner than is expected'.[24] It is not clear whether the Prime Minister had seen this intercept before he wrote to Eden, but it was certainly intelligence of the highest importance.

* * *

Vital intelligence was also available across the Atlantic. President Roosevelt and his closest advisers had by now, 2 December, seen the four important MAGIC messages which had been translated the day before: Ribbentrop encouraged the Japanese to take military action; Tōgō confirmed that the Washington talks had failed, that the 29 November deadline for negotiations had passed (but that the pretence of talks should continue); Japanese troops were moving, and war with Britain and America might come 'quicker than anyone dreams'.[25] At some point during the 2nd the codebreakers decrypted the Japanese 'stop' code set-up message, sent to a number of foreign embassies and consulates on 27 November. This comprised a list of fifty-four codewords to be inserted into normal messages. The codewords stood for words, numbers and phrases, mainly relating to communications procedures, evacuating embassy personnel, breaking relations or going to war. The message did not specify Japan's relations with any particular country, but it was evidence, like the 'winds' message, that Tokyo was taking the current international crisis very seriously indeed.[26]

Despite all this remarkable intelligence, the administration in Washington continued to unroll the cautious diplomatic strategy that the President had discussed with Ambassador Halifax and Harry Hopkins the day before. Ambassador Nomura and Special Envoy Kurusu were summoned to the State Department for the implementation of step one. Secretary of State Hull, ill with a bad cold, was spending the day in bed; it was Under Secretary Sumner

Welles who handed the Japanese a letter from President Roosevelt requesting an explanation for the concentration of Japanese troops in Indochina.

The letter fell well short of an ultimatum, but in it the President set the Japanese concentration alongside similar actions taken by the Germans in Europe. The letter mentioned various areas threatened by the build-up: the Philippines, the Dutch East Indies, Burma and Malaya; last of all was the threat, by coercion or occupation, to Thailand. Ambassador Nomura agreed to pass the message to his government.[27]

Later in the day the fit members of an informal American 'war cabinet' assembled for another strategic lunchtime meeting: the President, Welles, Secretary of War Stimson, and Secretary of the Navy Knox. Welles was a professional diplomat and a personal friend and confidant of the President. Stimson and Knox were powerful Republican politicians whom FDR had brought into his Cabinet in 1940 to develop bipartisan support for his foreign policy. Frank Knox was a Midwestern newspaperman who had had been the Republican candidate for Vice President in 1936. 'Colonel' Henry L. Stimson, a grey-haired seventy-four year old, was a wealthy Wall Street lawyer whose robust views on American patriotism and national defence dated back to his experience fighting in the Spanish-American War.

The President walked the group through the events of the last days. It was never altogether clear where FDR stood, but the hawkish Stimson thought he had 'made up his mind to go ahead' – that is, to take a firm stand against Tokyo. Roosevelt was considering a direct appeal to the Emperor. '[I]n addition to that he is quite settled, I think, that he will make a Message to Congress and will perhaps back that up with a speech to the country.'[28]

From the vantage point of the White House the overall situation appeared highly threatening. Japan, it was becoming increasingly clear, meant business. All the same, things looked more dangerous for the British and the Dutch than they did for the United States. The problem for President Roosevelt seemed to be one of timing. Time was needed to prepare American public opinion and rally Congress, and meanwhile the President could neither make open promises nor despatch open warnings. Roosevelt did not realise that the assault was only hours away, and that it would directly affect the United States as much as it would its partners.

CHAPTER 6

## WEDNESDAY, 3 DECEMBER
# The President's Secret Promise

*I told him that the situation is more critical than is imagined, and therefore, we are very anxious to have the formal reply as soon as is possible. From my past experiences with Ribbentrop I feel fairly confident when I say that you will not be mistaken if you assume that there will be no objections.*

Ambassador Ōshima to Foreign Minister Tōgō

*On Far East PM wishes to wait for Americans and see a Jap-American war start (which we would immediately enter) rather than a Jap-British war which the Americans might or might not enter.*

Oliver Harvey

*[T]he signs seem to point to the Japs going ahead, unless things are really going against the Germans in Russia, which may possibly give them cause for pause.*

Lord Halifax

### Japan

For the Japanese, 3 December remained a day of preparation rather than action. The ships of the Imperial Navy were nearly in position. The main transport convoy for the Southern Operation was gathered at Hainan. At airfields on Formosa and in Indochina the pilots of the Navy's twin-engined attack planes were briefed about their targets in the Philippines and Malaya. In Tokyo, Imperial General Headquarters decided on 3 December that the RAF forces were sufficiently weak that the invasion of the Kra Isthmus and Malaya could be carried out at the very beginning of the war, and without an extended series of air attacks to neutralise British airfields in northern Malaya. Admiral Yamamoto, the C-in-C of Combined Fleet, went to the Imperial Palace in

Tokyo for an audience with the Emperor, to brief him on the naval aspects of the coming war with America and Britain. The Admiral had travelled up by train on Monday afternoon, from the main fleet base at the western end of the Inland Sea.[1]

## Moscow

This Wednesday, 3 December, was the day the Red Army's counterattacks against the northern and southern wings of Army Group Centre were supposed to have begun. Zhukov's plan of 30 November, approved by Stalin, had envisaged an all-out attack by four of his armies. As late as Tuesday morning, Zhukov's headquarters had ordered 20th Army to begin its drive into Panzer Group 4 at dawn on the 3rd.

But there was no major attack on the northern side of Moscow on the 3rd. The same was true south of the city, for Golikov's new 10th Army facing 2nd Panzer Army. Zhukov's forces were still fully occupied reacting to German attacks. The General Staff Situation Report recorded that the forces of Western Army Group were still fighting 'fierce defensive battles' all along their front, although some rifle brigades of 1st Shock Army had expanded the Soviet hold on the western side of the Moskva-Volga Canal. Guderian's forces were in the process of cutting off Tula. The sudden cold weather and Luftwaffe air strikes were making it harder to assemble the new armies. The forces of Konev's Kalinin Army Group had not moved. During the 3rd, Stalin allowed Konev to delay his part of the offensive from 4 to 5 December, due to the late arrival of promised tank reinforcements.[2]

The most favourable development on 3 December was the abandonment by the cautious General Kluge (4th Army) of his offensive drive in the centre of the front, due west of Moscow, which had met with stiff Soviet resistance. At midday Kluge informed Bock at Army Group HQ that he would have to withdraw his two advanced corps back behind the Nara, and he actually began the retreat before obtaining permission to do so.

Back at Smolensk, Bock was becoming increasingly alarmed at the state of his Army Group Centre. He contacted General Jodl, operations chief at the Wehrmacht High Command (*OKW*), to ask whether the atrocious circumstances in which his army group found themselves were being accurately reported to Hitler. He also painted a bleak picture for General Halder at the Army General Staff. He had continued moving his troops forward, but 'the hour was in sight' when they would be exhausted and would find it difficult to go over to the defensive. Both Halder and von Bock were in favour of continuing to attack just to keep the Russians off-balance, and because it would be so hard to defend what was held. 'The disadvantages of the defence,' as Halder put it, 'were also a reason for holding to the attack.' But a shift to the defence was certainly growing in both their minds.[3]

The situation was complicated by Hitler's continued absence from WOLFSSCHANZE. The departure of his aircraft from Poltava, HQ of Army Group South, was delayed by bad weather until the morning of the 4th. His visit to the front had convinced the Führer – much to the Army's relief – that neither the army group nor 1st Panzer Army had acted wrongly during the Battle for Rostov. But the dismissal of Field Marshal von Rundstedt still stood.

* * *

Despite the crisis on the battlefield around Moscow on 3 December, Joseph Stalin found time for two and a half hours of talks in the Kremlin with General Sikorski, the head of the London-based Polish government in exile.[4] 'It is really rather remarkable', wrote Stafford Cripps, the British Ambassador, 'that Stalin should have entertained Sikorski at Moscow within 40 miles of the front line trenches. It shows confidence in the Red Army and its continued power of resistance. So does the planning for Anthony's [Anthony Eden's] visit in ten days time.'[5] The Sikorski meeting was among the first major diplomatic initiatives by the Kremlin since the start of the war.[6]

Władysław Sikorski had travelled from London, via Egypt and Iran, to Kuibyshev (Samara); this was the city on the Volga where the diplomatic corps, including Ambassador Cripps, and many commissariats had moved after the October crisis. On 2 December Sikorski flew on to Moscow with Stanisław Kot, the Polish Ambassador, and Władysław Anders, the commander of the new Polish Army being formed in the USSR.[7]

Soviet-Polish relations were extremely important, despite – or because of – the long-running hostility between the two governments. In September 1939, Soviet Russia had struck a deal with Nazi Germany which divided the territory of Poland between themselves; Moscow accepted the extinction of the Polish state. Many ethnic Poles from the regions annexed by the USSR and refugees from the German-occupied regions had ended up in Soviet internment camps or even the GULAG. Several thousand imprisoned officers had been murdered by the Soviet secret police at Katyn and elsewhere early in 1940. Then came the epiphany of the German invasion of Russia on 22 June 1941. The Kremlin sanctioned the organisation of Polish military formations on Soviet territory. Aside from having to deal with the 'Allied' Poles, Stalin knew improved relations with Poland were important for improved relations with Britain and America.

Sikorski had joined the Polish nationalist movement before 1914. In 1920, as a senior commander of the new Polish Army, he defended Warsaw against the attacking Red Army. All the same, he moved into political opposition after Marshal Józef Piłsudski's coup in 1926, was retired from the army and joined the opposition to the increasingly dictatorial government. When Poland was defeated and the old regime discredited, Sikorski formed a new government based in Paris, which later moved to London. On 3 December he explained to Stalin that he, unlike other leaders of inter-war Poland, had never been an advocate of an anti-Soviet policy, and he complimented Stalin on the Soviet war effort.

The substance of the talks with Stalin and Viacheslav Molotov (the Foreign Commissar) concerned the fate of the hundreds of thousands of Polish internees in the USSR. Sikorski argued that it was impractical for these people to be formed into military units in Russia, and that it would be preferable to get them out to British-controlled territory, where conditions were better and equipment more readily available. The Russian leaders grudgingly accepted, but feared the Poles would thereafter make little contribution to the common war effort. 'We will conquer Poland and then we will give her back to you,' Stalin grumbled.

When they talked at a banquet in the Kremlin the following evening (4 December),[8] Sikorski raised the even more difficult question of the post-war Soviet-Polish borders. Despite mutual toasts and Stalin's 'salesman's joviality' (Anders' description) nothing was really cleared up. All the same, on the 5th Stalin and Sikorski would sign a Declaration of Friendship and Mutual Assistance. This effectively nullified the Nazi-Soviet Pact and permitted the release of Polish prisoners and internees.

Stalin made a number of remarks about Britain and Japan at his meeting on 3 December, which show that he – like other world leaders – thought a British-Japanese war was imminent. His comments, however, were meant to suggest to the Poles the danger of throwing in their lot with the British; they would be reduced to serving as garrison troops at such outposts of the British empire as Singapore.

* * *

There are a number of close descriptions of Stalin in these days, at one of the crucial moments of his career. General Anders, imprisoned in the USSR after 1939 and for a time held and tortured in Moscow's Lubianka Prison, not unsurprisingly painted a negative portrait after that first meeting with the Soviet leader. Stalin's eyes, he recalled, 'black, cold and dull, wrinkled into a smile which somehow seemed to be only skin deep'. Stalin, he recalled, spoke with a thick Georgian accent (Anders had grown up in Russia and knew the language).

Ambassador Kot (an historian by profession), had had an earlier introduction to Stalin, on 14 November. He recalled the Soviet dictator's appearance: 'Short, stocky, with calm, cold eyes, well-tended, plump hands, his tunic of half-proletarian and half-military cut buttoned up to the chin, and made of very fine greyish-blue cloth, his trousers thrust into legboots, a thick crop of hair, heavily grizzled and brushed up – only his bushy black eyebrows indicated its original colour. On the whole he gave the impression of a self-satisfied Armenian merchant.' Ambassador Kot did not, however, underestimate the little man: 'His look, at times calm and controlled, then glinting with cunning and suspicion, then again cold, steely, almost cruel, witnessed to his craftiness but also to his wisdom, and above all to great strength.'[9]

The British diplomat, Alexander Cadogan, who met Stalin in the Kremlin three weeks later, also left a description: 'Difficult to say whether S. is impressive. There he is – a greater dictator than any Czar. . . . But if one didn't know that, I don't know that one would pick him out of a crowd. With little twinkly eyes and his stiff hair brushed back he is like a porcupine. Very restrained and quiet. Probably a sense of humour.'[10]

These visitors, whatever their reservations, saw Stalin at his most diplomatic. To Russian generals, no doubt, he showed another personality, although perhaps not an entirely different one.[11] Stalin's effect on the Battle of Moscow remains a subject of controversy. Zhukov later stressed Stalin's positive role in the battle, although he himself would be sidelined by the Soviet dictator after 1946. In the 1960s Zhukov took part in a 'round table' discussion with Russian military historians. He recounted to them how the censors had cut from his account of the Battle of Moscow the following comment: 'People often asked me where Stalin was during the Battle of Moscow. And I replied, "Stalin was in Moscow, where he worked and achieved nearly impossible things in the organisation of the defence of Moscow".' 'This was, in my opinion,' Zhukov told the historians, 'the very highest praise for the Supreme Commander-in-Chief.'[12]

As a military leader Stalin made many mistakes, both before and after December 1941. He was partly to blame for the way the Red Army was caught by surprise in June 1941, and for the over-ambitious counteroffensive in early 1942. But when Moscow was under threat in October, November and December 1941, Stalin kept his nerve. As the battle was fought on the outskirts of the city, he was directly involved in the day-to-day decision making, by telephone and teleprinter, especially the deployment of vital reinforcements and equipment. Above all, his was the ultimate decision about whether or not to fight for the Soviet capital.

## Rome and Berlin

Late on the morning of Wednesday, 3 December, Horikiri Zenbei, the Japanese Ambassador to Italy, met Mussolini and his Foreign Minister, Count Ciano. Like Ambassador Ōshima in Berlin, Horikiri had received instructions to contact the government leaders to give them Tokyo's message. It had taken him more than a day to do so, possibly because he had arranged a meeting with the head of the government, rather than the Foreign Minister. In any event Horikiri, like Ōshima, transmitted the message that war with Britain and United States was imminent, and called for Japan's partners in the Tripartite Pact to declare war on the United States and not to sign a separate peace. Mussolini stated that in principle he was in favour, although he would have to consult with the Germans about timing. For his part, the *Duce* declared, he did not have any objection to a declaration of war on the United States, because that country was already de facto fighting Italy. 'So now we come', he said, 'to the war between continents, which I have predicted since September 1939'; it would be a prolonged struggle in which national 'stamina' would be crucial. 'A stunning move by the Japanese', noted the shrewd Ciano, observing that Roosevelt had forced the Japanese to move towards making war on America, and was getting, in a roundabout way, his wish to enter the war against the Axis.[13] Count Ciano would not be the last person to think this.

Ōshima in Berlin had begun to carry out his instructions more quickly than Horikiri. He had met Ribbentrop (on the evening of the 1st), and sent a preliminary report home, before Horikiri spoke to the government in Rome. But to Ōshima's frustration he had still not been able to get an authoritative commitment from the Germans. On Wednesday afternoon he visited Ribbentrop at the Wilhelmstrasse again, hoping for a decision. The Reich Foreign Minister told him that Hitler was 'at a distant place at present' – evidently Russia, where snow was interfering with air transport. Ribbentrop did not want to use the long-distance telephone. He would, if necessary, go to Hitler's East Prussian headquarters to make personal contact. 'As I have told you before,' he explained to Ōshima, 'we cannot make an official reply until the Führer has given his approval. The Japanese Government is undoubtedly very anxious to have our reply as soon as possible. I, myself, am in agreement . . . and I have no objection to your advising your home government of this fact. Moreover, I am of the opinion that the Führer will be in agreement too'.

Ōshima sent an optimistic message to Tokyo about his talk with Ribbentrop: 'I told him that the situation is more critical than is imagined, and therefore, we are very anxious to have the formal reply as soon as is possible. From my past experiences with Ribbentrop I feel fairly confident when I say that you will not be mistaken if you assume that there will be no objections.'[14]

The Japanese general – Ōshima was an army man – might well have wondered what had drawn the Führer into the depths of the Russian winter. Ribbentrop reassured him that any news coming from Britain and America about a setback at Rostov was a 'fabrication'; General von Kleist had withdrawn 'voluntarily' to a prepared position to avoid unnecessary losses to his Panzers. More truthfully (although not more accurately), the Foreign Minister stated that he had received a report that the encirclement of Moscow was progressing favourably.[15]

## London and Washington

Various war fronts, and not just the peril in Southeast Asia, commanded Whitehall's attention on 3 December. Churchill was still far from sure about the outcome of Operation CRUSADER, the British offensive in Libya. In a letter to General Ismay, his link with the Chiefs of Staff Committee (COS), Churchill now expressed doubts about plans that were under discussion in London to send British divisions from the Middle East to fight in the Soviet Caucasus. (This initiative was on the agenda for Foreign Secretary Eden's talk with Stalin in Moscow, scheduled for the end of the following week.) 'It is too soon', he told the General, 'to decide how CRUSADER will go.' There was no point in planning a further advance in Tripolitania or French North Africa, and there was a chance Auchinleck would be beaten, although the enemy would also have been 'severely mauled', and the British 8th Army would be able to dig in at its starting point.[16]

Meanwhile the top leaders in Whitehall had now had time to digest Tuesday's decrypts about Japanese intentions. The Joint Intelligence Committee met late in the morning, but the Far East was not on the agenda. In the course of the day even more damning evidence arrived from Bletchley Park: a decrypt of the Japanese Foreign Ministry message of 1 December instructing the London embassy immediately to destroy its cipher machine and other cryptographic materials. By 6.30 p.m. on Wednesday, London also knew that the order had been carried out.[17]

The top-level Defence Committee (Operations) of the War Cabinet, including Churchill, Eden, the service chiefs and a representative from

Australia, met at 5.30 p.m. The agenda touched on both Russia and Southeast Asia. The British Chiefs of Staff finally convinced Churchill and Eden that there was no point in sending British ground troops to southern Russia, especially given the unresolved battle in Libya. Russia, it was agreed, wanted machines and not men. In Asia the most concrete danger now seemed to be to the Dutch East Indies, and the question was how Britain – and the US – would respond to an attack there. Oliver Harvey, Eden's private secretary, summed up Churchill's response in his diary: 'On Far East PM wishes to wait for Americans and see a Jap-American war start (which we would immediately enter) rather than a Jap-British war which the Americans might or might not enter.'[18]

Later that evening, at 8.55 p.m., Eden's reply to the Halifax note of Monday night was despatched. Lord Halifax had forwarded President Roosevelt's vague promise that 'we will all be in it together'. All that the Foreign Secretary could suggest in his reply was to repeat the request for some kind of simultaneous 'warning' by the British and American governments, along with the Dutch government in exile. This was what the Prime Minister had proposed on Sunday. Before Japan tried to use occupied Indochina as a base for further aggression, the country would be told 'she will do so at her peril'. But what, Eden wondered, would happen if the warning was ignored? Operation MATADOR remained an option, but that would only be possible if there was a real guarantee of American 'armed support'. The problem, as Eden was clearly aware, was Thailand. The British would be asking the Thais to accept their fate; 'It would, we feel, be asking a good to deal of them to expect them to accept the virtual certainty of partial extinction in order to ensure their ultimate independence.'[19]

* * *

Eden's telegram arrived in Washington in the afternoon, and Lord Halifax immediately contacted the American government. Perhaps the most important meeting of the whole December crisis – the tipping point of American policy – took place in the White House between 7.10 p.m. and 7.45 p.m. Present were Halifax, the President, and Under Secretary of State Sumner Welles.

No known American records of this meeting exist. During the post-war Congressional investigation into the outbreak of the Pacific War there seems to have been an attempt to make the meeting disappear. Roosevelt was dead, and as for Welles, he testified that he knew nothing about military guarantees to the British and had not met Halifax after 28 November.[20] The only written account was, again, Lord Halifax's report to the Foreign Office.

According to Halifax, he read out Eden's new telegram to the President and Welles. The Foreign Secretary had been responding to Roosevelt's question about what Britain would do in two hypothetical cases: either that Japan occupied some part of Thailand other than the Kra Isthmus, or that Japan put unacceptable pressure on the government in Bangkok. Eden's telegram affirmed that 'we should still think it wise to put into operation the same plan [i.e. Operation MATADOR], provided that we had a[n]. . . assurance that we would have the armed support of the United States if our actions resulted in hostilities with Japan'. Halifax later described how the President then 'indicated assent to our putting Kra Isthmus plan [MATADOR] into operation in this eventuality, and I have no doubt in this case you can count on the armed support of the United States'.[21]

Eden had also, in his telegram of 3 December, pointedly put 'on the record' the President's assurance of support: 'We note particularly President's statement that in case of any direct attack on ourselves or the Dutch we should obviously all be together. We fully endorse this statement.'[22] Now, meeting with Halifax and Welles, Roosevelt again assented to this. He thought that Japanese attacks might be directed against the Dutch East Indies, north of Sumatra, and said that would make the 'presentation to the United States public opinion' easier than defending the Kra Isthmus, as an advance into the northern Dutch East Indies would threaten the Philippines with encirclement.

The British had now received as good a promise of American armed support in the Far East as they were going to get. They would take – or not take – important decisions in the following days based on the President's words. But these developments also made the grave danger of war with Japan more likely. When he wrote up his diary at the end of Wednesday, 3 December, Lord Halifax was more pessimistic about the chances of avoiding war with Japan. He made one especially interesting observation: 'the signs seem to point to the Japs going ahead, unless things are really going against the Germans in Russia, which may possibly give them cause for pause.'[23]

The sense of snowballing crisis, fed mainly by the diplomatic intercepts, also influenced the US Navy Department. During 3 December a message went out over Admiral Stark's name (OPNAV) to the US Navy C-in-Cs in the Far East and in the Pacific, Admirals Hart and Kimmel. It was drafted by Commander Laurance F. Safford, chief of the Navy's codebreaking organisation in Washington, OP-20-G, and detailed the Japanese Foreign Ministry circular (sent to the Washington embassy and translated on 1 December) concerning the destruction of Japanese code machines in London, Hong Kong, Singapore and Manila. This was an extraordinary message on two levels. Firstly, it was itself a serious breach of security, as it potentially compromised the American codebreaking effort; the Japanese circular was mentioned by its official number (no. 2444) and the code machine was referred to (albeit as PURPLE). Fortunately, the Japanese never decrypted the message themselves. Secondly, the warning was ignored. In summarising the intercept Safford's intention was to alert Hart and Kimmel to a warning about the immediacy of the Japanese threat, but according to the later testimony of Admiral Kimmel, no special importance was attached to this intelligence in Hawaii.[24]

CHAPTER 7

## THURSDAY, 4 DECEMBER

# Hitler and Japan's War of Conquest

*With the goals of wrecking the enemy's preparations for a further offensive against Moscow and for the defeat of the exhausted enemy, I order you to go over from the defensive to a decisive offensive . . .*

General Georgii Zhukov

*Such a pity. God knows where we would be without him, but God knows where we shall go with him.*

General Alan Brooke

*Everything looks exactly like the Japanese balloon going up in the course of a day or two – cyphers being burnt, secret messages in that sense, etc.*

Lord Halifax

### The Central Pacific and Southeast Asia

The outbreak of a great war in the Far East was now only three days away. Thursday, 4 December, was the day that forces began to move into position in the Pacific and Southeast Asia. It was not just the Japanese who were taking steps. At 7.00 a.m., shortly after sunrise, the American aircraft carrier *Enterprise*, at sea about 650 miles west of the International Date Line, turned into the wind and launched the twelve Marine fighters that she had ferried from Hawaii. Their new base was to be the remote Wake Atoll. *Enterprise* flew the flag of Admiral William F. Halsey – later, as 'Bull' Halsey, one of the great American heroes of the Pacific War. Task Force 2, the carrier and her escort of three heavy cruisers and nine destroyers, had sailed from Pearl Harbor on 28 November.

Remote Wake occupied a strategic position, where American and Japanese power met. For well over three thousand miles from east to west, from the Hawaiian Islands to the Marianas, there was little but the empty sea, with a scattering of coral atolls. The islands of the atolls themselves were tiny, only a few feet above the sea line, mostly uninhabited and uninhabitable. A ring of these islands sometimes formed a lagoon broad and deep enough to provide a landing place for flying boats. In a few instances there was safe passage into the lagoon to provide an anchorage for big ships. Some of the islands were sufficiently large to lay out compact air fields for long-range land planes; these served as invaluable and unsinkable coral aircraft carriers. The lagoon at Wake was used as a commercial flying boat station, and in addition a single landing strip had recently been built by contractors working for the US Navy. In August 1941 a detachment of Marines was put ashore as a garrison.

Stretching to the south of Wake were the Japanese-held Marshall Islands, a vast archipelago of coral atolls. They were the most easterly of the 'Mandates', the islands the Japanese obtained at the expense of a defeated Germany after 1918. Kwajalein Atoll had a huge lagoon and a couple of islands with airfields; the field nearest Wake was on the island of Roi, where the Imperial Navy had laid out a triangle of runways. A new long-range bomber had been detached here for a special mission. On this Thursday morning the streamlined cigar-shaped airplane took off from Roi for the arduous 740 mile flight north to Wake. Unseen by the Americans the spy plane overflew the atoll at a height of 30,000 feet. The crew reported the arrival of the twelve Marine fighters on the landing strip.[1]

Elsewhere in the Pacific the US Navy would belatedly attempt to reinforce its exposed island outposts. A second big American carrier, *Lexington*, sortied from the narrow entrance to Pearl Harbor on the morning of Friday, 5 December, nearly forty-eight hours after *Enterprise* launched her Marine fighters off Wake.[2] *Lexington* was the largest ship in the US Navy, converted from a battlecruiser in the 1920s. The carrier and her escort of three heavy cruisers and five destroyers were designated as Task Force 12, and their commander was Admiral John H. Newton. *Lexington*'s mission was to fly off eighteen Marine 'scout bombers' to Midway, another Pacific atoll. Midway was further than Wake from any Japanese-ruled territory, and nearer Oahu, but distances in the vastness of this ocean were relative; the tiny atoll was still 1,500 miles to the northwest of Oahu. Late that Friday afternoon the cruiser *Indianapolis* would rush out of Pearl Harbor headed for the remote Johnston

Island, 700 miles to the southwest, with a party of fifty Marines and food supplies.

Wake and Midway were so far from Oahu as to be beyond the ferry range of fighters and scout bombers, which was why carriers had to be used. And although miniscule, the two atolls were of growing importance. Their air strips provided the most direct route by which US Army heavy bombers could leapfrog to the Philippines. They would also be vital for providing cover to the movement of the US Pacific Fleet into the Central Pacific, should war break out with Japan.

* * *

Admiral Kimmel, C-in-C of the US Pacific fleet, had been ordered to deploy his forces for war.[3]

Blue-eyed, with a prominent aquiline nose, Husband Kimmel was a solid man, nearly six feet tall. He was a Midwesterner from Kentucky, and in December 1941 he was fifty-eight years old. Kimmel took over his command in February 1941, after the unexpected departure of Admiral Richardson.[4] He had been selected over nearly a dozen more senior officers and was himself greatly surprised by the appointment. He had clearly demonstrated his abilities as an efficient and energetic officer serving (since 1939) as 'Commander, Cruisers, Battle Force', in charge of thirteen light cruisers that offered direct support to the fleet's heavy battleships. Having gained his new post, Kimmel based himself ashore at the Submarine Base, adjacent to Pearl Harbor. He oversaw a rigorous fleet-training programme and created an effective headquarters staff. Kimmel was preoccupied with training his fleet, and it would be fair to say that he lacked strategic and technological imagination.

Admiral Kimmel and the Pacific Fleet were subject to the national strategy of the United States. Since the winter of 1940–41 Washington had increasingly come to see Nazi Germany as the most likely opponent of the US Navy. Indeed, one of the main architects of that 'Germany first' strategy was Kimmel's immediate superior, the Chief of Naval Operations, Admiral 'Betty' Stark.[5] This strategy was confirmed by the secret American-British staff talks held in Washington in early 1941, and by the RAINBOW FIVE war plan, which placed the emphasis on contesting German control of the Atlantic. This was not unreasonable. In the first half of 1941 (particularly before the invasion of Russia), Nazi Germany seemed quite likely to attempt to extend its power south into the Mediterranean, and west into the Atlantic.

All the same, the United States was trying to do a great deal with limited means, and it was still exposed to a Japanese threat, especially in the

Philippines. Admiral Kimmel himself had complained about the anomaly in a letter to Stark in May 1941:

> [O]ne cannot escape the conclusion that our national policies and military moves to implement them, are not fully coordinated. . . . We have . . . made strong expressions of our intention to retain an effective voice in the Far East, yet have, so far, refused to develop Guam or to provide adequate defense for the Philippines. We retained the Fleet in Hawaii, last summer, as a diplomatic gesture, but almost simultaneously detached heavy cruisers to the Atlantic and retained new destroyers there, and almost demobilised the Fleet by wholesale changes in personnel.[6]

This complaint was no doubt also fuelled by Washington's order in April 1941 to transfer a large part of his forces to the Atlantic.

Within RAINBOW FIVE the US Navy operated under its own war plan, designated WPL-46.[7] The Navy's plan was now different from the series of plans developed in the 1920s and 1930s and often referred to as War Plan ORANGE. These had all assumed a war between the United States and Japan (ORANGE was the Navy's code name for Japan), in which the US Navy carried out a drive across the Central Pacific, established forward bases, and destroyed the Imperial Navy en route. In 1940–41, for the first time, the planners had to consider the possibility that their country might be at war with a number of enemies concurrently (hence the 'RAINBOW' plan), and that this enemy coalition would be led by Nazi Germany. For the first time, too, the war plans assumed that the United States would be fighting alongside allies, cautiously described by the planners as 'associated powers'. Of these allies by far the most important would be the British Empire.

In WPL-46 Washington did assign to the US Pacific Fleet one 'task' that followed the tradition of the ORANGE plans: 'Prepare to capture and establish control over the Caroline and Marshall Island area, and to establish an advanced fleet base in Truk'.[8] This expedition, however, was set a long way in the future. Admiral Kimmel's immediate task was more limited, and it very much followed from the new strategic partnership with Britain: 'Support the forces of the associated powers in the Far East by diverting enemy strength away from the Malay barrier, through the denial and capture of positions in the Marshalls, and through raids on enemy sea communications and positions.' (The 'Malay barrier' meant Singapore, Malaya and the Dutch East Indies.) One of the most peculiar features of the plan was that it gave no clear indication of what the US Navy would do to defend the American possessions of the Philippines and Guam, both of which were directly exposed to Japanese attack.

Kimmel was extremely dissatisfied with his situation. In a personal 'Dear "Betty"' letter to Admiral Stark, dated 15 November 1941, he had stressed the 'real and immediate' needs of the Pacific Fleet and complained that his command was becoming 'a training fleet for support of the Atlantic Fleet'. In case of war in the Pacific,

> [w]e must be in a position to minimize our own losses, and to inflict maximum damage to the Japanese fleet, merchant shipping, and bases. We should have sufficient strength in this fleet for such effective operations as to permit cruising at will in the Japanese Mandated Island area, and even on occasions to Japanese home waters. We should have the strength to make any operations against Wake a highly hazardous undertaking. To do these things substantial increase of the strength of this Fleet is mandatory.[9]

All the same, ten days later, on 25 November, in his war warnings to the Pacific Fleet and the Asiatic Fleet, Admiral Stark set the US Navy's war plan in motion: 'Execute an appropriate defensive deployment preparatory to carrying out the tasks assigned in WPL-46.' He effectively repeated this order two days later. As for Admiral Kimmel, he was under no illusions about what the Pacific Fleet could do to 'divert enemy strength', let alone capture positions in the Marshalls. He pointed out to Admiral Stark on 2 December that even a small-scale amphibious operation would not be possible until February 1942, when the Marines in San Diego arrived after having completed their training. Any thought of occupying the Marshalls and Carolines 'in an advance across the Pacific' would require 'a thirty to fifty percent increase in the fighting strength of the Fleet', as well as thirty to forty transports and an equal number of supply ships.[10]

* * *

To understand the tragic fate of the American Pacific Fleet – still three days away – it is essential to know what it was supposed to do if and when war came. Admiral Kimmel's staff had drafted their own sub-plan for the implementation of WPL-46 back in July 1941. It was designated WPPac-46 and it was still in effect in December.[11] WPPac-46 took into consideration a range of circumstances, with the most likely starting point being the United States becoming involved in war with Germany, which in turn might or might not lead to war with Japan. The plan for the opening weeks of war had two variants. What was called 'Phase 1' assumed that America was at war with Germany but that Japan was still neutral; 'Phase 1a' was a variant based on the assumption that hostilities had already started with Japan.

When war came the Pacific Fleet was to be organised into a number of 'task forces'. Task Force 1 was to be the anchor point of the fleet, providing ultimate but distant support for forward operations. Admiral Pye, 'Commander, Battle Force', would have charge of the most powerful battleships – *Maryland*, *West Virginia*, *Tennessee*, *California* and *Nevada* – and these would be joined after the first days of the war by *Arizona*, *Pennsylvania* and *Oklahoma*. Admiral Kimmel probably intended to fly his flag in *Pennsylvania*. The battle line was supported by four light cruisers and about twenty destroyers.

Task Force 2 was the 'reconnaissance and raiding force'. Under Admiral Halsey, 'Commander, Aircraft, Battle Force', were the carrier *Enterprise*, four heavy cruisers and ten destroyers. In peacetime, and in the first days of the war, three of the oldest battleships, *Arizona*, *Pennsylvania* and *Oklahoma*, were to be attached to this task force to provide support. Task Force 2 existed in late November 1941, and it was this force (without the battleships) that had transported the Marine fighters to Wake. Task Force 3, which would eventually carry out landing operations, was assigned a range of other duties at the beginning of the war, including the protection of shipping routes. To Admiral Newton, 'Commander, Scouting Force', were assigned the carrier *Lexington*, a powerful force of eight heavy cruisers, about twenty destroyers, transport ships, and ultimately – so the plan went – a division of US Marines. Task Force 7 comprised the fleet's submarines.

An important, and later controversial, part of the plan was to be played by Task Force 9, the fleet's long-range patrol planes. These aircraft, all twin-engined PBY 'Catalina' flying boats, were grouped into three patrol wings ('PatWings'). PatWing 1 and 2 were based on Oahu, at the Naval Air Stations on Ford Island and at Kaneohe respectively; PatWing 4 was divided between Ford Island and the US West Coast. Admiral Kimmel would later be asked to explain why, with this very large number of PBY flying boats available to him (the total was no fewer than 81) he could not establish an effective patrol perimeter around Oahu. Kimmel replied that his first priority had been training new crews and preparing for the forward operation into the Marshalls. His senior air officer later wrote that extensive patrols by the PBYs would have resulted in 'rapid automatic attrition' and they could not then be used for the Marshalls operation.[12]

Kimmel's mission was offensive; his task was not the passive defence of his base. The main fleet effort under WPPAc-46 would be directed towards the

Marshall Islands. Task Force 2, supported by Task Force 1, would reconnoitre and raid them in preparation for a landing. Kimmel designated Eniwetok Atoll, at the northwest end of the archipelago, as the likely objective – although it was clear that the actual landing would be some months in the future. Phase 2 of the plan, set even further in the future, envisaged the establishment of a forward anchorage for the Pacific Fleet in the Marshalls, and a campaign to capture the Japanese base at Truk in the Caroline Islands. Even if there were not enough Marines to mount an amphibious operation, the Japanese did not necessarily know this, and it might be possible to lure part of their fleet south and defeat it.

Kimmel and his staff had thought through in some detail the first weeks of the coming war – as they hoped it would occur.[13] The carrier *Saratoga* and the five large new light cruisers would be temporarily assigned to Task Force 2, as would the carrier *Lexington*, if she were available. This reinforced task force would sortie from Pearl Harbor on 'one J-day' – one day after hostilities with Japan began – with carriers and cruisers pushing forward at twenty knots. At this rate they would cover nearly 500 nautical miles each day. The carriers would then spend four days sending their scout planes over the Marshalls, paying special attention to Eniwetok. The battleships of Task Force 1 would leave Pearl Harbor on 'five J-day', the sixth day of the war. On the eleventh day they would rendezvous with Task Force 2 northeast of the Marshalls and southeast of Wake. Task Force 1 would provide distant support, nurse damaged ships, and serve as a rallying point towards which Task Force 2 could retire at the end of the raids. After the rendezvous, Task Force 2, with elements of Task Force 3 merged into it, would commence raids on the Marshalls on 'twelve J-day'.

It was this probe into the Marshalls that made Midway and Wake, and the PatWings, so important. Offensive operations required long-range air reconnaissance; advanced bases for the PBYs needed to be protected by garrisons and air defences. Kimmel's plan specified that by the fifth day of operations, 'maximum practicable patrol plane strength' would be deployed to Wake, Midway and Johnston. Wake was especially important, as it was furthest west, most remote from Oahu and most exposed to attack. PBYs from Wake could scout the northeastern part of Marshalls; most importantly, they could also cover the approaches to those islands from the direction of Japan.

* * *

The tentative American steps to reinforce Wake and Midway, and to prepare a diversion in the Marshalls, were one thing. More ominous naval movements were taking place four time zones to the west. Shortly after dawn on

4 December the main Japanese invasion convoy of fifteen transports left the harbour at Samah on Hainan Island. The ships headed southwest at sixteen knots, bound for Malaya and Thailand (two slower vessels had left the day before to obtain a head start).[14] The convoy observed radio silence, and there were no British or American aircraft, submarines or surface ships patrolling off the coast of Indochina. The convoy would not be sighted for over forty-eight hours. This was to be a critical failure for the defenders.

The Japanese were well ahead of other countries, including the United States and Britain, in the theory and practice of amphibious warfare. General Yamashita, commander of Japanese 25th Army, had his forward headquarters aboard the 7,100 ton *Ryūjō Maru* (or *Shinshu Maru*), which had been completed for the Japanese Army in 1935, and was the world's first purpose-built landing ship. The decks of the other transports were covered with nested landing craft. The convoy transported the first wave of Yamashita's Army: three of four regiments of 5th Infantry Division, and a regiment of 18th Infantry Division, some 27,000 men in all, including 17,000 combat troops. Both the 5th and 18th Divisions had completed intensive training in landing operations.

The fast battleships *Haruna* and *Kongō*, with three cruisers and eight destroyers, the 'main body' of the Southern Force, left Mako in the Pescadores (between Formosa and the mainland) for the south on 4 December. Their mission was to provide distant cover for the convoy. Admiral Kondō, C-in-C of the Southern Force, flew his flag in heavy cruiser *Atago*. Another squadron of heavy cruisers sortied from Hahajima in the Bonins on the 4th, bound for the American possession of Guam.

* * *

In Tokyo the 75th Liaison Conference assembled for two hours in the afternoon of the 4th, the last such meeting to be held before the outbreak of the Pacific War. The main item discussed was the 'Final Communication to the United States'. The actual content was left to Foreign Minister Tōgō, and the timing of the delivery of the note was also to be determined by discussion between the *Gaimushō* and Imperial General Headquarters. Tōgō stated that the message should include Japan's response to the Hull Note of 26 November, as well as the Imperial Rescript declaring war.[15]

## East Prussia

Hitler's aeroplane finally touched down near his headquarters in East Prussia on Thursday, 4 December, probably at midday. What happened next remains something of a mystery. The decision about what kind of support to promise Japan – first raised by Ambassador Ōshima on Monday evening – still awaited resolution. It was not until the evening, however, that Ribbentrop, from his office in the Wilhelmstrasse, was able to make contact with the German dictator by telephone and obtain general approval to support Japan against America – including in a case where Japan was the attacker, rather than the attacked. Even then, the decision would not be formally dealt with, in consultation with the Italians, until the small hours of 5 December.

The Italian Foreign Minister, Ciano, thought this delay demonstrated German reluctance to make such a commitment, although he also noted that Mussolini had no such reservations. But there is no other evidence of German reluctance, and a more mundane explanation may be advanced: the Führer had to sleep. Hitler had suffered two uncomfortable nights in Poltava, and then a flight of three or four hours from Poltava to the airfield at WOLFSSCHANZE squeezed into a small converted bomber. In any event, in the evening Foreign Minister Tōgō, Ambassador Ōshima, Reich Foreign Minister Ribbentrop – and presumably the *Duce* – got what they wanted. Hitler verbally approved a strengthened Tripartite Pact with Japan and Italy, he agreed to support Japan against America, and he accepted that there would be no separate peace with the USA or Britain.[16] Hitler had given his crucial approval to Japan's war of conquest.

## Russia

Thursday, 4 December brought even more severe weather conditions onto the battlefields around Moscow. The temperature now stood at –20°C (–4°F). The sky was overcast, with heavy snow showers in places.

Another day had passed with heavy fighting, and still the Soviet counterattacks planned by General Zhukov for 3 December had not begun. The Soviet General Staff situation report mentioned defensive fighting around Zvenigorod against the German 4th Army, and some minor advances against the enemy in the north.

Early in the day Zhukov ordered General Golikov to prepare his attack for the morning of the 6th. Golikov's new 10th Army, south of Moscow, was to defeat Guderian's 2nd Panzer Army and reach Stalinogorsk and Uzlovaia within four days. Zhukov also issued a detailed directive to three of his other armies – 5th, 16th and 20th – to plan for an attack against Hoepner's Panzer Group 4 in the Istra area (north of Moscow). The offensive was set for the morning of 7 December, and it was to consist of 'well-prepared sequential operations'. Once again, the C-in-C of Western Army Group tried to stir his commanders into action: 'With the goals of wrecking the enemy's preparations for a further offensive against Moscow and for the defeat of the exhausted enemy, I order you to go over from the defensive to a decisive offensive.'[17]

Zhukov's assessment of the German situation was critical: 'According to all available information, the enemy forces [Panzer Groups 3 and 4] which are operating against the right wing of Western AG are exhausted and cannot now resume a general offensive without further preparation.' The enemy had expended all his reserves in the eighteen-day battle. The recent fighting on the Nara River had demonstrated that it was no longer difficult to force the enemy's infantry to take flight. Zhukov calculated that Panzer divisions were now down to 30 per cent of personnel and forty to fifty tanks; they had very little fuel or ammunition.[18]

The Germans also attempted an assessment of their enemy on 4 December. More errors in judging the situation around Moscow were now made by Colonel Kinzel's Foreign Armies East (*FHO*). 'The enemy's strength,' the *FHO* concluded, 'comes from complex minefields and much use of heavy tanks, aircraft and rocket launchers. On the whole his combat strength cannot be so highly rated that it would be, at present, capable of a large-scale offensive without substantial reinforcement.' The intelligence reports of Army Group Centre were also overly optimistic: 'What the enemy is doing has become clearer in the attack battles of recent days. He has freed up forces from quiet sectors of the Moscow front to use for counter-attacks in places where he is especially threatened.' The danger was limited: 'In other respects his combat strength is not high enough *at the present time* to mount a major offensive against the Army Group.'[19]

Whatever the situation at the front, the problems at the top of the German high command continued. The position of Field Marshal von Brauchitsch was discussed at midday by Halder and General Bodewin Keitel; Keitel was head of the Army's Office of Personnel and the younger brother of Field Marshal Wilhelm Keitel (military head of the *OKW* under Hitler). General Keitel stated that it was necessary to remove the German Army C-in-C on health grounds, and that he would consult with his brother. Halder consented to the removal of his chief, but hoped to avoid being directly involved in the procedure.[20]

## London

The USSR was also a major concern for the British war leadership in Whitehall on Thursday, 4 December. Foreign Secretary Eden was scheduled to depart for

Moscow on Sunday the 7th. The meeting of the British War Cabinet at 6.00 p.m. that evening was unusually tense. The political objectives of Eden's visit did not arouse open controversy, but there was disagreement about what aid could be promised to Britain's Russian allies.

The Foreign Secretary had discussed his visit with Ivan Maiskii, the Soviet Ambassador to Britain, on the 1st. The round-faced, white-haired Ambassador had served in London since 1932, and made excellent contacts. As an intellectual of Polish-Jewish background and a former Menshevik, Maiskii was a remarkable survivor of the terrible blood-purge of the Commissariat of Foreign Affairs in 1937–38. He was given some extravagant promises. 'Eden said,' Maiskii reported to Moscow, 'that he was getting ready on his arrival in Moscow to lay his cards on the table, to give us information about the deployment of British forces and tell us what help the British government could give us now and in the future. As the first instalment Eden cited a figure of up to 70,000 troops, including a significant amount of mechanised forces.' If the battles in Libya went well the forces to be sent to Russia might be increased beyond these three or four divisions.[21]

Within two days it had become clear that the Foreign Secretary had promised too much. On the evening of 3 December the War Cabinet's Defence Committee had concluded that, in view of the undecided battle in Libya, Britain would not, as had been briefly considered, send two divisions to Russia. At the War Cabinet on the 4th, however, Churchill began by proposing that the Russians be sent 500 tanks and 500 aircraft 'in the spring'. But the new Chief of the Imperial General Staff, General Alan Brooke, who was attending his first War Cabinet, poured cold water on the plan.[22] The best that could be offered, Brooke suggested, was 300 of the new 'Churchill' medium tanks, fifty a month for the next six months. And he could not recommend 'such a gift' as it would mean 'seriously denuding this country and prematurely disclosing a new pattern of tank'. At the same time Air Marshal Portal, the RAF C-in-C (Chief of the Air Staff), said that his service could provide no planes, but that 300 might be diverted from planned American Lend-Lease deliveries to Britain.

The Foreign Secretary, according to Brooke, took all this badly: 'Anthony Eden like a peevish child grumbling because he was being sent off to Uncle Stalin without suitable gifts, while Granny Churchill was comforting him and explaining to him all the pretty speeches he might make instead.' Eden went so far as to suggest that if he had to go empty-handed the visit should be postponed; Churchill said he thought this would be 'disastrous'. Eventually it was agreed to send 300 tanks and 300 aircraft. A typically shrewd and pithy assessment of the discussion was made by Alexander Cadogan, one of the most important participants. 'Alec' Cadogan was the senior civil servant in the Foreign Office ('Permanent Under-Secretary'), and the keeper of a most important – and often outspoken – personal diary. He described Anthony Eden's response to the reduction of promised arms to Russia: 'A. – rightly – made a stink about this, but agreed to go.'[23]

In the late evening, after dinner, the principals reassembled. Present with the Chiefs of Staff were Churchill, Eden and Clement Attlee (Lord Privy Seal and Churchill's de facto deputy). The Prime Minister had decided not to offer tanks and aircraft, but instead to promise ten RAF squadrons as soon as the Libyan offensive was over. Portal, for the RAF, agreed in broad terms but opposed too 'definite' an offer. This provoked, as Brooke put it, 'the most awful outburst of temper' from Churchill. He accused the military chiefs of being persistently negative and of not seeing the larger picture. Now it was Eden's turn, along with Attlee, to try to soothe Churchill, but to no avail. The Prime Minister looked at his papers for five minutes, then slammed them together, closed the meeting and stalked out of the room in a rage.

General Brooke recorded his impressions that evening: 'It was pathetic and entirely unnecessary. We were only trying to save him [Churchill] from making definite promises which he might find hard to keep later on.' The General put the Prime Minister's outburst down to overwork and too many late hours. 'Such a pity,' he noted in his diary. 'God knows where we would be without him, but God knows where we shall go with him.'[24]

* * *

The intensity of emotion at these meetings came partly from an expectation that the Foreign Secretary's visit to Moscow would be a turning point in Allied relations (and it should not be forgotten that at this moment the USSR was Britain's only serious ally). Eden had explained the background of the trip to the American Ambassador, Gilbert Winant, on 3 December: 'Stalin was in a mood of suspicion and even resentment to an extent that might adversely affect the cooperation of the two Governments in the prosecution of the war, and His Majesty's government decided that every effort must be made to dissipate those feelings.' Churchill had decided, as a result, to despatch the Foreign Secretary himself. Eden saw his role as allaying Stalin's suspicions that Britain and the US aimed to exclude Russia from the peace settlement, and in particular that they would not be prepared to take sufficient steps to 'render Germany innocuous'. The purpose of his trip, Eden assured Ambassador

Winant, was 'to give Stalin as much satisfaction as possible without entering into commitments'.[25]

In truth, all of this had only begun to come together within the last ten days, and it followed an especially frosty period in British-Russian relations. Earlier in November the Prime Minister had decided that the relationship with Moscow was strained and that there were important issues that could be resolved only by high-level discussion; he and Eden may even have been concerned about a separate Russian-German peace being brokered. Churchill offered to send two senior generals, Wavell and Paget, to Russia 'in order to clear things up and to plan for the future'. On 8 November – the day after the famous Revolution Day military parade in Red Square – Stalin had issued a curt reply.[26] He turned down Churchill's proposal as a waste of time for both the generals and himself, unless the British delegation was able to discuss serious issues. British-Soviet relations, Stalin complained, lacked clarity. No agreement had been made about war aims and the post-war organisation of world affairs; neither had any treaty been signed between the two states regarding mutual co-operation against Hitler. Without these things, 'if it is possible speak completely openly', there could be no mutual confidence. One particular concern raised by the Soviet leader was Britain's failure to declare war on Finland, Hungary and Romania, all of which had taken up arms alongside Nazi Germany in its invasion of the USSR in June 1941.[27]

Churchill persisted, encouraged partly by expectations of early military success in Operation CRUSADER in Libya. In a personal letter to Stalin on 21 November he suggested that the Foreign Secretary himself could go to Moscow. This time Churchill received a very positive reply two days later. 'I agree with you,' the Soviet leader said, 'that differences in the state structure of the USSR, on the one hand, and of Great Britain and the USA, on the other, must not and will not interfere with us in the favourable resolution of the basic questions of securing our common security and legal interests. I hope that if there are any sort of reservations and doubts in this area that they will be dispelled as a result of the conversations with Mr Eden.'[28] (Eden had particular significance as a representative of Britain. His official visit to Moscow in 1935 was the first by a senior British politician, and had to some extent broken the ice of British-Soviet relations.)

Major issues were indeed at stake. Communist Russia and the British Empire had been arch-enemies from the 1917 revolution until the mid-1930s. Hostility had resumed in August 1939 when Stalin signed a pact with Nazi Germany, Soviet propaganda viciously criticised the British-French war effort, and the Red Army invaded Finland; the Soviet Union also annexed a third of

Poland, part of Romania and all of the three Baltic States. In addition, whatever its own interests, the British government had to stay highly attuned to American sensibilities, and both London and Washington were unwilling to recognise border changes achieved by Moscow's aggression against its neighbours. The Atlantic Charter, proclaimed by Roosevelt and Churchill in August 1941, rejected any territorial alterations without the consent of the peoples concerned.

Eden told Ambassador Winant on 3 December that he hoped to secure Stalin's agreement on several points. Two of these seemed straightforward: an agreement not to 'interfere in the internal affairs of other nations', and the disarmament of Germany. The British, more contentiously, also wanted to promote federations of weaker European states (such as Poland and Czechoslovakia) to make them a better bulwark against foreign aggression. The final point touched on compensation (reparations) by Germany, which had been such a great issue after 1918. Eden explained that the British government had made no decision about this, and would try to keep Moscow from committing itself to a reparations policy at this moment. The Foreign Secretary confided to Winant that Britain was aware that any participation of the Russians in post-war planning, including economic planning, would eventually require 'consent of other participating governments' (including the government in Washington). But since the Soviet government had made British readiness to discuss post-war problems 'a test of confidence', it was 'indispensible . . . to give an indication of our own attitude'.[29]

* * *

Churchill's outburst of temper late on Thursday evening was directly provoked by military foot-dragging over aid to Russia, as well as overwork and tiredness. But a more general cause may well have been a growing realisation of the limits of British power, and part of that related to the confrontation with Japan.

Earlier in the evening, at its 6.00 p.m. meeting, the War Cabinet had also discussed the situation in the Far East. Those present were made aware of Lord Halifax's report of his trips to the White House, especially the meeting on the previous evening (3 December) with Roosevelt and Welles. The President, the War Cabinet were told, had repeated his assurance that 'we would obviously all be in it together' if British territory or the Dutch East Indies were attacked by the Japanese. Churchill argued that this meant Britain could promise help to the Dutch and put Operation MATADOR into effect in Thailand 'if the circumstances made this necessary'. He also proposed 'joint assurance' with the US towards Thailand.[30] (Cadogan also recorded this in his diary:

'We had had a very good telegram from Roosevelt [sic] about Far East, which removed many of P.M.'s doubts, and he said we could now [sic] guarantee Dutch.')[31]

About nine hours later, at 3.30 a.m. on Friday, 5 December, the British War Office would send a message to Air Marshal Brooke-Popham in Singapore, numbered FE 50. 'His Majesty's Government have now received an assurance of American armed support in the following contingencies,' the message began. One 'contingency' was a direct Japanese attack on Britain; a second was a Japanese attack on the Dutch East Indies, with Britain supporting the Dutch. The third, and most important, involved Thailand; 'if we undertake Matador either to forestall a Japanese landing in Kra Isthmus or as a reply to a Japanese violation of any other part of Thailand'.

Telegram FE 50 authorised Brooke-Popham to execute Operation MATADOR 'without reference home' if he had 'good information that a Japanese expedition is advancing with the apparent intention of landing on the Kra Isthmus' or if the Japanese violated any part of Thailand. The Air Marshal was also authorised, without referring to London, to execute existing joint war plans agreed with the Dutch.[32]

It was a remarkable message and a remarkable decision. America could not provide serious 'armed support' – to uphold the British Empire or for any other reason – unless it went to war. America could not go to war unless Congress declared war; this was still not a decision the President could make. It is most likely that the decision in London was influenced by strong, if still vague, vocal messages of support from President Roosevelt, and also by increasing evidence (including decrypts) that the Japanese were actually going to take military action against Britain *and* the United States.[33]

Evidence of intended Japanese aggression certainly continued to mount. On Thursday Bletchley Park produced BJ 098540, a decrypt of the message sent on Tuesday (2 December) from Tokyo, instructing the Washington embassy to destroy codes and code machines.[34] This followed the previous day's decrypt (sent from Tokyo on 1 December) about destroying code materials in London. In the first days of January 1942 the British War Office's Director of Military Intelligence (DMI), General Francis Davidson, wrote a post-mortem about the failure of the British Joint Intelligence Committee to anticipate the outbreak of war in the Far East. In Davidson's paper, this destruction of code materials was singled out as *the* giveaway of Japanese hostile intentions, and one which should have alerted British intelligence.[35] (Commander Safford, head of the US Navy codebreaking unit, OP-20-G, had come to the same – correct – conclusion in Washington on 3 December.)

The very next BJ (098541) processed on 4 December was a decrypt of Ambassador Ōshima's report of his meeting in Berlin with Ribbentrop on 28 November. In it the Ambassador reported that the German position versus the US had 'stiffened', that Ribbentrop was urging Japan to take action now, and that he had promised that Germany would 'join the war immediately'.[36]

## Washington

Meanwhile, in Washington, there was an unexpected and remarkable new twist to the pre-war crisis. On the morning of 4 December, the *Chicago Tribune*, a Republican, isolationist newspaper and flagship of the Hearst Press, ran a major story under the headline: 'F.D.R.'S WAR PLANS! GOAL IS 10 MILLION ARMED MEN; HALF TO FIGHT IN AEF'. The scoop was also published by the similarly-minded *Times Herald* in Washington. The article, by the reporter Chesly Manly, leaked details of secret American war plans, based on the so-called 'Victory Program', a copy of which he had been given overnight access to.[37] The document disclosed both the level of American planned mobilisation of human resources and manpower, and the government's strategic intentions for using them.

American military and civilian officials had been working on an economic mobilisation programme since the summer of 1941, and any such plan had to include estimates of how and where the war would be fought, and the number of troops and amount of equipment that would be required. The programme envisaged US armed forces of 10 million, with an army of no fewer than 215 divisions and thousands of fighter and bomber aircraft. Some 18 million tons of shipping would be required. 'It is a blueprint,' as Manly put it, 'for total war on a scale unprecedented in at least two oceans and three continents, Europe, Africa, and Asia.'

Even more striking than the statistics was the plan's broad-brush outline of American strategic intentions. Half the force of 10 million men would be deployed in an American Expeditionary Force (AEF) – the term used in the First World War – to be launched against Germany in July 1943. The vast bomber force would also be used against the Third Reich. It was hoped that Japan could be held in check 'pending future developments'. The United States was described as presently being in a first, preparatory, phase. In Phase 2, beginning most likely in April 1942, the country would actually enter the war against Germany. Phase 3, beginning in July 1943, would complete the task: 'Total defeat of Germany'. The article also quoted a passage in which one objective was listed as preserving the British Empire. This was then interpreted by Manly: 'Thus it appears that the No. 1 military objective of sending American armed forces outside the western hemisphere is the preservation of the British Empire.' Manly's account was, it must be said, generally a fair report of military strategy behind the Victory Program, although the document was itself a poor predictor of what would actually happen in 1942–45.[38]

The reaction to the *Tribune*'s story in the Third Reich, in the seven days remaining before Hitler declared war on the United States, was both interesting and important. Hans Thomsen, the Chargé d'Affaires in Washington, sent an accurate précis of the news story back to Berlin, with his opinion that it was accurate. Goebbels commented on its importance in his diary on the following day.[39] The news was also, as we will see, taken seriously by the Wehrmacht planners, when they considered the implications of war with the United States. And Hitler would certainly refer to the *Tribune* story in his speech of 11 December declaring war on the United States. But in the end it was Japanese action that brought America and Germany into the war, and from Hitler's point of view there were many other American provocations.

How the *Tribune* leak came about remains unclear. The documents were made available to Chesly Manly by one of the most prominent isolationists in the Senate, the Montana Democrat Burton K. Wheeler. Senator Wheeler claimed that he was given them by an Army Air Force officer who opposed the government's policy. No one was ever prosecuted for the breach of security, and even now it cannot be said who this officer was.[40] Two other explanations have been suggested, although both are farfetched. One is that British 'political warfare' officers put the material in the hands of the press, using Senator Wheeler as a stooge; their intention was to increase tension between Nazi Germany and the United States.[41] The other is that the Victory Program was leaked by the White House itself, in order to provoke a reaction from Berlin.[42] This does, however, seem implausible, and would certainly have risked alienating the US military leadership, as well as key officials in the Cabinet like Hull, Stimson and Knox.

In any event, Senator Wheeler and the *Chicago Tribune* were certainly involved in the leak and their motives were clear. They wanted to embarrass the Roosevelt administration and to illuminate what was going on out of sight of Congress and the American electorate.[43] The affair was indicative of the deep rifts within American politics, the strength of isolationist feeling and hostility to Roosevelt and the New Deal. It also highlights the caution with which the President needed to act in early December. To take the United States to war in order to defend an obscure part of the British Empire was a very serious political challenge indeed.

The *Tribune* story of 4 December was surely one of the most extraordinary leaks in the history of American journalism. This is true not only because it was a gross violation of national security, but also because the 'scandal' lasted little more than seventy-two hours. President Roosevelt himself wisely decided to make no public response to the leak (although Secretary of War Stimson held a press conference at which he expressed his outrage). Everything was forgotten when the United States was actually plunged into war at midday on 7 December. By 9 December Senator Wheeler would be declaring himself an advocate of 'total war'.[44]

* * *

For all the clamour about the *Tribune*'s war-plans leak, the main concern for the White House remained the explosive situation in the Far East.

One thing did *not* happen in Washington on the morning of 4 December. That was the arrival of an intercepted 'winds' message (the so-called 'winds execute'), making it clear that Japan was about to break off relations with the United States and Britain.[45] Laurance Safford, by this time promoted to Captain, later claimed that he saw such a message while on duty in the Navy Department between 8.00 a.m. and 9.00 a.m. that morning, and passed it to his superiors. This was part of his testimony made during various official hearings into the outbreak of the Pacific War; his argument was that crucial intelligence was mishandled and suppressed. Safford was certainly an important witness; he was the administrator of the US Navy's codebreaking unit in Washington, OP-20-G. In later testimony, however, he was inconsistent, and there was no supporting information from anyone else in the organisation.

There is no evidence that a 'winds execute' message was transmitted before 8 December. In general, too much time was spent in the post-war hearings, and consequently by later historians, arguing about the 'winds execute' message. Even if it had been sent before 8 December (which it was not) there was by that time abundant *other* information, decrypted and circulated, which showed that Japanese relations with Britain and the United States were at breaking point.[46]

President Roosevelt had yet another meeting with Lord Halifax in the White House late in the evening of 4 December; the British Ambassador left half an hour after midnight. The two men returned to the subject of a warning to Japan, which had been raised by Prime Minister Churchill four days earlier. Halifax wanted the warning to extend not only to Thailand, but also to Malaya, the Dutch East Indies and the Chinese part of the Burma Road. The President generally agreed, although he removed the Burma Road from the list.[47] He also requested that the United States be allowed to deliver its warning to Japan before Britain did, so that the White House would not appear – to Congress and to the US public opinion – simply to be following the British lead.

In addition, President Roosevelt wished to make his warning only after he had taken one further step: he proposed to write directly to the Japanese Emperor. If no reply was received by Monday evening (8 December), the United States would proceed with the warnings to Japan in the latter half of Tuesday (9 December), and the British and the Dutch would follow with warnings on Wednesday (10 December). The view of the British Ambassador was that Roosevelt believed this timetable to be realistic, given the stage of Japanese preparations. Halifax reported that Secretary of State Hull, with whom he had talked on another occasion on the 4th, was less optimistic about the amount of time available for diplomacy.[48]

The notes in Lord Halifax's diary at the end of this day show that in his opinion, too, armed conflict with Japan was now imminent: 'Everything looks exactly like the Japanese balloon going up in the course of a day or two – cyphers being burnt, secret messages in that sense, etc.' In mid-November he had offered to bet Lady Halifax that Britain would not be at war with anyone new by 1 January 1942. He now thought that wager lost.[49]

CHAPTER 8

## FRIDAY, 5 DECEMBER

# The Lull Before Two Storms

*Should a state of war begin between Japan and the United States, Germany and Italy for their part will consider themselves to be in a state of war with the United States, and shall conduct this war with all the forces at their disposal.*

German note to Ambassador Ōshima

*v. Bock. No more strength. Tomorrow's attack by Panzer Group 4 is no longer possible.*

General Franz Halder

*Japan, already extended militarily, has a multiplicity of strategic objectives; but for a variety of reasons, she cannot concentrate the required forces to attack any of them on a large scale and with assurance of success.*

General Sherman Miles

### Southeast Asia

On Friday, 5 December, General Terauchi Hisaichi secretly flew into Saigon to take charge of the headquarters of Japan's new Southern Army.

One remarkable thing that did not happen on 5 December was a sighting of the big Japanese invasion convoy carrying the lead elements of one of Terauchi's four armies to the Kra Isthmus and Malaya. The transport ships, loaded with troops and equipment, with escorting warships, had left the Samah anchorage on Hainan Island on the previous morning. They were now proceeding along the coast of French Indochina, making an average speed of about twelve knots. Over the twenty-four hours of 5 December the armada covered another 290 miles. Strict radio silence was observed.[1]

The route of the convoy on that day was 800 to 900 miles distant from the Philippines and Singapore – at the limit of the practical range of the search planes based in the area. Flying weather on the 5th was also poor. It is not known if the flying boats of PatWing 10 in the Philippines patrolled over the convoy route, but there were no reports of a sighting; in any case, American attention was concentrated on Camranh Bay, further south down the Indochina coast. The large US submarine flotilla was tied up in Manila Bay, and only one of the little picket ships ordered out of the bay by President Roosevelt's personal order of 1 December was in place. This was the yacht USS *Isabel*, and she approached the coast of Indochina – probably near Camranh Bay – in the evening of the 5th, after a two-day cruise. Almost immediately she was ordered back to the Philippines.[2]

During Friday morning one Catalina flying boat did cross over the South China Sea – but it was operated by the RAF, and flew well southeast of the convoy route. The mission was VIP transport rather than reconnaissance, and aboard were Admiral Phillips (C-in-C, Eastern Fleet) and two members of his staff. After an arduous journey from Singapore, including about ten hours in the air, the Admiral and his party alighted in Manila Bay. They were to confer about overall strategy with the American commanders in the Philippines.[3]

The British party were met by Admiral Thomas C. Hart, who had been C-in-C of the US Asiatic Fleet since July 1939. 'Tommy' Hart was five years older than Admiral Kimmel – indeed he was considerably senior to the CNO, Admiral Stark. The US Asiatic Fleet was largely a token force representing American interests in the Far East, rather than providing real defence for the Philippines; it was a separate command from the US Pacific Fleet, and came under the direct control of the Chief of Naval Operations in Washington. In the autumn of 1940 Hart had pulled his ships back from Shanghai to Manila Bay; a year later he despatched them out of harm's way to the southern waters of the archipelago. In December 1941, the surface ships under his command consisted of the heavy cruiser *Houston*, a light cruiser, twelve old destroyers and an exotic miscellany of Chinese river gunboats and other vessels. On paper the Asiatic Fleet also had powerful submarine forces – Hart was himself a submariner by speciality – and most of the twenty-eight boats were still in the Manila Bay area, but their effectiveness was an unknown quantity. The Asiatic Fleet also contained twenty-eight PBY patrol planes, but there were no other Navy or Marine aircraft in the Philippines.

Hart and the British visitors had a preliminary talk for most of the afternoon. In London Tom Phillips had a reputation for impatience bordering on rudeness, but he made a good impression on Hart. The American Admiral wrote in his diary that he had mentally pictured a 'big, husky, personably magnetic sort' but found Phillips quite different: 'He's a bare 5 ft. two and decidedly the intellectual type – good stuff all right and has a first-rate brain.'[4] Hart kept the visit of Phillips and his team very quiet, and put them up in the *Comandancia* in Cavite. The officers who were to take part in the main conference the following day met for a preliminary dinner in the evening. Admiral Hart's main guest, aside from the British Admiral, was General Douglas MacArthur, C-in-C of US Army forces in the Philippines.

* * *

Early in the morning of 5 December the British War Office had sent signal FE 50 to Singapore. This gave the C-in-C (Brooke-Popham) extraordinary powers. In the event of a Japanese expedition being sighted approaching Thailand, or if the territory of that country were to be violated, he had permission to mount Operation MATADOR without reference to London. The message was a long time in transit, and it was received only in the afternoon, at 3.31 p.m. local time.

The fact that Admiral Phillips had, on the previous day, decided to fly to Manila was a sign that, whatever the warnings of the previous week, he did not expect immediate action by the Japanese. Equally significant was the detachment of half the strength of Force 'G' for a courtesy visit to northern Australia. On 5 December, *Repulse*, with an escort of four destroyers, departed for Port Darwin. The round-trip distance of 5,500 miles meant the battle-cruiser would have been away from Singapore for the better part of two weeks. *Repulse* would not have been detached had an attack been anticipated in this period.[5]

## Berlin and Moscow

On Thursday evening, rested after his arduous his trip to south Russia, Hitler had finally agreed that the Reich would give unconditional support to Japan. This triggered a night of hectic diplomatic exchanges between Berlin, Rome and Tokyo. At 9.30 p.m. the German Ambassador in Rome, Hans von Mackensen, received a phone call from his Foreign Ministry telling him that an important document was to be received in the very near future (no exact time could be given) and that he was to take it up with Foreign Minister Count Ciano, and possibly Mussolini, immediately.

Four hours later, at 1.30 a.m. on Friday, 5 December, a draft agreement with the Japanese government arrived in Rome by teletype from Ribbentrop. The text required advance approval by the Italians, and this approval was to be obtained with all possible haste. At 2.20 a.m., Mackensen telephoned Ciano and read the text – consisting of a preface and four short articles – to him, translating from German into Italian as he spoke.

The Preface explained that this new agreement of the three governments stemmed from 'the increasingly obvious intention of the United States and England, with all the powers at their disposal, to frustrate a just new order and to cut off the means of existence of the German, Italian, and Japanese people'. Article 1 committed Germany and Italy to war with America: 'Should a state of war begin [*der Kriegszustand eintritt*] between Japan and the United States, Germany and Italy for their part will consider themselves to be in a state of war with the United States, and shall conduct this war with all the forces at their disposal.' This proviso went well beyond the terms of the September 1940 Tripartite Pact, under which this mutual support would only apply if one of the signatories was 'attacked by' a power (*von einer Macht angegriffen wird*) not currently involved in the war (i.e. the United States).

In Article 2 the Germans agreed to the Japanese request that the three Axis countries would not make any armistice or peace with the United States or Britain without mutual consent. The third article stipulated that the agreement was to be kept secret, although the point about not making a separate peace would be announced when, and if, Germany, Italy and Japan found themselves jointly in a state of war with the United States or Britain, or both. The final article specified that the agreement would enter into force immediately and would run for the same term as the original Tripartite Pact, that is until 1950.[6]

Ciano said that it would not be necessary to awaken the *Duce*, as he knew the terms would be acceptable to him. The approval of the Italians having been assured, Ribbentrop now summoned General Ōshima to the Wilhelmstrasse. At around 4.00 a.m. he handed the Japanese Ambassador the draft agreement, which gave him the assurance of unqualified support that he had requested thirty-six hours earlier. Ōshima immediately sent the text – a Japanese translation and the German original – back to Tokyo.[7] The Japanese Ambassador in Rome, Horikiri, was given the same (German) text by Count Ciano in mid-morning, Mussolini's formal approval having been granted.

Hitler and Ribbentrop – and Mussolini and Ciano – now knew that war between Japan and Britain was likely, as probably was war between Japan and the United States. They could guess, too, that this war would be initiated by Tokyo and not by Washington. Hitler and Ribbentrop did not know that war was two days away, but they knew it was coming.[8] They had now formally committed their countries to a global struggle.

* * *

In front of Moscow the weather conditions turned even colder on 5 December, dropping to between –25°C and –31°C (–13°F and –24°F).

Meanwhile, the Soviet counterattack finally began, the first blow being delivered by part of General Konev's Kalinin Army Group. This represented yet another Soviet change of plan. The original intention, put forward by Zhukov on 29 November, had been for Konev to move into action from the north against the German 9th Army, two or three days *after* the armies of his own Western Army Group had commenced attacking Panzer Groups 3 and 4 from the east.

The first attack was executed in the middle of the night, at 3.00 a.m., by 31st Army, east of the German-occupied town of Kalinin. The headquarters of Kalinin Army Group reported: 'Units of VANGUARD [the codeword for 31st Army] sent their forward battalions into an offensive in the period 03:00 to 05:00 with the objective of establishing a bridgehead on the south side of the Volga River. By 09:00–09:40 they had taken Staroe Semenovskoe and the western part of Gorokhovo.' The 29th Army (also in Konev's army group) began the second strike at about midday, on the other (western) side of Kalinin. In both battles Soviet troops gained a foothold on the southern bank of the Volga.[9]

Kalinin Army Group was on the move, but Zhukov's Western Army Group still did not launch concerted attacks on the 5th. All the same, the Germans in the two bulges north and south of Moscow were unable to push any further forward. In the afternoon of the 5th, General Reinhardt reported to Field Marshal von Bock that his Panzer Group 3 had exhausted its offensive strength and had no reserves, and that the cold was having a detrimental effect on his forces. The line on the Moskva-Volga Canal, he said, would have to be given up as soon as possible. By the evening, General Guderian, commanding 2nd Panzer Army south of Moscow, had also decided that even the attack on Tula was impossible, and that it was necessary to retreat – the first time in the whole war that the aggressive Panzer General had had to take such a decision. Field Marshal von Bock, by the early evening, had reported to German Army headquarters in East Prussia that his forces were too weak to carry out the offensives planned for 6 December. 'No more strength', was Halder's comment that evening. 'Tomorrow's attack by Panzer Group 4 is not possible. Whether a withdrawal is necessary will be reported tomorrow.'[10]

As the Germans troops on the front line reached the end of their capacity, so the crisis in the highest ranks came to a head. At the very end of the day, Field Marshal von Brauchitsch told Halder that he finally had made his decision to resign as C-in-C of the German Army.[11]

## London and Washington

The British military authorities in London did little on 5 December, at least after despatching – in the middle of the night – telegram FE 50 to Singapore. Cavendish-Bentinck's Joint Intelligence Committee met, and prepared a paper on the pros and cons of Russia entering a hypothetical war between Japan, Britain and the United States. The conclusion was that the 'decisive consideration' should be the maintenance of a strong front against Germany.[12] There were meetings of the Chiefs of Staff, but they were mainly concerned with the details of combined strategy with Russia. An evening meeting of the Defence Committee (Operations) dealt with projected operations in the Mediterranean. Foreign Secretary Eden did give the Dutch government a written pledge of support, but no formal document had been drawn up before the Japanese struck.[13]

On Friday, 5 December, Churchill set off for a weekend stay at Chequers, located about thirty-five miles northwest of London in Buckinghamshire. Before he left, however, he received Soviet Ambassador Maiskii. The Prime Minister was, according to Maiskii, 'extremely pessimistic about developments in the Far East'. Britain and Japan were on the brink of war. On the other hand – according to Maiskii's interpretation of Churchill's words – 'the general situation in this part of the world was not that bad for Great Britain, as the United States had just informed Britain that they would give the British government full support in the event of a Japanese attack to the south'.

The main business of the meeting was a final consultation before Eden and the Soviet Ambassador set off for their long trip to Russia (scheduled to begin on 7 December). Maiskii reported back to the Moscow that the Prime Minister was now stressing that RAF squadrons would be sent to support the Red Army, rather than ground forces; setbacks in Libya and logistical problems meant the British could no longer spare troops.

Churchill also raised important political issues, going further than Eden had dared in his own talks with Maiskii on the 1st. The Prime Minister agreed that Germany would have to be disarmed, and broken up, above all by the detachment of Prussia. But this, he said, could not be spoken of publicly. He expanded on his vision for a Europe in which the major states would survive but the 'petty states' would be grouped into new federations: Balkan, Central European, Scandinavian, and so on. He would support the creation of a federation of Poland and Czechoslovakia. All of this would be overseen by a European Council able to use military means to enforce its decisions. (Many of these threads would be picked up by Stalin, when he met Eden in the Kremlin in less than two weeks' time.)

The difficult issue of Britain going to war against the Axis allies was brought up, and Maiskii insisted on a formal statement. 'Oh well,' replied Churchill, 'if Stalin wants this we will declare war on Finland, Romania, and Hungary'.[14] This, at least, was easy to deliver, despite considerable British sympathy for the Finns. At midnight, the United Kingdom declared war on Germany's small Axis allies.

* * *

Meanwhile, in Washington, Secretary of State Hull had both the Russians and the Japanese to worry about. In the early evening of 5 December he penned a brief reply to Eden's letter of the previous day, in which the British Foreign Secretary had set out the purposes of his upcoming trip to Moscow. Ambassador Winant in London was instructed to read Hull's reply to Eden personally, and to leave no written text. As Hull put it, he was 'very frankly' setting out the American position 'in order that in view of the short time before Mr. Eden's departure he may have no misunderstanding as to the general lines of our [Washington's] position'.

Hull's letter was a classic statement of the idealism of President Woodrow Wilson, and it stood in marked contrast to more pragmatic British notions of diplomacy. It was not all that different from the more famous note Hull issued to the Japanese on 26 November. The implication was that Eden's trip was both premature and unnecessary. For Hull the 'test of our good faith' to the USSR was for America and the British Empire to send war supplies, and this was already being done. (Eden had argued that the Russians required, as a test of confidence, a readiness at least to discuss post-war problems.)

For Hull, a statement of basic principles, the 'Atlantic Charter' (announced by Roosevelt and Churchill at Argentia in August 1941), was sufficient. The charter had laid out eight points. First, the signatories did not intend any territorial aggrandisement. There should be no border changes without the consent of the peoples concerned. People had a right to choose their own form of government, and those who had been forcibly deprived of sovereign rights should have them restored. All states should have access to raw materials and trade. Economic collaboration was to be brought about. All nations would live at peace within their own boundaries. Freedom of the seas would be assured. Pending creation of a global security system it was essential that nations 'which threaten aggression outside of their frontiers' should be disarmed. It was a programme at odds with the actions of the USSR in 1939–40, in regards to Poland and the Baltic states. (There were also evident tensions concerning the global situation – political and economic – of Britain and its dependent colonies.)

There should, Hull argued, be no discussion of the post-war settlement beyond these eight points. '[I]n our considered opinion,' Hull complained, 'it would be unfortunate were any of the three governments . . . to express any willingness to enter into commitments regarding specific terms of the post-war settlement.' Above all, there should be no secret accords. 'Given the limitations of this Government, it would be difficult if not impossible for us to implement this common understanding by agreements of a more detailed nature at this time. Furthermore the constitutional limitation to which this Government is bound must be kept in mind.'[15] (What Hull was stressing here, of course, was that under the American Constitution any agreements would have to be approved by the US Senate.)

Fortunately for Secretary Hull's peace of mind, he had no inkling of what Churchill had proposed to Ambassador Maiskii that same day.

* * *

From the perspective of later relations between the Allies, and the origins of the Cold War, Secretary Hull's thoughts about Russia were not so unimportant. But, inevitably, he was more concerned with the immediate confrontation with Japan.

Earlier in the day Ambassador Nomura and Special Envoy Kurusu had made their penultimate call on the State Department and Secretary Hull. This time they brought Tokyo's reply to President Roosevelt's written question of 2 December regarding the Japanese troop build-up in Indochina. The explanation, the note from Tokyo stated, was that these forces had had to be strengthened to guard against an attack from China. Reports of troop movements had, in addition, been exaggerated. Hull subjected this explanation to withering criticism; indeed, the two Japanese diplomats cannot themselves have taken the explanation seriously. Hull asked how the Japanese could request the US to stop aiding China, when Japan was aiding Hitler's Germany by keeping American forces tied down in the Pacific (an argument the Japanese, with some reason, found hard to understand). At one point Ambassdor Nomura was heard to mutter to himself (in Japanese), 'This isn't getting us anywhere.'

As the discussion came to an end, Kurusu again argued for some kind of *modus vivendi*. Hull replied that American public opinion made it unthinkable that there could be any loosening of the oil embargo. As Secretary Hull knew from the MAGIC decrypts, the two Japanese were only going through the motions of negotiation. Nomura and Kurusu then withdrew, according to the State Department minute, 'after making the usual apologies for taking so much of the Secretary's time when he was busy'.[16] They would not return until the afternoon of Sunday, 7 December.

Washington also reconsidered the military picture on 5 December. US Army Intelligence (G-2) presented General Marshall, the Army Chief of Staff, with a singularly wrong-headed 'Brief Periodic Assessment of the Situation', outlining the global strategic position over the next four months (from 1 December 1941 to 31 March 1942). The document is valuable for understanding the perceptions at the very pinnacle of the US Army, and the preliminary actions that the military took – or failed to take. Written by General Sherman Miles, the Army's Assistant Chief of Staff (for intelligence), the Assessment followed the official line of emphasising the danger from Germany and minimising that from Japan: 'Germany . . . will remain the only power capable of launching large strategic offensives.' There was less of a general threat in the Far East than in Europe: 'Japan, already extended militarily, has a multiplicity of strategic objectives; but for a variety of reasons, she cannot concentrate the required forces to attack any of them on a large scale and with assurance of success.' The Assessment listed a number of possible Japanese objectives, including an attack on the Philippines or an attempt to isolate them prior to attacking Singapore or the Dutch East Indies. Hong Kong and Malaya, however, had recently been reinforced: 'Both of these localities present a very strong defence against any possible Japanese attack.' The most likely Japanese course of action, the Assessment concluded, was an occupation of Thailand.[17]

* * *

It had been a hectic working week in Washington. On Friday afternoon, at 2.00 p.m., President Roosevelt's Cabinet assembled for its regular meeting in the White House. One of those present was Frances Perkins, Secretary of Labor and the first woman ever to hold Cabinet rank in the American government; she later dictated her recollections. Secretary of State Hull had opened the proceedings by expressing his 'gloom and disgust' at the insincere behaviour of the Japanese negotiators with whom he had, of course, met earlier in the day. 'He was so gloomy,' Perkins recalled, 'that the gloom fairly stood out all over him.'

The discussion at the Cabinet meeting was premised on a possible Japanese attack on the British, and in particular on Singapore. Frank Knox, the rather excitable Secretary of the Navy, declared that he was about to reveal secret information that must not leave the room, and then confided that the Japanese fleet was at sea, and that it was probably moving south towards Singapore.[18] The President then put forward a hypothetical question: 'If they proceed towards Singapore, what's the problem for the United States? What should the United States do?' He then went around the room, asking the members of the Cabinet, in turn, for their opinion. According to Perkins almost all of those present felt they should go to the aid of the British, even if that meant war with Japan. Roosevelt had described the consultation as non-binding, she recalled. (This was just as well; two days earlier he had – not hypothetically – made a verbal commitment to Britain.)

'I think we all felt shattered by this discussion,' Perkins recalled, 'because the problem seemed so near. You were aware as you went out of the room that the President and Frank Knox had got to decide something very soon. We were going out, getting our cars, and going off for the weekend, but the President, Frank Knox, and a few others had got to make some decision in a very short time.'[19]

CHAPTER 9

# SATURDAY, 6 DECEMBER
# General Zhukov Throws in his Armies

*1 BS 5 CR 7 DR 25 MV, bearing 090°, approx. course 270°, position 08°N 106°08′E*

RAAF sighting report

*The Russians have never given anything away voluntarily; we also must not do that either.*

Adolf Hitler

*This means war.*

Franklin D. Roosevelt

## The Philippines

The secret British-American talks in Manila about the practicalities of joint operations began at 9.30 a.m. on Saturday. Superficially, the three main participants got on well. Tom Phillips, the visitor, was (aged fifty-three) a decade younger than the others, but he was used to the corridors of power and had diplomatic experience. Admiral Thomas Hart was C-in-C of the US Asiatic Fleet (CINCAF), and described by the historian Samuel Eliot Morison as 'small, taught, wiry, and irascible' with the reputation of a strict disciplinarian. Hart was, at sixty-four, beyond the usual age of retirement from active service. The astute British General Pownall, who met Hart two months later on Java, when the Admiral was commanding the Allied rear-guard naval force, came away with a negative impression: 'Poor old Hart is quite unfitted for his job, he has no kick in him at all.'[1] To be fair to Hart, however, he had by then suffered the physical and psychological strain of repeated defeat.

Douglas MacArthur is, of course, the best known of the three. The C-in-C of US Army Forces in the Far East (USAFFE) – meaning, essentially, in the Philippines – he was already sixty-one years old. He had been a national hero of the First World War, a Brigadier General at thirty-nine, and had even served as Chief of Staff of the US Army from 1930–35, directly under Presidents Hoover and Roosevelt. MacArthur's roots in the islands ran deep. His father, General Arthur MacArthur, had fought here against Spain in 1898 and was Military Governor after the US took control. Douglas had served as his father's aide during the campaign, and had seen duty again in the Philippines in the 1920s.

MacArthur believed himself to be a man of destiny and – to the annoyance of his many enemies – this turned out to be true. The General would survive the collapse of the Philippines in 1942, a debacle for which he deserved no small share of the blame. He ended up leading the main Army command in the Pacific. His genuine successes in the southwest Pacific and the Philippines (in 1944) would eventually take him to the deck of the USS *Missouri* in Tokyo Bay in September 1945, where he personally accepted the surrender of Imperial Japan. MacArthur then, even more extraordinarily, presided for four years over the successful reconstruction of the defeated enemy country.

In December 1941 MacArthur's greatness lay in the future. Beneath a surface politeness, Hart had little time for his Army counterpart, either professionally or personally. He was the older man and, as a full Admiral, outranked MacArthur, who was only a Lieutenant General – although he had been 'field marshal' of the Liliputian Philippine Army. After a preliminary dinner on Friday evening Hart had grumbled that MacArthur 'talked interminably'. Things were no better at the morning session on the 6th, where Hart gave the General a chance to present his views to Phillips: 'Of course I had in MacArthur and arranged so that he would pretty much have the floor at first, get off his wordy spiel . . . clear out and let me get down to business.'[2]

Given his head, MacArthur launched into a bullish account of the defences being prepared. The air danger to the Philippines was limited, the Amercan and Filipino ground forces could cope with an invasion, and any Japanese operations in Southeast Asia would be mounted in only one direction at a time. All the same, he believed that the expansion of his forces, especially aviation, over the next four months would be critical. From this and other evidence it seems clear that MacArthur did not believe that his command was going to be thrown into war in the next few weeks, let alone the next few hours.[3]

Admiral Phillips outlined a similar potential strengthening of the British forces. He admitted that the current British Eastern Fleet was still weak, but he hoped to receive two more battleships in the course of December, then two more in January, and another after that, bringing the total of his capital ships to seven. If war broke out, Singapore would be too far south to allow offensive action by the Royal Navy. Hong Kong, the nearest British base to Japan, was exposed to air attack and the harbour was not suitable for operational naval use. Manila was the best forward base, provided it could be protected from air attack. All this came as surprising news to MacArthur, but he sent a very positive report back to General Marshall, the Army Chief of Staff, in Washington: 'Phillips stated that in British naval opinion, in order to wage offensive war it was necessary as soon as possible to establish an advance naval operating base in the Philippines'. The General also thought the meeting had gone very well at a personal level: 'Complete coordination and cooperation most satisfactorily accomplished in an atmosphere of entire cordiality.'[4]

After MacArthur departed, the two admirals got down to more detailed discussions; these were, after all, meant to be primarily naval talks. 'We were quite frank with each other,' Hart recalled, 'laid our cards down, and wore no gloves.' The meeting evidently went on without a break until 8.30 p.m. that evening, although very startling messages came through in the afternoon about Japanese shipping movements off the coast of Indochina. Overall, Hart's impression of his opposite number in Singapore was very favourable: 'Well I acquired considerable respect for Phillips – looks like as good an Englishman to work with as I have had for some time.' As for Tom Phillips, his brief report to Their Lordships after his return to Singapore was favourable: 'Discussion with Admiral Hart very friendly and we can expect full cooperation.'[5]

The results of the naval deliberations were laid out in a joint message sent by Hart and Phillips to their respective naval headquarters in Washington and London. While not so rashly confident as MacArthur, they both anticipated war, but not military disaster. In the early stages of the conflict the initiative would inevitably rest with the Japanese, and specific planning – beyond the disposition of forces to meet 'the probable Japanese action' – could not yet be carried out. Joint plans for use of submarines and naval aircraft, however, were reported as 'definite and ready'. Surface ships were divided into four groups, the most important of which would be a multinational fleet based in Singapore including three British battleships, six to eight British, Australian and Dutch cruisers, and twenty destroyers. Hart's own two big ships (cruisers *Houston* and *Marblehead*) would operate in the Philippines and the Dutch East Indies, along with some British ships.

One revealing part of the discussion concerned general strategy. Phillips and Hart reported home that they considered it important that action in the Far East should be co-ordinated with the operations of Kimmel's US Pacific Fleet: 'We hope we may be informed of the timetable visualised for the movement of this fleet to Truk in accordance with plan "Rainbow Five". The release of cruisers from Australia and New Zealand is intimately connected with the movements of this fleet.'

The admirals also looked into an easier future, 'as our forces in the Far East grow', when they could undertake more offensive operations. They returned to what Phillips had told MacArthur in the morning: 'We consider that we should aim at having Manila available as a base by the first of April 1942, if this can be done.'[6] This would turn out to be an April Fool's joke, and a cruel one. (Manila was abandoned by MacArthur on 26 December and occupied by the Japanese on 2 January. On 1 April 1942 the only places in the Philippines under American control were the besieged peninsula of Bataan and the small fortress island of Corregidor, both west of Manila; Bataan surrendered on 9 April and Corregidor on 6 May.) The Manila talks were to prove one of the last moments of British-American optimism in the Far East for many months to come.

* * *

The threat of war was not unexpected, at least for Admiral Hart. From the end of November, Washington had issued alarms of growing intensity. On 25 November a top-secret and pessimistic assessment of future relations with Japan had arrived from Admiral Stark in Washington. The Chief of Naval Operations judged the chances of a favourable outcome to the Washington negotiations to be very doubtful. Statements made by Tokyo, and the movements of Japanese naval and military forces, indicated that 'a surprise aggressive movement in any direction including attack on Philippines or Guam is a possibility.'[7]

Three days later General Marshall sent warnings to MacArthur (and General Short in Hawaii). Negotiations with Japan now appeared to have terminated: 'Japanese future action unpredictable but hostile action possible at any moment.' Marshall advised MacArthur that it was better for Japan to 'commit the first overt act', but told him he should not limit himself in a way 'that might jeopardize the successful defense of the Philippines'. Active preparations were encouraged: 'You are instructed to take such reconnaissance and other measures as you deem necessary. Report measures taken.' MacArthur replied the following day that air reconnaissance had been extended, in conjunction with the Navy, and that efforts had been made to strengthen ground security. 'Within the limitations imposed by present state of development of this theater of operations,' reported the general, 'everything is in readiness for the conduct of a successful defense.'[8] In the circumstances, this was the most naïve over-confidence on the part of Douglas MacArthur.

Admiral Hart was more realistic. After he received the message sent by CNO Stark on 25 November – 'straight from the horse's mouth', as Hart put it – he made the following note in his diary: 'I'm told that the barometer is so very low that the storm pretty much must break, somewhere. It's really a war warning and one which I must heed.'[9]

Admiral Stark's fuller 'war warning' was sent from Washington on 27 November: 'The number and equipment of Japanese troops and the organization of the naval task forces indicates [sic] an amphibious expedition against either the Philippines Thai or Kra Peninsula [sic] or possibly Borneo. Execute an appropriate defensive deployment preparatory to carrying out the task in WPL 46.' Admiral Hart in Manila took this warning badly. 'The air,' he complained, 'is full of words from Washington acting on and deciding things that could and should have been all buttoned up months ago. It quite likely now is much too late for much of it.'[10] The old Admiral was absolutely right.

CINCAF had access to his own US Navy intercept and codebreaking organisation, Station CAST. Hart's diary entry on the evening of 28 November had included the comment: 'Well – It looks like rain!' This was without doubt a reference to the 'winds' set-up message which Hart would have seen on this day. 'East wind rain', in the recently-arranged Japanese code system, indicated the contingency that Japanese-American relations were in danger.[11]

While Hart thought that a Japanese amphibious strike could be made in any direction, he seems to have assumed there would be only one major offensive at the start of the war, and that it would not come directly at him. On 3 December he wrote: 'I'm guessing that – having to do something that is pushful they [the Japanese] will push at what is softest, and looks softest. That will be the Siamese [Thais]. Then see what we will do about it. Well that push wont [sic] help them out of their dilemma, and Mr. Jap is in one all right.' The following day he wrote that things had gone well beyond bluff: 'the possibility of a reversal, by the Japs or by us seems infinitesimal.'[12]

In truth, US planning for the defence of the Philippines represented a low point, both of strategic thought and of Army-Navy co-ordination.[13] The Americans had been uncomfortable about their big Pacific colony since seizing it from Spain in 1898. For most of the inter-war years the armed forces had assumed the islands were indefensible. The Washington Treaty of 1922 prohibited fortification, and in any event Congress would not provide the funds. The Tydings-McDuffie Act of 1934 accelerated the movement towards Philippine independence, setting out a ten-year preparatory period under a self-governing 'commonwealth'. The following year the task of organising the Philippines' armed forces was assigned to MacArthur, on secondment from the US Army but with a very generous salary paid by the Philippine government.

Almost no one in Washington thought through the implications, for this exposed US outpost, of the 'Germany first' strategy of RAINBOW FIVE,[14] or the economic boycott of Japan. On 26 July 1941, immediately after the Japanese occupation of southern Indochina and the declaration of the American-led economic embargo, MacArthur was recalled into American service as C-in-C of USAFFE. He had sufficient political power to obtain some ground and air reinforcements, as well as equipment for local forces. His project for ten divisions of Filipino militia was quite impractical, however, in view of the level of training facilities and the amount of equipment. Admiral Hart tartly remarked in September on the 'lack of AS-IS realism of the Army's planning'.[15]

Even more lacking in 'as-is' realism – indeed, stunningly unrealistic – was a proposal developed that autumn by US Army air power visionaries, and endorsed by Secretary of War Stimson and General Marshall. This was the project to defend the Philippines and even to exert control over much of the western Pacific using the heavy bombers of the US Army Air Force. The four-engined B-17 'Flying Fortress' was supposed to be able to destroy any invading force far out to sea, picking off its ships from high altitude. In the near future the even longer-range B-24 'Liberator' would, it was hoped, be able to bomb Japan from bases on Luzon in the Philippines (shuttling back and forth using bases in the Russian Far East around Vladivostok).

The tactical concepts had never been tested, and it would transpire that heavy bombers were nearly useless against moving surface ships at sea. Strategic bombing of Japan was (with the technology of 1941) also tactically impractical, and politically hopeless in view of its dependence on Russia. Very little thought was given to the creation of an adequate base structure even in the Philippines, with protected air fields and supply bases. As the basis of national strategy it was completely unsatisfactory. To be fair to him, President Roosevelt was never closely identified with this project, and – as might be expected – the US Navy also took a dim view of it.

In any event, in August 1941 the Philippines command was promised four entire heavy-bomber groups amounting to 272 aircraft – at that time the largest heavy-bomber force in the world. A squadron of B-17s flew out across the Pacific in September, and by December much of the first group had arrived.[16] It was destined to be wiped out on the ground in the first days of the Pacific War.

The unworkable bomber strategy was not MacArthur's, but it did not lessen his confidence that the US Army could defend the Philippines on its own. There was certainly very little attempt to co-ordinate plans with the Navy. MacArthur and Hart very seldom met, although they lived in the same hotel in Manila.

## Malaya and London

As Admiral Phillips sat conferring with his American counterpart in Manila, the alarm bells began ringing in Singapore. Saturday, 6 December, was when intelligence about Japanese intentions was confirmed by the reality of the threat: at midday the invasion convoy from Hainan had suddenly come within range of scout planes from Malaya.

No. 1 Squadron, Royal Australian Air Force (RAAF), was carrying out searches over the sea from its base at Kota Bharu in northern Malaya, using its American-built 'Hudson' light bombers. The first sighting of three Japanese ships was made just after noon by the crew of Flight Lieutenant J.C. Ramshaw. At 12.46 p.m. Ramshaw sighted a much larger group of ships, which was eventually (at 2.00 p.m.) logged at General Headquarters (GHQ) in Singapore: '1 BS 5 CR 7 DR 25 MV, bearing 090°, approx. course 270°, position 08°N 106°08′E'. The report was not entirely accurate. There was no battleship (BS) and Ramshaw probably mistook destroyers (DR) for cruisers (CR). But there were indeed about twenty-five merchant vessels, and the position was correct, about ninety miles southeast of Cape Cambodia, the southern tip of Indochina. The sighting was confirmed by a second Hudson. Ramshaw's first sighting was 380 miles east of the Kra Isthmus, and if the ships maintained their course and speed they could arrive there late on the following afternoon (7 December). The northeast monsoon was blowing, there was low cloud cover, and at least three groups of Japanese ships were at sea, so the sightings (by Ramshaw and other pilots) were confused. By mid-afternoon, however, the scout planes had revealed that the largest convoy consisted of twenty-one merchant ships steaming in two columns.[17]

One of the Hudsons was pursued by a Japanese float plane, catapulted from an escorting seaplane tender. The GHQ, Far East, war diary later recorded that this was the first Japanese hostile action. At 3.00 p.m. Admiral Ozawa, commander of the 'Malaya Force' – the main escort of the convoy – had issued orders permitting his ships and aircraft to engage shadowing aircraft, although in the event no actual air fighting took place on Saturday. In the afternoon the weather deteriorated, and the British patrol planes lost contact with the convoy. Based on the direction in which some of the Japanese ships were sailing, Brooke-Popham's GHQ in Singapore made the fatally incorrect assumption that the convoy was making not for the Kra Isthmus but for the capacious anchorage at Koh Kong in Cambodia. Only after stopping in there, the British believed, would it head for its ultimate destination, which might well be Bangkok.

At 3.15 p.m. Air Marshal Brooke-Popham's staff at GHQ raised the command to the first degree of readiness, which meant it was to be 'ready for immediate operations and prepared for enemy attack without prior warning'. There was not much else that could be done at that moment. The main anti-shipping force, a handful of obsolete biplane 'Vildebeest' (sic) torpedo planes, were ordered to deploy north from their base at Singapore to Kota Bharu, some Blenheim light bombers were put on standby, and photographic reconnaissance aircraft were readied, but nothing could happen until the following day. Singapore informed Admiral Phillips in Manila, who ordered that the visit of *Repulse* to Darwin be cancelled; the battlecruiser was immediately recalled to Singapore to join *Prince of Wales*.

The other possible action was to set in motion Operation MATADOR, the pre-emptive strike to occupy the ports of the Kra Isthmus in southern Thailand. In the crucial signal FE 50 of the previous day, London had given Brooke-Popham permission to do this at his discretion. Indeed, the ground-force commander in Malaya, General Percival, had flown up to central Malaya on the morning of the 6th to consult with General Lewis Heath in Kuala Lumpur. Heath's III Corps would have to carry out MATADOR; his 11th Division (two brigades) was located some 250 miles to north, near the Thai border. At 3.10 p.m. General Percival verbally ordered Heath to put his corps on standby for the commencement of MATADOR.[18]

* * *

In Whitehall it had seemed likely to be a quiet Saturday. Churchill had driven down to Chequers on Friday afternoon, and General Ismay and Air Marshal Portal joined him there. Eden was at his Binderton country house, preparing for Sunday's departure to Russia. Singapore was six hours and thirty minutes ahead of London, so news of the midday convoy sighting south of Indochina ought to have reached the British capital early on Saturday morning. There would, in fact, be a considerable delay.

Eden's Permanent Secretary, Alec Cadogan, was due to depart with him for Russia on the following afternoon, but he was drawn into events, as he recalled in his diary: 'Found report of reconnaissance of Japanese armada moving west, south of Cambodia point. Rang up A [Eden]. Broke into meeting of COS [Chiefs of Staff Committee] who didn't seem to know quite where they were. Informed Winant.' Cadogan contacted Winant, the American Ambassador, and then met representatives of the Dutch government in exile to explain Friday's plans to give a warning to the Japanese. 'But all may now be melting-pot,' he grumbled to himself, 'if the monkeys are going for the Kra Isthmus.'[19]

General Brooke (Chief of the Imperial General Staff) later recalled that he had a quiet morning that Saturday, and caught up with office work. It was not until mid-afternoon that news of the convoys reached him, and it was only then that Admiral Pound had summoned the meeting of the COS. 'We examined the situation carefully,' recalled Brooke, 'but from position of the transports it was not possible to tell whether they were going to Bangkok, to the Kra Isthmus, or whether they were just cruising around as a bluff'. More information came through during the meeting. '[I]t did not clear up situation in the least, and it said only that convoy had been lost and could not be picked up again.' Cadogan attended this meeting, and made his own interpretation: 'Later hear that they [Japanese convoy] had gone into west coast of Indo-China. This gives us more time.'[20]

The COS sent cautious advice to Churchill at Chequers: 'From the military point of view, it would pay to attack these convoys at sea, but our present political instructions prevent us from doing so. Unless we are absolutely assured that an attack delivered in these circumstances would have the armed support of the United States, we ought not to make the first move.' Since the minute was telephoned to Chequers at 6.15 p.m. there could be no thought of immediate action; it was already 1.45 a.m. in the South China Sea. Churchill later minuted this: 'If it is not physically possible, the political issue does not arise.'[21]

Nearly ten hours passed between the time that GHQ, Far East, put its forces on high alert after the convoy sighting (8.45 a.m. in London), and the time that the Chiefs of Staff in London made any response (6.15 p.m.). Aside from the long delay, it is not clear whether the COS factored into its analysis of the situation the latest diplomatic decrypts about Japan's intentions. By 10.00 a.m. that morning the British codebreakers at Bletchley Park had decrypted and made available their version of the telltale Japanese circular of 2 December, which ordered various diplomatic posts to burn most of their codes and to send confirmation back to Tokyo. Chargé d'Affaires Kamimura in London was also instructed to destroy all correspondence and secret papers '[t]aking all possible care not to arouse outside suspicion'. The 'stop' code set-up circular of

27 November, creating an emergency communications system for Japanese embassies and consulates abroad, was also decrypted on this day.[22] In the end, however, no order went out from London to prepare air attacks or to launch Operation MATADOR; decisions were left with the local commanders.

For practical reasons, attacks by British warships or aircraft on the Japanese convoy were never a serious possibility on Saturday. And only preliminary steps were made for attacks on Sunday. Admiral Phillips was absent from Singapore, and neither Brooke-Popham nor Air Marshal Pulford (the RAF commander in Malaya, subordinate to Brooke-Popham) pressed for action. This was also not a contingency authorised under FE 50, as Brooke-Popham was later to explain: 'Until the Japanese had committed some definite act of hostility against the United States, the Dutch or ourselves, permission had not been given to attack a Japanese expedition at sea.'[23] More surprising was the failure to activate Operation MATADOR.

The man on the spot who had to make the decision to launch MATADOR was Air Chief Marshal Sir Robert Brooke-Popham. Brooke-Popham had been appointed to the new post of C-in-C, Far East, in October 1940, in an attempt to smooth out the difficult relations between the Army, the RAF and the Royal Navy in that area. Brooke-Popham was something of a combination of Biggles and Colonel Blimp, 'a big, untidy man, going bald, with [reddish] moustache that might have shrunk from one he had proudly borne as an officer in the cavalry in his youth.' 'Brookham' was a pioneer aviator but had now reached the age of sixty-three, and was at the end of a distinguished career which had included very senior posts in the RAF and the governorship of Kenya. His energy was limited – 'quite out of the business from dinnertime onwards,' as one colleague later put it – and he was now out of date with military affairs.

By the summer of 1941 it was clear that the C-in-C, Far East, needed to be replaced with someone more technically competent, but the decision was not made in London until 1 November. Brooke-Popham was informed of his impending departure, and the news circulated in Singapore. There were problems selecting a replacement – resulting from the demands of other theatres of war – and it was not until the end of November that the decision was made to appoint General Henry Pownall in Brooke-Popham's place. Pownall was still en route to Singapore from London on 6 December, while the lame duck Brooke-Popham remained at GHQ Far East, with his authority limited. The Conservative MP Alfred Duff Cooper, who had been sent out by Churchill earlier in the autumn to assess the Far Eastern situation, wrote a damning appraisal of Brooke-Popham just after the war began: 'He is a very much older man than his years warrant, and sometimes seems on the verge of nervous collapse. I fear also that the knowledge of his own failing powers renders him jealous of any encroachment on his own sphere of influence'.[24]

The other officer involved in the MATADOR decision – or non-decision – was the ground forces commander (GOC, Malaya), General Arthur Percival. His superior, Air Marshal Brooke-Popham, had the bitter good fortune to be removed from his post in Singapore at the end of December, thus avoiding the worst. The unfortunate Percival would have to bear responsibility for Britain's greatest ever military defeat and three years of Japanese captivity. A protégé of the former Chief of the Imperial General Staff, Sir John Dill, Percival had pre-war experience in Malaya, before returning there as 'General Officer Commanding' in April 1941. He had a thin sharp face, an unfortunate moustache set above prominent front teeth, and large ears; when wearing his pith helmet and tropical shorts he did not achieve a commanding presence. He was a thorough staff officer, not an inspiring leader, nor one with much initiative – though the worst descriptions of him date from the terrible days before the fall of Singapore in January and February 1942. It was not his decisions or advice on 6 December that were fatal for Singapore. Percival later wrote that he had initially expected implementation of MATADOR on Saturday when GHQ received news of the convoy sighted off Indochina. He was then advised (according to his own account) that other sightings suggested the convoy was headed north into the Gulf of Siam in the direction of Bangkok.[25]

Brooke-Popham and Percival actually had thirty-six hours – the time allowed in British contingency plans – to implement MATADOR. The Japanese landing would not begin until the small hours of 8 December. It is, however, hard to believe that British forces could have been in a strong position on the beaches of the Kra Isthmus when the formidable General Yamashita arrived. An energetic commander might have achieved a daring victory, but Brooke-Popham and Percival were not the men to take such a chance.[26]

## Tokyo

The Japanese military remained confident that they would achieve success with the main 'Southern Operation' and other planned attacks. Still, Admiral Yamamoto and Admiral Kondō must have been mightily relieved that the main convoy was not spotted on Friday. Indeed, the only sighting was more than halfway through the daylight hours on Saturday. The Japanese were lucky with the stormy weather. Even so, the convoy's route was planned precisely to be ambiguous, with Bangkok and northern Thailand as possible destinations. The Japanese planners certainly succeeded in confusing the defenders, and delaying their reaction.

Less smoothly executed were Japanese diplomatic preparations, which reached their final stages on 6 December. In the evening the Foreign Ministry in Tokyo transmitted an encrypted warning telegram (later known as the 'pilot message') to the Washington embassy, informing Ambassador Nomura and Special Envoy Kurusu that a detailed 'memorandum' for the United States had been prepared, responding to Secretary Hull's Note of 26 November. This message was going to be 'very long' and would be sent as fourteen transmission instalments. The time for presentation of the memorandum would be given in a separate message. Meanwhile, embassy staff in Washington were to prepare a text in a 'nicely drafted form'.[27]

Transmission of the first thirteen instalments of the memorandum itself began that same evening, about an hour later. The *Gaimushō* had produced the text in English, and the memorandum had then been encrypted using the Type 'B' (PURPLE) Cipher Machine.

The memorandum was a robust defence of Japanese policy, and a critique of that of the United States, especially of Secretary Hull's Note. Half the document consisted of a long preamble, which was to be followed by seven numbered points, of which six were included in the transmission instalments sent that evening. In the preamble the Japanese declared that they had negotiated in good faith and wanted to bring peace to Asia and to end the war in China. The United States and Britain, however, had blocked this. American policy was described – not altogether inaccurately – as 'always holding fast to theories in disregard of realities, and refusing to yield an inch of its impractical principles'.

The thrust of Tokyo's first six (of seven) points was straightforward. American diplomacy had made demands that were unacceptable, including Japanese abandonment of the Tripartite Pact. The United States condemned Japanese military steps, while using economic pressures which could be even more inhumane. Meanwhile it attempted to buttress the unacceptable status quo of European imperialism. The Americans demanded that Japan deal only with the Chungking government, ignoring Japan's four-year sacrifice in China. (The Chungking government was that of Chiang Kai-shek; the Japanese had set up a puppet government in the old capital of Nanking in 1940, under Wang Ching-wei. They claimed that this had now become the real government of China.) Finally, the US had colluded with Britain, Australia, the Netherlands and China against Japan.[28]

This was the communication that had been discussed in Tokyo at the 75th Liaison Conference on 4 December. It was not a declaration of war and, despite what had been said by Foreign Minister Tōgō at the Liaison Conference, it was not accompanied by such a declaration. No comparable note was sent to the British government.

On the previous day the Germans and Italians had given their approval for a new Tripartite agreement, under which they would support Japan even if it attacked the United States. The German Ambassador to Japan, Eugen Ott, had now fallen behind developments. Just after noon on the 6th a telegram from him arrived in Berlin. Ott included an outline of the proposed Japanese reply to Hull, but also said that he had given the Japanese advice to avoid a direct attack on the United States, so that Washington should bear responsibility for the outbreak of war. Late that evening Ribbentrop shot back a reprimand: 'it would seem inappropriate to me in the present situation to suggest to the Japanese government this or that course of action in the event that a show-down should come with the United States.' If the matter was discussed again the Ambassador should take the view that 'the Axis Powers and Japan find themselves faced with a struggle upon which hangs their fate, which they must fight through together, regardless of the form of the tactical moves taken by one or other partner in the individual case.'[29]

## Washington

The fateful weekend had begun in Washington as well. At 10.40 a.m. the State Department received a telegram from Britain. Ambassador Winant, having been briefed by Alec Cadogan, sent (at 4.00 p.m. London time) vital information: 'British Admiralty reports that at 3 a.m. London time this morning two parties seen off Cambodia Point, sailing slowly westward toward Kra 14 hours distant in time. First party 25 transports, 6 cruisers, 10 destroyers. Second party 10 transports, 2 cruisers, 10 destroyers.' In a later telegram (sent at 7.00 p.m. London time) Winant relayed another report from Cadogan: at a further British meeting it had been concluded that the convoy could be heading for either the Kra Isthmus or Bangkok, and in the latter case arrival would not be before Monday.[30]

Much the same information arrived in Washington for the Chief of Naval Operations. Admiral Hart sent a telegram from Manila in the late evening (8.55 p.m.) of 6 December (corresponding to 7.55 a.m. in Washington). In the telegram he relayed the report about the convoys, which had been sent to him by Admiral Layton, the acting British naval commander in Singapore. Two additional pieces of information were included. One came from the British, who attached importance to the movements of the most westerly Japanese group: 'This indicates all forces will make for Kontron.' The second was the following sentence: 'Sighted by my scouting force anchored Camranh Bay – 30 ships and one large cruiser.' Hart copied the message to Admirals Kimmel and Bloch in Hawaii. Stark discussed the sighting of the Japanese ships with Secretary of the Navy Knox at 11.25 a.m. on the morning of 6 December, and the Navy forwarded this information to the State Department.[31] It is most unlikely that this information was not also passed to the White House.

The Japanese Embassy in Washington began to receive the warning telegram (the 'pilot message') and the bulk of the fourteen-instalment memorandum before lunchtime on Saturday. There was still no indication that the presentation of the message to the Americans was imminent.

President Roosevelt's diplomacy, as outlined to Lord Halifax on the previous Monday (1 December), plodded forward. The Japanese had on Tuesday been questioned about the build-up of their forces in southern Indochina; on Friday they had responded with an explanation. President Roosevelt then wrote a personal letter to the Japanese Emperor, which was despatched at 9.00 p.m. on Saturday evening, 6 December. The contents demonstrated the President's indecision and his preoccupation with Indochina. In the past few weeks, Roosevelt wrote, the Japanese had deployed such forces in southern Indochina as to create a 'reasonable doubt' that this was not defensive. '[T]he people of the Philippines, of the hundreds of Islands of the East Indies, of Malaya and of Thailand itself are asking themselves whether these forces of Japan are preparing or intending to attack. . . . None of the peoples . . . can sit either indefinitely or permanently on a keg of dynamite.'[32] As the President had known for some hours that a large convoy was heading for Thailand (or Malaya) his message was not wholly innocent.

By the evening of 6 December the American codebreakers had decrypted and translated all thirteen instalments of the memorandum which Tokyo had sent to its Washington embassy. At 11.30 p.m. a junior naval officer brought the decrypt to the President, who was with Harry Hopkins in his study in the White House. The officer was Lieutenant Lester R. Schulz; he was acting as Communications Assistant to the President's naval aide. In testimony after the war Schulz admitted he could not remember full details of the conversation in the President's study. All the same, his version of FDR's words after reading the Japanese message has gone down in history: 'This means war,' the President declared. He and his closest adviser then discussed the situation in Schulz's presence for five minutes. Hopkins agreed with the President's pessimistic prediction, and they talked about (in Schulz's words) 'the situation of the Japanese forces, that is their deployment'. As the young lieutenant recalled it, Hopkins said that the Japanese were going to strike first when their forces were properly deployed to their advantage, and specifically referred to Indochina.[33]

## Russia

Nearly twenty-four hours before Roosevelt and Hopkins's late-night conversation, dawn had broken over Moscow. General Zhukov's offensive finally began in earnest. On 6 December the sky above the city was mostly clear, but the frost was extreme. The temperature now plummeted to an extraordinary −38°C (−36°F). Zhukov's overall plan, sent to Stalin on 30 November, involved attacks on both extended wings of German Army Group Centre. On this day, however, the attacks were concentrated in the area north of Moscow, around the Klin-Istra bulge. The Soviet General Staff's secret situation report, written that night, would record the events:

> In the course of 6 December in the area of the Western Army Group our forces, repelling the enemy's counter-attacks, continued to carry out determined offensive battles in the Dmitrov, Solnechnogorsk, Istra, Zvenigorod directions and drove off the attacks of enemy tank and motorised formations in the regions north and north east of Tula.
>
> The forces of the left wing of the Kalinin Army Group, repelling repeated enemy counter-attacks, continued to carry out offensive battles on the right bank of the Volga to the southwest and southeast of Kalinin.

The most significant Soviet advance of the day was at the northern end of Zhukov's front. The left flank of Panzer Group 3 ran southeast some forty miles from the Volga Reservoir to the Moskva-Volga Canal at Dmitrov. This line, running through snow-covered woods and fields, with no natural obstacles, was very thinly held by two German motorised divisions. At 6.00 a.m. General Leliushenko's 30th Army, on Zhukov's right flank, began concerted attacks. Spearheaded by Colonel Pavel Rotmistrov's 8th Tank Brigade, the Russians made good progress in the direction of Klin.

To the left of Soviet 30th Army, on the Moskva-Volga Canal, was 1st Shock Army, commanded by General V.I. Kuznetsov. This was one of the 'new' armies committed from the Stavka Reserve, but over the past few days it had been thrown into action piecemeal, before it was fully assembled. Zhukov had needed it to stop Panzer Group 3 consolidating a bridgehead east of the canal, and to regain territory on the western bank. Even so, Kuznetsov's army was able to make some progress on the 6th.

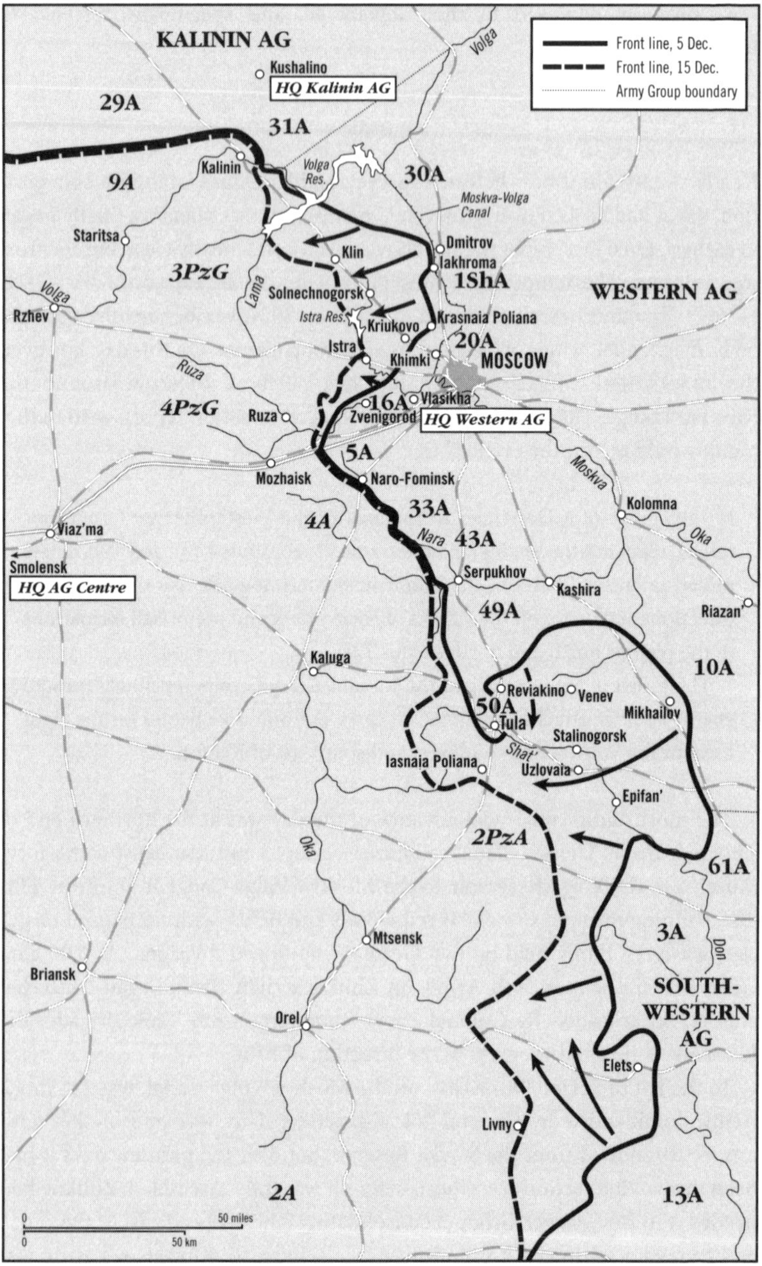


**Map 4.** Battle of Moscow: Soviet Counterattack.

Andrei Vlasov's new 20th Army, to the left of 1st Shock Army, also advanced west against the hard-pressed Panzer Group 3, attacking in the general direction of Krasnaia Poliana and Solnechnogorsk; behind those two places lay Klin.

Elsewhere the situation at the front was quieter. Rokossovskii's 16th Army was recovering from two weeks' hard fighting, and was not yet ready to move west again towards Istra. The central armies of Western Army Group were also relatively static on this day, although 5th Army kept up the pressure in the direction of Zvenigorod. The 33rd and 43rd Armies stood in place, while the forces of 49th and 50th Armies attempted to break the German stranglehold north of Tula at the village of Reviakino. South of Moscow the Stalinogorsk bulge of Guderian's 2nd Panzer Army was beginning to deflate, but the new Soviet 10th Army was still not ready to go into action on its east side. The same was true of the left-flank 13th Army of Marshal Timoshenko's Southwestern Army Group, facing German 2nd Army in the Elets area.

The events of 6 December and the preceding days demonstrated that German Army Group Centre was approaching its physical limits. On the bleak snow-covered battlefields around Moscow the exhausted German troops were hard-pressed, and their commanders felt a deepening sense of doom. But the Army Group command in Smolensk and the high command at MAUERWALD and WOLFSCHANZE in East Prussia had not yet grasped the full extent of the crisis.

The comments in Field Marshal von Bock's war diary, written at the end of the day, detailed the varied circumstances of his army group. Guderian's retrenchment of 2nd Panzer Army was progressing well enough, and Kluge's 4th Army had had a quiet day. Panzer Group 3 was, however, under serious attack from the north, forcing General Reinhardt to throw in his last reserves, and to begin a withdrawal to a more readily defended line. On the far left, German 9th Army, on either side of Kalinin, was not able to throw the Soviets back across the Volga. The high command, Bock concluded, had to be informed that pulling back Panzer Group 3 and the northern flank of 4th Army was unavoidable.[34]

The response of the supreme command in East Prussia on 6 December was complicated by the deteriorating interaction between Hitler and the Army C-in-C. This was Hitler's second working day at WOLFSSCHANZE since his expedition to the Rostov front, and his relations with Field Marshal Brauchitsch were even nearer breaking point. There had been a very bad atmosphere at the 'situation conference'. '[T]rust between F. [Hitler] and OB [*Oberbefehlshaber*, i.e. Brauchitsch] can no longer be patched up,' noted Engel, Hitler's Army adjutant. In private conversation Brauchitsch told Engel again that he would have to resign.[35]

All the same, at MAUERWALD the daily report of the Army General Staff for 6 December did not allude to serious problems, except for the pressure on Panzer Group 3. During the day Hitler discussed the situation with General Halder at WOLFSSCHANZE. There had been discussions over the past few days about shortening the front line by tactical withdrawals, in order to refit exhausted formations, but in the afternoon the Führer decided not to take any immediate action. According to Halder, Hitler was not opposed to straightening out – shortening – the front line, but he wanted to do so only when the fall-back position had been prepared. He did not want to give ground too rapidly: 'The Russians have never given anything away voluntarily; we also mustn't do that either.'[36]

On 6 December Hitler made an even more profound misjudgement when he discussed with Halder a draft directive on manpower. He estimated that total Soviet losses since June had been around 8–10 million men, and he played down the possibility of an enemy recovery in the near future: 'If we have lost 25% of our combat strength the Russians have lost much more of their combat strength – even with a three-fold increase of replacement formations. If [each of] our divisions can hold [a front line of] 30km it is proof of the insufficient strength of the enemy. Numbers prove nothing.'[37]

* * *

This was not the first time that Hitler had revealed his underestimation of the Russians. He did this before the war, and during the campaign; he was, in particular, influenced by the Red Army's autumn defeats. The German dictator had probably expressed this most clearly in his Munich speech of 8 November. Anticipating what he would say to Halder in December, Hitler announced in Munich that the Soviets had lost 8–10 million soldiers in the first four and a half months of the war. '[N]o army in the world,' he declared, 'can recover from this, not even the Russian one.'[38] The stated size of the losses was roughly accurate, but not the prediction about the Red Army's inability to recover. The Führer, however, was by no means alone in his view. It was shared by German Army intelligence, by Brauchitsch and Bock, and by many of the senior front-line commanders. Hitler and the generals disagreed seriously on a number of points of strategy, but they were agreed about this.

The German Army intelligence experts who compiled the handbook 'Kriegswehrmacht der UdSSR' ('Armed Forces of the USSR'), issued on 1 December, had admitted their limited knowledge: 'Reliable data does not exist about how many Red Army replacement formations will be available as of 1 May 1942.' The Russians were reckoned to have at least 16.5 million men of military age, but many of these would be required for the labour force. There were a limited number of trained officers and NCOs, and the enemy would have difficulty supplying replacement armies with equipment. 'What is clear is that *the combat effectiveness of the new formations will be relatively limited*, due to the low cultural level of the mass of the population, and the lack of trained officers, non-commissioned officers, technicians and crews.' Equipment and supplies as well as personnel were judged to be inadequate: 'The new formations which have been encountered are often poorly equipped, and there are numerous prisoner of war statements about difficulties with regards to matériel. This suggests that the Soviet armaments industry *does not have sufficient reserves of raw materials and completed weapons to do more than make up for current losses*.'

The 'Kriegswehrmacht' handbook included a detailed order of battle of the Red Army as of 1 December. According to this, total Red Army strength facing the German Army on the Eastern Front as a whole included 202 rifle divisions, 35 cavalry divisions, and 40 tank brigades. Red Army strength in Zhukov's Western Army Group (*Westfront*) was estimated to consist of 50 rifle divisions (with an 'effective value' [*Kampfwert*] of 23⅔) and 19 armoured brigades ('effective value' of 11). There were also 11 ('effective value' of 5) cavalry divisions.[39]

The strength available to Zhukov and his generals was indeed limited, in terms of personnel and equipment, and in terms of quantity and quality.[40] The three armies that Stalin released from his reserves at the end of November were hardly first-class formations.

Kuznetsov's 1st Shock Army, thrown prematurely against the German northern wing on 1 December, was a 'shock (*udarnyi*) army' in name only. It consisted of one rifle division, eight rifle brigades, and a two tank battalions (with a total of fifty tanks). The artillery of the 'army' consisted of 145 field guns and 35 anti-tank guns, roughly the establishment of a single pre-war rifle division. Much of its 'shock' effect was provided by eleven lightly-equipped ski battalions, and these were not very effective.[41]

Vlasov's 20th Army, which began operations north of Moscow on 4 December, was initially made up of two rifle divisions, three rifle brigades, and two tank battalions; there were only 130 field guns and 60 tanks.

The third new army of Western Army Group, Golikov's 10th, was not able to get into action south of Moscow at all on 6 December. Although a sizeable force, with seven newly-formed rifle divisions, and a cavalry division – 60,000 men in all – this army was mostly made up of raw recruits, and it had no tanks. As Zhukov would remember in a candid 1960s interview: 'We threw in many divisions which were completely untrained, and poorly equipped; one day they arrived at the front, the next day we pushed them into combat. What happened next was only to be expected.'[42]

And yet the sheer weight of Soviet numbers, coupled with the courage and determination of the troops, and the exhaustion of the Germans, would turn the tide, not on one day, but over weeks and months of that winter. German assessments significantly underestimated Soviet potential. The Germans believed Zhukov had fifty rifle divisions, whereas he actually commanded (on 1 December) the equivalent of fifty-six; they credited him with nineteen tank brigades and eleven cavalry divisions, while he actually had the equivalent of thirty-one of the former and sixteen of the latter.[43]

Even less accurate was the German reckoning of the strength that General Zhukov would deploy against the northern and southern wings of Army Group Centre, and it was there that he concentrated his counterattacks. Against the northern wing they expected thirteen rifle divisions and three tank brigades (in 16th and 30th Armies), and were actually engaged by the equivalent of nearly twenty-four rifle divisions and thirteen tank brigades (in 16th, 20th, 1st Shock and 30th Armies). The same would be true in the south, where they expected nine rifle divisions (in 50th Army) and were by 7–8 December engaged with thirteen (in 10th and 50th Armies). They expected one tank brigade here, and would actually be engaged by the equivalent of five.

Stalin's Russia and the Red Army had shown remarkable – and, for the Germans, unexpected – powers of recuperation. August 1941 was a critical period in the history of the Battle of Moscow, because it was then that many of the divisions and brigades that took part in the battle began to be formed.[44] The Russians had turned to the creation of emergency formations. The great bulk were infantry. By the end of 1941 no fewer than 159 'rifle brigades' had been formed.[45] Similar developments occurred with armour, although on a smaller scale. The big pre-war tank formations – mechanised corps, tank divisions and motorised divisions – had been destroyed or broken up. In their place in front of Moscow were much smaller elements, tank brigades and independent tank battalions.[46] Some contribution was made by the arrival (from October) of the first British Matilda and Valentine tanks; nearly a hundred fought in the Battle of Moscow (mostly west of the city) and they made up as many as 15–20 per cent of tanks on hand.[47]

The global war also played a part in the turnaround at Moscow. The Stavka had transferred a number of divisions from the Far East. Although the *Sibiriaki* were not in themselves decisive, they were certainly important in the defence of Moscow from the middle of November onwards. In total, some thirteen

'Siberian' divisions took an active part in the fighting during in this period. A fair estimate would suggest that nearly a fifth of tank formations came from Siberia, and 15 per cent of the infantry.[48]

* * *

General Zhukov recalled the December battle at a 'round table' of Soviet military historians twenty years later. There had been, he reminded his listeners, no 'classic counter-offensive, as we understand it' at Moscow. It was not even a separate stage of the battle; rather, it was an improvisation which grew out of the course of events.[49]

In truth, Saturday, 6 December, on the Moscow front, did not stand out as dramatically as would the following day, Sunday, in the Far East. Sunday was clearly the beginning of the Pacific War; Saturday's level of fighting around Moscow was not that very different from the days immediately before, or the days immediately afterward. Zhukov's counterattack was not like the Stalingrad offensive, Operation URAN, which on 19 November 1942 smashed into both flanks of German 6th Army after a cleverly masked concentration of Soviet mobile forces. There was no Red Army order laying down 6 December 1941 as 'D-Day' for the offensive, and the operation had no codename. If anything, it might be more accurate to say that the Moscow counteroffensive began with attacks by Konev's army group on 5 December, around Kalinin. On 12 December, however, when the first major Soviet press reports appeared about the success in front of Moscow, they stated that the Western Army Group offensive had begun on 6 December. Since then historians have made this the beginning of the offensive stage of the Battle of Moscow.[50]

It would be several days after 6 December before the German high command realised how bad things were. In four days Hitler would give a major speech to the German people which made no mention of any setbacks in Russia at all; it was not until 22 December that the press announced that Hitler was taking over command of the German Army. The Soviet government, for its part, would not claim a major victory for nearly a week. All the same, 6 December was – probably more than any other – the red-letter day. With it ended the Blitzkrieg, and with it began a terrible and bloody struggle that would end in Berlin forty-two months later.

CHAPTER 10

SUNDAY, 7 DECEMBER

# Date of Infamy: Japan's Undeclared Wars in Malaya and Hawaii

*[T]he stage certainly is set . . . We know of upwards of 50 ships, no doubt stuffed full of little brown brothers and their equipment, in waters of southern Indo China. Their attack is all mounted and at present it appears pointed at the Malay Peninsula.*

Admiral Thomas Hart

*Japanese are presenting at one pm eastern standard time today what amounts to an ultimatum also they are under orders to destroy their code machine immediately. Just what significance the hour set may have we do not know but be on alert accordingly.*

General George C. Marshall, Order to
US Army overseas commands

*I received a radio report that hostilities had broken out between Japan and America, and at once called on Ribbentrop. He said that from reports which he too had received he thought this was true, and that therefore, although he had not yet secured Hitler's sanction, the immediate participation in the war by Germany and Italy was a matter of course.*

Ambassador Ōshima to Foreign Minister Tōgō

## The Far East

Japan's 'Greater East Asia War' claimed its first victims a couple of hours after dawn on Sunday, 7 December, over the Gulf of Siam.

The Japanese convoys had been spotted south of Indochina early on the previous afternoon. During the evening and on Sunday morning, four of the five American-built Catalina flying boats of RAF No. 205 Squadron took off from Seletar, at the Singapore naval base.[1] Their mission was to scout out the northern part of the Gulf of Siam. Australian Flying Officer P.E. Bedell, with a crew of seven, took off two hours after midnight. His task was to check anchorages where the Japanese transports might have put in. Some six hours later, lumbering along at 125 knots, his Catalina reached the southern coast of Indochina. There it was attacked by Japanese Army fighters operating out of Konpong Trach airfield in southern Cambodia. Riddled with machine-gun fire, the flying boat exploded and fell into the sea. All the crew perished. Bedell's wireless operator had been unable to send an alarm back to his base.[2]

The time was around 8.20 a.m. (local time). It was just after midnight (7 December) in London, and early on Saturday evening (6 December) in Washington. The real beginnings of the Pacific War, however, were still nearly sixteen hours away.

The large Japanese invasion convoy from Hainan, with General Yamashita and his expedition on board, reached what the Japanese called point 'G' (9°25´N, 102°20´E) in the centre of the Gulf of Siam at 10.30 a.m., just over two hours after Bedell's Catalina was shot down. The convoy split, its various elements heading toward different points on the east coast of Thailand and Malaya, with the intention of arriving at the scattered landing sites in the middle of the coming night. Stormy weather over the South China Sea favoured the invaders, but there were a number of sightings by British scout planes. However, the commanders in Singapore could not be sure whether the Japanese ships were heading for Malaya or Thailand, and indeed whether the shipping movements were now a feint to provoke a British violation of Thai neutrality and to give Japan a justification for going to war. Later that Sunday, at 3.45 p.m., an RAAF Hudson light bomber patrolling in the Gulf of Siam sent a report about a transport ship with 'a large number of people on deck in khaki'. Other patrol aircraft in the course of the afternoon and evening radioed sightings of merchant ships and warships.

Even as the invasion convoy crossed the Gulf of Siam, Prime Minister Churchill was returning to the idea of sending a warning to the Japanese government. Drafts were cabled to Washington and the Dominion

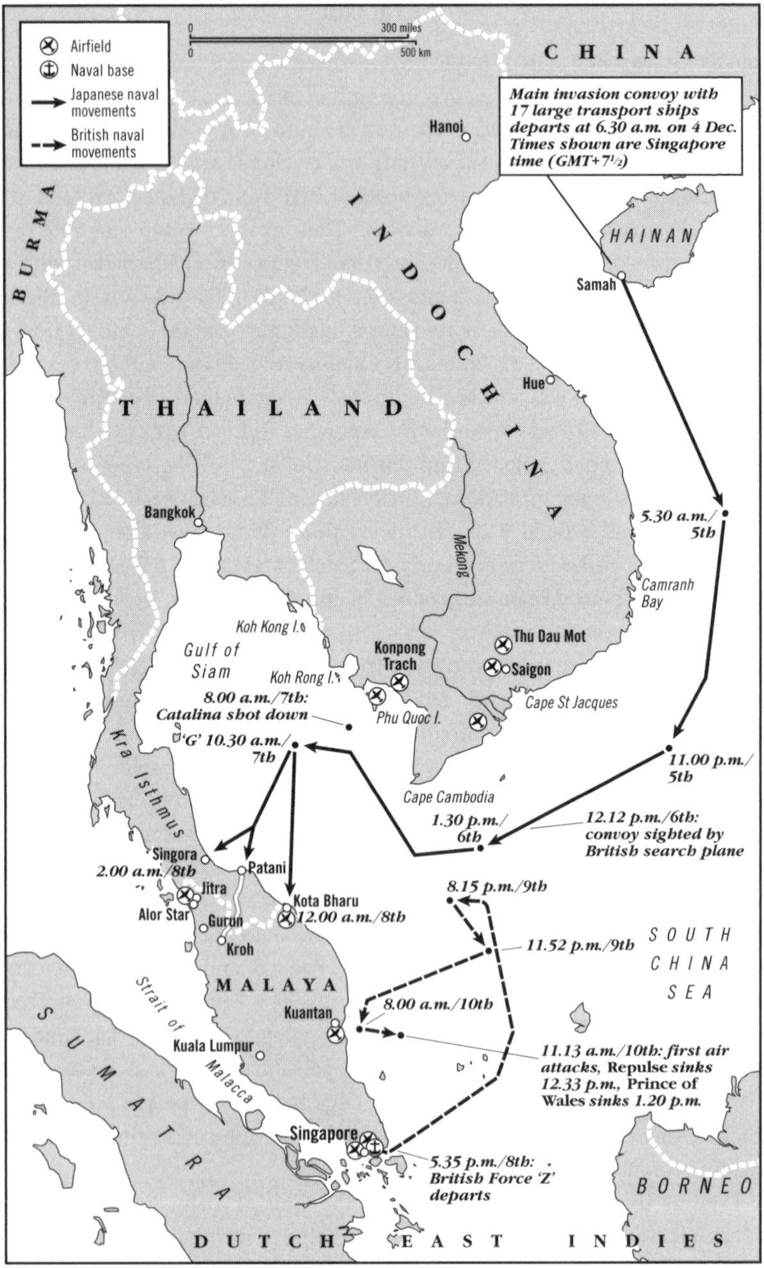


**Map 5.** Southeast Asia.

governments, stressing the unity of British and American concerns: 'if Japan attempts to establish her influence in Thailand by threat or force she will do so at her own peril and His Majesty's Government will at once take all appropriate measures. Should hostilities unfortunately result the responsibility will rest with Japan.'[3] But the British warning could certainly not be ready that day.

Just before 8.00 p.m. on 7 December (London time) the Admiralty sent a signal to the naval command in Singapore which encapsulated the fatal British inconsistency. On the one hand, the message outlined leisurely diplomatic measures, stretching over the next two or three days; an American warning about a Japanese 'hostile act' with respect to Thailand, Malaya, Burma and the Dutch East Indies, could be expected on Tuesday afternoon (9 December), and the British and Dutch would follow on Wednesday morning. But on the other hand, the message suggested that in military terms the Admiralty was thinking in terms of hours, not days: 'We will let you know shortly whether you can attack expedition at sea.' The message arrived in the Far East well after midnight on 8 December (local time). The Japanese armada was already lying in the dark off the beaches at Singora, Patani and Kota Bharu. Japanese bombers were droning towards Singapore and were just an hour or two away.[4]

Admiral Phillips's own Catalina flying boat had arrived back from Manila a few hours after dawn on 7 December, and he was soon conferring with the Australian, New Zealand, Dutch and American representatives in Singapore. Unfortunately, far more than alliance-building would be required today. The Admiral, along with his RAF and Army opposite numbers, were still following Whitehall's advice to wait and see. *Prince of Wales* remained at the Singapore naval base, and air activities were confined to reconnaissance.

Back in Manila, Admiral Hart was now even more sure of the imminent outbreak of hostilities. '[T]he stage certainly is set,' he wrote in his diary that evening. 'We know of upwards of 50 ships, no doubt stuffed full of little brown brothers and their equipment, in waters of southern Indo China. Their attack is all mounted and at present it appears pointed at the Malay Peninsula. But an amphibious expedition can be thrown at anything.'[5]

The veteran American Admiral had discovered, in an infuriatingly roundabout way, that Washington was thrusting his command into the front line. Very late on Saturday evening Captain Creighton, the US Navy observer in Singapore, sent him a cable reporting an extraordinary development. The War Office had informed Brooke-Popham that Britain had 'received assurance of American armed support' if it executed plans (i.e. Operation MATADOR) to forestall a Japanese invasion of the Kra Isthmus or any other part of Thailand, if it went to the defence of the Dutch East Indies, or if British territory was attacked. This was certainly a reference to the message (FE 50) that Brooke-Popham had received from London on Friday afternoon.[6] Two days later, on Sunday afternoon, when the news percolated down to him, Hart sent an urgent and very angry missive to CNO Admiral Stark in Washington: 'Learn from Singapore we have assured Britain armed support in event of three or four eventualities. Have received no corresponding instructions from you.'[7]

The annoyance and confusion of the C-in-C of the Asiatic Fleet are understandable, especially since he had spent the previous day in discussions with the British Admiral Phillips. Tommy Hart saved the real outrage for his diary that evening: 'my Government has assured the British of armed support in any one of four contingencies having to do with the Jap's [sic] going into Thailand, the NEI [Dutch East Indies] etc. And not a word to me about it. Of course in ordinary times such treatment as that would force me to ask for my immediate relief. And now it is too late.' He had made the biggest mistake of his life, Hart thought, when he agreed to stay in the Asiatic Fleet beyond retirement age.[8]

Despite London's instructions, and despite the naval movements in the Gulf of Siam, General Percival, commander of British ground forces in Malaya, still urged caution. Late on the evening of 7 December he advised Brooke-Popham that launching Operation MATADOR was not advisable. The Japanese were already so near Singora in the Kra Isthmus that, if they *were* coming, they would get there before any British expedition. 'Conditions for reconnaissance were very bad and there can be no real certainty that ships were an expedition,' Brooke-Popham informed London. He was concerned about a 'Jap "switch movement" designed to get us to break Thai neutrality'. All the same, the MATADOR force was not stood down; General Heath of III Indian Corps was told just after 11.15 p.m. that he should hold his troops ready to act on the following morning.[9]

* * *

From Tokyo, the bulk of the Japanese Foreign Ministry's long memorandum for the American government had been transmitted to the Washington embassy late on Saturday evening, 6 December. Now, late on Sunday afternoon, 7 December (Tokyo time), the *Gaimushō* sent two final messages. One was the fourteenth and final transmission instalment of the memorandum. It concluded with the following words: 'The Japanese Government regrets to have to notify the American Government that in view of the attitude of the American Government it cannot but consider that it is impossible to reach an agreement through further negotiation.'[10] It was not a declaration of war. The second message set the time for the delivery of the fourteen-instalment message.

Marked 'Urgent – very important', it read, in its entirety: 'Will the Ambassador please submit to the United States Government (if possible to the Secretary of State) our reply to the United States at 1.00 p.m. on the 7th, your time.'[11]

At 8.50 p.m. on 7 December (Tokyo time) the *Gaimushō* also sent an urgent circular warning message to its diplomatic posts around the world. This was sent using the 'stop' code arranged on 27 November. The decoded meaning was: 'Relations between Japan and Great Britain and United States are extremely critical.'[12]

President Roosevelt's direct message to the Emperor, sent from Washington late on Saturday evening, had been received in Tokyo at noon on Sunday (with the ten-hour time shift, an hour after it left the State Department in Washington). It arrived at the American Embassy some ten and a half hours after that, in the late evening of the 7th, having been diverted by the Japanese Army. When he finally received the message, Ambassador Grew requested an immediate meeting with Foreign Minister Tōgō.[13]

## Russia

The sun rose in Russia on 7 December, as the Japanese convoys were still making their final approaches to landing beaches in Malaya and Thailand. The weather over the sprawling battlefield around Moscow had improved slightly. The day began clear and frosty, with temperatures down to –25°C (–13°F), but clouded over in the afternoon and some snow fell, increasing the temperature to –15°C (5°F). Despite the slight improvement, frostbite was causing numerous casualties on both sides.

The Soviet General Staff recorded the continuing offensive towards Klin, Dmitrov, Solnechnogorsk and Istra to the north of Moscow. South of the city Zhukov had opened a new counterattack against Guderian's Panzers; he ordered forward Belov's 1st Guards Cavalry Corps from his reserve. Part of Soviet 50th Army, north of the Tula salient, also went into action. Both attacks threatened, from the north, Guderian's line of retreat. To the south of the Stalinogorsk bulge the forces of Southwestern Army Group (Marshal Timoshenko) were also beginning to take the initiative against German 2nd Army. Timoshenko's right-flank force, 13th Army, was not as yet having much success against the most advanced German divisions, in the Elets area, but Timoshenko had thrown in a 'striking group' to hit them from the flank. He had put in charge Fedor Kostenko, his own deputy. (General Kostenko was an energetic cavalryman who would be killed at the Battle of Kharkov in May 1942.) 'Operational Group Kostenko' began its attack to the northwest with the aim of cutting off Elets (forty miles to the northeast); it advanced approximately ten miles on 7 December.[14] For the next couple of days the Germans would perceive this as one of the most crucial threats to their forces in Russia.

Although the Wehrmacht press release on the morning of the 8th would announce that on large stretches of the front the fighting had been reduced to 'local engagements', the secret *OKW* Situation Report was more frank: 'To the northwest of Moscow [the enemy] continued his attacks in undiminished strength and also carried out vigorous new attacks across the Volga southwest of Kalinin.' It also noted that 'enemy attacks were carried out with artillery and rocket-launcher support. Bombers and strike aircraft have also been frequently used. North of Moscow our forces have established a line 10km west of the Moscow-Volga Canal.' Indeed, the last German toehold on the Moskva-Volga canal had been given up on this day, when the Soviets recaptured Iakhroma. The Chief of the Army General Staff, General Halder, noted in his own war diary 'great pressure' on Panzer Groups 3 and 4 north of Moscow.[15]

At Smolensk, Field Marshal Bock was increasingly concerned about the flanks of his army group. In his diary for this day, under the heading 'Causes of the Severe Crisis,' Bock listed what had gone wrong: one, autumn mud; two, the inadequacy of the railways; and three, an underestimation of the enemy's ability to resist, and his reserves of personnel and matériel. He played down his own responsibility:

> The orders for relentless pursuit were justified as long as the High Command believed there was a basis for this, that the enemy was fighting for his life with the very last of his forces; the effort to overthrow him in one short push was worth the 'maximum effort' that the Army High Command demanded. That, however, was a mistake and the army group is now forced to go over to the defensive under the most difficult circumstances.[16]

From the point of view of the German Army High Command the whole Russian front was under strain. Aside from the dangers around Moscow, bitter fighting raged around Tikhvin for control of the vital railway to Lake Ladoga and Leningrad. The Russians had thrown in reinforcements, and the overstretched forces of Army Group North were now in a critical position. Brauchitsch gave Field Marshal von Leeb permission to pull his forces back, but ordered him to stay within artillery range of the railway line through Tikhvin.[17]

At MAUERWALD, General Halder was worried both about Russian successes at the front and the malfunctioning of his own side's command structure. 'The experience of recent days is both depressing and shameful,' Halder complained, after long telephone conversations with Field Marshal von Leeb, Field Marshal von Bock and General Jodl. 'The *ObdH* [Army C-in-C Brauchitsch] is scarcely even a postman. The Führer goes over his head directly to the C-in-Cs of the Army Groups.' The 'high command' did not grasp what a bad state the German troops were in, and was tinkering with their position when big decisions were needed. For Halder, 'big decisions' now meant 'big withdrawals' – on the northern flank he believed it was necessary to pull Army Centre back a good distance from Moscow to the line of the towns of Ruza and Ostashkov.[18]

Franz Halder was not the only person to sense that the command structure of the Third Reich was approaching breakdown. On the morning of 7 December Colonel Rudolf Schmundt spoke confidentially with Hitler. The Führer's influential *Chefadjutant* at the OKW made the proposal – which he had been dwelling on for some weeks – that if Brauchitsch had to be replaced as C-in-C of the Army, and if there was no satisfactory military figure to replace him, then Hitler himself might take on the responsibility, with Halder supporting him. Hitler said he would think about the suggestion and consult with *Reichsmarschall* Goering and Field Marshal Keitel.[19]

## London, Chequers, Washington I

In London it was a Sunday, and the Prime Minister and Foreign Secretary were away from Whitehall. The war, nevertheless, went on, as did the confrontation with Japan. At midday the Chiefs of Staff Committee (COS) met in London with a representative of the Foreign Office, discussing, as General Brooke put it, 'all the various alternatives that might lead to war [with Japan] and trying to ensure that in every case the USA would not be left out.'[20]

Saturday's order blocking any attacks on the Japanese convoys remained in force. At 1.29 p.m. the Admiralty despatched a signal to Tom Phillips in Singapore. 'No decision has yet been taken by H.M. Government,' Phillips was informed. This was followed by a decidedly unhelpful request for information: 'on the assumption that it may be decided that a Japanese expedition is located in the South China Sea in such a position that its course indicates that it is proceeding towards Thailand, Malaya, Borneo, or Netherlands East Indies report what action it would be possible to take with air or naval forces.'[21]

The Americans had intercepted late on Saturday evening (the middle of Saturday night, London time) the bulk of the fourteen-instalment message from Tokyo on American-Japanese relations. There is, however, no evidence that this information was communicated to Lord Halifax, nor that the text was available in London on Sunday morning or afternoon. The British military command, and Prime Minister Churchill, were also evidently unaware of the later Japanese message that ordered Nomura and Kurusu to deliver the fourteen-instalment message to the State Department at 1.00 p.m. (7.00 p.m. London time).[22]

Meanwhile Eden and Cadogan – the Foreign Secretary and the civil-servant head of the Foreign Office – began their odyssey to Moscow. They were accompanied by a high-level British delegation, as well as Ambassador Ivan Maiskii and some staff from the Russian Embassy. The party left London by train early on Sunday afternoon. They were en route to northeast Scotland to embark on a destroyer for the trip to the Scapa Flow naval base in the Orkneys. There, a cruiser awaited that would take them to North Russia. Eden had come up to London from his country house at Binderton in Sussex (where he had gone on Friday), and brought a bout of gastric flu with him.

Churchill had been at Chequers since Friday. It was here, during Saturday evening or Sunday morning, that the draft warning to the Japanese government was written, and then forwarded to Washington and the Dominions. It was here, too, that Churchill wrote to the Thai Prime Minister warning him of the 'possibility of imminent Japanese invasion', urging his country to defend itself, and declaring that Britain would regard an attack on Thailand as an attack on Britain.[23]

The Duchess of Marlborough and her young son, Lord Blandford, had been invited to lunch at Chequers, along with Gilbert Winant, the American Ambassador to Britain. Winant had been at Binderton (where he had discussed with Eden the latter's forthcoming trip to Russia), and he was running rather late. Churchill was waiting outside the entrance door. The two men discussed the vital topic of the day: whether there was going to be a war with Japan, and whether Britain or the US would be involved. Winant was, he later maintained, non-committal. 'He turned to me,' Winant recalled, 'with the charm of manner that I saw so often in difficult moments, and said, "We're late, you know. You get washed and we will go into lunch together." '[24]

Although it was a country Sunday, Churchill continued to work after lunch. He took care to stay in contact with his most important war front, in Libya. In other circumstances, 7 December would have been a day of triumph for British war history. Two and a half weeks after the launch of Operation CRUSADER the desert battle had reached its turning point. That morning, Rommel conferred with his most important subordinate, General Ludwig Crüwell (commander of the *Afrika Korps*), and the two commanders reluctantly decided to fall back to a new defensive line at Gazala, forty miles to the west of Tobruk. The five days since 1 December had seen Rommel's weakened Panzer Group Afrika come under increasing pressure, as the British brought reinforcements and supplies into the battle and from the south threatened Panzer Group headquarters at El Adem. Rommel's decision meant giving up the seven-month siege of Tobruk; it also meant abandoning thousands of Axis troops who were dug in a hundred miles to the east of Gazala, on the Egyptian border at Bardia and Sollum, along with their supply dumps.

The British did not yet know of Rommel's decision to retreat. Full-scale movement of the two German Panzer divisions and other troops would only begin on the night of 7–8 December. But the tide was clearly flowing in the right direction. General Auchinleck, C-in-C, Middle East Command, sent a message to the Prime Minister reporting the successes of his forces. Churchill's reply, sent early in the evening of the 7th, showed his pleasure at this development, but he was still unwilling to make public the dismissal of General Cunningham (commander of 8th Army) – which had occurred on 25 November – until the news from North Africa was 'decidedly good'.

The Prime Minister also briefed Auchinleck on the general strategic situation, especially in the Far East. President Roosevelt, he reported, had now said that the United States 'will regard it as hostile act if Japanese invade Siam, Malaya, Burma, or East Indies'. He expected Roosevelt to warn the Japanese to this effect in the near future, probably on Wednesday (10 December). 'This is an immense relief, as I had long dreaded being at war with Japan without or before United States. Now I think it is all right.'[25]

* * *

In Washington, President Roosevelt had a quiet Sunday morning on 7 December. He received the Chinese Ambassador, Dr Hu Shih, shortly after noon, and had lunch at 1.15 p.m. with Hopkins.

Maksim Litvinov arrived at National Airport that morning, to take up his duties as the new Soviet Ambassador to the United States. Litvinov was the personification of the new relationship between the United States and the USSR. As People's Commissar of Foreign Affairs from 1930–39 he had been the instrument of the Collective Security policy in the 1930s and, for a time, a pillar of the League of Nations. (His replacement as Foreign Commissar by Molotov was followed by the Nazi-Soviet Pact of August 1939.) With his British-born wife and his secretary, he was completing an epic flight which had started two weeks earlier in Kuibyshev on the Volga and had taken him through Iran, India, Singapore, Manila, Guam, Wake and Hawaii. The party had arrived on the 6th in San Francisco, after a nineteen-hour flight on the Pan American China Clipper from Honolulu. From San Francisco Litvinov and his party boarded an Eastern Airlines aeroplane for the transcontinental flight. In Washington the travellers – no doubt now exhausted – were met by American and British diplomats.[26]

More immediately important was the arrival of the decrypted text of the fourteenth instalment of the Japanese note, plus the message setting 1.00 p.m. as the hour of delivery. This was seen by Colonel Rufus Bratton (Chief of the Far Eastern Section of US Army intelligence) between 8.30 a.m. and 9.00 a.m. Bratton had already circulated translations of the first thirteen transmission instalments to senior officials during the previous evening, but these two messages were even more significant. The fourteenth transmission instalment contained the final paragraph in which the Japanese notified the US government that the diplomatic talks had failed. Meanwhile Tokyo's rigidly-fixed hour of delivery – early on a Sunday afternoon, Washington time – obviously corresponded to a specific event or events that were to occur somewhere else in the world.

Secretary of State Hull was with Stimson and Knox from 10.30 a.m., in a meeting which had been arranged the previous evening. The three key members of FDR's Cabinet were now shown the two new Japanese messages. The intercepts, coming on top of the previous day's news about the advance of the Japanese convoy across the Gulf of Siam, fostered a growing sense of alarm.

It is likely that a third piece of intelligence drew the attention of Washington decision-makers still more towards Southeast Asia. The codebreakers provided Hull, Stimson and Knox with a garbled version of the Japanese 'stop' code warning, which had been despatched from Tokyo at 8.50 p.m. (6.50 a.m., Washington time). The American leaders were told that this message meant 'Relations between Japan and England are not in accordance with expectations', when in fact it meant 'Relations between Japan and Great Britain and United States are extremely critical.' The reference to the United States had been omitted, and the emphasis on a deterioration between Britain and Japan in the garbled text seemed to be supported by news of Japanese convoy movements in the South China Sea.[27]

The 'stop' code messages were potentially as signficant as the better-known 'winds' code. Unlike the latter the 'stop' code warning *was* actually sent before the Japanese attack. Events were now happening very fast and mistakes are understandable. Nevertheless, American forces overseas might have received a few hours' warning of the impending attack if Washington had understood the correct meaning of the 'stop' message.

In the Navy Department, at about 10.40 a.m.,[28] 'Betty' Stark decided that the two new messages relating to the Japanese diplomatic note did not justify another warning to the Pacific commanders. This was a decision which probably cost the Chief of Naval Operations the best part of his career. Stark's opposite number in the Army, General Marshall, had gone riding in Rock Creek Park that morning, and several hours were wasted attempting to reach him. The Army Chief of Staff arrived at the War Department only at 11.25 a.m. and slowly read the messages. Eventually, and after consulting Admiral Stark, Marshall drafted a warning telegram to the overseas bases: 'Japanese are presenting at one pm eastern standard time today what amounts to an ultimatum also they are under orders to destroy their code machine immediately. Just what significance the hour set may have we do not know but be on alert accordingly. Inform naval authorities of this communication.'

This warning was sent just after noon to the Panama Canal Zone, the Philippines and San Francisco. Because of unsuitable atmospheric conditions for long-range radio transmission to Hawaii, the Army despatched the message at 12.17 p.m. through Western Union and RCA, civilian telegraph companies. For various technical reasons this telegram was only read by a responsible Army officer in Hawaii over eight hours later, at 2.58 p.m. local time; Admiral Kimmel saw it somewhat later. During the morning, events in Hawaii had intervened.[29]

## Kota Bharu

Japan's war with the West began with the first landing at Kota Bharu, on the northeast edge of Malaya.[30] Carried out in the darkness, in rough seas, by small craft launched in batches from several different mother ships, there was inevitably an element of confusion. Timing was of critical importance, in view of events elsewhere. The first of the Emperor's soldiers probably came ashore on the beaches of Malaya at about 12.25 a.m. on Monday, 8 December. In London this corresponded to the late afternoon (5.55 p.m.) of Sunday, 7 December. In Washington it was midday (11.55 a.m.). In Hawaii, most significantly, it was 6.35 a.m. The three big transport ships had arrived off the shore an hour or so earlier, where they lowered flat-bottomed lighters and transferred troops aboard them. Japanese ships had been sighted by British observers on shore just before midnight, at 11.45 p.m.[31]

Kota Bharu was, in 1941, a small town located near the mouth of the Kelantan River, around fifteen miles south of the border with Thailand. From Kota Bharu a narrow gauge railway ran into central Malaya, and then on to Singapore, but the town's real importance to the Japanese was due to the three

RAF 'aerodromes' nearby. One, with a 1,600 yard grass runway, was situated between Kota Bharu and the sea; two more, with hard runways, were fifteen miles to the south.

The landing at Kota Bharu was one of the most daring phases of the whole Japanese Southern Operation. The British believed an incursion into Thailand was a distinct possibility – or at least they had for the past two days, since the Japanese convoy was sighted. They did not suspect, until the very last moment, a landing at Kota Bharu.[32] This was because a landing in Malaya would categorically mean war with Britain, and also because it was (or seemed to be) operationally very risky. The Japanese Army itself had been very wary about making an opposed landing in Malaya, but Admiral Ozawa, commander of the 'Malaya Force', had insisted that the RAF airfields at Kota Bharu be neutralised in order to prevent attacks against his vulnerable ships in the Gulf of Siam.[33]

The three transports off Kota Bharu were *Awazisan Maru*, *Ayatosan Maru* and *Sakura Maru*, and they were part of the convoy which had sailed from Hainan on the 4th. These were large modern ships of about 10,000 tons. In view of the danger from British air attacks three of the fastest vessels, capable of seventeen knots, had been selected for this landing. They were accompanied by a small naval escort, a light cruiser and four destroyers. The invasion force was relatively small: a regiment from 18th Division and supporting troops, numbering altogether some 5,600 men. About two-thirds probably landed on the first night, and the remainder on the night of 8–9 December. Many of the officers and soldiers of 18th Division were veterans of the war in China; in 1937 they had come ashore behind the Chinese positions covering Shanghai and forced the enemy to give up the city; in 1938 the division landed at Bias Bay east of Hong Kong and marched inland to occupy the great southern port of Canton. Later they received more specialised training in landing operations.

Kota Bharu was defended by four battalions of Indian infantry, supported by some field-artillery batteries. The Japanese came ashore on a ten-mile stretch of shoreline near the mouth of the Kelantan, held by the 3/17th Dogras.[34] Some barbed wire and 'pill boxes' had been positioned on the sandy beach, but it was a thin defence for a ten-mile stretch of coastline.

British air attacks taking off from the Kota Bharu aerodrome from around 2.00 a.m. onward were able to cripple the *Awazisan Maru* and damage some of the enemy ships and barges. The two transport ships still able to move withdrew up the coast to the relative safety of Patani. Nevertheless the Japanese had been able to establish a position ashore during the night, and British infantry counterattacks, supported by artillery, were unsuccessful. By the afternoon of the 8th the Kota Bharu aerodrome was coming under threat and was then precipitately abandoned. RAF personnel made no serious attempt to block the runway, or even to blow up stores of fuel and bombs. The naval transports returned on the night of 8–9 December to offload the remainder of the Japanese regiments. Once the northern airfield had fallen the surviving defenders began to pull back. The town of Kota Bharu was abandoned on the morning of the 9th.

The Japanese suffered some 800 casualties in the landing and two days' fighting at Kota Bharu, which made it a costly action for them compared to later fighting in Malaya. But it had achieved its objective; it wrested control of the air from the British over the Gulf of Siam.

* * *

A pre-dawn air raid on 8 December was mounted against Singapore by the Japanese Navy. The Mihoro Wing had taken off from Thu Dau Moi airfield near Saigon, late on the evening of the 7th. Struggling through bad weather over the South China Sea, only seventeen of the thirty-one bombers which set out completed the very long outward flight, covering some 675 miles. They dropped their payloads in the moonlight at about 4.15 a.m. on 8 December (9.45 p.m., 7 December, London time). The raiders had been picked up by British radar at 3.20 a.m., and some anti-aircraft fire was put up, but Singapore city was not 'blacked out' and the local ARP (civil defence) headquarters was unmanned. A few bombs landed in the brightly-lit city, where a number of civilians were killed, but the air attacks on Singapore's harbour, the naval base and the airfields at Seletar and Tengah – the main target – only caused damage to three aircraft on the ground. No attempt was made to sink *Prince of Wales* and *Repulse*.[35] Compared to other air raids that the Imperial Navy mounted during 7 and 8 December, this one was not successful.

## Pearl Harbor I

Over the past few days, senior government officials and military leaders in London and Washington, and in Berlin, had watched and waited on events in Southeast Asia – the 'Malay barrier' and the region to the north of it. In the last thirty-six hours – since at least Saturday morning – they had begun to realise that a major development in that region, perhaps even war, was not weeks hence, but days or even hours away. The question was whether that the forces that the Japanese were assembling would target Thailand, Malaya, British Borneo, the Dutch East Indies or the Philippines. Then came the bolt from the blue. Some 6,800 miles to the east, nearly a quarter of the way around the earth's surface, Japanese planes attacked the US Pacific Fleet at Pearl Harbor, on Oahu in the Hawaiian Islands.

The Japanese Navy's carrier raid was, in its planning and execution, perhaps the most skilful military operation of the Second World War. The strike was carried out by the Mobile Force (*Kido Butai*) of Combined Fleet, commanded by Admiral Nagumo Chūichi. Six aircraft carriers formed the striking force of the Mobile Force: *Akagi*, Nagumo's flagship, was a large ship converted from a battlecruiser in the 1920s; *Kaga* was a converted battleship; *Hiryū* and *Sōryū* were smaller, but new and purpose-built; and *Shōkaku* and *Zuikaku* were two large vessels that were commissioned in the early autumn of 1941 – their paint was hardly dry, and the crews of their air groups were not yet fully trained. Two fast battleships, two heavy cruisers, a light cruiser, eight destroyers and three submarines screened the carriers, accompanied by a vital refuelling element of eight tankers.

Secrecy and surprise had been paramount. The sleek grey ships of the Mobile Force began to steal away in small groups from Saeki Bay in Japan's Inland Sea on the night of 17–18 November. That was a full week before Secretary of State Hull presented his famous Note in Washington. (Indeed, the advance force of submarines had begun to leave Japan even earlier; the first nine boats departed for their advanced base in the Marshall Islands on 11 November.) The destination and rendezvous point was 1,200 miles away at Hitokappu Bay, a remote anchorage at Etorofu Island in the Kurile Islands. Admiral Nagumo himself arrived in Hitokappu Bay on the 21st, and the rest of his ships joined him over the next two days.

The Mobile Force departed Hitokappu Bay for the Pearl Harbor raid on the morning of 26 November. It crept secretly across 3,700 miles of the northern Pacific. During the voyage the ships observed strict radio silence; to make doubly sure the transmitter keys were detached from some of the wireless sets.[36] Refuelling at sea was the critical technical problem, as the escorting destroyers needed frequent topping up. The procedure required relatively calm seas, and in the first week the weather was unseasonably fine. 'We were blessed by the War God,' wrote the C-in-C of Combined Fleet shortly after the attack.[37] A high-pressure zone extended 2,000 miles across the North Pacific, the first time in three years that it had come this late in the season. The weather was good, but with heavy swells.

On the seventh day, 2 December, Nagumo received the order 'Climb Mount Niitaka, 1208', which had gone out to the whole Combined Fleet. This confirmed that the date of the start of hostilities would be 8 December,

Japanese time. The Admiral was worried that his Mobile Force might be spotted by American planes from Midway Atoll or Dutch Harbor in the Aleutians, but no patrols had in fact been organised. No one on the American side had thought to station patrol vessels here either, and there were very few merchant ships in this part of the Pacific, remote from the main shipping lanes. The likelihood of an accidental sighting was slight.

Most remarkably, there were no aircraft flying from Oahu to patrol the seas north of the island. The war warnings issued by the US Army and Navy at the end of November had not led to any change of routine. The US Army, which in theory had responsibility for air reconnaissance around Oahu, had sent most of its long-range four-engined bombers to the Philippines, and it was not carrying out any patrols. The Pacific Fleet had over eighty big flying boats, but Admiral Kimmel, the fleet C-in-C, was saving most of them for the planned advance toward the Marshall Islands. It occurred to no one in authority that the first priority should be ensuring the security of the Hawaiian base.

Admiral Kimmel, C-in-C of the Pacific Fleet (CINCPAC), believed that the most likely danger would come from the southwest or northwest. He trusted that those two directions would be covered, at least for the next few days, by carrier planes from the *Enterprise* and *Lexington* task forces. These were operating, respectively, in the direction of Wake (and the Marshall Islands) and Midway. Kimmel did not expect that an attack force could approach from the empty seas to the north.

So it was that, on the evening of 6 December (Hawaiian time), still not sighted by the American patrol planes or ships, the carriers of the *Kido Butai* began their final dash through the night to the launch point, 240 miles north of Oahu. The first wave, 183 attack planes and escorting fighters, began to take off from the Japanese ships at 6.00 a.m.

* * *

The American military made three fatal mistakes that morning. The first has already been mentioned: at 10.40 a.m. (5.10 a.m. in Hawaii), the Chief of Naval Operations in Washington decided not to inform the overseas commands about what he had recently learned concerning Japanese intentions. The final MAGIC intercepts revealed that Tokyo had ended negotiations with the US; the American government was to be informed of this fact at a particular and peculiar time, 1.00 p.m. this Sunday afternoon (7.30 a.m. in Hawaii). Three years later the Naval Court of Inquiry would conclude that by not passing on this information, Admiral Stark had 'failed to display the sound judgement expected of him.'[38]

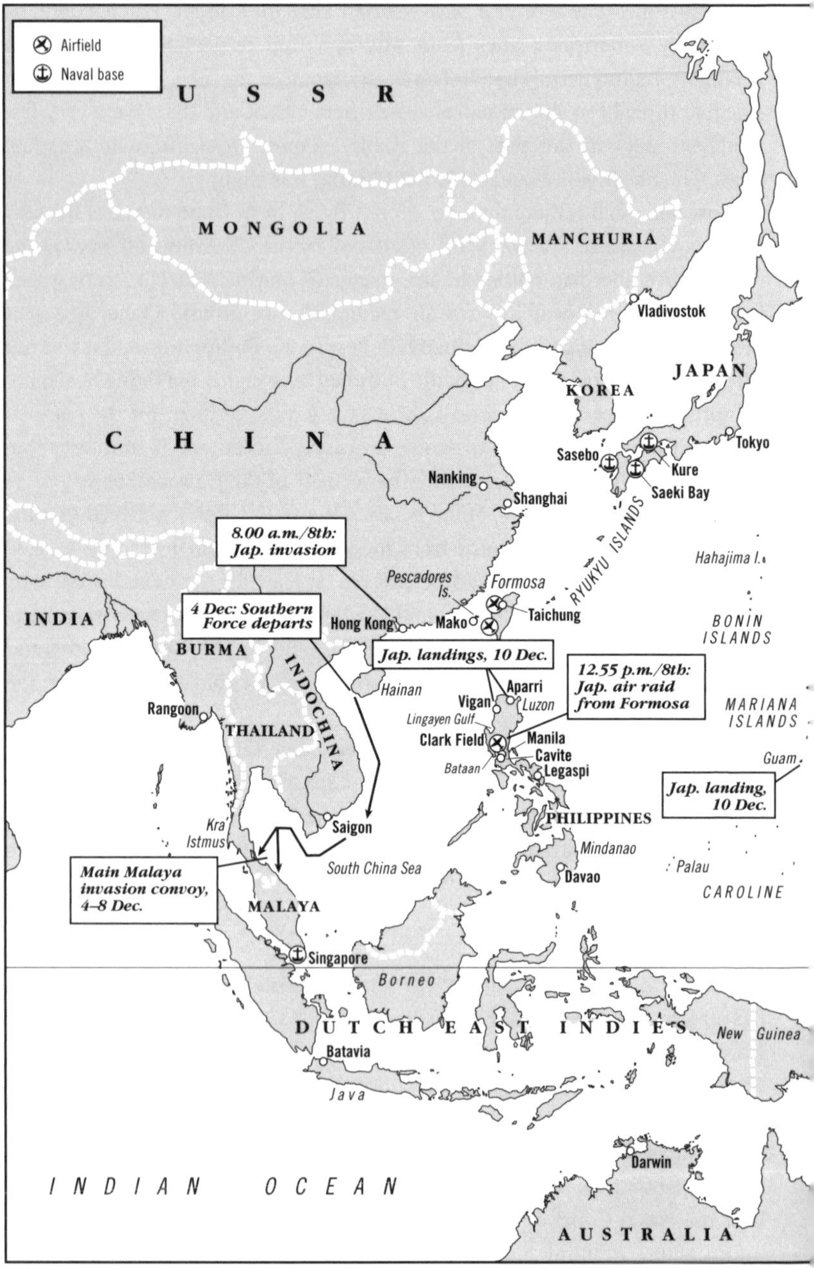


**Map 6.** The Pacific and East Asia.

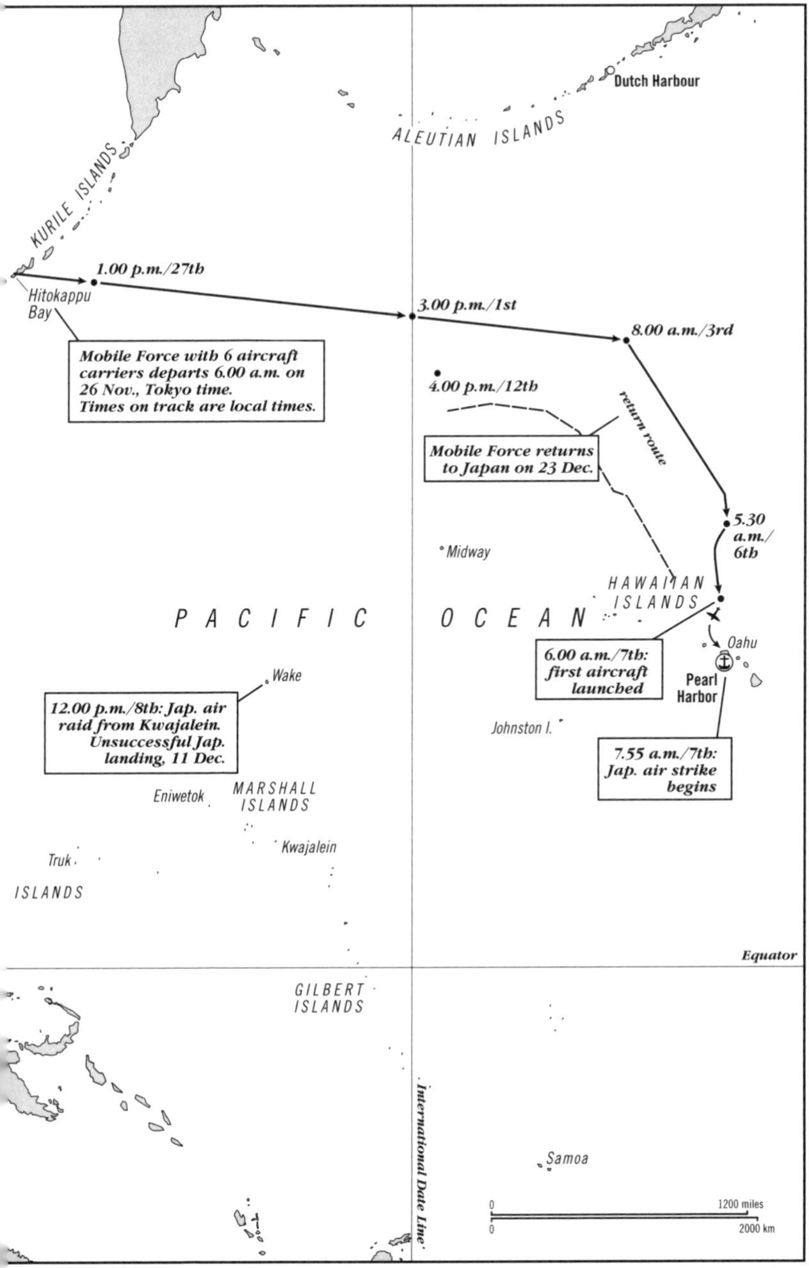

Dutch Harbour
ALEUTIAN ISLANDS
KURILE ISLANDS
1.00 p.m./27th
Hitokappu Bay
3.00 p.m./1st
8.00 a.m./3rd
Mobile Force with 6 aircraft carriers departs 6.00 a.m. on 26 Nov., Tokyo time. Times on track are local times.
4.00 p.m./12th
return route
Mobile Force returns to Japan on 23 Dec.
5.30 a.m./ 6th
Midway
HAWAIIAN ISLANDS
PACIFIC OCEAN
Oahu
6.00 a.m./7th: first aircraft launched
Pearl Harbor
Wake
12.00 p.m./8th: Jap. air raid from Kwajalein. Unsuccessful Jap. landing, 11 Dec.
Johnston I.
7.55 a.m./7th: Jap. air strike begins
Eniwetok
MARSHALL ISLANDS
Kwajalein
Truk
ISLANDS
Equator
GILBERT ISLANDS
International Date Line
Samoa
0
1200 miles
0
2000 km

Stark and his staff, in Washington, pondered intelligence and options. Meanwhile five two-man Japanese submarines were attempting to slip through the narrow entrance of Pearl Harbor. Each had been launched from a 'mother' submarine.[39] Between 6.30 a.m. and 6.45 a.m. the destroyer USS *Ward*, patrolling off the harbour mouth, spotted – and promptly attacked and sank – one of the little craft. Although the captain of *Ward* immediately reported his attack to the watch officer at the headquarters of 14th Naval District (responsible for the defence of Hawaii), it took crucial minutes for the report to pass up the naval chain of command. Even then, the original incident was not confirmed. No attempt was made to inform the Army. This failure to respond quickly to the *Ward* incident was the second mistake.

The third mistake was an ignored radar warning. A small US Army Mobile Radar Station was positioned above the north coast of Oahu at Opana. Two conscientious privates, who had been at their post since 4.00 a.m., were supposed to close down their operations at 7.00 a.m. The men remained on duty when their oscilloscope suddenly registered a very large flight of aircraft approaching from the north, around 130 miles distant. They telephoned the Information Center (IC) at Fort Shafter, which was designed to co-ordinate the air defence. Most of the staff of the IC had gone off duty at 7.00 a.m. The inexperienced Army Lieutenant who had been left in charge thought the sighting was a group of American heavy bombers scheduled to fly in from the mainland that morning. 'Well, don't worry about it,' was his final response to the Opana privates, at 7.20 a.m.[40] How much there was to worry about would become clear thirty-five minutes later.

By 5.10 a.m. that Sunday morning – when Admiral Stark considered sending a warning, and the Japanese planes were still three hours away – there was nothing the American forces on Hawaii could have done to move the fleet to safety, fend off a major attack, or prepare a counter-strike. But if Admiral Stark had warned the Hawaiian command that morning, and if an alert from Washington had meant the *Ward* incident or the Opana radar sighting was accurately interpreted, then the damage could have been greatly reduced, and the Japanese compelled to pay more heavily for their success. The hulls of warships are greatly sub-compartmentalised, and if all watertight hatches had been secured – and the ships' damage-control parties put on alert – then some of the American vessels sunk at Pearl Harbor might have stayed afloat. The anti-aircraft guns, at least those of the fleet's ships, could have been fully manned and ready to fire. Some Army fighter planes might have been able to get into the air, and others could have been put on alert.

* * *

At around 7.40 a.m. the Japanese mass formation reached the north point of Oahu. The aeroplanes, bombers and escorting fighters, were all single-engined machines. Most were painted light grey with a slight greenish tint. A few were dark green. All had their wings and fuselage adorned with the red circles of the Japanese national markings.[41] The plane of Commander Fuchida Mitsuo, the raid leader, had a garishly-painted red tail for easy identification. Fuchida fired off a flare, signalling his belief that surprise had been achieved, and his intention that the torpedo planes should attack first. The gaggle of planes flew together for two or three more minutes along the sparsely populated north coast of Oahu, then broke up into half a dozen groups, each group assigned to a particular target.

The US Army was responsible for the protection of the islands against air attack. Two weeks later, Oahu would boast serious air defences: a third of the Army and Navy fighters would be in the air from half an hour before sunrise until 8.00 a.m., with the remainder on ready status with their engines warmed up. On the morning of 7 December, however, there was no 'dawn patrol', and no fighters on the ground ready to scramble.[42] The response of General Walter Short, commander of US Army forces on Hawaii, to the war warnings from Washington had not been to institute long-range air patrols, or to put his fighters in a state of readiness, or even to disperse his aircraft to sheltered revetments. Rather he ordered his planes lined up in tight rows in front of their hangers, so they could be guarded against sabotage by suspected 'fifth columnists' from among the local ethnic Japanese population. The neat rows of fighters and bombers made an easy target for air attack.

Two groups of Japanese torpedo bombers – a total of forty planes – flew south along either side of the Waianae mountain range on the west side of Oahu. Further west still, forty-nine 'level bombers', led by Fuchida himself, followed the coast around the shoreline. At 7.49 a.m., and still about twenty miles northwest of the main target, Fuchida told his radio operator to tap out a message to the entire air attack force: '*To, to, to*', the abbreviation of '*totsugeki-seyo*' ('Charge'). A few minutes later he sent another radio message back to the flagship *Akagi* and Admiral Nagumo: '*Tora, tora, tora*', meaning that surprise had been achieved, and that the air attack was about to begin.[43] Arcing slowly round the south side of the island, Fuchida's bombers were still ten or fifteen minutes from their first bomb drop, although the torpedo and dive-bomber squadrons which had cut directly across the island were only five or six minutes from their targets.

Events exploded almost simultaneously – just after 7.55 a.m. – as Japanese planes roared into the vortex of the naval base area from several different directions. The very first attacks here were by a group of dive bombers against the airfield on Ford Island (in the middle of Pearl Harbor) and the nearby army base at Hickam Field. It was the Ford Island strike that triggered the famous report, at 7.58 a.m.: 'Air raid, Pearl Harbor. This is not drill!'[44]

A few moments before this warning was transmitted, a group of sixteen planes, coming in very low from the northwest, launched torpedoes against ships on that side of Ford Island or against the long 'Dock 1010' to the south. Both were locations where the American aircraft carriers were sometimes docked, but on this morning it happened there were only second-line vessels here.[45] The carriers *Enterprise* and *Lexington* were at sea, and *Saratoga* was picking up aircraft on the West Coast.

So it was that the most deadly attack came from the south, executed by some twenty-four low-flying torpedo planes, formed in groups of three. Their target was 'Battleship Row' on the southeast side of Ford Island, especially the exposed vessels, those moored on their own, or the outer ship of a pair. Here were seven of the capital ships Admiral Kimmel was preparing for the task forces that would attack the Marshall Islands if and when war broke out with Japan.[46] Many of the crewmen were still below decks, unable to see or hear the attacking planes. 'Man your battle stations! This is no shit!' was the message over the loudspeaker on the battleship *Oklahoma*.[47]

*California*, moored nearest the harbour entrance because she was flagship of the Battle Force, was hit by two torpedoes. *Oklahoma*, next in line, was hit by five torpedoes in seventy seconds, *West Virginia* by no fewer than six, and *Nevada* by one. With fatal flooding to her port side, *Oklahoma* capsized. Frantic counter-flooding in *California* and *West Virginia* enabled those vessels to sink upright, with their decks still exposed, to the bottom of the harbour. *Nevada* was able to cast off and move toward the harbour entrance, but during the second wave of attacks she was run aground to keep her from blocking the way in.

Surprise was complete. The American ships were at 'Condition 3' of readiness. A quarter of the light anti-aircraft guns in the fleet were manned, but none of the heavy 5-inch guns. Even the machine guns that were manned had ready ammunition stowed away in locked boxes, with the keys held centrally. The Army had a dozen anti-aircraft installations in the Pearl Harbor area, but few of the crews were on duty, and all ammunition was stored in remote depots.

About ten minutes after the first torpedo strike, Fuchida's mass of level bombers arrived from the southwest, flying more than two miles above the harbour. Their mission was to pick off the ships that the torpedo planes could not reach. Each plane carried a very heavy special weapon – a single 800kg (1,800lb) bomb adapted from a 16-inch battleship shell – which they were to drop from a height of 12,000 feet. Flying in 'vic' formations, the bombers were able to lay down a tight pattern of destruction. The high-altitude bombing turned out to be less effective than the torpedoes. The bombs, when they hit, could damage the superstructure of the target, but not cause fatal flooding below the armoured decks. The spectacular exception was USS *Arizona*. One of two hits led, directly or indirectly, to a fire, and to the ignition of one of Arizona's main magazines. The ensuing catastrophic explosion blew off the forward part of the ship and killed 85 per cent of the crew of 1,400 officers and men; the wreck burned for two days.[48]

Admiral Kimmel was at his quarters, ten minutes' drive away from his headquarters in the Submarine Base. He was preparing to go into work to follow up the report of the *Ward* incident, when he was informed by telephone that Pearl Harbor itself was now under attack. From a neighbour's garden the Admiral was able to watch the first part of the strike against his fleet. He reached his HQ at just about the time the torpedo attack finished. As Kimmel stood with Commander Maurice Curts, the communications officer of his staff, surveying the scene of devastation through the window, a spent .50 caliber round hit him on the chest, and fell harmlessly to the floor. 'It would have been merciful,' CINCPAC murmured to Curts, 'had it killed me.'[49]

Meanwhile other elements of the Japanese first strike, dive bombers and fighters, were attacking American air fields elsewhere on Oahu. Their objective was to paralyse any air defence, and to prevent a counterattack against the Japanese carrier force. They caused heavy damage to the rows of Army and Marine fighters and bombers. The Japanese fighters were each armed with two 20mm cannon, whose explosive shells ripped their targets apart. They also devastated the vital Patrol Wings. PatWing 2 at Ford Island and PatWing 1 at Kaneohe Naval Air Station, suffered the loss of twenty-seven PBY flying boats destroyed and six damaged; only the three Catalinas that had been aloft on anti-submarine patrol that morning would be usable.

The second Japanese attack wave, comprising 168 planes, arrived an hour after the first, at about 9.00 a.m. This time the high-level bombers targeted air fields where long-range American planes were based. Special attention was paid to Hickam Field, just east of the entrance to Pearl Harbor. The second wave was less dangerous to Kimmel's fleet than the first. There were no torpedo planes; the surviving ships were left to the dive bombers, whose 250kg bombs could not penetrate heavy armour. Anti-aircraft fire was now intense, and a few American fighters had even made it into the air. By 9.45 a.m. most of the second wave had also departed. The whirlwind had come and gone.[50]

* * *

The overall commander of the Japanese attack force, Admiral Nagumo, had been pessimistic about his prospects. But in the event, the Hawaiian attack had been carried out with greater damage to the target, and lower losses to the attacking planes and ships, than anyone had dared to hope. Nagumo broke radio silence to send a lengthy and exultant 'action summary' back to Yamamoto in Japan. In spite of close clouds and extremely heavy defensive fire in the later stages, the targets in Hawaii had been successfully attacked, Nagumo reported. '[W]e can assume that we have practically annihilated the enemy's main fighting forces of the Pacific as well as the air, land, and sea strength in the Hawaiian Areas within one and a half hours after opening battle.' By 12.30 p.m. (Hawaii time) all aircraft had been recovered, and the entire Mobile Force withdrew to north-northwest as planned. It had not come under any attack: 'Although we were pursued by a few seaplanes, there was no enemy counter-attack this date.' Nagumo reported twenty-nine of his own planes lost to defensive enemy fire.[51]

Based on photographs and the debriefing of aircrew, the Admiral believed that his planes had sunk four American battleships, two cruisers and a tanker; they had inflicted heavy (and hopefully irreparable) damage to two battleships, two cruisers and two destroyers; they had caused medium damage to two further battleships and two light cruisers. Eleven of the forty-nine level-bombers were said to have had scored hits, and thirty-five of forty torpedo planes. Great numbers of American aircraft were claimed to be destroyed on the ground, some 450 burned out by fire and many others damaged.

Fortunately for the Americans the success was exaggerated. In reality only two of eight battleships – *Arizona* and *Oklahoma* – were total losses, and they were among the oldest big ships present that morning. *California* and *West Virginia* had sunk upright in shallow water, and they would be repaired (and modernised), but would not be back in service until 1943 and 1944 respectively. *Nevada*, run aground, would also return to the fleet only in 1943. *Maryland* and *Tennessee* had been protected against torpedoes by the hulls of the outboard ships, and *Pennsylvania* had been in dry dock. None of the three carriers had been in port. The large and powerful American cruiser force was also intact. Of the twelve Pacific Fleet heavy cruisers only two had been in Pearl Harbor, and neither had suffered damage. Of five modern light cruisers present only one (*Helena*) required major repairs in the US; several older light cruisers and destroyers were damaged.

But it was a fact that the entire American battle line had been put out of service. Over 2,000 US Navy personnel were killed as well as 100 Marines, 200 Army personnel and 68 civilians. None of the eight battleships at Pearl Harbor was ready to go to sea, and even the three lightly damaged ones would not re-enter service until the spring of 1942. The military establishment of the United States had suffered a profound psychological shock. From belittling the Japanese threat, the President and his advisers now, for the next few weeks at least, would see danger everywhere, even fearing the invasion of the Hawaiian Islands and air strikes on the West Coast and the Panama Canal.

## London, Chequers, Washington II

At 1.40 p.m. in the early afternoon of 7 December (8.10 a.m. Hawaii time – fifteen minutes after the first bombs were dropped), the Secretary of the Navy telephoned the White House to report the attack on Pearl Harbor.[52] Ambassador Nomura and Special Envoy Kurusu arrived at the State Department at 2.05 p.m., bearing the fourteen-instalment message. They were over an hour late, because the staff of the Japanese Embassy had taken so long to decrypt and type out the text. Secretary Hull frostily perused the paper. He had already read most of it on Saturday evening, and the final instalment four hours earlier. 'In all my 50 years of public service,' he exclaimed, 'I have never seen a document that was more crowded with infamous falsehoods and distortions.'[53]

It took some time for Washington to obtain a full picture of what had happened on Oahu. Late in the afternoon (Washington time) General Short's first report arrived in the White House, via General Marshall. It understated the damage to the Army airfields, although Short did note that there had been little sabotage. Approximately four hours after the attack Admiral Kimmel made his initial report, which arrived in Washington late on Sunday afternoon: 'Despite security measures in effect surprise attack by Japanese bombing planes damaged all battleships except Maryland X Moderate damage to Tennessee and Pennsylvania X Arizona total wreck West Virginia resting on bottom still burning Oklahoma capsized California resting on bottom Nevada moderate damage beached.' There was no speculation about the nature of the attack, but countermeasures were reported: '2 carriers 7 heavy cruisers 3 squadrons destroyers and all available planes searching for enemy X Personnel behaviour magnificent in face of furious surprise attack.'[54]

At 2.15 p.m. Roosevelt telephoned the British Ambassador and caught him as he was about to go out for a horseback ride. He asked Lord Halifax to inform London of the attack. 'So that's that,' Halifax noted in his diary that evening. 'If war was to come with Japan I can't imagine any way in which they could have acted so as more completely to rally, united [sic] and infuriate American opinion.'[55]

* * *

General Brooke attended a second meeting of the British Chiefs of Staff in London from 5.00 p.m. to 7.00 p.m. After dinner, at home, he learned that Japan had attacked America. There was no longer any question of Britain going to war with Japan on its own. 'All our work of last 48 hours wasted! The Japanese have now ensured that the USA are in the war.'[56]

At Chequers Churchill had dinner with Ambassador Winant and Averell Harriman, FDR's Special Envoy in Britain. Harriman recalled that Churchill seemed tired and depressed; 'He didn't have much to say throughout dinner and was immersed in his thoughts, with his head in his hands part of the time'.[57] The party listened to the BBC nine o' clock bulletin.

> The news has just been given [the announcement began], that Japanese aircraft have raided Pearl Harbor, the American naval base in Hawaii. The announcement of the attack was made in a brief statement by President Roosevelt. Naval and military targets on the principal Hawaiian Island of Oahu have also been attacked. No further details are available.

A few minutes later came a transatlantic telephone call from Washington telling the Prime Minister the news directly. Churchill later recalled the conversation; 'It's quite true,' the President had said, 'They have attacked us at Pearl Harbor. We are all in the same boat now.'[58]

Shortly afterwards news also arrived from Malaya. John Martin, Churchill's secretary, passed on a message from the Admiralty. He jotted down Admiral Layton's report from Singapore, relayed by telephone from Whitehall: 'Report from Kota Bharu. An attempt is being made to land from 3 or 5 (? Transports). One landing craft is already approaching mouth of river.'[59]

The remainder of the evening was filled with official telephone conversations and, no doubt, discussion. As the Prime Minister himself put it, having the United States on Britain's side was to him 'the greatest joy'. He was clearly thrilled at the news of the Japanese attack on the United States. (Churchill had little information about the scale of the damage to the US Pacific Fleet, and he may well have expected that the effect of the 'raid' would be far less harmful than it actually was.) Even the uncontested landing in Thailand's Kra Isthmus and the unexpected assault on Kota Bharu in Malaya seemed less than a fatal threat. We have seen that Churchill and his advisers expected a delay of several months before the Japanese forces could attempt an advance through northern Malaya to Singapore. 'So we had won after all!' was the phrase in his memoirs. Famously, Churchill recalled his final response to the day: 'Being saturated and satiated with emotion and sensation, I went to bed and slept the sleep of the saved and thankful'.[60]

* * *

In the evening, probably after Churchill had retired to his bed, a crucial meeting was held in the Oval Room of the White House. It began as a Cabinet meeting, and later added some invited Congressional leaders, both Democrats and Republicans. The President's aim was to discuss the statement he hoped to make to a joint session of Congress on Monday. Frances Perkins, Secretary of Labor, later dictated a colourful account.[61] It was only six or seven hours since news of the attack had arrived. The room was in a state of confusion as telephones rang and people hurried in and out. Secretary of the Navy Knox was flustered at the failure of his department. Secretary of State Hull was silently enraged at Japanese bad faith. The President was not at all himself. 'He was very serious,' Perkins recalled. 'His face and lips were pulled down, looking quite gray. His complexion didn't have that pink and white look that it had when he was himself. It was a queer gray, drawn look'.

When President Roosevelt finally spoke, he described this as the most serious Cabinet session since the outbreak of the Civil War in 1861. He explained how the situation, diplomatic and military, had developed on the eve of the Japanese attack. He stressed especially the responsibility of Berlin. Talks with Japan had continued until two weeks ago 'when we received indications from various sources – Europe and Asia – that the German government was pressing Japan for action under the Tripartite Pact. In other words, an attempt to divert the American mind and the British mind, from the European field, and divert American supplies from the European theatre to the defense of the East Asia theatre.' They had begun to realise, the President continued, 'that the probability of Japan being in earnest was so slim, that it was time to make a definite and final effort to pin them down', to make them agree to cease actions of aggression and try to bring the China war to a close. The result had been the 'Hull Note' of 26 November.

After 26 November the United States had received, the President continued, 'more and more definite information that Japan was headed for war', and that

Tokyo would not accept Secretary Hull's proposals. About a week ago, the build-up in the strategically vital area of Indochina had become evident. '[W]e believed that under pressure from Berlin the Japanese were about to do something', and so the President had written directly to the Emperor. But war had begun. 'We have reason to believe that the Germans have told the Japanese that if Japan declares war they will too. In other words a declaration of war by Japan automatically brings . . .'.

The President read out an outline of his message to Congress, one which focused mainly on the treachery of the attack, rather than any larger issues. Some of the Cabinet members, notably Secretary of State Hull and Secretary of War Stimson, were unhappy that the speech did not (as Stimson put it) connect Japan 'in any way with Germany', and they thought such a connection should be made immediately. Stimson actually spoke up for making a declaration of war on Germany on the following day, but no one supported him.[62]

When the legislators arrived for the second part of the meeting, Roosevelt asked to be allowed to present a short message to Congress. He kept the nature of this message vague, ostensibly because the situation was developing hour by hour, but really (according to Hopkins) because Roosevelt knew that if he said he was going to ask for a declaration of war 'it would be all over town in five minutes'.[63]

Naturally, the President outlined what he knew about the tragic military situation, and there were questions and comments by those who were present, especially after the Congressmen arrived. Stimson recalled that the President's account had a stunning effect: 'They sat in dead silence and after the recital was over they had very few words.' Roosevelt gave the shocking details of the losses at Pearl Harbor (which he put at three or four battleships), and poured cold water on the prospect of any quick offensive. The war would be long, and there was no chance of an immediate revenge blow against Japan. Victory would come through slow strangulation.

## Pearl Harbor II

The Congressional leaders who met in the White House that evening raised the question of what had gone wrong, and who was to blame for the national humiliation at Pearl Harbor. 'I am amazed at the attack by Japan,' said Senator Tom Connally, the powerful Democrat from Texas, 'but I am still more astounded at what happened to our Navy. They were all asleep. Where were our patrols? They knew the negotiations were going on.'[64]

Five years later a Congressional inquiry, after an exhaustive review of the evidence, would set out 'one enigmatical and paramount question': 'Why, with some of the finest intelligence available in our history, with the almost certain knowledge that war was at hand, with plans that contemplated the precise type of attack that was executed by Japan on the morning of December 7 – Why was it possible for a Pearl Harbor to occur?'[65]

Why indeed? The United States government, at its very highest levels, had extraordinary sources of information, mainly the diplomatic intercepts of MAGIC. This information was shared with the professional heads of the Army and Navy; indeed it was generated within the military. The MAGIC intercepts showed that Tokyo had effectively ceased negotiating. They revealed, as well, technical preparation by the Japanese in the area of communications which strongly suggested that their armed forces were contemplating – somewhere, against someone – a form of military action.

The 'war warnings' sent to overseas commands by Admiral Stark and General Marshall from 24 to 27 November were unambiguous. Further diplomatic intercepts and other intelligence became available in Washington after 27 November. Diplomatic intercepts gave details of talks between Tokyo and Berlin, and more information became available about Japanese communications preparations. On 3 December Admiral Stark's office warned the American commanders overseas about the Japanese disposal of cipher machines in London and the Far East. Meanwhile the Japanese build-up, in and around Indochina, was revealed, and early on 6 December an invasion convoy was sighted heading south. This news also was made available to the overseas commanders.

The largest share of responsibility for the scale of disaster on Oahu must lie with the commanders on the spot, Admiral Kimmel and General Walter Short.[66] Kimmel was preoccupied with training the fleet and with readying it for strikes against the Marshall Islands in the event that the US declared war on Japan. Short, an infantryman, was preoccupied with preparing for an enemy invasion and for coping with potential 'fifth column' activity from within the large ethnic Japanese population. Neither fully addressed the danger of air attack, nor requested appropriate resources from the continental US.

The first investigation into the causes of the Pearl Harbor fiasco, the Roberts Commission, produced its conclusions in January 1942. It placed the principal blame squarely on the two local commanders. There had been a 'dereliction of duty' on the part of these two officers in that they did not fully consult with one another, and an 'error of judgement' in that they 'failed properly to evaluate the seriousness of the situation' or to make 'suitable dispositions' to meet an attack. Kimmel and Short were removed from their posts in Hawaii almost immediately after the raid, and in February 1942 they were retired from military service. The definitive Congressional Investigation, in 1946, also blamed the local commanders, although it did also consider broader problems of military organisation and cuture, as well as military shortcomings in Washington. The Joint Committee concluded, moreover, that the mistakes made by the Hawaiian commanders were 'errors of judgement' rather than 'derelictions of duty'.[67]

Some historians have attempted to show that the fault for the defeat at Pearl Harbor lies elsewhere, especially with poor handling or transmission of intelligence in Washington.[68] Such shortcomings certainly existed, but they do not excuse Kimmel or Short. Other writers have put forward a different line of argument. They blame key figures in the American government (notably President Roosevelt) or in the governments of its future allies (notably Prime Minister Churchill). These leaders, it is alleged, were not only aware of the general threat of war with Japan, but they also knew about the plan to attack Hawaii. Because they wished to bring the United States into the war (either against Japan or Germany), and to galvanise American public opinion, they allowed the surprise attack to go ahead and did not send a warning to Hawaii. There is, however, no evidence to support these theories, nor is it plausible that a high-level conspiracy involving the political and military leadership of two major democracies could be kept secret for seventy years.[69]

What is true is that the political and military leaders in Washington did not, any more than Kimmel or Short, expect a Japanese air attack on Pearl Harbor. The war warnings which they issued did not specifically mention a threat to Hawaii. The American high command also had not sent sufficient equipment and personnel to allow the defenders of Hawaii to detect with certainty, let alone to fend off, an attack. The overall strategy of the United States – for which Admiral Stark and General Marshall, as well as President Roosevelt, Secretary of the Navy Knox, and Secretary of War Stimson, were responsible – was poor. Especially significant was the failure to ensure closer Army-Navy collaboration in the overseas bases or to order that long-range patrol aircraft were to be used first and foremost to screen and defend the essential base area in Hawaii, rather than being earmarked for impractical schemes in the Philippines or the Marshall Islands.

Arguments will no doubt continue about the responsibility and fate of the Hawaiian commanders, particularly Admiral Kimmel. But we can condense what happened to its essentials. The attack on Oahu was the greatest single defeat in American military history. Kimmel and Short were the officers in charge. Neither could be left in post after the fiasco. The two men had been clearly warned by Washington about the danger of war, and they failed to make adequate preparations.[70]

* * *

There were shortcomings on the part of the commanders in Hawaii, and mistakes were made in Washington. But absolutely essential for any answer to the question – set by the Congressional enquiry – 'Why was it possible for a Pearl Harbor to occur?' is an awareness of events in Southeast Asia. This factor is often overlooked today, but contemporaries were certainly aware of it. The 1945–46 Congressional Inquiry put it as follows:

> [J]ust about everybody was blinded or rendered myopic by what seemed to be the self-evident purpose of Japan to attack toward the south – Thailand, Malaysia, the Kra Peninsula [sic], and perhaps the Philippines and Guam. Japan had massed ships and amphibious forces, had deployed them to the south, and had conducted reconnaissance in that direction. So completely did everything point to the south that it appears everyone was blinded to significant, albeit somewhat disguised, handwriting on the wall suggesting an attack on us elsewhere.

Admiral Kimmel said as much when he explained to the Congressional Investigation why he and his staff had thought the Japanese were destroying their codes. 'This information,' he testified, 'fit in with the information which we had received about a Japanese movement in southeast Asia. Japan would naturally take precautions to prevent the compromise of her communication system in the event that her action in southeast Asia *caused Britain and the United States to declare war*, and take over her diplomatic residences.'[71]

* * *

The blame for defeat at Pearl Harbor must, on balance, rest with the American commanders on the spot. In mitigation, it should be said that the Pearl Harbor raid had been a daring, indeed reckless, gamble on the part of the Japanese.[72] Planning and preparing the operation had provoked strong debate in the upper ranks of the Imperial Navy. It is worth pausing the narrative here to recount this remarkable story.

The Pearl Harbor raid was the vision of one man. Admiral Yamamoto Isoroku had been C-in-C of the Japanese Combined Fleet for fourteen months when, in January 1941, he wrote to the Minister of the Navy about the need to further develop the naval air force and to prepare, if war with America became inevitable, to undertake a first strike against the US Navy. At the same time Yamamoto set up, on his own initiative, a small planning team to assess whether an operation against the main base of the Pacific Fleet, at Hawaii, was feasible.

The round-faced, clean-shaven little Admiral – Yamamoto was only five feet three inches tall, short even by Japanese standards of the time – enjoyed enormous authority and popularity in the Imperial Navy.[73] He was self-confident, energetic and intelligent, somewhat eccentric in his personal habits, and very well-informed both about changing technology and the world outside Japan. He was an enthusiastic games-player – of bridge, poker, *Mah-jong* and *Shogi*. Calculated risk was an outstanding feature of his way of thinking, and of the operation for which he is most famous.

Born into a samurai family, Yamamoto entered the fleet through the Naval Academy in 1901. The war with Russia began before he graduated, and in 1905 he took part as a midshipman in the crushing victory at Tsu-shima, where he was injured (in a gunnery accident). The young man was identified as an officer of great potential, and promotion was rapid. He was selected for foreign duty; he had two years at Harvard University after the First World War, and a tour in the mid-1920s as naval attaché in Washington, as well as postings to London in 1929 and 1934 for naval disarmament conferences. In December 1936 he became Vice Minister of the Navy, a post he held until August 1939.

Yamamoto was a truly remarkable officer.[74] In the 1920s he realised that the future of naval warfare lay with the aeroplane, and one of his first major commands was the new *Akagi* (the future Pearl Harbor flagship). He was a champion of carrier- and land-based naval aviation in the 1930s, with his work in the Naval Air Department. It was due to Yamamoto, more than anyone else, that the Imperial Navy could, in late 1941, assemble a task force of six aircraft carriers, with over four hundred combat aircraft. This was much the most powerful naval force in world. The US Navy would not match it until late 1943, and a British admiral would not command such a fleet until 1945. As fate would have it, Yamamoto would be killed sixteen months after Pearl Harbor when the Navy bomber in which he was travelling to make a front-line inspection was shot out of the sky over the Solomon Islands by American long-range fighters.

Yamamoto also overturned existing conceptions from the 1920s and 1930s about how a war against United States Navy would be fought. The strategy of Combined Fleet had been focused on a 'battle of interception' (*yōgeki*

1 **Ambassador Ōshima Hiroshi and Adolf Hitler**

This photograph dates from 1939. In the first days of December 1941, Ōshima, the Japanese Ambassador to Berlin, had difficulty contacting Hitler, as his government attempted to obtain support for the attack on Britain and the US. Ōshima was a General in the Imperial Japanese Army; he served in Berlin as Military Attaché and then as Ambassador. His intercepted messages to Tokyo were a vital source of intelligence for the Allies throughout the war.

2 **Field Marshal Fedor von Bock**

Von Bock was C-in-C of Army Group Centre, the largest German command on the Eastern Front. An enthusiastic supporter of a continued advance on Moscow in mid-November 1941, Bock eventually realised that his men were being pushed beyond endurance. Physically exhausted himself, he was removed from his post in late December.

3 **General Franz Halder and Field Marshal Walther von Brauchitsch**

From 1938 until late December 1941 these two men led the German Army. Brauchitsch (*r.*) was C-in-C of the Army, Halder was Chief of the General Staff. Both strongly urged an unrelenting attack on Moscow in November 1941, believing the Red Army had been fatally weakened. Hitler blamed Brauchitsch for the subsequent defeat and took over his post.

4 **General Georgii Zhukov**

In October 1941, when the Moscow front seemed in danger of collapse, Stalin installed General Zhukov as C-in-C of Western Army Group. Resolute and ruthless, Zhukov led the successful defence of the city and carried out the successful counterattack. He is shown here, in November 1941, reading an incoming message from a teletype tape.

5 **President Roosevelt and Prime Minister Churchill aboard *Prince of Wales*, 10 August 1941**

The relationship between these two leaders was crucial to the events of December 1941. They first met, face to face, during the August 1941 conference at Argentia Bay, Newfoundland. The meeting was held partly aboard the British battleship *Prince of Wales*, which would be sunk four months later off Malaya. The conference developed plans for a possible war with Germany and its allies. Standing behind Churchill are Admiral King (*l.*) and Admiral Stark. Harold Stark, as Chief of Naval Operations, was a close adviser to FDR and an advocate of a strategic policy which prioritised war with Germany. Errors of judgement made at the time of the Pearl Harbor attack would lead to his replacement by Admiral King.

6 **Lord and Lady Halifax**

E.F.L. Wood, Viscount Halifax, served as the British Ambassador to Washington, and was a key intermediary between Churchill and Roosevelt. In mid-November he bet Lady Halifax that Britain would not be at war with anyone new before the end of the year. On 4 December he concluded, on the basis of intelligence revelations, that the wager was lost and that 'the Japanese balloon' would go up in a day or two. The previous evening FDR had given him a verbal promise of support if Britain became involved in a war with Japan.

7 **Operation CRUSADER, November–December 1941**

A German Panzer IV tank on fire in the Libyan desert; in the background a British 'cruiser' tank. In December 1941 Churchill and his generals were preoccupied with their offensive in Libya, where they hoped for a decisive victory over Rommel's armour, followed by the rapid conquest of North Africa and the collapse of Italy. What forces Britain could spare were sent to Libya; there were no British tanks at all in Malaya. Although not as quick a victory as first hoped for, CRUSADER eventually threw the Axis out of eastern Libya. In the event, the demands of the Far East enabled a rapid German counterattack.

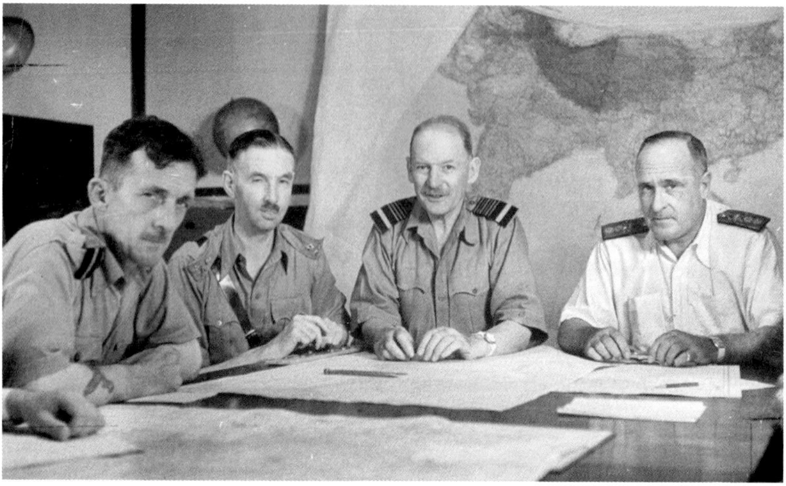

**8 The British commanders in Malaya, 1941**

Seated (*l. to r.*) around the table are Air Marshal Pulford, General Percival, Air Marshal Brooke-Popham and Admiral Layton. Robert Brooke-Popham, overall C-in-C of British ground and air forces in the Far East, was well out of his depth; he was awaiting replacement when the Japanese attacked. Percival conducted the shambolic defence of Singapore, and signed the surrender of the fortress in February 1942. Pulford died tragically during the evacuation. Layton (who was temporarily replaced by Admiral Phillips) later wrote a scathing condemnation of British policy.

**9 RAF Catalina flying boat**

This patrol bomber, known in the US Navy as the PBY, was bought in quantity for the RAF and assigned the name 'Catalina'. One of the RAF Catalinas was shot down by the Japanese over the Gulf of Siam on 7 December, sixteen hours before the outbreak of the war. The US Pacific Fleet operated eighty-one PBYs but was unable to organise adequate search patrols around Hawaii.

10 **Joseph Stalin signs the Declaration of Friendship and Mutual Assistance with Poland, 4 December 1941**

German troops were only twenty miles from the Kremlin. The five men nearest Stalin are (*l. to r.*) Politburo member Malenkov, General Anders, Ambassador Kot, General Sikorski and Foreign Commissar Molotov. Sikorski, head of the Polish government in exile, had come to Moscow to normalise relations with the Russians and make an agreement about evacuating Polish prisoners and internees. Two years earlier Stalin and Hitler had partitioned Poland; now Poland and the USSR were uneasy allies.

11 **Tending to German wounded on the Moscow front**

As German Army Group Centre attempted to envelop Moscow in November and December its losses increased in the face of fierce Soviet resistance and its men became progressively more exhausted. The cold and snow further reduced German combat strength. The Russians calculated that the enemy would not be able to resist a counterattack.

12 **The air raid on Pearl Harbor, 7 December 1941**

This photograph (facing southeast) was taken at the very beginning of the attack, just after 7.55 a.m. Above Ford Island, in the centre of the photograph, eight ships are lined up in 'Battleship Row'. Spray from a torpedo hit rises next to the battleship *Oklahoma*; she eventually capsized. Two ships on the west side of the island (*l.*) are on fire and one is listing. On the extreme right, black smoke rises from the seaplane base on Ford Island.

13 **Admiral Yamamoto Isoroku**

Yamamoto commanded the main force of the Imperial Japanese Navy, the Combined Fleet. Dubious about the long-term prospects of a conventional naval war with the wealthier United States, he single-handedly pushed forward the plan for a surprise attack on Pearl Harbor.

14 **Admiral Tom Phillips**

Phillips (*r.*) sailed from Britain to take command of a new Eastern Fleet. His capital ships, *Prince of Wales* and *Repulse*, arrived in Singapore on 2 December. Admiral A.F.E. Palliser (*l.*) was his Chief of Staff. Seven days later Palliser, ashore in Singapore, sent Phillips a report warning of a possible landing at Kuantan on the southeast coast of Malaya. This turned out to be a false alarm, but Phillips's Force 'Z' was caught off Kuantan by Japanese bombers. His ships were sunk, and he was killed.

15 ***Prince of Wales* and *Repulse* under Japanese air attack, 10 December 1941**

The sinking of the two capital ships of Force 'Z' by Japanese land-based planes off Malaya was a greater disaster than Pearl Harbor. It meant the end of British sea power in the Far East, and led to the fall of Singapore. The picture shows battlecruiser *Repulse* bracketed by bombs dropped from 10,000 feet. These could do little damage to armoured ships; the fatal hits came from low-level torpedo planes.

16 **Hitler declares war on the United States, 11 December 1941**

A grand meeting of the German Reichstag was held in the Kroll Opera House in Berlin. In a long speech Hitler boasted of successes in Russia, denounced President Roosevelt and explained Germany's reasons for declaring war on the United States; his words were also broadcast over the radio. Goering, the President of the Reichstag, is seated directly behind Hitler.

17 **Senior German leaders at the Reichstag meeting, 11 December 1941**

This rogues' gallery of Nazi leaders, on the stage of the Kroll Opera House, heard Hitler deliver his declaration of war on the US. Seated (*l. to r.*) Propaganda Minister Goebbels, Interior Minister Frick, Field Marshal Keitel, Field Marshal von Brauchitsch, Admiral Raeder and Foreign Minister Ribbentrop. These men doggedly obeyed the Führer's commands, but they often loathed one another.

18 **The Old Reich Chancellery, Berlin**

Hitler held a secret meeting of around fifty senior Nazi Party leaders in his private quarters in the Old Reich Chancellery (*Alte Reichskanzlei*) at Wilhelmstrasse, 77, on 12 December 1941. After discussing setbacks in Russia and the implications of America's entry into the war, Hitler laid out a policy for the deportation and mass murder of Europe's Jews.

*sakusen*) in the mid-Pacific, wearing down and then destroying the Americans as they made their way west towards Japan. On this strategy had been based much of the Navy's pre-war procurement: the long-range land-based attack planes (*rikkō*), heavily-armed cruisers and destroyers, big 'cruiser' submarines, and even midget submarines with their support ships. But the war games and map exercises carried out in the late 1930s had convinced Yamamoto that Japan could not win such a war, once America had mobilised its forces.

In April 1941 Yamamoto had taken the radical organisational step of concentrating most of his carriers into the 1st Air Fleet, under Admiral Nagumo. This was not self-evidently linked to the Pearl Harbor plan – Nagumo and his Chief of Staff were highly alarmed when they first learned about the Hawaii project later in the spring – but it was a vital step. The 1st Air Fleet, reinforced with fast battleships and cruisers, and given the tactical designation 'Mobile Force', would be the instrument of the offensive strike.[75]

Meanwhile the secret planning team set up in in January 1941 had been at work. During the summer of 1941 the torpedo planes, level-bombers, and dive bombers of the 1st Air Fleet received extensive training, partly under conditions similar to those around Pearl Harbor. The Navy's technical workshops developed special attack ordnance – shallow-running torpedoes and the 800kg heavy bombs. In March 1941 Oahu was put under closer surveillance, when a naval intelligence officer, Yoshikawa Takeo, arrived in the consulate in Honolulu with a false name and under diplomatic cover.[76]

In his attack Admiral Yamamoto also intended to make use of the submarines which came under his command (as 6th Fleet). A force of big long-range submarines had been built in the 1920s and 1930s to engage the Americans as they advanced across the Pacific. In late July 1941 it was decided that much of this force would be concentrated in Hawaiian waters, in order to ambush the US Pacific Fleet as it sallied forth from Pearl Harbor, or fled to the east after the air attack. On 7 December there were no fewer than twenty-six big Japanese submarines ringing Oahu.[77] During the summer the submarine command also suggested that some 'midget' submarines might be used to penetrate Pearl Harbor and sink surviving ships after the air attack; this was approved only in the middle of November, and it was one of these boats that was sunk by the destroyer *Ward* at dawn on 7 December.[78]

Up to mid-October, all the thinking about the Hawaii project had taken place within the staff of Yamamoto's Combined Fleet. There was no official participation by the highest authorities of the Navy, let alone the Army or the government. The Imperial Navy's existing 1941 plan in the event of war with

America – the plan was updated annually – envisaged the seizure of the Philippines and Guam. No mention was made of a strike nearer the potential enemy's homeland.[79] The planning situation grew more complicated, and more problematic with regards to an all-out raid on Hawaii, as the requirements of the simultaneous Southern Operation became apparent. The highly ambitious invasion of Malaya, the Philippines and the Dutch East Indies would require a large commitment of ships and aircraft from Combined Fleet. There was information, too, that what the Japanese called the 'ABD' powers – the Americans, British and Dutch – were building up their own naval and air forces in Southeast Asia.

On paper Yamamoto did not control the Imperial Japanese Navy. However, the Navy ministers in 1941, successively Admiral Oikawa and Admiral Shimada, had little role in operational matters, and as individuals were not especially strong-willed.[80] The real counterweight to Combined Fleet, and theoretically superior to it, was the Naval General Staff (*Gunreibu*) or NGS, located in Tokyo; from April 1941 this important organisation was headed by Admiral Nagano Osami. Nagano was two years senior to the C-in-C of Combined Fleet. He had served as Minister of the Navy (indeed he had prevailed on Yamamoto to serve as his Vice Minister in 1936). He had commanded Combined Fleet for eleven months in 1937. The Chief of the Naval General Staff was committed to war with Britain and America – it will be recalled that he spoke at the Imperial Conference of 1 December 1941. He knew all about the Southern Operation. But he was not officially informed about Yamamoto's high-risk Hawaii project until August 1941, when a series of war games were held at the Naval Staff College in Tokyo.

There was also growing pressure from Admiral Kondō and the other officers now assigned to command the Southern Operation (they were also part of Combined Fleet) to be given more resources for their difficult task in Malaya and the Philippines. These operations would be greatly eased if they had the support of some of 1st Air Fleet's carriers. The NGS decided in October to assign three of the best-trained Mobile Force carriers – *Akagi*, *Hiryū* and *Sōryū* – to support the 'Southern Operation', along with half the vital tankers Yamamoto had earmarked for the Hawaii voyage.

Not until near the end of October – only six weeks before the actual attack on Pearl Harbor – did Admiral Yamamoto finally get his way. Early in the month, when Combined Fleet staff representatives travelled to Tokyo to explain the details of Hawaiian operations, they were met by opposition from the NGS. Tokyo argued that it would be impossible to achieve surprise, that taking such a great risk was strategically unnecessary, and that the problem of refuelling the Pearl Harbor task force was insurmountable. Admiral Fukudome, Nagano's chief planner, later recalled that the NGS estimated that the air attack by the Mobile Force had only a 50 per cent chance of success.[81] The NGS only gave in when Yamamoto sent a senior officer to Tokyo (on 18 October) with the ultimate threat: the C-in-C and his entire staff would resign unless Combined Fleet was allowed to mount the Hawaiian operation, and with the full force of six carriers.

Six days later, on 24 October, Yamamoto made the case for the Hawaiian operation for one final time. This time he wrote to his Naval Academy classmate and friend Shimada, who had just taken over as Navy Minister. Yamamoto now couched the argument he had been making since January 1941 in global terms. The planned Southern Operation would inevitably involve heavy losses, leaving the Navy weakened when the inevitable American counterattack began. 'I have come to the conclusion,' the Admiral wrote, 'that the only way is to have a powerful [carrier] air force strike deep at the enemy's heart at the very beginning of the war and thus to deal a blow, material and moral, from which it will not be able to recover for some time.' The venture was risky, but no more so than 'the idea of going to war against America, Britain and China [sic] following four years of exhausting operations in China and with the possibility of fighting Russia.' Such a conflict might involve ten years of war over a vast area. 'If in the face of such odds, we decide to go to war . . . I, as the authority responsible for the fleet, can see little hope of success in any ordinary strategy.' The samurai Admiral then cited three battles in medieval Japanese history which had been won by surprise attack.[82]

It was only on 5 November that the orders for the Hawaiian Operation were officially issued, alongside those for the Southern Operation. This was only a week before the first ships began to sortie for the Pearl Harbor attack. It was a reflection of the peculiarities of the Japanese constitution that very few individuals outside the top echelons of the Navy were told about the mission, just as they had not been consulted about the feasibility studies and planning that had been conducted in Combined Fleet throughout 1941. It is possible that the charmed circle excluded even General Tōjō Hideki, Minister of the Army until 18 October, and Prime Minister thereafter. Tōjō later testified that he did not know about the Pearl Harbor plan when he met Army and Navy leaders after becoming Prime Minister, and that he was only informed about the operation at a conference in November. Indeed, Tōjō maintained that he had thought it might be possible to go to war with Britain and the Netherlands without involving the United States, and that even if the Americans were directly involved, Japanese action would be confined to an attack on the Philippines.[83]

We need, then, to have some sympathy for the American commanders who thought in terms of 'ordinary strategy'. For them a mass air raid on Hawaii was unfeasible. A number of Admiral Yamamoto's most senior colleagues in the Imperial Japanese Navy thought just the same thing.[84]

## East Prussia

It was late on the evening of 7 December when the historic news from the Far East arrived at the WOLFSSCHANZE headquarters in East Prussa. Adolf Hitler knew that the Japanese might take action in Southeast Asia, but he had no inkling of the attack on Hawaii. The Führer was in the lounge of his bunker, relaxing after dinner and talking with colleagues – including his female secretaries and his Foreign Ministry liaison Walther Hewel – about the winter supply for the army in Russia. It was very late in the evening when Heinz Lorenz, a press officer, burst in with news that the American radio had announced the attack on Pearl Harbor. A delighted Hitler then rushed, in turn, to the quarters of Field Marshal Keitel and Jodl, his senior military subordinates at Wehrmacht headquarters, waving a telegram. It was the only time in the whole war (according to Keitel) that the Führer did anything of the sort. General Warlimont recalled that a 'frenzy of joy' seized the entire HQ complex, including the sober specialists of the Wehrmacht planning staff – who should have known better.[85]

For Goebbels in Berlin the news came 'like lightning out of a clear sky'. The Führer telephoned, and the Propaganda Minister found that Hitler was 'extremely pleased by this development'. Hitler arranged with him to summon the Reichstag on Wednesday, 10 December (the meeting would later be moved back to the 11th). It is possible that Hitler did not explicitly say he would use the session to declare war on United States, but Goebbels recorded in his diary that German involvement could probably not be avoided. (Hitler had for some weeks been planning, according to Goebbels, to make a major speech to the Reichstag on the war situation.)[86]

Ambassador Ōshima, who heard the news at 11.00 p.m., immediately went to call on Ribbentrop. When the two men met that night, the Reich Foreign Minister confirmed that America and Japan had indeed commenced hostilities, and then informally promised German support. In a message to Tokyo, Ōshima reported Ribbentrop's comments: 'although he had not yet secured Hitler's sanction, the immediate participation in the war by Germany and Italy was a matter of course'. This being the case, Ribbentrop had concluded, the secret agreement drafted on the 5th would no longer be required. The form of Germany and Italy's entry into the war would be determined on the following day.[87] Ribbentrop telephoned Italian Foreign Minister Ciano in the middle of the night of 7–8 December, exultant at the news of the Japanese attack.[88]

All this should not be seen too much from hindsight. On the night of 7–8 December Hitler could not know with certainty how successful the initial strike against Hawaii had been. He could not predict the run of later Japanese successes after the raid – the invasion of Malaya and the Philippines, followed by the fall of Burma and the Dutch East Indies. On the other hand he could now be sure that the worst outcome – a *modus vivendi* between the US and Japan – had been avoided. In that case President Roosevelt might have been able to bring America into the war against Germany with all its resources (along the lines of the Victory Program) while Japan remained neutral.

We know that Prime Minister Churchill 'slept the sleep of the saved and thankful'. What ran through Adolf Hitler's mind at WOLFSSCHANZE that night is guesswork. Hitler was pleased by these developments, and once he heard the news about the Japanese attack on American territory he almost certainly had no reservations about Germany making its own declaration of war against the United States. In a conversation with Goebbels on 21 November he had predicted that US entry into the war was not an 'an acute danger', and the Americans had no means to shake Germany's hold on the European continent.[89]

From Hitler's perspective there were advantages, both long- and short-term, in declaring war on the United States. To his private circle in January 1942 he proclaimed his perception of the country: 'I have feelings of hatred and deep repugnance against *Amerikanismus*. . . . America is in its spiritual attitude half Judaised and negrified.'[90] The German dictator hated Roosevelt and his 'Jewish advisers'. Neutral America was already conducting a policy which heavily favoured Britain, and for the next year or so could do little more to help Britain even if it were a belligerent. Involvement in a Pacific War would preoccupy the American forces and keep them away from Europe.

In the shorter term, there were political and propagandist benefits. By declaring war on the United States the Führer would still be seen to be in control of Germany's destiny. The Axis as a whole would regain the strategic momentum. Japanese victories would mask problems in Russia – events which had preoccupied Hitler throughout that Sunday. They currently amounted to an embarrassing setback for the Wehrmacht, and perhaps they were something worse.

In any event, Sunday, 7 December, had been a momentous day. 'Now this war is a World War in the truest sense of those words,' Goebbels recorded in his diary. 'From the smallest beginnings its ripples now affect the entire globe.'[91]

CHAPTER 11

# MONDAY, 8 DECEMBER
# The Beginning of the End of the British Empire

*We are ready. We have had plenty of warning and our preparations are made and tested.*

Air Marshal Brooke-Popham

*The unexpectedly early onset of severe winter conditions in the East, and the supply difficulties which follow from this, force the immediate adjustment of major offensive operations and a transition to the defensive.*

Adolf Hitler, *OKW* Directive No. 39

*Today all of us are in the same boat with you and the people of the Empire and it is a ship which will not and can not be sunk.*

Franklin D. Roosevelt to Winston Churchill

## Wake, Guam, the Philippines, Japan

The sun rose on a new day, Monday, 8 December 1941, at Wake Atoll in the Central Pacific. Malaya and Thailand lay three time zones to the west; there it was still a few hours after midnight, and Japanese troops were still coming ashore at Kota Bharu and on the Kra Isthmus. Far to the east was Oahu, two time zones away and beyond the International Date Line; the day there was still Sunday, the 7th, and the second Japanese air strike was still hammering Pearl Harbor and the air fields on Oahu. The Marine garrison on Wake learned about the Hawaiian attack from a radio report at 7.00 a.m.[1] By that time another Japanese strike force from the Imperial Navy, numbering twenty-seven long-range bombers, had taken off from Roi, 740 miles to the south in the Marshall Islands. At noon, after a six-hour outward leg, the Japanese force would arrive over Wake. The Marines were caught by surprise when the Japanese bombers dropped out of a rain squall and carried out a low-altitude formation attack. Many island facilities, including the Pan American flying-boat terminal, were damaged. Most important, seven of the Marine fighter planes that had been flown in during the previous week were destroyed where they stood on the tiny airstrip.

The American possession of Guam lay 1,500 miles further west across the expanse of Pacific, about halfway between Wake and the Philippines.[2] Guam was no tiny atoll; it was a proper island, a third the size of Oahu, with an indigenous population of 20,000. The United States had provided no defences beyond a token detachment of Marines. Guam learned of the Pearl Harbor attack before sunrise, and around three hours later seaplanes arrived from the Japanese island possession of Saipan, 150 miles to the north. The enemy flyers attacked the handful of local military targets, principally the small Marine barracks on the Orote Peninsula and some small craft in the harbour.

* * *

The Japanese began their raid on Pearl Harbor at 7.55 a.m. on Sunday, 7 December (Hawaiian time). In the Philippine Islands this corresponded to 2.25 a.m. in the small hours of Monday, 8 December.[3] Admiral Hart heard the news at 3.00 a.m., General MacArthur just after 4.00 a.m. Both men had received the war warnings from Washington, and unlike Admiral Kimmel in Hawaii they would realistically expect some form of direct attack if war broke out.

General Lewis Brereton was C-in-C of the Far East Air Force (FEAF), with his headquarters at Nielson Field outside Manila. At about 5.00 a.m. Brereton presented himself at MacArthur's offices in the old Spanish Citadel, hoping to urge a heavy-bomber strike with his B-17s against Japanese targets on Formosa. General Sutherland, MacArthur's Chief of Staff, refused access to his boss, who was involved in making other preparations concerning his ground forces and the Philippines civilian authorities.[4]

Douglas MacArthur, at this moment in his epic career, possessed only a limited grasp of air power. The decision to base a large B-17 bomber force in the Philippines was made in Washington, and had nothing to do with him. His discussion with the British Admiral Phillips on Saturday had made clear that he did not think the Philippines faced a fatal or immediate threat. He agreed with Phillips that the Japanese could only reach the central Philippines with unescorted bombers, while the Americans could deploy their fighters anywhere.

> The inability of an enemy to launch his air attack on these islands [MacArthur concluded] is our greatest security. Most fighters are short ranged. I repeat what I said. Even with the improvised forces that I have now, because of the inability of the enemy to bring not only air but mechanised and motorised elements [sic] leaves me with a sense of complete security.[5]

Even when, two days later, war became a reality in the Philippines, the opening shots did not unduy alarm MacArthur. At 6.00 a.m. a handful of Japanese carrier-based fighters and bombers flying in from the east made a raid against the southern Philippines port of Davao on Mindanao Island, nearly 600 miles south of Manila. They attacked (without result) a small US Navy seaplane tender, but destroyed two patrol planes at their moorings. At the other end of the island chain, Japanese planes from Formosa appeared at 8.30 a.m. and bombed two American army camps in northern Luzon, including one at Baguio that served as MacArthur's country residence. Neither of these northern raids had much effect; they were carried out by unescorted Japanese Army bombers, flying at their extreme range.

The Americans' air defence 'system', such as it was, ranged across central Luzon. Manila was the headquarters of both MacArthur and of Brereton (at Nielson Field). At Nichols Field, in the suburbs, were based a pair of 'pursuit' squadrons equipped with the Curtiss P-40E, the most modern fighter in the USAAF inventory. (The Army had complete responsibility for the air defence of the Philippines; there were no Navy or Marine fighters.) The new Army 'filter room' and communication hub, the Air Warning Service (AWS), was also located at Nielson. A rudimentary ground observer system set up by the army in northern Luzon was intended to warn of an approaching air attack over land; the exposed flank on the South China Sea was covered by the coastal airfield at Iba, eighty-five miles northwest of Manila, with a functioning SCR-270B radar and another squadron of twenty-four P-40Es. The main operational bomber base in the Philippines was Clark Field, forty miles inland from Iba, and fifty miles northwest of Manila; Clark was home to about twenty four-engined B-17s of 19th Bombardment Group; Clark was also the headquarters of 24th Pursuit Group.

The Japanese Army's northern strike in the early morning was detected by the radar at Iba Field, as was a Japanese reconnaissance plane out in the South China Sea. The American fighters were sent up to patrol above their bases. Nearly the whole B-17 force at Clark was put into the air and sent out of harm's way. The Far Eastern Air Force, as far as it could be, was on alert.

Then disaster struck. At 10.14 a.m., after waiting four or five hours, MacArthur telephoned Brereton, giving approval for an air strike against

Formosa. The B-17s were to return to Clark Field and prepare for the attack. Most of the fighters, running low on fuel after their morning sorties, were also ordered to land. There was now no air patrol over Clark, and the B-17s were lined up along the runway. Just after noon, at 12.35 p.m., tight formations of twin-engined Japanese bombers suddenly appeared from the north, flying high at around 20,000 feet, and executed an accurate carpet bombing of Clark Field and its aircraft. After the bombers departed, Japanese single-engined aircraft from the escort dove down to ground level to strafe the air base with their cannon and machine guns. This phase of the attack went on for an hour and caused even more damage. A similar raid hit the fighter field at Iba, five minutes after the strike began at Clark. The attackers destroyed many more US aircraft on the ground and put the Iba radar permanently out of commission.

The few American interceptors that got off the ground from Clark and Iba suffered badly from the attacks of roving Japanese Navy fighters, as did planes that got into the air from other bases. This was a military catastrophe on the scale of Pearl Harbor. In the course of the day FEAF lost as many as fifty-five of its seventy-two modern fighters. Only seventeen of the original thirty-five heavy bombers were operational, and nearly all of these were 500 miles away, at remote airfields in the south.[6]

* * *

The Imperial Japanese Navy had arrived in the skies over central Luzon. This was the third strategic mission of the Navy's long-range bombers in the Southern Operation; each involved flights – to target and back – of over 1,200 miles. The first had been the fruitless raid on Singapore twelve hours before, launched from Indochina. The second was the raid on Wake Atoll. The Luzon raid, the largest and most successful thus far, came from Formosa. As far as the British and Americans were concerned the Japanese had revealed a 'secret' weapon.

MacArthur's calculations might have been correct had the Japanese Army been his only opponent. Army aircraft were designed for a war on the continent with Russia, and they had limited range. The Army escort fighters could not reach the Philippines from Formosa; the Army bombers could only reach the northern part of Luzon, and there were only about fifty of them available. It was these aircraft that had mounted the early morning raids on northern Luzon on the 8th.

The Japanese Navy, with Pacific Ocean distances in mind, had designed aircraft with much longer range. Avoiding the inter-service demarcation disputes and funding limitations that hobbled the armed forces of Britain and the United States, the Imperial Navy had developed its own long-range bomber force. Nearly 140 of these aircraft were available on Formosa, and they could fly all way to the central Philippines. Even more remarkable was a single-engined navy fighter, the Zero, which could escort the bombers all the way to their targets, and carry out ground-attack strikes once they got there; ninety of these planes were available. Both fighter and bomber crews had gained much operational experience in China.[7] The most important cause of the destruction of American air power in the Philippines on 8 December, and the days that followed, was the superior training, equipment and experience of these elite Japanese Navy air units.

In addition, on 8 December, the Japanese were lucky that fog on Formosa delayed the take-off of their strike force, because otherwise the American fighters would still have been in the air over their bases. When the delayed strike did arrive, some poor tactical decisions were made by middle-ranking American officers.[8] An airborne American fighter squadron was vectored south to cover the city of Manila – which the Japanese did not attack – rather than to provide defensive cover at Clark Field. Although the Iba radar spotted the approaching Japanese formation, there was a delay in passing the warning to Clark Field, and when it actually arrived there it was inexplicably lost.

Although the big Navy bomber formation would have been flying over the Philippine countryside for at least twenty minutes before reaching its target, the attackers achieved complete surprise. The air raid alarm went off at Clark as the bombs rained down. Another squadron of fighters was kept on the ground at Clark by Army controllers, despite the approaching Japanese force; it was destroyed before it could get airborne. The squadron protecting Iba was called in too late to cover Clark, but just in time to expose its home base to attack.

For the US Army Air Force, the disaster in the Philippines was as bad as Pearl Harbor, and the FEAF command did not have the excuse of tactical surprise, in terms of either timing or distance from Japanese-held territory. The American commanders in Manila knew that some form of Japanese air attack from Formosa was a possibility, and they had nine or ten hours' warning before the Clark Field raid. There were also deeper reasons for the fiasco. The tactical blunders of the morning of 8 December could have such a devastating effect only because of the shortcomings of the vaunted heavy-bomber strategy. A force of bombers had been sent to the Philippines without anything like adequate airfield construction, let alone airfield defences (and even more B-17s were on the way). Clark Field was still under construction, and the aircraft had to be parked together on the limited space of the hardened runways and aprons.

It remains something of a mystery as to why MacArthur took no pre-emptive action with his bombers on the morning of 8 December.[9] A priority should certainly have been consulting with Brereton, his senior air commander. The most likely explanation is that MacArthur did not yet think the air threat to central Luzon was a serious one. Likewise he probably also believed that he had time to assess the overall situation before launching offensive raids on Japanese territory – and by 10.14 a.m. he did indeed give permission for an air strike.

However, even if, before dawn on 8 December, General Brereton had been allowed to launch an immediate attack against Formosa, his bombers could not have prevented the Japanese air attacks, nor achieved any other significant results. There were only fifteen or so operational B-17s at Clark Field; they would have had to fly without fighter escort, and intelligence about the airfields on Formosa was poor.[10] It was, however, a reflection on the quality of Brereton's Far East Air Force that it was never able to mount *any* raids on the Japanese bases on Formosa, either on 8 December or later.

Douglas MacArthur may have been arrogant, blinkered and ignorant of aviation, but he was not to blame for what happened. It was Brereton who was in charge of the functioning of the air defence system and the dispersal of the bomber force. And it was the men in Washington – Secretary of War Stimson, General Marshall, General Henry Arnold (commander of the USAAF), and to some extent the President himself – who attempted a half-baked strategy which provided the Philippines with aircraft but inadequate bases.

* * *

Some 1,700 miles to the north, it was also a new day in Japan. There was a clear blue sky, with no clouds. At 7.30 a.m. on 8 December, Ambassador Grew was beckoned to the residence of Foreign Minister Tōgō. What ensued must surely count as one of the stranger diplomatic encounters of modern history. The attack on Hawaii had begun four hours earlier, but Foreign Minister Tōgō made no mention of this. He informed Grew that the Emperor had asked his government to reply to President Roosevelt's query about the presence of Japanese troops in Indochina. 'We believe the President must be fully aware of the fact that the object of our wishes is the establishment of peace in the Pacific and throughout the world, and that, in accordance with our desires, the Japanese Government has up to the present time striven to attain that goal.' Tōgō courteously saw Grew to his car after the meeting.

The British Ambassador, Sir Robert Craigie, was summoned by Tōgō for a meeting at 8.00 a.m. The Japanese Army had invaded British territory at Kota

Bharu five hours earlier. 'I sensed a certain tension in the atmosphere,' Sir Robert recalled, 'but although the Minister's manner was somewhat stiff, there was nothing to indicate that this was to be our last interview.' Tōgō outlined the note that had been sent to Washington (the fourteen-instalment message). Craigie then mentioned the reports of the previous evening about the approaching Japanese convoy, to which the Foreign Minister professed ignorance. Tōgō bade farewell, expressing regret that Craigie's efforts to maintain peace had failed. 'I cannot but regard it as unfortunate,' Sir Robert would recall in 1943, 'that Mr Togo should have failed to inform me in person either at this interview or at a subsequent one, that the Japanese Government had decided to declare war on my country.'[11]

Under happier circumstances, Eugen Ott was summoned to meet Tōgō during Monday afternoon. Like his American and British colleagues, the German Ambassador was shown a copy of the Japanese note. Ott declared that he was certain that 'Japan's great and momentous decision was attended by the best wishes of the entire German people.' Getting down to business, Tōgō said he hoped Germany would declare war on the United States very soon. Tōgō did explain that no change had occurred to the relationship between Japan and the USSR. Ott raised several times the question of what the Japanese could do to block the port of Vladivostok on Russia's Pacific coast. The port was strategically important to the Germans, as it was one of the last routes by which American supplies could be sent to the Red Army. It would gain in significance if (as was expected) the Wehrmacht was able to seal off Murmansk and Arkhangel'sk in north Russia, and cut the route through Persia. Tōgō replied that the matter was 'not altogether simple,' and he asked for more time to consider it. Thus far, he explained, very little in the way of armaments had been sent by the Vladivostok route.[12]

At 11.00 a.m. the Imperial Rescript declaring war on the United States and the British Empire was issued in the Emperor's name, co-signed by the members of the Cabinet. In the document the Emperor expressed his confidence that the armed forces, public servants and the population as a whole would do everything for the war effort. Much of the third paragraph was devoted to elucidating the peaceful traditions of Japan. War, however, had become inevitable, forced on Japan by America and Britain. Having, as they did, an 'inordinate ambition to dominate the Orient,' those two Powers had continued support for the illegitimate regime in Chungking (i.e. Chiang Kai-shek), they had increased military preparations against Japan and induced other states to follow suit, and finally they had resorted to 'direct severance of economic relations, menacing gravely the existence of our Empire.' They had unduly delayed negotiations. 'The situation being such as it is, Our Empire for its existence and self-defence has no other recourse but to appeal to arms and to crush every obstacle in its path.' It was hoped that 'the sources of evil will be speedily eradicated and an enduring peace immutably established in East Asia, preserving thereby the glory of Our Empire.'[13] This was hardly an objective view of the situation in East Asia, and to some extent it stood reality on its head. All the same, Japanese policy was at least consistent, and it was now out in the open. The question remained: whether the drastic initiative taken by the agressive nationalists who led the Japanese government had successfully met the fundamental challenges that were enumerated in the Rescript, or whether they had, in the long term, only made things worse.

That morning the Main Body of Combined Fleet raised anchor in Hashirajima Bay. Admiral Yamamoto flew his flag aboard battleship *Nagato*. The column of six massive dreadnoughts debouched through the Bungo Channel into the open Pacific. The Japanese, ever cautious, had swept the channel for mines and they proceeded on strict watch for American submarines. Yamamoto set course 140° (SE). This squadron's mission was to provide very long-range support for Nagumo's Mobile Force in case it was pursued from Oahu. No doubt the sortie also had a morale-boosting role for the big-gun ships and their crews, too slow to accompany the carriers. They were destined to play little active role in the war until October 1944.[14]

## Malaya and Thailand

The Japanese had struck everywhere, simultaneously. The big convoy in the South China Sea, originally from Hainan Island, had broken up, with three of the ships proceeding to Kota Bharu in Malaya and arriving there shortly after midnight (on 8 December).

At around 2.00 a.m. on 8 December the sixteen transport ships of the main Japanese invasion force arrived off Singora and Patani on the Kra Isthmus, carrying three regiments of 5th Division. Cranes were used to lower about a hundred landing craft, and within an hour the troops had begun to climb down rope ladders into the tossing boats. The sea was rough, with waves as high as three metres, and many landing craft foundered.[15] Some smaller ports farther north were also occupied to open the route into southern Burma.[16]

For the Japanese invasion force the really dangerous moments came on 7 and 8 December, when their transport ships were most exposed to British air attack. A combination of skilful Japanese manoeuvres, poor weather and British political uncertainty had prevented any air attacks during the approach on the 7th (local time). The main RAF air attacks, early the following morning, were concentrated off Kota Bharu rather than targeted against Singora or Patani, let alone the Japanese bomber bases in Indochina. An attempted mass strike by five 'Blenheim' light-bomber squadrons, operating from four aerodromes, found no targets off Kota Bharu aside from the mortally damaged *Awazisan Maru*, and some landing craft. The weather conditions, with a low cloud base, were far from ideal for air attacks.

By the end of 8 December the Japanese had passed through the period of highest risk. The RAF aerodromes in the north of Malaya had been neutralised or captured. The bulk of 5th Division was ashore, and Japanese Army fighters could provide cover from landing strips at Singora. In the post-war discussion on the draft of the British official history General Percival claimed that the local RAF command had assured the Army that the air attacks would inflict 40 per cent damage on a 'hostile seaborne expedition before it reached the shores of Malaya'. In reality, Percival claimed, 'the maximum loss inflicted by the Air Force was one ship (which was also claimed by field artillery)' – surely a reference to *Awazisan Maru* off Kota Bharu. There was much justice in this particular claim; the attempt to defend Malaya by air power had proved to be a dismal failure.[17]

The landings thus went off more or less as planned, and with low losses. Nevertheless, the Japanese forces available for the invasion of southern Thailand and Malaya and for the operations of the first weeks of the war were small, as a result of shipping and supply limitations. Although on paper the 25th Army consisted of four divisions, the initial force involved in the main fighting south of the Kra Isthmus comprised only three regiments from 5th Division, with some supporting troops. On 8 December, 13,500 men were landed at Singora, and 7,550 at Patani, and only two-thirds of these men were combat soldiers. Another regiment (from 18th Division) had landed at Kota Bharu, but its operations would be confined to eastern Malaya. The three regiments of the Imperial Guards Division crossed into Thailand by land from Indochina, but that division had to assure control of Thai territory, and it was not scheduled to be available in Malaya until the fourth week of December. Other Japanese troops were due to arrive in the battle zone when shipping and supplies became available at the end of the month. The fourth division of Japanese 25th Army, the 56th, was held in reserve in Japan and never deployed.[18]

Japanese strategy had been based on a careful calculation of relative strength. At the Imperial Conference of 5 November General Sugiyama, Chief of the Army General Staff, produced figures for the strength of potential opponents in the Far East. These may be taken as the Japanese Army's definitive intelligence assessment. British ground forces in Malaya were estimated to number 60–70,000 men. Only about 30 per cent were white 'homeland' soldiers; the remainder, although used to tropical conditions, 'did not have sufficient education and training, and their fighting ability is generally inferior'. British air strength in Malaya was more worrying. The RAF had 320 aircraft; it was believed that 'the quality of their aircraft is excellent and their pilots are comparatively skilled'. On 1 December Sugiyama reported on final British deployments; some 6–7,000 additional troops had arrived in Singapore, but there was no large-scale build-up. The Japanese estimate was impressively accurate, at least as far as ground forces were concerned. The initial strength of the British Empire in Malaya were actually the equivalent of three and a half divisions (thirty-one battalions), numbering 88,600 soldiers, including support echelons. The estimate of air strength, however, was too high. The RAF had available only 158 combat aircraft, and they were not of a high quality.[19]

In view of British numerical superiority on the ground the Japanese needed an outstanding commander and clever tactics. In charge of the forces of 25th Army was General Yamashita Tomoyuki, an able, energetic and determined senior officer who was to become Japan's best-known wartime general: 'The Tiger of Malaya'. Yamashita was a contemporary, and perhaps a rival, of General Tōjō. He had been head of the Army's air department, and had a keen sense of the importance of aviation in modern warfare. He was also well-informed about the recent Blitzkrieg campaigns in Europe, having been sent to Germany on an inspection tour earlier in the year; during this high-level visit he presented a ceremonial sword to Field Marshal von Brauchitsch.[20]

Yamashita was only assigned to the command of 25th Army in November 1941, and he did not take part in the initial planning of the Malayan invasion. But he had to give final approval to the plan of campaign, and it was critically important that he accepted the option of a rapid advance into Malaya, rather than a slower build-up of a base in southern Thailand. The tactical concept was known to the Japanese as *kirimomi sakusen* – 'driving charge' or 'dash advance'. It was hoped that superior Japanese morale, mechanised equipment and extensive air support would overcome numerically superior enemy manpower.

The tactic of *kirimomi sakusen* was put into action from the moment the Japanese came ashore at Singora and Patani. By midnight on the 8th the reconnaissance detachment of the 5th Division, under Colonel Saeki, had reached the Thai-Malaya border, a distance of some fifty miles from Singora. Only seventy-two hours later, the Japanese spearheads would hit the main British defensive position at Jitra. It was the speed of the advance, and the initiative and energy shown by Japanese officers and soldiers, which would doom the British defence of Malaya.

* * *

Unlike the experience of the Americans, the outbreak of war in the Far East did not take the British completely by surprise. At 6.30 a.m. on 8 December, Air Marshal Brooke-Popham and Admiral Layton issued an Order of the Day. This document had been drafted back in May, translated into several languages, and printed and distributed in advance to the various commands. It declared that confidence and enterprise were expected from the fighting services, and patience from the civilian population, be they Malay, Chinese, Indian or Burmese. The cause was 'the preservation in the world of truth and justice and freedom'. The text radiated optimism: 'We are ready. We have had plenty of warning and our preparations are made and tested. . . . We are confident. Our defences are strong and our weapons efficient.' As for the Japanese, the order said nothing about the capabilities of their forces. It did note, however, that Japan was exhausted by the war in China. '[H]er government has flung her into war under the delusion that, by stabbing a friendly nation in the back, she can gain her end. Let her look at Italy and what has happened since that nation tried a similar base action.' As the official British history would put it sixteen years later, 'the wording of this Order of the Day showed how much the official view of the situation on the outbreak of war was out of touch with reality.'[21]

There was still indecision about Operation MATADOR. At 8.00 a.m. on the 8th, the C-in-C, Far East, finally received permission from London to launch the pre-emptive strike into southern Thailand. But Brooke-Popham did not know whether the landing in Malaya (at Kota Bharu) had been accompanied by landings in Thailand (on the Kra Isthmus). 'Do not act' was the order he passed on to Army command in Malaya. He learned of the landings at Singora and Patani at 9.45 a.m. from the report of a British reconnaissance plane. Although this intelligence finally made implementation of the original MATADOR plan impossible – the Japanese had taken the strategic ports first – nobody bothered to tell the British troops in northern Malaya. Due to communications errors the orders were not relayed by the C-in-C to General Percival (the ground-forces commander), and from Percival to General Heath at III Corps, until 1.00 p.m. Only at 1.30 p.m. was the 11th Division finally ordered to stand down and hold the defensive line at Jitra, fifteen miles south of Thai-Malaya frontier. This was an important delay; the hours spent waiting in the rain to set out on an expedition that never took place had a damaging effect on troop morale.

In the afternoon of the 8th a small motorised company of Indian troops was actually sent ten miles into Thailand to conduct reconnaissance and to carry out demolition work. At 9.30 p.m. they ran into a Japanese tank column, moving south with its headlights on, and beat a hasty retreat.

Operation MATADOR has been abandoned, but the British still intended to send a column of troops into Thailand from Kroh (now Pengkalan Hulu), on the northern border of Malaya. They were to advance thirty miles up the rough road towards Patani. The intention was that the Kroh column (KROHCOL) would occupy a defensive position known as the 'Ledge'; this was a steep section of road dug out of a hillside where engineers could, if necessary, block the route. Brooke-Popham initially did not order the battalion (the 3/16th Punjabis)[22] to move, and KROHCOL only crossed the frontier at 3.00 p.m. that Monday afternoon. It was then stalled by roadblocks set up by Thai armed constabulary, and by dusk it was only three miles inside Thailand.

* * *

In Singapore, 600 miles to the south, Admiral Phillips had to make a decision about what the Royal Navy could do to interfere with the Japanese invasion. He must have thought through the options and discussed plans on the ten-hour flight home from the Philippines on the night of 6–7 December. In Singapore he was handed the Admiralty's request to know his plans in the hypothetical case that there was an invasion convoy. During the early hours of the 8th reports came in about the landings at Kota Bharu, Singora and Patani. Phillips signalled the Admiralty at 9.04 a.m. on the 8th. '[I]ntend to proceed with *Prince of Wales* and *Repulse* dusk tonight 8/12 to attack enemy force off Kota Bharu daylight Wednesday 10th.'[23] The big ships left Singapore in the early evening of 8 December, escorted by four destroyers. The squadron was given a new tactical designation: Force 'Z'.

Several different factors lay behind Admiral Phillips's decision to take his ships 'into harm's way'. The Royal Navy traditionally favoured offensive action, even in the face of superior enemy numbers; it assumed the qualitative and moral inferiority of any opponent. The Japanese may have been at war with China for four years, but their ships had not had recent combat experience. Admiral Phillips commanded two fast and powerful capital ships, both equipped with radar. Indeed, at this time *Prince of Wales* had the best radar suite of any operational warship in the world; she mounted air and surface search radars, radar for her main guns, and close-in radar for her anti-aircraft guns.[24] The strength of enemy surface forces in the South China Sea, as far as it was known, was limited. In any event only the four Japanese 'Kongō' class battleships could keep up with Force 'Z', and only one or two of these elderly modified battlecruisers were believed to be in the area.

The air danger was an unknown. Phillips was a surface-ship Admiral, but there was a general assumption that the ships and aircraft of the Japanese Navy were not especially 'efficient'. The Joint Intelligence Committee in London had concluded on 16 November 1941 that any Japanese operations in the South China Sea would require aircraft carriers. Support by land-based aircraft would not be a serious factor.[25] Phillips also knew on the morning of 8 December that at least a portion of the Japanese carrier fleet was nearly 7,000 miles away, in Hawaiian waters.

Phillips's view was based on his (second-hand) knowledge of war off Norway in 1940 and in the Mediterranean in 1941. Long-range multi-engined bombers, flying in tight formation and dropping bombs from high altitude, had had little success against fast moving warships. As for torpedo bombers, the few Italian squadrons had had little success. In his discussions with Hart and MacArthur in Manila on the 6th, Admiral Phillips had explained how British war experience showed that the danger came from dive bombers, based on the successes of German Stukas against cruisers and aircraft carriers in the Mediterranean. But single-engined dive bombers had short range, and they had never sunk a heavily-armoured British battleship.

A British raid against the Japanese off Kota Bharu, or even further north against Singora or Patani in the Kra Isthmus, would put Phillips's ships in a position 300–350 miles away from the new Japanese air bases in southern Indochina. The force would be able to make a night approach run, so the main exposure to daylight air attack would be during withdrawal after the morning of the 10th. The account of Captain L.H. Bell, one of Phillips's staff officers (made during the subsequent Royal Navy enquiry), summed up the intentions of the squadron. The Admiral, Bell recalled, planned a 'high speed descent' on Singora, relying on surprise to avoid damage: 'He calculated that the Japanese aircraft would not be carrying anti-ship bombs and torpedoes, and that his force would only have to deal with hastily-organised long-range bombers from Indochina during its retirement.'[26] That calculation proved to be highly inaccurate.

* * *

Some 1,700 miles north of Singapore, and 500 miles west of Luzon, the British crown colony at Hong Kong was another treasure of the British Empire that came under attack on the morning of 8 December.[27] Hong Kong proper was set at the foot of a large peninsula, with numerous bays and inlets, and rugged terrain. The main populated centres were Hong Kong Island (with the city of Victoria) and Kowloon, which faced it on the mainland. British territory extended a further ten miles north of Kowloon to the Sham Chun (Shenzhen) River at the neck of the peninsula.

The Japanese ground attack was not a tactical surprise, coming as it did hours after the air attack on Singapore and the landing in Malaya. British troops had been on alert since 6.45 a.m. The screening force on the Sham Chun, part of an Indian battalion, blew up the rail and road bridges. Around 8.00 a.m., the Japanese began bridging operations and the three regiments of the Japanese 38th Division – the formation that would carry out the whole Hong Kong operation – crossed the Sham Chun on a broad front. The British fell back on the range of hills north of Kowloon.

General Christopher Maltby's forces left much to be desired. The garrison totalled 12,000 men. The two British-manned infantry battalions were inexperienced and under-strength garrison units. As elsewhere in Asia, the British Empire relied for numbers on the Indian Army, and there were two Indian battalions. Finally, two Canadian battalions had arrived very recently, but these were green troops and far from home. There were no combat aircraft, and no naval forces beyond a few motor torpedo boats. Maltby also had responsibility for nearly two million Chinese civilians, mostly at Kowloon or on Hong Kong Island.

## Russia

On the Russian front the weather was somewhat warmer than on the previous day, but snow continued to fall in places. The Wehrmacht news bulletin covering 8 December was brief and reassuring: 'On the eastern front only local engagements.'[28]

The German Army Headquarters situation report outlined a much more difficult situation: 'Northwest of Moscow the enemy is mounting determined attacks, partly with tank support, against the Panzer Groups.'[29] What was actually happening was that General Rokossovskii's divisions (16th Army), now moving onto the offensive, forced the Germans out of Kriukovo and Krasnaia Poliana; these were the villages on the northern outskirts that had been lost on 30 November. During the night of 8–9 December Rotmistrov's 8th Tank Brigade, attacking with the 30th Army from the north, cut the Kalinin-Klin road. Klin was the central position of Panzer Group 3.

Both wings of von Bock's Army Group Centre were being rolled back. In the south, Guderian's embattled 2nd Panzer Army came under heavy attack. 'The enemy,' the Army Headquarters war diary reported, 'appears to have brought new forces up against the right wing of the Army Group and against Elets.' The 'new forces' were actually the raw levies of Golikov's 10th Army, which were finally making their weight felt. During the night of 7–8 December the town of Mikhailov, on the (north-south) Kashira-Ranenburg railway, was retaken by one of Golikov's divisions, inflicting heavy casualties on the Germans. And Soviet 50th Army in the Tula salient began to attack; Guderian, who for the last two days had been attacked from the east and north, now came under pressure from the west.

In a private letter written on the 8th, General Guderian grumbled – not without a degree of inconsistency – about how the high command had overreached itself. 'I would never have believed that a really brilliant military position could have been so buggered up [*so verbocken kann*] in two months. If a decision had been taken at the proper time to break off and settle down for the winter in a habitable line suitable for defence, we would have been in no danger. For months past now it has all been one great question mark'. In the evening the testy General telephoned the HQ of Army Group Centre in Smolensk. As Field Marshal von Bock put it, Guderian described his army's situation 'in the blackest colours' and implied there was a 'crisis of confidence'. 'He asked for the hundredth time', Bock recalled, 'if the high command was aware of this situation.' The Field Marshal's reply was stark: 'I could not give him reinforcements, either one held out or let oneself be killed. There is no other choice.'[30]

Bock, however, made a similar request for reinforcements to Halder at German Army headquarters in East Prussia. 'There was no single place,' he reported, 'where a strong attack by the Russians could be dealt with', and he went on to stress the urgent need for fresh divisions from the homeland.[31]

* * *

The Wehrmacht news bulletin, released on the morning of the 8th, hinted to the Reich population about an important change: 'The carrying out of operations and the nature of [war leadership] in the East will from now on be influenced by the Russian winter. On broad stretches of the Eastern front only local fighting is taking place.' It was probably no accident that on this same day Hitler released his secret Wehrmacht Directive No. 39.[32]

This directive was not a result of the events of 8 December or even a response to the beginning of Zhukov's offensive on the 6th; the document had been in the drafting process for several days. All the same, Directive No. 39 marked the halt – and failure – of the BARBAROSSA strategy: 'The unexpectedly early onset of severe winter conditions in the East, and the supply difficulties which follow from this force the immediate adjustment of major offensive operations and a transition to the defensive.' The general aim was to regroup and prepare for large-scale offensive operations in the spring of 1942, rather than to deal with an immediate winter crisis. A shorter front line created by tactical withdrawals would allow a reduction and refitting of forces, especially Panzer and motorised formations. The withdrawals were to be accomplished when the new 'rear position' had been established. The problem was that the directive had been issued a month too late, and an orderly regrouping was no longer possible.

Directive No. 39 showed that the Germans were still overreaching themselves. Hitler's orders were that even during the regrouping and reinforcement phase certain 'special tasks' were to be completed. It is true that these did not include the occupation of Moscow, but they were still ambitious and unrealistic: Sevastopol' was to be captured, the Tikhvin-Lake Ladoga railway was to be cut to seal off Leningrad completely, and the line of the lower Don and Donets Rivers near Rostov was to be taken and held by the Army Group South.

On this same day, 8 December, the C-in-C of the German Army issued a directive on 'Tasks of the *Ostheer* [Eastern Army] in the Winter of 1941–42'. 'With the onset of snow and cold,' Field Marshal von Brauchitsch announced, 'the operations of 1941 have essentially come to a conclusion; individual [operations] not terminated will need to be continued through.' Brauchitsch still claimed victory in the campaign, as a result of all the industrial strength than had been stripped from the Russians. 'The task assigned to the *Ostheer* was to smash the mass of the Red Army before it could be pulled back into the depths of Russia. Through the battles of this year this has been to a very large measure achieved. The combat strength of the enemy has been decisively weakened due to the high losses of personnel and materiel.' Further action followed a similar line to Hitler's Directive No. 39, with an emphasis on refitting 'fast troops'; Brauchitsch spoke of resuming the offensive in 1942, beginning with the southern part of the front in April, and followed by the central and northern parts in late May or early June.[33] The Army C-in-C would be proved right in some respects. The German offensive was resumed in 1942, and with considerable success. But Operation BARBAROSSA had been far from the complete triumph that Brauchitsch claimed. Germany had missed its one chance to destroy Soviet Russia.

Directive No. 39 was a medium-term plan, and one overtaken by rapidly changing events. During the course of 8 December, Hitler remained opposed to making withdrawals, at least in the Moscow area, and he was no doubt preoccupied with thoughts of how to deal with the entry of the United States into the war. Major Engel, Hitler's Army adjutant at WOLFSSCHANZE, made notes about the development of the German dictator's thinking. His initial idea was to stand firm, and perhaps to restart operations against the exposed town of Tula south of Moscow. 'F[ührer] . . . embarked – as so often – on an endless monologue. Did not believe in fresh Russian forces, considered it all a bluff, assumed it likely that these were the last reserves.' For Hitler too, there were memories of former setbacks, perhaps including 1914 and the Marne: 'It would not be the first time that Germans had lost their nerve at the fateful hour. He did not want to hear the expression "pull back" again.' General Jodl, head of operations at the *OKW*, expressed some doubts about this rigid policy, but Field Marshal Keitel – always sensitive to the Führer's wishes – did not back him up. Engel noted, however, that Hitler was unsettled and uncertain.[34]

Remarkably, on 8 December Hitler did allow the withdrawal of divisions from Army Group North that were threatened with a tactical encirclement at Tikhvin – despite the fact that the blocking of the Tikhvin-Ladoga railway was one of the 'special tasks' of Directive No. 39. Brauchitsch had approved this withdrawal on the 7th, after a request by the C-in-C of Army Group North, Field Marshal Leeb.[35]

In any event the German dictator now had to turn his attention from the battle front in Russia to questions of high policy and global strategy. On the evening of the 8th Adolf Hitler boarded his special train at WOLFSSCHANZE and set off on the overnight trip to Berlin.

## Germany

In Berlin, Ambassador Ōshima called in to see Reich Foreign Minister Ribbentrop at the Wilhelmstrasse at 1.00 p.m. on 8 December. He requested formal declarations of war on America, at once, by Germany and Italy. Ribbentrop informed him that Hitler was conferring with his senior commanders about how the details would be arranged. The Führer had already that morning, he reported, instructed the German Navy to sink American ships 'whenever and wherever' they met them, although this was to be kept secret for the moment.[36]

Later in the afternoon of the 8th, Ōshima and Ribbentrop discussed, along with legal experts, the new Tripartite declaration. The aim was to impart to this document, as Ōshima put it, 'the loftiest possible significance.' It was brief, with three substantial articles: one, the signatories would continue the war forced upon them by America and Britain, using all forces to bring the struggle to a victorious conclusion; two, they would not conclude an armistice with America and Britain without full mutual agreement; and three, they would continue to co-operate after the victorious conclusion. The text was closely based on what had been sent sent to Tokyo by Ribbentrop on Friday, 5 December, although that was before Pearl Harbor, and it had only been a hypothetical agreement about entry into the war.

The draft of the Tripartite declaration was sent to German Ambassador Ott in Tokyo by Ribbentrop, and to Foreign Minister Tōgō by Ōshima. Ribbentrop sent an accompanying telegram just after midnight on 8–9 December, in which he requested that the draft be approved by Wednesday morning (10 December) at the latest. 'You may mention casually,' Ribbentrop advised, 'that the Japanese Government itself has an interest in expediting this, since the agreement may be announced here in a special form.'[37] The 'special form' was to be Hitler's address to the Reichstag, although the session would soon be postponed from Wednesday afternoon to Thursday afternoon (11 December).

* * *

By chance, these global events coincided with a grave moment in the history of the Holocaust. On this day, 8 December, Hitler's SS began the first systematic use of gas vans to murder Jews, at Chełmno.[38] This event was not the beginning of the Nazi policy of genocide. The racial policies of the Third Reich had already led to large-scale deportations of German Jews to ghettos and concentration camps in Poland and other parts of Eastern Europe, where many had already perished from starvation or maltreatment. Jews in territories conquered by the Wehrmacht in 1939–40 – especially Poland – had also suffered terribly. After the outbreak of Hitler's 'war of annihilation' in Russia on 22 June 1941 the SS had unleashed mobile murder squads (*Einsatzgruppen*), which massacred hundreds of thousands of Soviet Jews of all ages and sexes. By November 1941 small-scale 'transport' of German Jews to killing centres in Latvia and Belorussia had begun.

For the most part, when Nazi policy changed from one of causing death by calculated neglect to outright murder, the method was mass shootings. By the autumn of 1941, however, Himmler and the SS were examining other means of 'extermination', and a pilot death camp was set up in little Polish village of Chełmno (German: Kulmhof), situated forty miles northwest of Łódź, in the part of Poland that had been annexed by the Reich. The apparatus of slaughter consisted of the personnel of SS *Sonderkommando Kulmhof* and a gas van. On 8 December Jews from the local area were brought to a makeshift mass execution centre in the *Schloss* at Chełmno. Stripped of their possessions, the victims were herded into a specially-built van and asphyxiated using carbon monoxide gas. (The method was a legacy of the earlier Nazi euthanasia campaign.) The bodies were then transported in the van to the nearby woods and buried in mass graves.[39] At first, in December and January, Jews from the neighbouring towns were the main victims of the Chełmno site. After that it became the murder centre for the thousands of Jews and Gypsies – from Poland, Germany and elsewhere – who had been concentrated in the Łódź ghetto.

This day, 8 December, was also the day that a proposed meeting of Nazi Party and state officials was postponed indefinitely. The meeting was supposed to have taken place on the 9th, at Wannsee in the suburbs of Berlin.[40] Invitations had been sent out on 29 November on the orders of Reinhard Heydrich, Himmler's deputy in the SS, and the Chief of the Reich Main Security Office (RSHA). The aim of the gathering would have been to discuss the fate, in particular, of the German Jews, and to determine which of them would be subject to deportation.

Unlike the initiation of the terrible little prototype death camp at Chełmno, which occurred by coincidence on the day after Pearl Harbor, there may well have been a direct link between the decision to put off the Wannsee meeting and developments at the level of grand strategy. Officially, the postponement was explained by 'events that were announced suddenly, and which required the attention of some of the gentlemen who had been invited'.[41] The rescheduling may have been due to the military and transport crisis at Moscow, which made immediate demands on key personnel; the retreat of Army Group Centre may have suggested that setbacks in Russia required a fundamental re-examination of plans to deport Jews there. The call for a grand Reichstag session that went out on 8 December (to convene on the 10th, later the 11th) was a response to the Japanese attack on the Americans and British, and was almost certainly a factor in the delaying of the Wannsee Conference. The infamous gathering at Wannsee would finally take place, after a delay of some six weeks, on 20 January 1942.

Four days after the postponement of the original Wannsee conference, there would be another important meeting of the top level Nazi leadership, where policies of genocide would be raised in the context of the new war with the United States.

### London, Washington, Oahu

By early on the 8th – having 'slept the sleep of the saved and thankful' – Winston Churchill had decided that he should go to Washington to confer with the American President in person. He telephoned Scotland at 8.00 a.m. to inform Foreign Secretary Eden of his plans, and he wrote a letter to George VI during the day, formally requesting permission to be out of the country. Churchill had 'little doubt', he told the King, that 'such a course is agreeable to President Roosevelt'. The visit, he thought, was crucial: 'The whole plan of Anglo-American defence and attack has to be concerted in the light of reality'. He expressed special concern that Britain continued to receive its share of munitions and other aid.[42]

Oliver Harvey, Eden's private secretary, was with the Foreign Secretary on the quayside at Invergordon in Scotland when he spoke with Churchill. The Prime Minister 'was in the highest spirits at America and Japan', he recalled, and full of enthusiasm for his own proposed trip to America. Eden, who was ill with gastric flu, was not so keen. Harvey thought a Washington summit would make the Russians suspect that Churchill and Roosevelt were plotting against them. He also suspected that Eden was concerned about his own reputation; Churchill's trip would take 'all the limelight off the Moscow visit'. Alec Cadogan, who was also in Eden's party, spoke directly with the Prime Minister. 'I said A. [Eden] was distressed at idea of their both being away together. He said, "That's all right: that'll work very well: I shall have Anthony where I want him!"'[43] Having failed to put off Churchill, Eden and his party boarded a destroyer for a five-hour trip to Scapa Flow, where they were transferred to a heavy cruiser. HMS *Kent* departed for Russia after tea at 6.00 p.m.

Meanwhile, in London the Cabinet had met at 12.30 p.m. and authorised a declaration of war against Japan. Churchill had repeatedly asserted, that autumn, that if the US went to war Britain would follow 'within the hour'. As it turned out, President Roosevelt had, at 7.30 a.m. (1.30 p.m. London time) requested a short delay in the British declaration of war: 'I think it best on account of psychology here that Britain's declaration of war be withheld until after my speech at 12:30 Washington time [6.30 p.m. in London].'

The Prime Minister ignored this request, explaining (not altogether candidly) that when it transpired that British territory had been attacked, there was 'no need to wait'. Churchill probably did not wish the inconvenience of an evening session of the House of Commons. More importantly, after Pearl Harbor, he no longer had to worry so much about American sensitivities. Britain was, after all, a great power.

Instructions were sent to Ambassador Craigie in Japan, and at 1.00 p.m. Churchill informed the Japanese Chargé d'Affaires, Kamimura Shinichi, about the action that had been taken. Churchill's note to Kamimura mentioned the attempted landing on the coast of Malaya and the bombing of Singapore and

Hong Kong but made no reference to the simultaneous attack on the United States. The Prime Minister remarked on Japan's flagrant violation of international law, especially of Article 1 of the Third Hague Convention, which required states to declare war before beginning hostilities. He concluded courteously: 'I have the honour to be, with high consideration, Sir, Your obedient servant.' 'Some people did not like this ceremonial style,' Churchill quipped in his memoirs. 'But after all when you have to kill a man it costs nothing to be polite.'[44]

* * *

Churchill's speech to Parliament on the afternoon of 8 December reflected a rather peculiar interlude in the history of the war, during which the Americans had suffered a defeat in the Pacific, but the British forces – for three days – were still apparently intact. The Japanese had made moves into Thailand, including a landing in the Kra Isthmus, but that was not altogether unexpected. Compared to the Americans on Oahu and in the Philippines, British forces had been on full-scale alert. The air attack on Singapore had been unsuccessful, though this had little to do with the defences. The only surprising event was the reported Kota Bharu landing in Malaya, but that was in the extreme north of the colony, and 360 miles from Singapore.

The Prime Minister rose shortly after 3.00 p.m. (9.00 a.m. in Washington) to speak about 'this vast and melancholy extension of the war' to a crowded House of Commons. (Parliament met in the Church House Annexe, in Great Smith Street, after the Palace of Westminster was badly damaged by a German fire bomb in May 1941.) This was two hours before President Roosevelt began his own memorable 'Date of Infamy' speech to Congress. Churchill was damning about Tokyo's diplomatic tactics: 'Every circumstance of calculated and characteristic Japanese treachery was employed against the United States.' And he was careful to link the new front in Asia with the war in Europe: 'we can only feel that Hitler's madness has infected the Japanese mind.'[45]

Churchill's summary of the military situation was guardedly optimistic. He noted that British forces had been 'in readiness'. By this time the Members would have been aware of the successful Japanese surprise attack on Oahu, and the British leader was here perhaps making a subtle contrast with the American performance. He said that it was fortunate that Japan had not attacked Britain at an earlier date, when the country was really weak after Dunkirk. He referred to the widely-publicised arrival of modern capital ships (only *Prince of Wales* was publicly identified), with words he would, a few days' time, regret: 'The

House and the Empire will notice that some of the finest ships of the Royal Navy have reached their stations in the Far East at a very convenient moment. Every preparation in our power has been made, and I do not doubt that we shall give a good account of ourselves.' He referred to co-operation with the United States: 'The closest accord has been established with the powerful American forces, both naval and air'. He may have had in mind here co-operation in intelligence, especially codebreaking. But the Prime Minister did not minimise Japanese strength: 'the enemy has attacked with an audacity, which may spring from recklessness but which may also spring from a conviction of strength.' Churchill said nothing about American participation in the European war against Germany and Italy. Churchill also referred to 'our heroic Russian allies', but made no reference to the improvement of the situation there or to the battles at Rostov and Moscow; the picture was perhaps considered too unclear.

One Member who was present, 'Chips' Channon, would record in his diary that it was a good speech and had the advantage of moving beyond the North African offensive (CRUSADER), for which so much had been hoped and but which after three weeks still seemed stalled in the sands. 'Now Libya will be forgotten,' he wrote. But the MP and diarist Harold Nicholson recalled it as 'a dull matter-of-fact speech'.[46] The Prime Minister concluded his address with a flourish of Churchillian rhetoric, one which he must have hoped would have lasting affect: 'In the past we have had a light which flickered, in the present we have a light which flames, and in the future there will be a light which shines [calm and resplendent] over all the land and sea.' The words did not turn out to be his most memorable or prescient; grave setbacks would have to be faced in the weeks ahead.

That night the Prime Minister also spoke on the radio, essentially repeating what he had said in Parliament. Aside from an embellishment about Japanese 'government by assassination', the main addition to the speech delivered earlier in the day was a call for workers to keep up the flow of arms production. Output would be especially important, he said, in the coming months, when war material was being diverted to Russia, and when the United States would be retaining its production to meet its own crisis. Like the earlier version, the Prime Minister's radio address was not inspiring. Churchill's PPS, George Harvie-Watt, provided his chief with some honest criticism: 'you were very tired'.[47]

* * *

The President drove from the White House to Capital Hill on the Monday morning, to address a joint session of Congress. The presidential party occupied six limousines. FDR was accompanied by his Cabinet; Mrs Roosevelt came with the widow of Woodrow Wilson, the Democratic President who had declared war on Germany in 1917.

At 11.00 a.m., Franklin D. Roosevelt began what would become one of his best-known speeches. It was very short – six and a half minutes long, interrupted by applause – but a powerful and effective public address. Astutely, Roosevelt kept the message simple. 'Yesterday, December 7th, 1941 – a date which will live in infamy – the United States of America was suddenly and deliberately attacked by naval and air forces of the Empire of Japan.' The President took pains to make clear that the message brought to the State Department by Nomura and Kurusu, after 2.00 p.m. on the previous day, had 'contained no threat or hint of war or of armed attack.' In view of the distance from Japan to Hawaii it was clear that the attack was 'deliberately planned many days or even weeks ago', and, meanwhile, the Japanese had deceived the US with falsehoods and 'expressions of hope for continued peace'. The President called for a declaration of war against Japan; he said nothing about Germany or Italy. The Senate unanimously passed the declaration of war. In the House, 388 Representatives voted in favour, and one voted against. The famous 'no' vote was cast by the pacifist Republican Congresswoman from Montana, Jeanette Rankin.[48]

The President sent a message to Churchill, reporting the near unanimous vote in Congress: 'Today all of us are in the same boat with you and the people of the Empire and it is a ship which will not and cannot be sunk.'[49]

Frances Perkins, the Secretary of Labor, later wrote about that morning: 'I don't recall anything except the terrible tenseness, and the absolute lack of the usual loose-mouthed jollity that goes on whenever Congress meets in full session.' Cabinet and Congressmen were stunned by the events of the previous day: 'we had all been trained to think of the United States as indomitable and invincible, that it was a terrible to thing to have to be faced with the fact that our navy had cracked'.[50]

Hans Thomsen, the German Chargé d'Affaires, sent two reports to Berlin on the 8th, relating to Roosevelt's speech. No doubt with the *Chicago Tribune* leak in mind, Thomsen speculated that the President would use this opportunity to get from Congress 'the full grant of authority he needs for carrying on a total war and effecting a total mobilization of industry'. He was not sure that the US would declare war on Germany and Italy, as 'it would seem logical to avoid a war on two fronts'. After he actually heard the contents of the speech Thomsen noted that the President had made no reference to Germany or Italy. This, Thomsen suggested, 'indicates for the present he wants to avoid any worsening of the situation in the Atlantic.' But the main development was clear enough:

'There is no such thing as an opposition any more, although some newspapers are reserving their right to make constructive criticism. For the first time all segments of political life are joined in eagerness for war, hatred of Japan, and desire for unity.'[51]

Secretary of War Stimson thought the President's speech was a very effective document, but 'not one of broad statesmanship', because it spoke only of the surprise attack and not Japan's long-term conduct.[52] Stimson was probably wrong about 'the broad statesmanship', and he certainly underestimated the political shrewdness of what the President had done and not done.

Franklin Roosevelt had mishandled much of America's confrontation with Japan. Both the Administration and Congress had been naïve. As Commander-in-Chief he bore responsibility for a flawed grand strategy and, to a lesser extent, for the unpreparedness of American forces on 7 December. But FDR had excellent political instincts, and he understood the essentials of the situation. His next basic decision and calculation was fundamentally sound: he did not use the occasion of the Pearl Harbor attack to declare war on Germany and Italy, as some of his closest advisers had suggested.

There was a gamble and calculation involved here, as Roosevelt was counting on declarations of war by Germany and Japan. If these two Axis countries did *not* in fact go to war against the United States, then a bitter duel against Japan in the Pacific Ocean might take up the nation's energies. That was certainly not the President's intention.

We cannot know exactly what information the President had available, even less what information he acted upon. He did see one relevant report dated 13 November from 'Bill' Donovan, the head of what in 1941 passed for an American security service (the Bureau of Coordination of Information, later to become the OSS). This was an account of a conversation earlier in the month between Hans Thomsen – the most senior German diplomat in the US – and the prominent Quaker Malcolm R. Lovell. 'If Japan goes to war with the United States,' Thomsen had said (on 3 November), 'Germany will immediately follow suit.' He had also accurately predicted that American pressure would lead to war in the Pacific: 'Japan is . . . forced to strike now whether she wishes to or not.'[53]

More important for the President, however, were surely the recent MAGIC intercepts of the conversations between Ribbentrop, Tōgō, and Ambassadors Ōshima and Ott. Ōshima's report of his meeting with Ribbentrop on 28 November – at which the German Foreign Minister had urged Japan to push forward and promised German support – was especially significant. This intercept had been available in Washington for a week (since Monday,

1 December). On 6 December the US codebreakers had translated Ambassador Ōshima's report of his meeting with Ribbentrop on the afternoon of the 2nd, at which the Reich Foreign Minister had – in Hitler's absence – made a personal promise of German participation in a Japanese war against the United States and Britain. (Churchill, who had access to the same intelligence sources, was on 8 December confident enough to inform the King of the situation: 'I am expecting that Germany and Italy will both declare war on the United States, as they have bound themselves by treaty to do so.')[54]

The President, whatever led him there, certainly arrived at the correct decision. Ribbentrop took a rather different view. 'A Great Power,' he remarked, 'does not permit any other power to make war on it. It declares war itself.'[55] This may have been true for the Third Reich and the Empire of Japan. It was not necessarily true for a great democracy, especially one whose people had shown such grave doubts about intervening in the 'European' war. A declaration of war against America by Germany and Italy would be of extreme political value for President Roosevelt. Even if Germany and Italy were not currently in a position to take direct action against the United States, they would identify themselves with the treacherous attack on Pearl Harbor. Their declarations of war would swing American public opinion, and the American electorate, unanimously behind a general struggle against the Axis.

* * *

Later in the morning Litvinov, the new Soviet Ambassador who had arrived in Washington from his trans-Pacific trip on 7 December, presented his credentials in a meeting with Secretary of State Hull. The two men discussed supplies, and whether Vladivostok could still be used. Hull did not directly press for Soviet entry into the war against Japan, but he clearly favoured it. 'It would probably be found best for all concerned among the Allied nations,' Hull declared, 'to effect a complete line-up and bring about a terrific forward movement all along the line.' Litvinov did not directly respond to this, but the Secretary of State was impressed that in general he showed 'an excellent reciprocal state of mind'. A 'complete line-up', of course, also implied American entry into the war against Germany and Italy.

In the early afternoon of the 8th, Litvinov was received by President Roosevelt. In his 'letter of credence' the Russian emphasised 'the unswerving desire' of his government for 'the maintenance of the friendliest possible relations and closest cooperation with the Government of the United States of America'. In the informal discussion that followed, the President asked if Litvinov thought Japan would also attack Russia; the Ambassador replied that he thought it unlikely. Roosevelt also broached the subject of using Vladivostok for shuttle-bombing attacks on Japan from the Philippines.

Litvinov found the President 'tired and preoccupied' after his speech in the Congress. Roosevelt admitted that American losses were heavier than had so far been reported, and he doubted that the Philippines could be held (by this time the White House would have had some details of the Clark Field attack). Litvinov's main concern was whether America's war with Japan would affect the supply of war material to Russia. Roosevelt replied that it would not, although aircraft would be a bigger problem than tanks.[56]

* * *

The American military establishment began to come to terms with new realities on the day following the attack on Pearl Harbor. At noon CNO Stark issued orders to Admiral King, C-in-C of the US Atlantic Fleet, to begin the transfer of ships to the Pacific. Included were battleships *Idaho*, *Mississippi* and *New Mexico*, carrier *Yorktown*, a squadron of modern destroyers, and three squadrons of patrol planes. King was also authorised to strip all naval forces from Iceland.[57]

Early in the evening Stark sent out a directive to the C-in-C in the Pacific, altering Kimmel's tasks within the Navy's war plan (WPL 46). Although set out in the most schematic and bureaucratic language, it reflected the disaster at Pearl Harbor and set out a fundamental change of strategy that would dominate the Pacific War for the next seven months.

Paragraph 3212, headed 'Tasks', was to be changed. Sub-paragraph 'a' was to be deleted. It had read: 'Support the forces of the associated powers in the Far East by diverting enemy strength away from the Malay barrier, through the denial and capture of positions in the Marshalls, and through raids on enemy sea communications and positions.' Sub-paragraph 'b' was also struck out: 'Prepare to capture and establish control over the Caroline and Marshall Island area, and to establish an advanced fleet base in Truk'.

The war plan now had a new high-priority task: 'Support the Army in the defence of the Hawaiian Coastal Frontier'.[58]

CHAPTER 12

# TUESDAY, 9 DECEMBER
# FDR Begins the American Century

*Now that we are, as you say, 'in the same boat', would it not be wise for us to have another conference?*

Winston Churchill to Franklin D. Roosevelt

*In any case our position is so favourable, especially after the entry of Japan into the war, that there can certainly be no doubt about the outcome of this enormous continental struggle.*

Adolf Hitler

*[W]e must begin the great task that is before us by abandoning once and for all the illusion that we can ever again isolate ourselves from the rest of humanity.*

Franklin D. Roosevelt, radio address

## Hong Kong, Malaya, Thailand

Sunday and Monday had been days of stunning Japanese action in the Pacific and the Far East. Tuesday, 9 December, was relatively quiet. Admiral Nagumo's Mobile Force was speeding back towards Japan after the Oahu raid. Bad weather in the Philippines prevented further mass air attacks there. Wake and Guam came under small-scale Japanese air attack from Kwajalein and Saipan respectively. Elsewhere the Japanese spent their time consolidating their first steps, and the British and Americans tried to repair the damage.

Hong Kong was an exception, as the distances involved were short. The Japanese commander of 38th Division, General Sano, spent 8 December and the daylight hours of 9 December taking over the larger part of the 'Leased Territories' (the northern part of Hong Kong) by pushing back a screen of Indian troops. Sano moved his troops towards the high ground above Kowloon, where the British had their main defensive position. The so-called 'Gin Drinkers' Line' was held by four battalions, two British and two Indian. The terrain was rugged, with some small forts built in the late 1930s, but it was a long line and thinly defended.

Active probing by Japanese scouts during the night of 9–10 December determined that one of the key positions was undermanned and vulnerable. This was the Shingmun 'Redoubt', a group of concrete pill boxes with an observation post. The energetic colonel of one of the Japanese regiments decided to attack at once. Assault squads took the redoubt during the night against half-hearted resistance, and cracked open the entire position. Disheartened, the British made no counterattack the following day. General Maltby, the British commander, decided that the whole position on the 'mainland' would have to be abandoned and ordered a withdrawal to Hong Kong Island. With this ended any prospect of a prolonged defence.

* * *

In Malaya on the ground the situation was deceptively quiet on the 9th, although the Japanese consolidated their hold on Kota Bharu. They had taken the northern airfield on Monday afternoon, and on Tuesday the British garrison abandoned the town.

On the Kra Isthmus General Yamashita organised his forces. The first column, a detachment under Colonel Saeki, had set off on Monday down the main road towards Malaya. The British land forces, which had been ordered to abandon the MATADOR advance, now stood by in northwestern Malaya, in Kedah State, near Jitra. Further east KROHCOL, which had started late on Monday, was only able to advance a mile or two further north during the course of Tuesday, although the resistance of the Thai gendarmerie had expired.

In the air over northern Malaya and the Kra Isthmus Tuesday's fighting was heavier, despite bad weather.[1] Japanese Army bombers flying from Indochina blitzed the system of RAF aerodromes. Some of these bases had hard runways but many were grassy (or swampy); protection for aircraft, facilities, and personnel on the ground was limited or non-existent. None had more than a handful of anti-aircraft guns. There were a few RAF radar sets in the north but they were not yet operational (including two sets at Kota Bharu). The working radars were 350 miles to the south, protecting Singapore or its immediate approaches.

Japanese air strikes neutralised other RAF airfields in northern Malaya or forced their abandonment. During Tuesday the British, under the weight of repeated air attacks, withdrew all their surviving aircraft from Alor Star (which had a 1,400 yard hard runway), Sungei Patani and Butterworth in northern Malaya, as well as the Kuantan aerodrome on the east coast. The surviving planes went to smaller airfields in central Malaya or to Singapore itself. There was a panic at the Kuantan. Located 200 miles down the coast from Kota Bharu, the big aerodrome was not threatened by Japanese ground or naval forces. But after Japanese air raids forced the temporary withdrawal of the two Kuantan-based RAAF squadrons to Singapore, the Australian ground crews fled to the nearest railhead, and the base was effectively abandoned. (The shambles at Kuantan, and the failure or inability to base fighters there or at Kota Bharu, would play a significant part in the fate of *Prince of Wales* and *Repulse* the following day.)

On Monday the main RAF offensive effort had been directed against the Japanese ships off Kota Bahru. On Tuesday there were belated attempts to attack Singora. The British were able to mount only two offensive strikes on the 9th, each by half a dozen Blenheim light bombers. Neither had any success. (However, Squadron Leader Arthur Scarf would be awarded a posthumous Victoria Cross after the war for a single-handed attack on Singora airfield.) There was no attempt to attack the airfields in Indochina from where big Japanese Army bombers were flying. At the end of the first two days the force of fifty Blenheims had been reduced to ten machines, of which only two were ready for operations. More Japanese aircraft were lost due to the bad weather or to 'friendly fire' than were lost to British aircraft or ground fire. Imperial GHQ in Tokyo announced the victory on the 13th: 'Within three days from the start of hostilities the main body of the British Far Eastern air force had been practically destroyed.'[2]

* * *

At sea off Malaya, the day passed with manoeuvre rather than battle. Admiral Phillips's ships, *Prince of Wales*, *Repulse* and their escort of four destroyers, now known as Force 'Z', steamed north through the night of 8–9 December. Force 'Z' bypassed newly-laid Japanese minefields, and outflanked the patrol line of enemy submarines.[3] In the very early hours of the 9th, naval headquarters in Singapore sent a signal warning that air cover could not now be provided off Singora, due to the loss of the Kota Bharu aerodrome.

Phillips could count on speed, surprise and poor weather. At 1.15 p.m. his intentions were signalled by Aldis lamp to the ships of Force 'Z': 'My object is to surprise and sink enemy transports and enemy warships before air attack can develop. Objective chosen [Singora, Patani or Kota Bharu] will depend on air reconnaissance. Intend to arrive objective after sunrise tomorrow 10th.' Little was known, his long message read, of enemy forces in the vicinity; reports had mentioned the presence of battleship *Kongō*, four heavy cruisers, and two light cruisers. The operation would be conducted at high speed (twenty-five knots), and the force would then retire at the maximum speed endurance would allow.

The Admiral gave a further sign of his intentions an hour later (2.25 p.m.) when he sent a signal to *Tenedos* for relay to Singapore (as the destroyer was to be detached from the force at dusk). Phillips reported that the earliest he expected to return to the approaches of Singapore was dawn on the 11th, off the Anamba Islands (some 200 miles northeast of the naval base), and he requested that escorting destroyers, possibly including American ships, meet him at a rendezvous near there.

Success depended on surprise and some knowledge of the enemy's disposition. Admiral Phillips had neither. He did not know it, but at about the time of his first signal (1.15 p.m. on the afternoon of the 9th) Force 'Z' had been sighted by *I-65*, positioned at the eastern end of the Japanese submarine patrol line. This gave the Japanese the first intimation that the British were at sea and not moored at the Singapore Naval Base. The weather was overcast, with low cloud, but the sky did clear for a few hours later in the afternoon. Force 'Z' was spotted by three seaplanes catapulted from Ozawa's cruisers; *Prince of Wales* saw them at 5.40 p.m., and they shadowed the force until dusk. The chance of surprise had been lost. Meanwhile Phillips received no useful report of the situation off Singora, Patani and Kota Bharu from the RAF, so he would be proceeding blindly.

At sunset – 6.30 p.m. – on Tuesday, having reached a position 250–300 miles east of the invasion beaches, Phillips gave up the idea of attack. He did, however, turn and run west in the direction of Singora for an hour or so, in order to confuse the last Japanese aerial 'snoopers' before full darkness. At 8.15 p.m. Force 'Z' finally changed course to begin a high-speed night run south towards its home base.

Force 'Z' should have ended its abortive raid at the Anamba Islands and the distant approaches to Singapore in the early morning of the 10th, a day earlier than planned. Just before midnight, however, a fateful signal was received from Singapore: 'Immediate. Enemy reported landing Kuantan, latitude 3°50′ North.' Kuantan, only 200 miles from Singapore, represented a greater and more immediate threat to the British fortress than anything that had happened so far. At 12.52 a.m. *Prince of Wales* signalled a turn of 90 degrees towards Kuantan to investigate.

* * *

In Tokyo, in the early hours of Tuesday, 9 December, Ambassador Ott met the Japanese Foreign Minister again, to present Ribbentrop's draft of the new Tripartite agreement. Tōgō was not altogether happy with the draft. He insisted on some minor additions, despite urgings of haste by Ott, who knew a finished document was required in Berlin. The Japanese, unsure of the long-term commitment of their European partners, wanted some indication of what was meant by a 'just new order'. They also requested written confirmation that there would be a discussion of long-term co-operation before the pact expired. Tōgō asked when the German declaration of war on the United States could be expected. Ott replied that he considered it possible that his government planned, simultaneously, to announce the new Tripartite Pact and to declare war. Foreign Minister Tōgō was less keen about this order of things. He 'particularly desired', as soon as possible, a German declaration of war on the United States, even if this meant that the Tripartite agreement would be published somewhat later.[4]

## Russia and Berlin

In Russia the intensity of daily combat far surpassed that in the Far East. Tuesday morning saw the German Army on the defensive all along the front. By the evening of 9 December the Soviet 30th Army was threatening the outskirts of Klin from the north. The attacks on Guderian's bulge south of Moscow continued, with the mobile forces of 1st Guards Cavalry Corps taking Venev, twenty miles from its starting point, two days earlier.

For all the success of the 6 December offensive, the C-in-C of Soviet Western Army Group was dissatisfied. Three days later, from his HQ at Vlasikha, General Zhukov issued a directive to his ten army commanders, and to the commander of 1st Guard Cavalry Corps. The basic task, he explained, was 'to defeat as rapidly as possible the flanking groups of the enemy, to capture equipment, transport, weapons, and finally, driving swiftly forward and enveloping his flanking groups, to encircle and destroy all the armies of the enemy which are in front of our Western Army Group.' (The 'flanking groups' meant Panzer Groups 3 and 4 north of Moscow, and 2nd Panzer Army to the south.) However, Zhukov complained, 'some of our units are fighting in a completely incorrect manner' and were launching bloody head-on attacks on the enemy rear-guard, rather than carrying out swift encirclements. These methods played into the hands of the enemy, 'giving him the possibility, while suffering light losses to make a planned withdrawal to new positions, to regroup, and to organise a new resistance to our forces'. The proper technique was to pin down the rear-guard, and then outflank it. In no case were Soviet units to make head-on attacks, or to attack fortified positions.[5]

General Rudolf Schmidt's 2nd Army, southwest of Moscow and the extreme right flank of Army Group Centre, was spread widely but had still been advancing gradually eastwards. It faced increasing resistance from the Southwestern Army Group of Marshal Timoshenko, which covered Zhukov's southern flank. Suddenly its line was penetrated, and Schmidt had to give up the important railway junction at Elets (215 miles south of Moscow) that he had taken on the 7th. During the night of 8–9 December the Germans pulled out of the town, and forces of the Soviet 13th Army arrived the following day. The retreat of 2nd Army would, in turn, threaten the flank and rear of Guderian's 2nd Panzer Army.

Northwest of Moscow, on the far left of the Army Group Centre, the position of German forces holding the strategic town of Kalinin was put under threat. Units from the 31st Army of Konev's army group, attacking from east of the town, cut the highway to the south. Combined with the advance of 29th Army to the west of Kalinin, there was a serious danger of encirclement.

In Smolensk, Field Marshal von Bock was now thinking in terms of a general withdrawal. He selected a 'rear position' some fifty miles to the west of his exposed forward line. This position would run from Kursk to the Volga Reservoir, by way of Orel, Gzhatsk and Rzhev. The Gemans would still keep control of the important lateral railway line between Rzhev and Viaz'ma.[6]

It was not just German Army Group Centre that was in trouble. The *Ostheer* also had to consider major withdrawals in the great battle around Leningrad. On 9 December Russian forces re-entered the town of Tikhvin. The Germans began a withdrawal some fifty miles back to the line of the Volkhov River, where they would sit until 1943. With Tikhvin back in Soviet hands the vital rail supply line from central Russia to Lake Ladoga and Leningrad had been restored. Although the worst starvation of Leningrad's population had yet to begin, the city was no longer completely cut off from the 'mainland'. Hitler's hopes of a link-up with the Finns east of Lake Ladoga had also been dashed. Leningrad, another of the general objectives of the BARBAROSSA campaign, would not be captured by the Wehrmacht in 1941. Indeed, the German advance in the north would never be resumed; Tikhvin had been a high-water mark.

* * *

The Führer finally arrived by train at Berlin's Anhalt Station on Tuesday morning, 9 December, at 11.00 a.m. His arrival was not publicly announced. He set a meeting for the following day, 10 December, to which he summoned senior Nazi leaders; this would actually take place on the 12th.

Hitler had a long talk with Propaganda Minister Joseph Goebbels at midday.[7] Both men were delighted with the events of the last two days in the Far East and the Pacific. The actual outbreak of hostilities had come as a complete surprise, Hitler told Goebbels, and indeed he had not believed the news when he first heard it – Goebbels replied that he had reacted in the same way. Nevertheless, the German dictator claimed (not altogether accurately) that he had always expected that in the end the 'appeasers' in the Japanese government would lose the argument: 'There are certain situations in the life of a great power in which it must resort to the use of arms, if it does not want to give up everything. This had become just such a situation for Japan.'

At the same time Hitler was – at least while talking to Goebbels – more philosophical than his field marshals and generals about the situation in Russia. There had been local setbacks, but that was, he thought, inevitable in war. The offensive would be resumed in April and May 1942, after German forces had been built up. It might even be the case, Hitler argued, that the delay caused by the *rasputitsa* in October and November had been a good thing; the supply problems would have been greater had the Army Group Centre been deeper into Russia. It might well be necessary to make tactical withdrawals, in order to shorten the line of defence and to prepare for the spring 1942 offensive. But Germany need not worry about any loss of prestige, as any military developments would 'be overshadowed by events in the Pacific Ocean theatre'.

'In any case,' Hitler concluded, 'our position is so favourable, especially after the entry of Japan into the war, that there can certainly be no doubt about the outcome of this enormous continental struggle.' Goebbels was mightily relieved: 'The Führer radiates once again a wave of optimism and confidence in victory. It is good, after so many days of bad news, to come into direct contact with him.'

The German dictator also talked about his pivotal speech to the Reichstag, at which he now planned to declare war on the United States. So important was this Reichstag session expected to be that he had decided to postpone the event for a day (from 10 to 11 December) to give adequate time for preparation.[8]

## London and Washington

Perhaps surprisingly, Winston Churchill – like Hitler – was not downcast on 9 December. The news from Libya was now much clearer. 'Consider tide turned,' General Auchinleck had reported during the day. Even Japan's actions, on balance, were not so worrying. Whitehall could have little sense yet of the setbacks in northern Malaya, and the accepted wisdom was that it would be several months before the Japanese could move south and threaten Singapore. Meanwhile America was in the war on Britain's side. This was the thrust of a message sent by Churchill to Jan Smuts, the Prime Minister of South Africa. (Smuts was a Dominion leader to whom Churchill often turned for advice; he also shared his views of events with him.) 'I am well content with Sunday's developments in the Far East,' he told Smuts. Churchill also revealed that he was 'almost certain' that Germany and Italy had promised Japan that they would declare war on the United States.[9]

That 'almost certain' must have been the result of Churchill's reading of diplomatic intercepts. On this day the codebreakers at Bletchley Park had decrypted the two telegrams sent by Ambassador Ōshima to Foreign Minister Tōgō on 8 December. In the first the Japanese Ambassador reported his visit to Ribbentrop late on Sunday evening (7 December). The Reich Foreign Minister had assured Ōshima that, although he had not secured the formal sanction of Hitler, 'the immediate participation in the war [against the United States] by Germany and Italy was a matter of course'. In the second telegram Ōshima reported his afternoon meeting of the 8th (Monday), at which he had passed on Tokyo's request that Germany and Italy make formal declarations of war on the United States as soon as possible. Ribbentrop had replied that Hitler was currently discussing this at his headquarters and revealed that in the morning the German Navy had been given permission to attack American ships.[10]

Churchill wrote to President Roosevelt, urging that they meet as soon as possible. He was replying to the President's letter of the previous day, reporting Congress's declaration of war on Japan. 'Now that we are, as you say "in the same boat" would it not be wise for us to have another conference?' Churchill proposed bringing a number of his most senior commanders with him. It would provide a chance to consider war plans and production. Such a discussion needed to be done at the 'highest executive level'.[11] Churchill, as we know, had decided upon this course of action almost immediately after hearing the news of Pearl Harbor.

* * *

In Washington, Ambassador Halifax saw the President before lunch, and passed on the Prime Minister's proposal that he come to Washington. Roosevelt's opinion, Halifax wrote in his diary, was that Germany and Italy will declare war 'almost immediately'. This view, like Churchill's, was also probably informed by the MAGIC decrypts giving details of Ambassador Ōshima's secret talks with Ribbentrop.[12]

President Roosevelt's response to Churchill's self-invitation to Washington was initially cool. Halifax reported back to London that the President – ostensibly concerned about the riskiness of Churchill's return journey – preferred a meeting in Bermuda, and not for nearly a month; he suggested 7 January.[13] Aside from genuine worries about the short time available and the danger of the flight, the White House was eager not to be seen as being under the thumb of the British, ally or not.

The mood in military circles in Washington was, inevitably, sombre. The nation had been suddenly plunged into war with the disaster at Pearl Harbor on Sunday, and there had been heavy aircraft losses in the Philippines on Monday. Admiral Stark, in particular, now saw dangers everywhere. Early on Tuesday afternoon the Chief of Naval Operations sent a pessimistic message to Admiral Kimmel in Pearl Harbor. 'Because of the great success of the Japanese raid of the seventh,' his telegram read, 'it is expected to be promptly followed up by additional attacks in order render Hawaii untenable as naval and air bases, in which eventuality it is believed Japanese have suitable forces for initial occupation of islands other than Oahu, including Midway, Maui and Hawaii'. Stark doubted whether Pearl Harbor on Oahu could be used as an American base except in an emergency, and urged that the 'wounded vessels' be sent to the mainland as soon as possible.[14]

The Joint (Army-Navy) Board met in the Munitions Building in Washington on Tuesday afternoon. Those present, including the service chiefs, Admiral Stark and General Marshall, regarded Oahu as under threat. There was a discussion regarding what to do about the convoy of transport ships, escorted by the heavy cruiser *Pensacola*, which had departed San Francisco on 21 November with air and ground reinforcements for the Philippines. Admiral Turner, Stark's head of War Plans, said that the convoy would have to return to Hawaii, as the equipment and men on board were needed to defend the main Pacific base. This decision was accepted by the Board.[15]

* * *

In the evening President Roosevelt spoke to the nation over the radio from the Oval Room of the White House. Roosevelt's 'Date of Infamy' address, delivered to Congress on Monday, 8 December, is one of his most famous speeches, but there was little substance to it. Japanese treachery was obvious and nothing was said about Germany and Italy. Far fuller, and far more important, was the President's public radio address delivered to the American people on Tuesday, rather misleadingly termed and recalled as a 'Fireside Chat'.[16] The speech marked a turning point in American history.

The President did not underemphasise the danger of the situation in the Pacific. 'So far the news is all bad,' he said. '[T]he Japanese are claiming that as a result of their one action against Hawaii they have gained naval supremacy in the Pacific.' He could not give details of the losses, he said, because he himself did not know them, but Americans had to prepare themselves for the possible loss of Guam, Wake and Midway. He warned his countrymen to reject all rumours: 'These ugly little hints of complete disaster fly thick and fast in wartime.' Roosevelt stressed to his mass audience the importance of war production, as Churchill had done in his own radio address of the previous evening. He warned of shortages (but said there would be no food rationing), and he warned of higher taxes. Adolf Berle, Assistant Secretary of State, commented on this part of the speech in his diary. 'The President's speech last night was first-rate. There was a complete absence of drama; no heroics, nothing but a very sober statement of a very long and hard time ahead.'[17]

One remarkable aspect of the speech was that Roosevelt committed the United States to global war, not only against Japan but also against Germany and Italy. He did this in the absence of a formal declaration of war. He also tied the United States to allies about whom many of his countrymen still held grave doubts.

Roosevelt had not spoken to Congress on Monday about the link between enemies in Asia and in Europe; now that link was the centre of his powerful radio address. The President began by referring to 'a decade of international immorality'. 'Powerful and resourceful gangsters', he declared, 'have banded together to make war upon the whole human race.' He recited the actions not just of the Japanese, but also of Fascist Italy and Nazi Germany. There had developed a pattern of attack, which was made without warning in Europe and Asia. Germany was directly involved in what had happened on 7 December:

> Your Government knows that for weeks Germany has been telling Japan that if Japan did not attack the United States, Japan would not share in dividing the spoils with Germany when peace came. She was promised by Germany that if she came in she would receive the complete and perpetual control of the whole of the Pacific area . . . .

> We know also that Germany and Japan are conducting their military and naval operations in accordance with a joint plan. That plan considers all peoples and nations which are not helping the Axis powers as common enemies of each and every one of the Axis powers.
>
> That is their simple and obvious grand strategy. And that is why the American people must realize that it can be matched only with similar grand strategy. We must realize for example that Japanese successes against the United States in the Pacific are helpful to German operations in Libya; that any German success against the Caucasus is inevitably an assistance to Japan in her operations against the Dutch East Indies; that a German attack against Algiers or Morocco opens the way to a German attack against South America and the [Panama] Canal.
>
> On the other side of the picture, we must learn also to know that guerrilla warfare against the Germans in, let us say Serbia or Norway, helps us; that a successful Russian offensive against the Germans helps us; and that British successes on land or sea in any part of the world strengthen our hands.
>
> Remember always that Germany and Italy, regardless of any formal declaration of war, consider themselves at war with the United States at this moment just as much as they consider themselves at war with Britain or Russia.

There could be no possibility, after Roosevelt's words, of a war that was a limited confrontation with Japan only. War with Germany was inevitable. The war would be global, and the enemy would be defeated unconditionally: 'Not only must the shame of Japanese treachery be wiped out, but the sources of international brutality, wherever they exist, must be absolutely and finally broken.'

Lord Halifax thought this was a good speech with the main point being 'striking home the complete identification of Tokyo with Berlin'. 'I think,' the Ambassador noted, 'public opinion is pretty well fixed on that by now.'[18]

But there was more to the speech even than that. The President delivered a damning criticism of 'isolationism', and he well and truly launched the United States of America onto the world stage:

> [W]e must begin the great task that is before us by abandoning once and for all the illusion that we can ever again isolate ourselves from the rest of humanity.
>
> In these past few years – and, most violently, in the past three days – we have learned a terrible lesson. It is our obligation to our dead – it is our sacred

> obligation to their children and to our children – that we must never forget what we have learned.
>
> And what we have learned is this: There is no such thing as security for any nation – or any individual – in a world ruled by the principles of gangsterism. There is no such thing as impregnable defense against powerful aggressors who sneak up in the dark and strike without warning. We have learned that our ocean-girt hemisphere is not immune from severe attack – that we cannot measure our safety in terms of miles on any map any more.

The words of Franklin Roosevelt would echo beyond 1941, beyond 1945, and into an American century.

CHAPTER 13

# WEDNESDAY, 10 DECEMBER
# Force 'Z' and the Malayan Tragedy

*From Repulse. To any British man of war. Enemy aircraft bombing. My position 134NYT22X09.*

Signal from HMS *Repulse*

*The news is bad but it will be better.*

Franklin D. Roosevelt to Winston Churchill

### Guam, the Philippines, Malaya

Tuesday had seen a lull in the Far East. Wednesday, 10 December, turned out to be another day of successive and terrible defeats there for the new allies, Britain and the United States.

The Japanese assembled a substantial force for the invasion of the American possession of Guam.[1] The Army provided the 'South Seas Detachment' of 3,000 men; the covering force for the Navy was four heavy cruisers and as many destroyers. This was a hammer to crack a nut: Guam was virtually undefended, except for a detachment of US Marines and the native constabulary. The island was 4,000 miles west of Hawaii, and sandwiched between Japan's possessions in the Central Pacific – Saipan was only 140 miles to the north. Post-1918 treaties had prohibited fortifications, and the US Congress had not been ready, in the late 1930s, to pay to bolster the defences, even though Guam was a strategic link between Hawaii and the Philippines.

A few hundred Japanese naval infantry from Saipan carried out the attack on the main settlement, Agaña. They came ashore in the early hours of

10 December on Dungcas beach and marched a mile or so south to the town. Shots were fired around the Plaza de España, seat of the American administration. By dawn the governor decided that further resistance was useless and surrendered. Twelve American serviceman and five islanders were killed in the skirmish, along with ten Japanese. The majority of the tiny US Marine force, 130 men stationed ten miles south of Agaña, did not take part. The soldiers of the South Seas Detachment came ashore at three points on the island, but no fighting was necessary.

* * *

Wednesday also saw the arrival of Japanese ground forces in the Philippines, albeit only a small advance guard. The immediate aim was to secure the air fields in the north of Luzon Island, to prevent their use by the Americans and to provide forward bases from which Japanese Army aircraft could support the planned full-scale landing scheduled to take place in two weeks' time. These first landings were 200–250 miles north of Manila. Despite Japanese fears, the slow transport convoys, like the larger ones off Malaya, were not attacked by American planes during their voyage south; they were not even spotted. The bulk of a Japanese Army regiment came ashore on the north coast of Luzon, at the port of Aparri and at nearby Gonzaga, during the morning, despite heavy seas and bad weather. Luzon was a large island but only thinly defended. A company of Filipino troops, commanded by an American reserve lieutenant, melted away to the south. At Vigan, about a hundred miles away on the northwest coast, another small Japanese force also braved the rough seas to come ashore. Here there was no opposition by American or Filipino ground forces.[2]

American flyers took more action against the second Japanese convoy after it arrived at Vigan, including a strike by six B-17s and strafing attacks by fighters, but this was to be the last co-ordinated effort of MacArthur and Brereton's air force. The troops of the Kanno Detachment were safely ashore in the Vigan area by Thursday, 11 December. The dozen American B-17s left in service were kept well to the south over the following week. On 19–20 December the last of the big planes was flown to Australia. With this the heavy-bomber air strategy came to an ignominious end.

Neither did the US Navy interfere with the Japanese invasion in these first days or later. There were no major American surface warships in the northern Philippines, although the Japanese, taking no chances, had stationed two heavy cruisers out in the South China Sea. Admiral Hart's large force of submarines had no successes. Boats sent, on 8 December and later, to patrol off Formosa arrived after the Japanese invasion transports had left.

During 10 December – the weather on Formosa having improved since the previous day – the Japanese Navy's long-range bombers and fighters returned to execute another mass attack on central Luzon, this time targeting the fighter base at Nichols Field in southern Manila and the nearby naval dockyard at Cavite. The defending fighters were overwhelmed by the escort force of nearly a hundred Zeros. The day's strikes effectively finished off General Brereton's Far East Air Force, and thereafter there was no organised American air opposition; the few surviving fighters would be used mainly for reconnaissance.

Wednesday afternoon's attack on the dockyard was devastatingly effective. Cavite, a hook of a peninsula protruding into Manila Bay, was easy to locate and attack from the air. Two groups of Japanese high-level bombers carpeted the yard, and as many as 500 Filipinos were killed. After learning belatedly about the disastrous raids on US Army Air Force bases on 8 December, Admiral Hart had withdrawn two of his three submarine depot ships to the safer waters of the southern Philippines, but he could do little about the fixed installations at Cavite. The big submarine *Sealion*, under repair in the yard, was so badly damaged in the Japanese attack that she had to be scuttled. The bombing and fire in Cavite also saw the destruction of 233 torpedoes meant for the submarines. Hart watched the destruction from five miles away, standing on the roof of the Marsman Building on the Manila waterfront. That evening he would write of his bitterness about the US Army's failure, and his grudging admiration for the Japanese: 'We saw and heard of no opposition by the Army's fighters. It was an efficient attack all right; there is one good lot of airmen in this war.'[3]

* * *

Early on 10 December the lead elements of the Japanese brigade that had landed at Singora crossed the border into northern Malaya.[4] The Japanese intended to dash down to the road in the direction of the town and aerodrome at Alor Star, the main town of Kedah State, which was located some thirty miles to the south. They met a screening battalion of Indian troops on the frontier; the 1/14 Punjabis fell back towards Changlun, about six miles inside Malaya.

A second Japanese column marched south across the Kra Isthmus from Patani; it consisted of two battalions of the Japanese 42nd Regiment, supported by two companies of light tanks. Meanwhile the leading battalion of the Indian column, advancing north from the opposite end of the road from Kroh, had resumed the slow journey that it had begun on Monday afternoon towards the precipitate 'Ledge' defensive position inside Thailand. On 10 December, six miles short of the Ledge, KROHCOL ran into the Japanese force. The enemy had won the race; they covered three times the distance that the British-led forces did, over seventy-five miles of bad roads. The stalled advance of the 3/16 Punjabis on the Monday and slow progress made on Tuesday proved now to have been of critical importance. The opportunity to block the Japanese south from Patani had been lost; the British could not control the Patani-Kroh road, and enemy troops emerging at the southern end of the road threatened to cut off the defending forces in Kedah.

## The South China Sea

Off the coast of Malaya, *Prince of Wales*, *Repulse* and three escorting destroyers – *Tenedos* had been detached – were now withdrawing rapidly south through the night. Late on Tuesday afternoon Admiral Phillips had abandoned his 'high-speed descent' on Singora and the Kra Isthmus, having been spotted and shadowed by Japanese scout planes. Just before midnight, however, had come Singapore's signal about the reported landing on the central Malayan coast at Kuantan, and Force 'Z' turned west-southwest to investigate. Kuantan was a critical site, and the admiral was right to be concerned about it.

Admiral Phillips was delaying his departure south by the detour to Kuantan. He could assume (not unreasonably) that the air danger to his fleet was now much reduced. Force 'Z' was by this time 350–400 miles away from the Japanese air bases in Indochina (much further away than it would have been off Singora). Phillips's best guess was that the Japanese believed Force 'Z' to be still 200 miles further north. (As night fell on Tuesday the British ships had still been heading west towards Singora.)

Unknown to the Admiral, however, Force 'Z' had been shadowed for a time during the night by submarine *I-58*. The Imperial Navy had positioned no fewer than eleven of its submarines in the southern part of the South China Sea, six of them in a patrol line stretching for 150 miles, west to east, off the coast of Malaya. (Phillips and the Admiralty had anticipated this danger, and on the northbound course had given the Malayan coast a wide berth.) *I-58* was a fast 'cruiser' submarine, and she was able to stay in contact with the British force for several hours. The Japanese command now had a good idea of where Force 'Z' might be found on the following morning.

* * *

Phillips approached Kuantan and the Malayan shore at 8.00 a.m. on Wednesday, about an hour and a half after sunrise. The destroyer *Express*, sent ahead to investigate the port, found nothing. Phillips dawdled away some more time investigating a tug and some barges spotted to the east of Kuantan earlier in the morning. He did not switch on his powerful air search radar, because he did not want to give away his own position.[5]

At about 10.20 a.m. lookouts on *Prince of Wales* spotted an enemy scout plane.[6] The new air search radar on *Repulse* detected aircraft approaching from an unexpected direction, the southwest. The British crews went to battle stations. *Repulse* took a position astern *Prince of Wales*, and to starboard. Both vessels made course 135° (SE). Just after 11.00 a.m. a tight formation of eight Japanese twin-engined bombers began a high-level attack, flying at 10,000 feet. They were small shapes in the sky. Each dropped one bomb, then circled around and dropped another.

One of the main questions about the British naval disaster off Malaya is why Admiral Phillips did not call for help; once he had been spotted there was no need to observe radio silence. The answer probably is that, as he watched the high-level bombers from the compass deck of *Prince of Wales*, he was still relatively unconcerned. This was the kind of attack the Royal Navy had survived repeatedly, off Norway in 1940 and later in the Mediterranean. Although British anti-aircraft fire was relatively ineffective at 10,000 feet, despite fire-control radar, and no friendly fighter planes were in the air to break up the raid, the high-level attack could be discounted as a fatal danger. Fast-moving warships could manoeuvre out from under the pattern of bombs. In any event small bombs, even dropped from high altitude, could not penetrate the armoured deck of a capital ship. On this occasion the Japanese had only 250kg and 500kg bombs (the 'level bombers' at Pearl Harbor had carried special 800kg bombs). In this attack, at 11.22 a.m., one missile did hit *Repulse* – but it was a 250kg bomb and it caused only minor damage.

Twenty minutes later, events suddenly took a turn for the worse. More Japanese bombers appeared and were seen to cross in front of the British formation at long range, moving from starboard to port and gradually losing height. Making use of low cloud cover on the port beam of Force 'Z', they formed up in line astern. Then, breaking into three successive groups of two or three planes flying abreast, they began the first wave of a mass Japanese torpedo-bomber attack. The time was now 11.42 in the morning.

* * *

The fatal British mistake was ignorance of the equipment and capabilities of the Japanese Navy's long-range aircraft. The Formosa-based aircraft of the Imperial Navy's 21st and 23rd Air Groups had just devastated MacArthur's bombers and fighters at Clark Field and elsewhere in the Philippines. Now it was the turn of the 22nd Air Group, flying from Indochina, and based at Saigon and nearby Thu Dau Moi.

The attack on the Philippines had demonstrated the long range of the Japanese Navy's bomber force, but the key point about these aircraft was that they were *torpedo* planes, designed to attack enemy warships. Their crews were at least as highly trained as the men who attacked Pearl Harbor. In the 22nd Air Group the Genzan and Mihoro Wings each had thirty-six Mitsubishi G3M bombers (organised in three squadrons per wing). The third element, two squadrons of the Kanoya Wing, consisted of twenty-four of the newer Mitsubishi G4M bombers; these planes had been transferred to Indochina from Formosa in the previous week. (This was a last-minute change of plan, following news of the arrival of the British capital ships at Singapore.) The G3M was a spindly-looking machine with two engines, a huge wing and twin fins; the G4M was sleeker, with a cigar-shaped fuselage that could hold a torpedo internally. Both types carried a crew of seven.

Aircraft from the 22nd Air Group had mounted the ineffectual night attack on Singapore on the night of 8–9 December. On Tuesday the three Wings of the Air Group had been preparing for another mass attack on the Singapore area, when the early afternoon submarine sighting of Force 'Z' was received. The big planes were then hastily re-armed and despatched on an anti-shipping strike, but the lead bombers failed to find the target and the weather was poor. The force undertook a dangerous return to base by moonlight, with their bombs and torpedoes still loaded on board.

At 4.55 a.m. on Wednesday morning eight bombers were sent out on a search pattern. They turned back northwards after reaching the latitude of Singapore and then, five and a half hours after take-off, one of them spotted Force 'Z' and radioed the position to the rest of the air group: eighty-four bombers (fifty armed with torpedoes, thirty-four with bombs).

The first torpedo attack, begun at 11.42 a.m., was delivered by two squadrons of sixteen aircraft. British anti-aircraft fire again had limited effect. The torpedoes were dropped from a height of 100 feet and a distance of about 650–1,650 yards from the target. Speeding at forty-two knots, they took about a minute to strike home. *Prince of Wales* was struck at 11.44 a.m. by a torpedo, towards the stern on the port side.[7] It was a most unfortunate event. The single torpedo hit led to serious damage to engines, boilers and auxiliary machinery (the last was important for training guns and pumping water). The battleship's speed was reduced, control was largely lost, and three-quarters of the 5.25-inch heavy anti-aircraft guns ceased to function. *Repulse* turned sharply to starboard, away from the torpedo attack, and was able to avoid any hits. At 11.58 a.m., *Repulse* – not the flagship – finally broke radio silence with a broadcast: 'Enemy aircraft bombing. My position 134 NYTW 22 × 09.'

The third and deadliest torpedo attack began at 12.19 p.m. The more modern G4Ms of the Kanoya Wing, armed with heavier torpedoes and with the best-trained crews, had arrived, and there were twenty-four of them. Captain Tennant manoeuvred *Repulse* skilfully, but this time he could not avoid a torpedo hit amidships. *Prince of Wales*, now moving slowly, was unable to turn to evade torpedoes, and could put up only very limited anti-aircraft fire. Between 12.23 and 12.26 p.m. the battleship took three more torpedo hits, with the immediate effect that her speed was reduced to eight knots. *Repulse* was attacked again at about this time, and as many as four torpedoes struck home. Tennant knew his old and relatively thinly-armoured battlecruiser was doomed. He spoke on the ship's loudspeaker, ordered all the crew up from below, and launched the 'Carley float' life rafts. The old ship took on a heavy list to port, and at 12.33 p.m., about seven minutes after the last attacks commenced, she rolled over, taking more than a third of her crew to their deaths.

*Prince of Wales* had taken the first hits, but owing to her larger size and superior compartmentalisation, she took longer to sink. The battleship steamed slowly and out of control. The cumulative effect of four earlier torpedo hits and the loss of power meant that British damage-control efforts were now failing. Destroyer *Express* came alongside to take off some of the battleship's crew, and the Carley floats were launched. At 1.10 p.m. *Prince of Wales* began listing to port, *Express* hurriedly backed off, and the crew of the stricken ship were ordered into the water. Ten minutes later the great ship capsized. She stayed on the surface, her red under-hull uppermost, for a few minutes. Then the bow rose, and she sank by the stern. *Prince of Wales* would be the only modern Allied battleship lost during the Second World War.

*Express* picked up many of the survivors from *Prince of Wales*. *Electra*, the other destroyer that had escorted the battleship all the way from Scotland, arrived some minutes later, along with *Vampire*. Some 90 officers out of 110 were saved, as well as 1,195 ratings out of 1,502. Captain Leach of *Prince of Wales* was drowned. Admiral Phillips was not seen again. He was one of the most senior British or American officers to be killed in action during the war.[8] Earlier, *Electra* and *Vampire* had picked up 42 of 69 officers from *Repulse* (among them Captain Tennant), and 754 out of 1,240 ratings. Fortunately the sea was calm. The Japanese lost three bombers and twenty-one men.

The C-in-C of the Royal Navy's China Station, Admiral Layton, had hauled his flag down for the last time at sunset on the 8th and had embarked on the

SS *Empire Monarch* for the return to Britain. Now, in tragic circumstances, he resumed his post as British naval C-in-C in the Far East. The Admiral later recalled, with anger, the decisions that had been taken in Whitehall. The squadron of ships that arrived had been 'sufficiently large to make its loss a severe blow to prestige and morale at a critical moment, but inadequate, as it proved, to inflict appreciable loss on the enemy in the circumstances in which it was employed.'[9] In total contrast, the Japanese were jubilant. 'No greater victory than this will be won,' enthused Admiral Ugaki Matome, the Chief of Staff of Combined Fleet, as he pondered what to call the battle. Ugaki was at sea aboard battleship *Nagato*, which Admiral Yamamoto had taken out into the Pacific at the head of his battle line two days earlier. As for Yamamoto himself, one of the Combined Fleet staff officers recorded his reaction: 'The Admiral was . . . smiling, with both cheeks flushed. For the first time I saw a bright smile on his face, which usually was almost expressionless.' He had bet ten dozen bottles of beer that both British ships would be sunk.[10]

The 'Battle off the Malay Coast', as the Japanese quickly named the sinking of Force 'Z', was more important than Pearl Harbor. It extinguished British sea power in the Far East and it was the precise point in the history of warfare where air power overtook the battleship. Admiral Phillips made some poor decisions, but the British were also unlucky. Had *Prince of Wales* and *Repulse* arrived in Singapore a couple of weeks earlier, or a couple of weeks later, they might have avoided their fate. Phillips had the misfortune to arrive as war broke out. The defeat, however, was also the result of poor British intelligence, a fatal underestimation of the Japanese, and a failure to co-ordinate the operations of the Royal Navy and the Royal Air Force.

## Russia

In the vicinity of German Army Group Centre, the weather on 10 December was not as severe as it had been in the past few days. Snow had fallen heavily in places, and the roads were icy, but the temperature had risen to a comparatively clement 0°C (32°F). The brief Wehrmacht press bulletin detailing Wednesday's events more or less repeated that for Tuesday: 'In the East the enemy has incurred additional heavy losses while attempting local attacks.' The secret Soviet General Staff Situation Report was more accurate: 'In the course of 10 December our forces in Western Army Group, overcoming stubborn enemy resistance, developed an offensive in the Klin, Solnechnogorsk and Istra directions, and in the Stalinogorsk direction continued to pursue the retreating units of Guderian's tank group. Solnechnogorsk, Stalinogorsk and Epifan' were taken by our forces.'[11]

On the night of 10–11 December, Panzer Groups 3 and 4 began a withdrawal behind the line of the Istra Reservoir, while reinforcing Klin in an effort to hold the strategically useful town. On the Soviet side, 30th Army and 1st Shock Army were left to reduce Klin, while 20th Army and 16th Army were directed to push as fast as possible to the west, either side of the Istra Reservoir, in the direction of Volokolamsk; their objective was about forty miles away.

The situation on the far right of German Army Group Centre, south of Guderian's rapidly deflating Stalinogorsk bulge, was now becoming especially dangerous. The German 2nd Army, under the acting command of General Rudolf Schmidt, was under grave threat. At noon on the 10th, elements of General Kostenko's striking group reached the main road between Elets and Livny, cutting the line of retreat of the German corps which had given up Elets the day before.

During the day Field Marshal von Bock drafted a pessimistic report for the German Army High Command about the situation in Army Group Centre. The essence of the report was the need for reinforcements. The message was not sent, but Greiffenberg, his Chief of Staff, read it out over the telephone to General Halder: 'the army group's front cannot be held over the long term with available forces. Even if, somehow and somewhere, the existing breakthroughs were dealt with, [our] strength would be exhausted.' Bock maintained that all his army commanders agreed with this view. Very little had been done to prepare positions for defence. Considering the cold, the state of the roads and the exhaustion of the men, even the option of a general retreat was fraught with danger: 'All that remains is to put up a tough fight for every foot and only to withdraw locally where nothing else can be done'. But such a desperate defence did not promise success, in view of the limited remaining strength of German units: 'This . . . runs the risk that somewhere the troops will collapse completely, before the attacking power of the Russians weakens.'[12]

In reply, Brauchitsch sent an extraordinary teleprinter message to Bock and to his six Army or Panzer group commanders in Army Group Centre. This was at least partly in response to General Guderian's suggestion of the preceding day that there was a 'crisis of confidence'. 'Both the Supreme C-in-C [i.e. Hitler] and I,' Brauchitsch declared, 'are fully aware of the situation at the front in the struggle with the enemy and with nature. Everything is being done to improve supplies to the troops. I am aware of what demands I can place on the power of resistance of officers and men in the name of Germany, until such time as the situation improves. I place my trust in the will to victory of the German soldier.'[13]

## Berlin and Rome

Hitler and Goebbels discussed the military situation when they met in Berlin at midday on the 10th. Hitler admitted to his Propaganda Minister that things in Russia were 'not so good'. Goebbels thought the most important problem was the lack of winter clothing. In any event, he thought, the propaganda line had to be one which prepared the German population for difficulties and setbacks ahead, before the great offensive in Russia could be renewed in the spring.[14]

Fitful diplomatic negotiations continued among the Axis partners. The main issue for the German side was clearing the ground for the ceremonial declaration of war against the United States, to be delivered by Hitler to the Reichstag. This great event had now been set for Thursday afternoon (11 December), and was to be broadcast live at 3.00 p.m. Goebbels thought this was a good time to reach German listeners, and it could also be heard in Japan (at 10.00 p.m.) and the United States (at 8.00 a.m. on the East Coast). As of midday on the 10th, however, Hitler had still not begun to prepare his speech.[15]

Ribbentrop sent a reply to Ambassador Ott in Tokyo agreeing to those changes in the new Tripartite Pact that the Japanese government thought important. The wording of the Pact would now make it clear that – after the victorious end of the war – the Axis partners would co-operate very closely to bring about a 'just new order' on the basis of the original September 1940 pact. Moreover, future co-operation would be agreed before the Pact expired in 1950. The Reich Foreign Minister wanted quick action: 'Please insist with the utmost vigour that Ambassador Ōshima be issued full powers to sign the agreement in this version without any further delay'; these powers were to arrive in Berlin by noon on Wednesday, at the latest.[16]

At 4.30 p.m. on 10 December, Ribbentrop telephoned Mackensen, the German Ambassador in Rome. Mackensen was to seek a meeting with Mussolini and tell him that Hitler planned to speak to the Reichstag at 3.00 p.m. the following day, when he would make public the Italian-German treaty with Japan. Hitler wished to suggest that the *Duce* might take a similar step. The meeting was quickly arranged. Mussolini spoke with Mackensen at length about the different moral fighting values of the Japanese and the Americans. He also questioned the sanity of President Roosevelt 'who at the age of 40 years – a case that occurred only once in 10 million people, as the doctors had assured him – had contracted infantile paralysis; this was a development which had had a decisive effect on his mental condition.'[17]

The Nazi Foreign Minister was also concerned that the Americans did not anticipate Hitler. 'A Great Power does not permit any other power to make war on it,' he had told Weizsäcker; 'It declares war itself.' Ribbentrop ordered Thomsen, the Chargé d'Affaires in Washington, to make sure he had no contact with the US State Department before 3.30 p.m. on Thursday (German time). Ribbentrop struck from his draft cable the one sentence which explained his intentions: 'We want to avoid absolutely the American Government's stealing a march upon us by taking a step of that kind.' Covering another flank, Mackensen requested that the Italian press and radio be instructed to delay announcement of the declaration of war until 4.00 p.m. on the 11th, after Hitler was scheduled to begin his Reichstag speech.[18]

## London and Washington

Before breakfast on Wednesday morning, 10 December, a telegram was sent from Churchill to Anthony Eden, giving the Foreign Secretary the latest news: HMS *Kent* was now approaching the Arctic circle. The thrust of the message was an instruction not to promise Stalin even the proposed ten RAF squadrons. Things were becoming too difficult to make promises to the Russians. The Red Army was now, after all, achieving 'magnificent victories'; Britain had continuing needs in North Africa, new needs in Malaya, and there was no way of knowing how much equipment would be received from the embattled Americans in the future. Churchill informed Eden that the German Navy had already been ordered to attack American ships and that 'a tripartite declaration of implacable war against the British Empire and United States is expected either 10th or 11th.' The Prime Minister also made much of the losses at Pearl Harbor, which meant that Britain was going to be attacked 'in Malaya and throughout the Far East by Japanese forces enjoying command of the sea.'[19]

Little did Churchill know, when he dictated this message, how quickly the situation was going to worsen. The final event of the sea battle off Malaya, the sinking of *Prince of Wales*, occurred at 7.00 a.m. London time, so it must have been several hours later that the terrible news was communicated to him. 'I was opening my boxes [of official correspondence] on the 10th,' Churchill later recalled, 'when the telephone at my bedside rang. It was the First Sea Lord [Admiral Pound]. His voice sounded odd. He gave a sort of cough and gulp, and at first I could not hear clearly. "Prime Minister, I have to report to you that the *Prince of Wales* and the *Repulse* have both been sunk by the Japanese – we think by aircraft. Tom Phillips is drowned."'

'In all the war I never received a more direct shock,' Churchill wrote in his memoirs. 'As I turned over and twisted in bed the full horror of the news sank upon me. . . . We everywhere were weak and naked'. Kathleen Hill, Churchill's secretary, was present in the room and shared her memory with the historian Martin Gilbert in 1982: 'I sat in the corner silently and unobtrusively. When he was upset I used to try to be invisible. . . . That was a terrible moment. "Poor Tom Phillips," he said.'[20] Churchill had known Phillips very well, and had spent two weeks aboard the battleship with its crew in August during his visit to President Roosevelt. It was he who had despatched Phillips and the two capital ships to the Far East, against the better judgement of the Admiralty.

During the day the Prime Minister went to the meeting of the House of the Commons, and the Speaker permitted him to make a statement before Questions. 'I have bad news for the House,' he said, 'which I think I should pass on to them at the earliest possible moment.' Singapore had reported the loss of *Prince of Wales* and *Repulse*. No details were available, except what was in the official Japanese communiqué, which claimed that the ships had been sunk by air attack. The MP 'Chips' Channon recalled the scene in his diary: 'A dreadful day of despair and despondency. The Prime Minister stalked into the House and seemed anxious to speak. After a preliminary parley and getting up and sitting down twice, he announced the sinking. . . . The House was restive, the Government suddenly unpopular'. The King sent his commiserations to Downing Street: 'I thought I was getting immune to hearing bad news, but this has affected me deeply as I am sure it has you.'[21]

Ambassador Halifax had forwarded President Roosevelt's message of 9 December about a possible visit. What the Americans proposed was a meeting, not in Washington but in Bermuda, and not in a week's time, but on 7 January. Churchill sent another message to Roosevelt, via Ambassador Winant, urging haste. The Prime Minister pooh-poohed the danger of the return flight to Britain, but offered to meet in Bermuda nevertheless. Churchill pointed out that he had already planned his departure for the following day, the 11th, and reaffirmed that the danger was not the journey, but the world situation. 'It would be disastrous to wait for another month before we settle common action in face of new adverse situation particularly in Pacific.'[22]

At least the news from Libya was now good. Early in the afternoon of 10 December a signal arrived from General Auchinleck. The enemy was 'apparently in full retreat towards the west'. The former location of Rommel's headquarters, at El Adem, south of Tobruk, had been taken. 'I think it is permissible to claim that the siege of Tobruk has been raised. We are pursuing vigorously and pressing enemy hard at all points with fullest and most effective cooperation with RAF.'[23] This success, however, was now deeply overshadowed by the tragedy in the South China Sea.

* * *

In Washington the Administration marked time, after the declaration of war against Japan on Monday and President Roosevelt's remarkable radio address to the nation on Tuesday evening. There was a two-hour midday 'off the record' strategy conference in the White House, attended by the President and nine of his closest advisers on foreign policy and defence. Secretary of War Stimson recorded in his diary that this was one of the most satisfactory meetings he had had with Roosevelt: 'in spite of the terrific pressure that has been put upon him, he was businesslike, clear, and effective'. In reality nothing much came of this session. No record was made of the discussion, and the only decision of substance concerned the *Pensacola* convoy. It had been en route for the Philippines when the war started and was recalled to Hawaii on Tuesday. Now it would proceed to Australia, and the equipment on board would be sent north to reinforce the Philippines. Army pressure to support the Philippine garrison had overcome, at least for the moment, Navy caution and the realities of geography.[24]

The President made another decision on his own, one that would have a much greater effect on the war; he finally gave in and agreed to an immediate visit by Churchill. Bermuda was off, as he (FDR) preferred not to leave the United States; Churchill would come to Washington. 'Delighted to have you at White House,' Roosevelt graciously wrote that evening. This invitation would lead to the first British-American wartime conference, which assembled on 22 December under the codename ARCADIA. The President understood that Churchill's main concern was the continuation of war supplies, and he assured him that normal shipments would resume at the start of the new year. He ended his invitation on a positive note: 'The news is bad but it will be better'.[25]

* * *

Pearl Harbor was five and a half hours behind Washington. At 10.20 a.m. local time, Admiral Kimmel sent the Chief of Naval Operations a 'Briefed Estimate as of 10 December', an overall appreciation of the situation in the Pacific. This was undoubtedly a response of CINCPAC and his staff to Admiral Stark's pessimistic message, sent from Washington the previous day, which had predicted more attacks on the Hawaiian Islands – even an invasion – and the possible loss of the important outpost at Midway Island to the north. Kimmel was also anticipating the arrival of Secretary of the Navy Knox, due in Hawaii the following day. The 'Briefed Estimate' was probably drafted in the afternoon and evening of the 9th, but the final version did refer to the loss of *Prince of Wales* and *Repulse*.

Kimmel had kept his nerve, a remarkable achievement in the face of the catastrophe suffered by his command on 7 December. 'With the losses we have sustained,' he began, 'it is necessary to revise completely our strategy of a Pacific war.' The effective loss of four or five of its battleships would compel the United States to stay on the strategic defensive until its forces could be built up again. Nevertheless 'a very powerful striking force of carriers, cruisers, and destroyers' had survived. 'These forces must be operated boldly and vigorously on the tactical offensive in order to retrieve our initial disaster.' Kimmel was more realistic and professional than Washington about Japanese capabilities. 'It is believed that the great success of the initial surprise raid was not anticipated [by the Japanese]. Otherwise it would have been followed up immediately.' He thought that logistical factors would make it difficult for the Imperial Navy to operate a battle fleet again as far east as Hawaii. In view of the other commitments of the Japanese Army and the distances involved, it was also unlikely the enemy would attempt an invasion of Oahu, or other American possessions in the eastern Pacific, with the possible exceptions of Wake and Samoa. The most probable Japanese action was a further series of raids by carriers and cruisers into the central or eastern Pacific. To deal with this Pearl Harbor had to be retained as a major and active American base, reinforced by Army and Navy land-based aircraft. There should be no general withdrawal to the continental US.

Kimmel's proposed action was to organise three task forces around carriers *Enterprise*, *Lexington* and *Saratoga*, each screened by two or three cruisers and six to nine destroyers; a fourth task force would be created once carrier *Yorktown* arrived from the Atlantic. These task forces would remain at sea for as long as possible, countering the Japanese raids and gradually wearing down enemy strength. Significantly, the Admiral said nothing about relieving the Philippines, and he even urged that convoys to Australia should be kept to a minimum, in view of the lack of escorts. It was an impressive paper, certainly more sensible than Stark's assessment of the previous day, but it would not be enough to save Kimmel's career or reputation.[26]

* * *

When Goebbels met the Führer in Berlin at midday on Wednesday, after the news had been received about the loss of *Prince of Wales* and *Repulse*, Hitler could not have been more delighted. Finally, he told the Propaganda Minister, we have worthy allies who did not rely on Germany to pull their chestnuts out of the fire – a comparison, no doubt, between Japan and Italy. The Japanese were now masters of the Pacific, and the pool of Allied merchant shipping would be much reduced. The permanent loss of four battleships at Pearl Harbor and off Malaya would cause a great shock in both the US and Britain; it was early days, but there was sure to be a great *Katzenjammer* there. Japan's victories came at the time that Germany needed them, when there were so many difficulties in Russia.

Goebbels reflected to himself on how these developments dovetailed with Germany's own war:

> The situation both on the Eastern Front and in North Africa gives some cause for thought. To be sure, too much should not be made of these crises, but they also should not be overlooked. In any case it is, from the psychological standpoint, extremely useful that the Japanese through their aggressive actions have diverted the attention both of our own people and of the world in general to the Pacific. If the whole world was looking at the Eastern Front, we would be in an extremely embarrassing situation.[27]

CHAPTER 14

# THURSDAY, 11 DECEMBER
# Hitler's War on America

*Germany and Italy have finally seen themselves as obliged to fight, side by side with Japan, against the United States and England ...*

Adolf Hitler

*One man, one man only, a real tyrannical democrat, through a series of infinite provocations, betraying with a supreme fraud the population of his country, wanted the war and had prepared for it day by day with diabolical obstinacy.*

Benito Mussolini

*Our public opinion is fully aware that a Soviet declaration of war against Japan would weaken Soviet resistance to Hitlerite Germany and would be in the interests of Hitlerite Germany.*

V.M. Molotov

## Wake

Thursday, 11 December, began at Wake. Here occurred the one, small failure of Japan's march of conquest. Before dawn US Marine lookouts spotted an invasion force approaching the atoll from the south.[1]

For the attack on Guam on the previous day the Japanese had assembled an Army regiment and a naval support force with four heavy cruisers – and had encountered virtually no American resistance. In comparison, remote Wake was a purely Navy affair and the invading force was dangerously under-strength. The Japanese fleet, from Kwajalein Atoll in the Marshalls (two day's steaming from the south) consisted of two destroyer-transports and two troopships, carrying a total of 450 men of the naval infantry. Admiral Kajioka commanded the small support force of three light cruisers and six destroyers, all old ships dating back to just after the First World War.

Kajioka knew that Wake had considerable defences, but he counted on superior martial spirit, the softening-up effect of Japanese bombers over the last three days, and the guns of his ships. The US Marine garrison had only arrived on Wake in August and their installations had suffered some damage in the bombing raids, but they had six 5-inch coast-defence guns. The American gunners waited until Kajioka closed in to begin his bombardment, then accurate Marine artillery fire damaged the enemy flagship and the two other cruisers; destroyer *Hayate* was sunk. The morning had hardly begun when, at 7.00 a.m., Kajioka ordered a temporary withdrawal to Kwajalein; none of the assault force attempted to land. Four of the Marine fighter planes were still able to fly. An hour to the south of Wake the retreating Japanese fleet was hit by repeated strafing and bombing attacks, which caused destroyer *Kisaragi* to explode and sink.

*Hayate* and *Kisaragi* were among the older destroyers of the Imperial Navy, but they made up Japan's first major naval losses of the 1937–45 war. More immediately significant, a Japanese landing attempt had been beaten off.

## Hong Kong and Malaya

In Hong Kong, by contrast, the British defence become a rout on 11 December. During the night of 9–10 December the Japanese infantry had outfought and overwhelmed the key British position north of Kowloon, on the Gin Drinkers' Line. General Maltby had originally promised the governor that he could hold his positions on the mainland for seven days or more. Instead, at midday on the 11th, the fourth day of the battle, the General had to order his forces to begin the evacuation of Kowloon and most of the colony's mainland territory. Merchant ships were scuttled and, where possible, military installations blown up. Rioting and looting broke out among the Chinese population of Kowloon, who had not been told the British were leaving; this would later be described as 'fifth columnist' activity. Two of the three battalions left on the mainland were ferried across to Hong Kong Island. The Japanese, surprised by the British collapse, did not move fast enough to block the retreat. The third battalion, the 2/14 Punjabis, pulled back to Hong Kong Island in the early hours of 12th.

* * *

The situation was better in northern Malaya on 11 December, but only for the moment. The weather was cloudy and the Japanese Army concentrated its air attacks on the port of Penang, on the west coast. The spearhead of Colonel Saeki's detachment (landed at Singora on the 8th) raced down the trunk road south of the Thai border, fulfilling General Yamashita's directive for a 'driving charge' towards the British defenders.[2] Leading the advance were thirty to forty medium and light tanks of the 1st Tank Regiment. These tanks were not heavily armoured, but the British had no tanks at all, and some of their troops had never even seen a tracked armoured vehicle before; they would not be the first or last infantrymen that fell victim to 'tank panic'.

Jitra was in 1941 a small town and road junction located about fifteen miles from the border, on the main road that led down the western side of Malaya. The aerodrome at Alor Star, the most northerly of the RAF bases, was six miles to the south. It had been abandoned, under Japanese air attack, two days earlier. Nevertheless at Jitra was the only prepared British position on the Malayan mainland. Geography favoured the defenders here, with one of their flanks fixed on the sea, and the other, seven miles to the east, on jungle-covered hills. Trenches had been dug, but there was as yet no barbed wire or mines.

General David Murray-Lyon's 11th Indian Division, the main force in northern Malaya, defended this seven-mile line. Murray-Lyon had deployed one brigade on either side of the road. Total strength was seven battalions (two British and five Indian). One Indian battalion had been sent up the trunk road to cover the approaches to Jitra from the border, followed by another from Murray-Lyon's reserves. Both units were bowled over and dispersed, one after another, by the tanks and motorised infantry of the Saeki Detachment. Officers and men from the two Indian units were forced to abandon their equipment and take to the swampy ground either side of the road. Among those temporarily cut off from the main line of defence was one of the two Jitra brigade commanders. By the afternoon of 11 December the Japanese had reached the outskirts of Jitra and left the road, in an attempt to outflank the position from the east. They had captured a secret British military map on Monday and possessed a good knowledge of the layout of the local defences. Heavy skirmishing would continue through the night.

The British and Indian troops at Jitra had been disconcerted by changing directives in the past few days, as Operation MATADOR was prepared and then abandoned. They were shaken by the rapid appearance of the Japanese advance force. Murray-Lyon, for his part, was also alarmed about the fighting on the Patani-Kroh road some fifty miles to the east, which like Jitra came under his control. The small KROHCOL force was believed to be outnumbered, and Murray-Lyon gave it permission to pull back. The danger now was that continued Japanese movement down the Kroh road would cut the line of retreat of the whole 11th Division.

## Moscow

Fighting on a much larger scale – armies, corps and divisions, rather than battalions – continued on the Russian front on Thursday. The men on the ground in the Moscow area were spared the extremes of cold suffered over the past weekend. The temperature now ranged from 0°C to –5°C (32°F to 23°F), but there were snow flurries, and sheet ice made all movement difficult.

Zhukov's Western Army Group kept steadily pushing back both extended wings of German Army Group Centre. The most significant gain of the 11th was the small town of Istra, recaptured by the forces of Rokossovskii's 16th Army. The bulge of 2nd Panzer Army south of Moscow continued to deflate, under the slow pressure of Golikov's 10th Army. Guderian was attempting to pull back to the line of the rivers Shat' and Don. Further south, divisions of German 2nd Army were still cut off west of Elets, on the road to Livny.

The C-in-C of Army Group Centre, Field Marshal von Bock, made another pessimistic note in his diary: 'By constantly withdrawing we will never force the Russians to halt, and a mass withdrawal under pressure from the enemy could have unforeseeable consequences.'[3]

## London

In London, just before 12 noon on Thursday, a worn-looking Winston Churchill began a major statement to the Commons.[4] He did not yet grasp how bad the situation was becoming in the air and on the ground in northern Malaya. He needed, however, to address more fully the naval disaster off the peninsula in the South China Sea – which had occurred eighteen hours previously, and which he had announced briefly to the Commons on the previous day. The events of the war had taken a profound turn, and the Prime Minster strove, as far as possible, to put them into a favourable context for Parliament.

Churchill began by outlining the overall war situation, leaving the worst developments to the end. The 'three great spheres' before 7 December, he said, had been Libya, the Atlantic and Russia. 'The Libyan offensive did not take the course which its authors expected, though it will reach the end at which they aimed. . . . When all is said and done, on 18th November General Auchinleck set out to destroy the entire armed forces of the Germans and Italians in Cyrenaica, and now, on 11th December, I am bound to say that it seems very probable he will do so.' Churchill took this occasion to announce publicly the dismissal of General Cunningham, the 8th Army commander. His removal by Auchinleck had taken place two weeks earlier. Churchill revealed that Cunningham had since 'been reported by the medical authorities to be suffering from serious overstrain and has been granted sick leave'. In any event the situation in North Africa was now very satisfactory: 'all danger of the Army of the Nile not being able to celebrate Christmas and the New Year in Cairo has been decisively removed'.

The Prime Minister also announced that Britain's other campaign, the defence of the Atlantic convoy routes, was going well. The rate of sinkings in the autumn of 1941 had been a fifth that of the spring and early summer, and the November figures confirmed the trend: 'these matters of sea power and sea transport involve our lives.'

In Russia, too, the overall situation was much better, while '[s]ix weeks or a month ago things had looked bad'. Churchill described the change: 'The enormous power of the Russian Armies, and the glorious steadfastness and energy with which they have resisted the frightful onslaught made upon them have now been made plain. On top of this has come the Russian winter; and on top of that, the Russian Air Force.' He painted a verbal picture: 'The cold snow, the piercing wind which blows across the icy spaces, the ruined towns and villages . . .'. As for the Russians, 'their soldiers . . . are inspired by the feeling of advance after long retreat and of vengeance after monstrous injury.' It was here that Churchill acknowledged the significance of what had happened since 22 June 1941: 'In Hitler's launching of the Nazi campaign upon Russia we can already see . . . that he has made one of the outstanding blunders of history, and the results so far realised constitute an event of cardinal importance in the final decision of the war.' Britain, for its part, had to sustain deliveries to Russia of 'tanks, aeroplanes and vital raw materials'.

Then, however, the Prime Minister had to turn to the terrible new developments in the Far East. 'In my whole experience,' Churchill said, 'I do not remember any naval blow so heavy or so painful as the sinking of *Prince of Wales* and *Repulse* on [Wednesday] last.' He was full of praise for Admiral Phillips: 'Personally, I regarded him as one of the ablest brains in the naval Service, and I feel honoured to have established personal friendship with him.' Phillips's operation was not foolhardy: he 'was undertaking a thoroughly sound, well-considered offensive operation, not indeed free from risk, but not any different in principle from many similar operations we have repeatedly carried out in the North Sea and the Mediterranean.' The cause of the sinkings had been the number of Japanese bombers and torpedo planes, and the skill and determination of their crews, not any new weapon.

Churchill ended on a positive note. Now that 130 million Americans had joined the war effort 'the flow of munitions and aid of every kind will vastly exceed anything that could have been expected on the peace-time basis that has ruled up to the present.' The overall balance was in favour of one side:

> Not only the British Empire now but the United States are fighting for life; Russia is fighting for life, and China is fighting for life. Behind these four great combatant communities are ranged all the free spirit and hopes of all the conquered countries in Europe . . . I said the other day that four-fifths of the human race were on our side. It may well be an under-statement. Just these gangs and cliques of wicked men and their military and party organizations have been able to bring these hideous evils upon mankind. It would indeed bring shame upon our generation if we did not teach them a lesson which will not be forgotten in the records of a thousand years.

There were some complaints that the Honourable Members were not allowed to ask questions, but overall the Prime Minister's speech had the desired effect. 'Chips' Channon noted in his diary that Churchill dithered over the narrow issue of war reports from the Libyan front, but '[t]hen he turned to the larger theatre of war and [had] his usual exhilarating effect on the House.' The MP Harold Nicolson, often critical of Churchill, wrote: 'I like him best when he makes that sort of speech.'[5]

## Berlin and Rome

Shortly before Churchill began his speech to the Commons in London the new Tripartite treaty had been signed in Berlin. As the Germans had promised Ambassador Ōshima, it was agreed that there would be no separate peace with the US and Britain. The terms would not remain a secret for long; Hitler read them aloud to the Reichstag that afternoon. Article I stated that Germany, Italy and Japan would fight 'this war, a war that was forced on them by the United States of America and England', and bring it 'to a victorious end'. Under Article III the signatories promised they 'would continue to co-operate closely, even after the victorious conclusion of the war, as [a sign of] bringing about a just new order'. Article IV stipulated that, like the original Tripartite treaty, this new document would remain in force until September 1950.[6]

When it came, Germany's entry into the war was certainly more diplomatically 'correct' than that of Japan, although the event only lasted from 2.18 to 2.21 p.m. Reich Foreign Minister Ribbentrop summoned the US Chargé d'Affaires,

Leland B. Morris, to the Wihelmstrasse. Morris had headed the mission in Berlin since October 1940; America had not had an Ambassador in Germany since the Nazi *Kristallnacht* pogrom of 1938. Ribbentrop immediately presented the declaration of war. It was now about forty minutes before Hitler was due to begin his address to the Reichstag. Standing, the Nazi Foreign Minister read out the note. 'President Roosevelt had consistently followed a policy aimed at war,' Ribbentrop told the American diplomat; 'Now he had got the war he desired.'

> [T]he Government of the United States has finally proceeded from initial violations of neutrality to open acts of war against Germany. The Government of the United States has thereby virtually created a state of war. The German Government, consequently, discontinues diplomatic relations with the United States of America and declares that under these circumstances brought about by President Roosevelt, Germany too, as from today, considers herself as being in a state of war with the United States of America.

America, the German note stated, had initiated the war. It had violated 'in the most flagrant manner and in ever-increasing measure all rules of neutrality'. The United States had then moved to open acts of aggression; the note specified the President's speech of 11 September 1941, which had authorised action against German vessels and led to the attacks on U-boats and the seizure of merchant ships. Contrary to what Hitler would claim later that afternoon, the text made no reference to any German obligations under the Tripartite Pact of September 1940. The document closed on a courteous note: 'Accept, Mr. Chargé d'Affaires, the expression of my high consideration.'[7] (For Ribbentrop, like Churchill, it 'cost nothing to be polite'.)

* * *

In the political arena, Mussolini in Rome stole a march on Hitler. The German Foreign Office, and Mackensen, the Ambassador in Rome, had made ponderous efforts to embargo any Italian press announcement about war with the USA until after 4.00 p.m. that afternoon, so as not to conflict with the Führer's speech. The German Embassy was disturbed to learn, at 12.30 p.m., that Mussolini had arranged to address a mass rally from a balcony of his residence in the Palazzo Venezia at 2.45 p.m. Mackensen grumbled to Ciano's Chief of Staff, *Marchese* Lanza D'Ajeta, but the latter could only assure him that the speech of the *Duce* would be brief.[8]

A huge crowd, said to number 100,000 people, were gathered in the Piazza Venezia. Mussolini spoke from a first floor balcony, just as he had on the evening of 10 June 1940. Then, he had announced that the 'hour appointed by destiny' had struck 'in the heavens of our fatherland,' and he had told the Italian people about the declaration of war against Britain and France. Now, in December 1941 his speech lasted only four minutes. It was, for all that, probably better than Hitler's speech to come, and it was only slightly shorter than Roosevelt's 'Date of Infamy' address to Congress on the previous Monday. Today, Mussolini invoked the global scale of the conflict: 'This is another day of solemn decision in Italy's history,' he declared, 'and of memorable events destined to give a new course to the history of continents.' Like Churchill that morning, Mussolini attempted some grand demographic conclusions: Japanese manpower meant that the Tripartite Pact had become a military alliance of 250 million people. The 'soldiers of the empire of the rising sun' had already won victories across the 'immense Pacific expanse'; it was a 'privilege to fight alongside them'. As for responsibility, Mussolini blamed President Roosevelt personally: 'One man, one man only, a real tyrannical democrat, through a series of infinite provocations, betraying with a supreme fraud the population of his country, wanted the war and had prepared for it day by day with diabolical obstinacy.'[9]

Mussolini expressed no reservations about war with America, throwing his country into this 'war of continents'. The decision was foolhardy. The 'war of continents' was one in which Italy's limited military resources became even more marginal. In July 1943 four American divisions (and an equal number of British and Canadian ones) would invade Sicily. American and British bombers from North Africa would threaten an air campaign against the poorly defended Italian cities. Fascist Italy faced disaster, and the *Duce* was overthrown. But in December 1941 Mussolini could not be seen to be tagging along limply behind his German allies. And even more than them, he had needed some kind of Axis propaganda boost after humiliating defeats in East Africa and now in Libya.

Shortly before this, at 2.30 p.m., the American Chargé d'Affaires in Rome – George Wadsworth – had been summoned to the Foreign Ministry and given the declaration of war by Count Ciano.

* * *

The main event for the Axis took place in Berlin. Adolf Hitler addressed the Reichstag at 3.00 p.m. that Thursday afternoon in the Kroll Opera House. The building stood across the Königsplatz from the shell of the old Reichstag building, gutted by fire in 1933. Hitler stood at the podium, with senior Nazi officials behind him and flanking him on the stage. Behind and above them all hung a huge stylised silver eagle bearing the swastika symbol, with a sunburst behind it. Giant swastikas adorned the purple walls framing the stage. The event was broadcast live by German radio.

Hitler's speech was a long one, some eighty-eight minutes. As of midday on 10 December, however, little work had been completed on the speech, and the end result was decidedly unimpressive. The content was, essentially, a poorly structured and repetitive list.[10] As a piece of rhetoric, the text was inferior to Roosevelt's 'Date of Infamy' speech, made to Congress three days before, which gained from brevity. The speechwriters did an even better job on the President's 'fireside' radio address of Tuesday evening. And as a discussion of the war, Hitler's words were less candid or broad-ranging than those of Churchill when he addressed Parliament earlier on the 11th, or on Monday.

'Deputies! Men of the German Reichstag!' Hitler began by complaining that Germany's peace proposals of 1940 had been rejected, but he then boasted that the Reich had created impregnable European defences. He reminded his listeners that Germany had gone to war with the USSR to prevent a British-instigated *Mongolensturm*. (This was one of the few references to the British enemy, and Churchill was rarely mentioned by name.) The Führer moved on to an outline of European history from classical times, in which the Germanic peoples had succeeded the Romans as the defenders of the continent. The Wehrmacht's strike of 22 June 1941 had pre-empted an attack – planned and even scheduled – by the Red Army. Hitler then catalogued in detail the victories that had been won in the summer and autumn, up to the capture of Kerch' in the Crimea on 16 November – and not including recent events at Rostov, Tikhvin and Moscow. There was no hint in the speech that the German campaign in Russia had suffered major reversals within the last two weeks, or that two days earlier Wehrmacht High Command Directive No. 39 had ordered a winter break of offensive operations. The crisis that had led to the dismissal of Field Marshal von Rundstedt, and the Führer's dramatic flight to Mariupol', were secrets kept from the deputies of the Reichstag.

Hitler presented the losses of the two sides. As of 1 December 'captured Soviets' numbered 3.8 million personnel. The Wehrmacht had destroyed or captured in Russia 21,000 tanks, 33,000 artillery pieces and 14,000 aircraft. By comparison, in the course of the fighting the Wehrmacht had lost 162,000 men killed, 572,000 wounded and 31,000 missing. He noted that the German losses were 'in killed and wounded somewhat more than double the losses of the Battle of the Somme in the First World War'; it was no accident that Hitler chose for comparison the 1916 battle in which he himself took part.

Hitler devoted the second half of his speech to an extended attack on the American President, who now replaced Churchill as the firebrand of the war inflicted on Germany. In his diary entry after Hitler's speech, Goebbels noted that this was an effective propaganda technique. He recalled that the Führer's sarcasm aroused the audience in *Krolloper* to fits of laughter; the humour does not survive in the printed record.[11] This 'gentleman', Hitler claimed, was 'fanatically hostile' towards Germany. He was insane, he was a Freemason, he hungered for power, he was desperate to mask the failings of his economic policies. Then there was the ultimate sinister force: 'We know what force stands behind Roosevelt. It is the eternal Jew . . .'.

Hitler launched into another tedious catalogue, this time not of German victories but of the President's evil steps. These went from the 'quarantine' speech that he had made in Chicago in 1937 (in which he first openly criticised German and Japanese aggressive policy) to the US Navy's seizure of the German blockade runner *Odenswald* on 6 November 1941. Roosevelt's culpability included even the outbreak of the European war in 1939, when the President had supposedly talked the Poles out of accepting a peaceful settlement with the Reich. Some of what Hitler said about Roosevelt was ludicrous; some of it was true. The neutrality of the Roosevelt administration had been very one-sided in favour of Germany's enemies. And there is indeed no doubt that President Roosevelt dearly wanted to provoke the Germans into striking the first blow.

Hitler announced his declaration of war on the United States in a roundabout way:

> We, on our side, will now do what this provocateur has tried to achieve for years. This is not only because we are Japan's ally, but also because Germany and Italy, under their present leadership, possess enough insight and strength to understand that, in this historic time, the existence or non-existence of nations is being determined, perhaps forever. It is clear what this other world intends for us. They brought the former democratic Germany to starvation [i.e. in the blockade of 1918–19], and they would exterminate the present National-Socialist Germany.

'I have therefore,' he declared, 'had the American Chargé d'Affaires sent his passport today'; according to Hitler he had also ordered that this diplomat be notified of America's hostile acts.

There followed, awkwardly and with some repetition from the earlier part of the speech, Hitler's version of what this unfortunate American had been told. This did not align exactly with written accounts of the Ribbentrop-Morris meeting. Hitler said that two particular provocations of an 'unbearable' kind had been brought up. One was the attack on German ships (and submarines). The other was 'the plan by President Roosevelt to attack Germany and Italy in Europe itself by military means, at the latest in the year 1943'. This plan had been made public, and the American government had made no attempt to deny its existence.[12] 'In response to this,' Hitler continued, 'Germany and Italy have finally seen themselves as obliged to fight, side by side with Japan, against the United States and England, in the struggle for the defence of the freedom and independence of their peoples and states, in accordance with the terms of the Tripartite Pact of 27 September 1940.' He then read out the text of the new Tripartite agreement which had been signed earlier that day.

Hitler made only the sketchiest references to the events that had taken place in the Far East. Nothing was said about the Japanese military attacks on Hawaii, Malaya or the Philippines. The German dictator did not attempt to justify Japan's actions as part of the 'new order' or as an appropriate response to the American economic embargo. All he said was that Roosevelt had, in Asia as in Europe, agitated for war, falsified the causes when war occurred, made arbitrary declarations, and hidden behind 'a cloud of Christian hypocrisy'.

> I think that all of you will be relieved that one state [i.e. Japan] has finally taken this step of protest against this historically unique and unashamed abuse of truth and law. This man wished it upon himself and, therefore, he should not be surprised by it. It fills all of us . . . with deep satisfaction that the Japanese government, after negotiating with this liar for a year, has finally had enough of being treated so dishonourably.

Hitler made no special effort to link together the two halves of his speech, the war with Russia and the new war with the United States. He briefly acknowledged the bloc of Germany's enemies: 'That the Anglo-Saxon Jewish-capitalist world should find itself in a common front with Bolshevism is no surprise to us National Socialists.' He also noted that in July 1941 Roosevelt had sent 'an American promise of assistance to the Soviet Union,' although he said nothing about the later supply of Lend-Lease aid. Probably Hitler could not yet grasp the enormous importance of the link. In any event, some diplomatic caution was required, even for the German Führer. The Tokyo government had not gone to war with Russia, and it had no intention of doing so in the near future.

The Führer stressed his confidence in victory. The German state had built up a strong Wehrmacht. A powerful and loyal home front backed up the German forces. Anyone who opposed the sacrifice would 'die in disgrace'. He ended with a statement on unity: 'In the 2,000 years of German history known to us, our *Volk* has never been more unified and united than it is today.' Such unity, and such mass support for the global war Hitler and the Nazis had brought on Germany would, in truth, be needed to survive, let alone achieve further victories.

On the same day as Hitler's speech Ribbentrop cabled the German embassies in Hungary, Romania, Bulgaria, Croatia and Slovakia to secure declarations of war against the United States on the basis of the original Tripartite Pact. A formal declaration of war was required by Berlin, not a mere severing of relations.[13]

## Washington

There was no oratory in Washington that Thursday to match Churchill's speech in Parliament or Mussolini's address to the masses in the Piazza Venezia, no grand event comparable to Hitler's performance at the *Krolloper*. Woodrow Wilson had made a fuller speech to Congress in April 1917. Publicly the American declaration of war on Germany in 1941 was an anticlimax after the President's 'date of infamy' speech to Congress on Monday, and even more his radio address on Tuesday evening.

Two German diplomats had presented themselves at the State Department at 8.20 a.m. in the cold morning of the 11th (3.20 p.m. Berlin time), winter having finally arrived in the American capital. These were Hans Thomsen, the Chargé d'Affaires, and Heribert von Strempel, the embassy's Second Secretary. They brought with them the declaration of war. Three photographers crowded into the lift with them. 'This is not very dignified,' observed von Strempel. Secretary of State Hull declined to meet them. The pair were left cooling their heels until 9.30 a.m. when they were received by Ray Atherton, head of the Division of European Affairs. The declaration of war handed to Atherton was the same text that Ribbentrop had presented to Morris, the Chargé d'Affaires in Berlin.

In the middle of the morning President Roosevelt wrote a simple request to Congress (rather than appearing in person) asking for a declaration of war on Germany and Italy. He explained that Germany, 'pursuing a course of world conquest', had declared war that morning; 'the long known and the long expected has taken place'. Congress met at noon and passed two joint resolutions: 'All of the resources of the country are hereby pledged by the Congress of the United States.' Roosevelt's understated action was shrewd. The declarations passed the Senate and the House of Representatives without 'No' votes; Congresswoman Rankin abstained this time. At 3.00 p.m. Vice President Henry Wallace and a small delegation of Congressional leaders arrived at the White House with the Declarations of War on Germany and Italy. The President signed them.[14]

* * *

During the 11th, Ambassador Litvinov had an off-the-record meeting with the President, following an appointment in the White House with Harry Hopkins about Lend-Lease. Litvinov had received a directive on that day from Molotov, in which the People's Commissar of Foreign Affairs explained why Russia would not declare war on Japan at the current time. The first reason was that the USSR had a neutrality pact with Japan (signed in April) which it could not break. The second reason was that Soviet forces were concentrated against Germany, including half the forces normally based in the Far East. Japan, moreover, had also not provided any grounds for Soviet intervention. 'Our public opinion,' Molotov concluded, 'is fully aware that a Soviet declaration of war against Japan would weaken Soviet resistance to Hitlerite Germany and would be in the interests of Hitlerite Germany.' At his meeting with the President, Litvinov repeated these ideas, and the President – so Litvinov reported to Moscow – accepted them with regret. Roosevelt did ask that the USSR should try to make its intentions ambiguous, in order to keep the Japanese from sending all their forces south. He even requested a joint US-Soviet statement to the effect that Moscow reserved its freedom of action. Litvinov rejected both these suggestions, as they might incite the Japanese to attack the USSR.[15]

At 4.10 p.m., it was the turn of Secretary Hull, who had summoned Litvinov to the State Department. The Soviet Ambassador told Hull about the meetings with Hopkins and the President earlier in the day. He began by repeating that his government had made the final decision not to take part in the war at this time, in view of the heavy fighting against the Germans. This was, as Hull drily recorded, 'rather positively stated'. The Secretary of State, for his part, made a strong formal bid for the USSR to enter the war against Japan. His information was that Japan was 'under the strictest commitment to Germany' and planned to attack Russia. Hull stressed the need for Russia to provide two air bases, one on the Kamchatka Peninsula and one near Vladivostok. From these bases American bombers could mount air attacks on the fleet and cities of Japan. He also made a threat, not a very veiled one, to the effect that the continued flow of Lend-Lease would depend on Russian co-operation against Japan. Having already seen the President, the Soviet Ambassador evaded or ignored all these points, and the frustrated Hull was forced to conclude in his memo that 'there is not much, as far as I can see, for me to take up with him just now'. The Secretary of State cannot have expected much more. Earlier in the day, after his morning press conference, Hull had released a statement which mentioned nothing about possible Soviet participation in the war against Japan. It stressed that the President had, on Monday, publicly spoken of the government's 'firm intention . . . to carry out its program of aid to the Soviet Union'; this determination had been strengthened by the events of the past few hours.[16]

* * *

Alarmism continued, especially on the part of the Chief of Naval Operations and his War Plans subordinate, Admiral Kelly Turner. On the 11th Admiral Stark – ignoring Kimmel's sensible report from Hawaii on the 10th – sent Secretary of War Marshall a memorandum outlining the danger of Japanese landings on the other Hawaiian Islands (Maui, Hawaii and Molokai) which would enable them to blockade and besiege Oahu. 'Japan has available a very strong naval force which is now free to operate directly against Hawaii.' Japan now had no need to guard against a US attack into the Mandates, so the Japanese naval force 'could concentrate its entire attention on the offensive'. The Japanese could quickly take Midway and Wake and the other strategic American-held islands and atolls of the Central and South Pacific: Samoa, Canton, Christmas, Palmyra and Johnston. Estimates, based on radio traffic and other information, suggested a Japanese force available for offensive operations in the mid-Pacific area of eight to nine battleships ('including the most recent construction'), five to six carriers, twenty to twenty-two cruisers, fifty to sixty troop transports and cargo vessels. 'Japan is known to have an ample number of seasoned troops for use with this fleet.' 'This picture,' Stark concluded, 'is not overdrawn. The Hawaiian Islands are in terrible danger of early capture by Japan. Once captured, and with the Pacific Fleet greatly reduced in strength, the West Coast, Alaska, and the [Panama] Canal, as well as coastwise and trans-Pacific shipping would be subject to heavy raids, to say the least.' What Stark wanted was a co-ordinated concentration of effort in reinforcing and defending the four Hawaiian Islands.[17]

There was some irony here. 'Betty' Stark had since the end of 1940 been one of the leading advocates of a national military strategy directed against

Germany, rather than Japan. Now, on 11 December 1941, Stark – and the President – had their war with Nazi Germany. But the conflict in the Pacific had broken out in such a way that a whole new strategy of desperate national defence seemed to be required. For this strategic confusion, and for the failure to anticipate the Japanese attack, Admiral Stark bore a good share of the responsibility. His days as Chief of Naval Operations were numbered.

CHAPTER 15

FRIDAY, 12 DECEMBER

# World War and the Destruction of the Jews

*You guard a link between the Far East and Europe long famous in world civilisation. We are sure that the defence of Hong Kong against barbarous and unprovoked attack will add a glorious page to British annals.*

Winston Churchill

*Now the world war has come. The destruction of the Jews must be its necessary consequence.*

Joseph Goebbels

*It is clear to me that this is the most dangerous situation of the two world wars.*

General Franz Halder

## The Pacific Ocean, Southeast Asia, Hong Kong

The flurry of attacks on America's Pacific outposts continued on Friday, 12 December, although Wake Atoll, after the high drama of the previous day, was relatively quiet. Some 3,000 miles further west across the Pacific the Japanese Army mounted another preliminary landing in the Philippines. The first troops had come ashore in the north of Luzon on Wednesday; today's attack was 400 miles away, in the south, at the port of Legaspi. With this, the route between Luzon and the southern Philippines was blocked. There was no improvement in the co-operation between the two American commanders. Admiral Hart recorded in his diary that evening that he had seen General MacArthur only twice in the preceding five days: 'Anyhow, it matters little now whether we cooperate or not for there seems not so much for us to cooperate with.'[1]

* * *

The danger was more immediate in Malaya, where Friday saw a slide into disaster with the momentous defeat of the 11th Indian Division at the Battle of Jitra. Brian Farrell, in his magisterial history of the fall of Singapore, described Jitra as 'the most important battle Malaya Command ever fought'.[2]

The 'driving charge' of Yamashita's Japanese advance guard had on Wednesday and Thursday cut through two Indian battalions on the Singora-Jitra road, and effectively put them out of the battle; the speed of the enemy advance and the appearance of a few tanks had caused serious alarm. Two of the 11th Division's brigades, each composed of an Indian battalion and a British one, were deployed blocking the road south, in rain-soaked positions they had resumed after the abandonment of the MATADOR scheme. The brigades were a small force by the standards of Moscow or even Libya, but they constituted the main defence of northern Malaya and they outnumbered the approaching Japanese. During the night (11–12 December) the Japanese were able to infiltrate through the 2/9th Jats, the Indian battalion anchoring the east end of the position, and the British brigadier in direct overall charge of the Jitra line used up his last reserve to counter them.

General Murray-Lyon, commander of 11th Division, came up from his HQ at Sungei Patani to inspect the battlefield on Friday morning. Discovering the difficult situation, he requested permission from General Heath (III Corps commander) to withdraw to the south. With no reserves Murray-Lyon needed to conserve his division in being as a fighting force. He was concerned, too, that the enemy column moving south down the road from Patani towards Kroh – for which he was also responsible – might cut his line of retreat. The failure to secure the 'Ledge' position on the Kroh road was now looking more and more like a disastrous blunder. (On this same morning the Japanese mounted heavy attacks on the lead battalion of KROHCOL, which was already falling back to a position on the Malayan side of the border.)

During the day the Japanese succeeded in driving a wedge at Jitra between the Jats and the 1st Leicesters (who were covering the main road). The defending troops were not holding their own, and Murray-Lyon overreacted to rumours of Japanese breakthroughs. In the evening he again asked to pull back. Heath and his superior, General Percival (GOC of Malaya Command), countered – correctly – that the Japanese forces in front of Jitra were small. In the end, however, they sent a vague order instructing Murray-Lyon that his task was to defend Kedah state as a whole, rather than specifically the Jitra position.[3] That was enough for the division commander. Beginning at midnight (12–13 December) the 11th Division effected its retreat to the Sungei Kedah River near Alor Star, but only after a demoralising fifteen-mile night march in pouring rain. Some 3,000 Indian troops were left behind to be captured by the Japanese, along with much equipment (which the Japanese later put to good use, as what they called 'Churchill supplies'). The forces Murray-Lyon still commanded were demoralised and exhausted, and he decided to pull them back another twenty miles during Saturday night, to the town of Gurun. Jitra had at least been a prepared position; no defence work had been begun at Gurun, and it too was abandoned on Monday. The 11th Division was now very badly shaken and it would never again be able to make a stand; the pattern of retreat culminated in the fall of Singapore nine weeks later.

The rout of the British at Jitra had nothing to do with superior numbers; the attacking Japanese numbered about 1,500 infantry. The basic cause was the superiority of the experienced Japanese over poorly-led Indian troops who, for the most part, had never faced battle before. Murray-Lyon had not been enthusiastic about fighting a defensive battle in Kedah, and was preoccupied about the threat to his rear. As the British official history frankly put it: 'A Japanese advanced guard of a strength equivalent to two battalions supported by a company of tanks had, with comparatively few casualties, defeated 11th Division and driven it from its prepared position in some thirty-six hours.'[4]

* * *

The battle of Hong Kong also proceeded badly for the British on 12 December. Only one Indian battalion was still on the mainland, as a rear-guard. Japanese artillery fired across Victoria Harbour against targets on the island. The British Prime Minister sent a message of encouragement. 'You guard a link between the Far East and Europe long famous in world civilisation,' he declared. 'We are sure that the defence of Hong Kong against barbarous and unprovoked attack will add a glorious page to British annals. . . . Every day of your resistance brings nearer our certain victory.'[5] Both in Hong Kong and Malaya, Churchill's expectations were to be sadly disappointed.

## Moscow and Murmansk

In front of Moscow snow flurries and sheet ice were still much in evidence on 12 December, but there was a thaw, and a light rain fell. The Wehrmacht news bulletin still gave no hint of crisis: 'On the EASTERN FRONT only local engagements took place yesterday.' (The bulletin covering the 12th, issued on the 13th, would sound only slightly more worrying: 'On the EASTERN FRONT local enemy attacks were rebuffed.')[6]

In fact, desperate fighting was now taking place. Vlasov's 20th Army completed the recapture of the small town of Solnechnogorsk, east of Klin, on the 12th. Far away to the south, on the right flank of Army Group Centre, German 2nd Army was in deep trouble. Having given up Elets on the 9th it was still threatened with encirclement as it tried to pull back; German XXXIV Corps was now surrounded west of the town. On 12 December German 2nd Army was put directly under the command of Guderian in 2nd Panzer Army. In the middle of the morning General Halder and Field Marshal von Bock discussed the overall situation in a teleprinter exchange. They were especially concerned about the retreat of 2nd Panzer Army and Schmidt's 2nd Army. 'Can the enemy exploit his successes?' Halder enquired. Bock's reply was pessimistic: '*Jawohl!* He is doing it. Our own troops run away when a single Russian tank appears.' The Russians were still attacking with relatively small forces, but the Germans on the northern and southern wings of Army Group Centre were now weak and poorly supplied. At the end of the exchange the Chief of the General Staff was thoroughly alarmed. 'It is clear to me,' Halder announced, 'that this is the most dangerous situation of the two world wars.'[7]

From the Russian side of the front the situation on 12 December certainly looked much better. From Western Army Group HQ at Vlasikha, General Zhukov wrote to Stalin summing up what had been achieved and reporting that heavy losses had been inflicted: 'The pursuit and destruction of the retreating German forces continue'. In the evening the C-in-C of Western Army Group travelled into Moscow where, with Generals Shaposhnikov and Vasilevskii from the General Staff, he visited Stalin at the Kremlin. This was the first such meeting since the critical phase of the Battle of Moscow began.[8]

This meeting was probably linked to the decision to announce success. In the late-evening bulletin ('*V poslednii chas*' – 'In the last hour') the Soviet propaganda organs finally released the news to the public that a major victory was being won in front of Moscow, under the headline 'Defeat of the German plan to encircle and capture Moscow'. The radio announcement outlined in considerable detail the German advance since 16 November, and then described the counterattack:

> On 6 December 1941 the forces of our Western Army Group, having exhausted the enemy in earlier battles, went over to a counter-offensive against the attacking wings of the enemy. As a result of the offensive that has

> begun, both these forces have been defeated and they are rapidly withdrawing, abandoning equipment and weapons, and suffering huge losses.[9]

The bulletin reported that much territory west of Moscow had been taken back: 'Since going over to the offensive, in the period from 6 to 10 December, our formations have captured and liberated over 400 towns and villages from the Germans.' The encirclement of Klin and the capture of Solnechnogorsk, Istra, Stalinogorsk and other towns were announced.

The bulletin also released the identities of the main Soviet commanders of Western Army Group and named the specific German divisions which had been defeated. The newspaper *Pravda* repeated the bulletin on its front page the following morning. The announcement was accompanied by a large photograph of Zhukov, flanked by smaller photographs of his lieutenants: Leliushenko, Kuznetsov, Vlasov, Rokossovskii, Govorov, Boldin, Belov and Golikov. Kalinin Army Group was not yet awarded similar praise. However on 17 December, after the capture of the city of Kalinin, large photographs of Konev and two of his army commanders, Iushkevich and Maslennikov, would appear on page one of *Pravda*.[10]

* * *

On the morning of the 12th, the cruiser HMS *Kent* nosed through the Arctic winter darkness and thick fog into the Kola inlet in North Russia, with the British delegation on board. Foreign Secretary Anthony Eden, still shaky from his illness, was accompanied by Ambassador Maiskii, Cadogan and others. The cruiser finally dropped anchor at 3.00 p.m. Maiskii went ashore to investigate whether to proceed to Moscow by train or plane.

## London

Friday, 12 December, would be Winston Churchill's last day in London for five weeks. The news from North Africa, unlike the news from Malaya, was good. Churchill wrote a letter to General Auchinleck, who was about to launch his successful attack on Rommel's Gazala line, west of Tobruk. 'I am so glad things are going well in your grand campaign,' he wrote. The Prime Minister reported, too, that the embarrassing replacement of General Cunningham as C-in-C of 8th Army had passed off well, being 'submerged by larger events'.[11]

Another message, to Eden in Russia, scaled down promises of arms as a result of the Japanese attack. 'We think', Churchill confided, 'they will go for Philippines, Singapore and the Burma Road'. '[W]ith a Russian victory and our new dangers', it would not be possible to promise arms supplies to Moscow beyond the original quota. As to Russian involvement in the war against Japan, the Prime Minister did not regard it as being of chief importance; 'Victory on the European battlefield,' Churchill insisted, 'must have priority in our minds.' The United States, China and Australia might want the USSR to join the war with Japan, but Britain should not assert 'undue pressure'.[12]

Churchill also wrote to President Roosevelt on 12 December, expressing a hope that the rendezvous in Washington would be on 21 December, that is, in nine days' time. (Atlantic storms would in the end delay Churchill's arrival until the 22nd.) The Prime Minister made the remarkable comment (in the aftermath of Pearl Harbor) that he was 'enormously relieved at turn world events have taken'.[13] The party bound for Washington gathered at Euston Station in the evening. Their cover story was that Lord Beaverbrook, the Minister of Supply, was going to America, and that the Prime Minister was merely seeing him off.[14]

In view of the grave military situation facing the British Empire in the Far East, it was a most remarkable delegation, including two of the three service chiefs, Admiral Pound and Air Marshal Portal, as well as the former Army chief, Field Marshal Dill. The party totalled thirty-eight, including secretaries. Deputy Prime Minister Attlee was left in overall charge in London. General Brooke, Dill's recently appointed successor – in the post for less than two weeks – oversaw military operations (as General Nye, Brooke's deputy, was en route to Moscow with Eden). The fate of the Empire now depended on America and Russia, and Churchill and Eden were headed for the right places.

Churchill's party would board the brand new battleship *Duke of York* at Greenock in Scotland on the following morning (13 December). For those, like Churchill, who had taken part in the August trip to the Newfoundland conference, it would be an uncanny experience. The battleship was identical to *Prince of Wales*, which had carried the main British party in August 1941 and which now lay at the bottom of the South China Sea.

## Berlin

On Friday afternoon Adolf Hitler held an informal meeting of Nazi leaders – mostly the regional leaders or *Gauleiters* – in his private rooms at the Old Reich Chancellery (*Alte Reichskanzlei*) in the Wilhelmstrasse. About fifty people were present.

These were old comrades, so the Führer could be more frank about the situation on the Russian front than he had been in his long Reichstag speech of the previous day. On Russia, Hitler's explanation generally followed the line of the secret 8 December Wehrmacht High Command directive, and he declared his expectation that the troops would be pulled back to a more readily defendable line. The Panzers would come home to refit, in preparation for the spring 1942 campaign. Hitler said that he still had hopes for the capitulation of Leningrad in the next few weeks, and for the capture of Sevastopol'. Goebbels recorded his words: 'The spearheads which had, as one of their possible objectives the encirclement of Moscow, must now be pulled back, with the troops holding a defendable line.' Hitler tried to see the positive side. It was fortunate, he noted, that the Army had *not* advanced another 190 miles (300km) to the Volga, because then the supply problem would have been even more difficult. In an earlier conversation with Goebbels the Führer had been a little more frank: 'The situation on the Eastern front should not be seen too "dramatically". Obviously it is painful and embarrassing, but it can't be changed.' The aim was to fall back, without suffering heavy losses, to a defensive line which had been laid out, 'and from here to inflict heavy losses on the Bolsheviks'.[15] The German Army would able to renew the offensive, and the intention was to occupy Russia as far as the Urals in the course of the coming year.

At the Old Reich Chancellery Hitler also spoke about the outbreak of war in the Far East. His words made more sense of why he was prepared to accept war with America, a development which he described as being extraordinarily important. He expressed its value mainly in terms of giving freedom of action to the U-boat commanders. Even if Japan had not entered the war, he claimed, the Americans would have done so sooner or later. It was highly advantageous that the 'plutocratic powers' would have to split their forces across more theatres of war.

Most chilling that afternoon were Hitler's words about the Jews. Some historians argue that this meeting at the Old Reich Chancellery marked the point when the systematic murder of all European Jews became the 'official' policy of Nazi Germany.[16] There was no written transcript, but Goebbels summarised Hitler's speech:

> Regarding the Jewish question, the Führer is determined to clear the table. He warned the Jews that if they were to cause another world war [*Weltkrieg*], it would lead to their own destruction. These were not empty words. Now the world war has come, the destruction of the Jews must be its necessary consequence. This question should involve no sentimentality. We should have sympathy not for the Jews, but for our own German *Volk*. If the German *Volk* have to sacrifice yet another 160,000 victims in the campaign in the East,

then those responsible for this bloody conflict will have to pay for it with their lives.[17]

The link between the Holocaust – 'clearing the table' – and the outbreak of what Goebbels called the 'world war', is often forgotten. Hitler had indeed threatened publicly at the beginning of 1939 that if 'international financial Jewry, both in and outside Europe' should succeed in bringing about a new 'world war' then the result would be 'the extermination of the Jewish race in Europe.'[18] The war that began in September 1939 may or may not have been regarded by Hitler and the Nazis at the time as a 'world war', but its outbreak was not followed by the immediate mass murder of the Jews (either in Germany or elsewhere).[19] By the summer of 1940 – with the defeat of France, the entry of Italy into the war, and the continued neutrality of the USSR – the position of the Third Reich seemed considerably stronger than it had been earlier.

The wars with Soviet Russia and the United States in 1941 brought about a profound change. The titanic struggle in the USSR from June 1941 included, from the beginning, the cold-blooded shooting by SS death squads of any Jewish males of military age encountered on Soviet territory; this had been sanctioned centrally in Berlin. In the course of the next few months the executions were extended to both sexes, and to all ages of the Jewish population.[20] Large-scale mass killings also began in western Poland during the autumn of 1941, partly from local SS initiatives. The mass murder in Russia and Poland loosened any mental, moral and 'legal' inhibitions that the Nazis might have possessed.

A limited deportation of German Jews to Poland and the newly-occupied part of the USSR (Belorussia and the Baltic region) had begun in mid-October 1941. (Hitler had evidently approved this the previous month.) It was still not fully clear which German Jews would be deported, and which would be excluded – for example, those of 'mixed blood', those married to non-Jews, those with special status (e.g. Jewish war veterans). Nor had there been a clear decision about how to treat some, or all, of the German Jews once they had been deported. There had been cases of mass execution of German-Jewish 'transports', based on the decisions of local SS leaders, and this had not always been approved in Berlin. ('Soviet' or East European Jews did not, for the Nazis, benefit from any such scruples.) No clear decision had been made about the Jews of occupied Western Europe. The Wannsee meeting, arranged in later November, was intended to clear up these issues.

Meanwhile the struggle in Russia was different from what had gone before in the 'European War' of 1939–41. The scale of fighting was much greater, and even if the Third Reich won big victories the human cost was great – Hitler referred to the 160,000 German 'victims' in Russia, both in his public speech on Thursday and this secret speech on Friday. Hitler and his comrades may not have thought that they were losing the war in Russia, but the 'painful and embarrassing' winter crisis in Russia, the battles at Rostov and Moscow, suggested that the bloodshed would go on for some time, and might get worse.

Then there was the beginning of a genuine global war on 7 December. Hitler followed this with his speech to the Reichstag on the 11th, and his meeting with the Nazi leaders on the 12th. Hitler was here following through with his January 1939 prophecy about a 'world war'. The beginning of war with America also marked a psychological 'moment' in the history of the war, when the Nazi regime could rethink its deepest objectives. To some extent Nazi policy towards the Jews of Germany and the rest of Europe had been mitigated by a desire to preserve them as hostages to deter American intervention. Pearl Harbor and the German declaration of war now made that consideration irrelevant.

Like the uncompleted campaign in Russia, the entry of the United States into the war meant that the conflict was going to be extended. To Hitler and the Nazi leaders the position did not perhaps yet seem desperate, but no one could now think that Russia would be knocked out in a few months, or that an embattled and isolated Britain would sue for peace. The 'world war' meant a prolonged struggle for the survival of the Third Reich. The merciless elimination of the Jews was rationalised as a requirement of that struggle.

As the German historian Christian Gerlach put it, Hitler's words were a 'decision in principle', rather than a 'concrete directive' to begin the immediate liquidation of the Jews of Germany and Europe.[21] The postponed Wannsee meeting, when it finally convened on 20 January 1942, clarified some of the remaining technical issues. It would take some time – until May 1942 – before mass deportation and the construction of death camps and gas chambers brought about the full and awful reality of what we call the Holocaust. But Hitler's words on Friday, 12 December 1941, were a most significant step in its development.

CHAPTER 16

AFTERMATH

# The New War and a New World

*A declaration is algebra, while treaties are simple practical arithmetic. We want arithmetic rather than algebra.*

Joseph Stalin, 16 December 1941

*The great extent of the theatres of war, the close interconnection of the operations of the ground war and the political and war-economic objectives, as well as the numerical size of the army in comparison with the other branches of the Wehrmacht, compel the Führer to influence to the utmost the operations and supply of the Army and, following his intuitions, to reserve for himself all essential decisions in this field.*

German press announcement, 19 December 1941

## End of Empire

On 16 December, as *Duke of York* steamed steadily to the west, Churchill spoke to Charles Wilson about the 'new war'. Russia was now winning great battles, Japan had declared war, and the United States was directly involved – 'up to the neck.'[1]

For most observers, Japan's astonishing run of victories was the most remarkable feature of the 'new war'. In the weeks after 12 December, America's garrisons in the central and western Pacific were doomed to follow the fate of Guam. The American commands in Washington and Pearl Harbor dithered about defending or evacuating Wake. In the small hours of 23 December the Japanese returned in strength and effected a landing with 1,200 Japanese naval infantry – a force three times the size of the US Marine garrison. After a burst of sharp fighting the surviving Marines surrendered, and they and over a thousand civilian contractors were taken into captivity.[2]

In the Philippines it was the same story, but on a grander and more tragic scale. The Japanese sent an armada, nearly eighty transports, for the main landing on 22 December, two weeks after the start of the war. The main Japanese invasion force, a reinforced division (the 48th), would land in Lingayen Gulf, 100 miles north of Manila, just after midnight. There were no defensive attacks by US aircraft, and little activity by submarines. Another regiment, from the Japanese 16th Division, was landed on the east coast of Luzon, at Lamon Bay, on Christmas Eve.

General MacArthur now reversed his foolhardy strategy of trying to defend all of Luzon, and ordered a general withdrawal to the Bataan Peninsula, west of Manila Bay. Stubborn resistance during the three-month siege of Bataan did salvage some prestige for the US Army and the Filipino forces, and for Douglas MacArthur in particular. Nevertheless the Japanese quickly took control of the rest of the archipelago and marched into Manila on 2 January. Bataan surrendered on 9 April, and some 60,000 Filipino troops and 15,000 Americans fell into Japanese hands. It was the largest overseas military surrender in US history.

* * *

The fate of the British garrisons in Asia was no better. After Japanese demands to surrender, and several days of heavy artillery bombardment, the main attack on Hong Kong Island began on the night of 18–19 December. The three regiments of the 38th Division came across the harbour to the ten-mile long Hong Kong Island in small boats. The fighting was desperate, and bloodier and more brutal than it had been on the mainland, but the outcome was only a matter time. On the afternoon of Christmas Day, General Maltby surrendered.

Hong Kong was the first complete defeat of the western powers at the hands of the Japanese. Churchill was much dispirited. 'The worst that has happened,' he wrote to his wife two days before the landing, 'is the collapse of the resistance of Hong Kong; although one knew it was a forlorn outpost, we expected that they would hold out on the fortified island for a good many weeks, possibly for several months, but now they seem on the verge of surrender after only a fortnight's struggle.'[3] As for the victorious infantry of 38th Division, they were quickly moved on to Sumatra for the next stage of the Southern Operation. Much of the division was sent to Guadalcanal a few months later where they fought the Americans – unsuccessfully this time – in some of the pivotal battles of the Pacific War.

* * *

In an outline of grand strategy, written aboard *Duke of York*, Churchill had been optimistic about Southeast Asia. 'We expect,' he predicted, 'that Singapore island and fortress will stand an attack for at least six months, although meanwhile the naval base will not be usable by either side. A large Japanese army with siege train and ample supplies of ammunition and engineering stores will be required for their attack upon Singapore. Considerable Japanese forces also will be needed for the attack on Burma and the Burma Road.'[4]

In fact Singapore had been doomed by the events of the first days of the war – the destruction of the RAF bomber force, the sinking of *Prince of Wales* and *Repulse*, and the rout at Jitra. The British never regained the initiative. By the end of January 1942 General Yamashita had carried through his strategy of a 'driving charge' all the way down to Singapore. The great base, anchor of the British Empire's position in the Far East, fell on 15 February. Generals Percival, Heath and Murray-Lyon were captured, along with 70,000 British, Indian and Australian troops.

On 17 February, two days after the surrender, 45,000 Indian POWs were assembled in Farrar Park in Singapore, where a captain from the 1/14th Punjabis, Mohan Singh, addressed them, alongside a Japanese intelligence officer. He promised the liberation of the Asian peoples and proposed the establishment of an Indian National Army (INA). Mohan Singh had been cut off from his battalion during the Battle of Jitra on 11 December, and convinced by Bangkok-based Indian nationalists to help the Japanese. As many as 25,000 men eventually joined the INA, and Mohan Singh was its first leader.[5]

In the second part of the Japanese strategic offensive in the 'southern region', British Borneo and the Dutch East Indies, with all their resources, were brought under Japanese control. Rangoon fell in March, and shortly after that all of Burma and with it the last vestige of European power in Southeast Asia.

One thing Adolf Hitler did accurately predict, and very soon after the Japanese attack, was the collapse of colonial power in Asia. On 12 December, in his speech to the *Gauleiters* at the Old Reich Chancellery – and it should be recalled he was speaking to an audience of ardent racists – he explained the logic of these new developments: 'The interests of the white race must, for the moment, be subordinated to the interests of the German *Volk*.' On the 18th, speaking over lunch to his intimates and the fascist leader Anton Mussert (who was Dutch, with a clear connection to the East Indies) the Führer shed crocodile tears: 'I did not wish for what is happening in Asia,' he said; 'For years I told every British person I met: You will lose East Asia if you begin a conflict in Europe.'[6]

* * *

The Americans avoided the worst in the eastern Pacific. The Hawaiian Islands were not attacked again. Secretary of the Navy Frank Knox flew back into Washington on 15 December, having spent two full days at Pearl Harbor inspecting the damage. Knox's report to the President provided an impressive account of the raid.[7] The day after Knox saw the President, Admiral Kimmel and General Short were relieved of their commands. 'Betty' Stark, the Chief of Naval Operations, although on close terms with FDR, was also edged out of overall command. On 31 December the formidable Admiral Ernest King became C-in-C, US Fleet, taking over many of Stark's duties. In March 1942 King replaced him as CNO (Stark was made commander of US naval forces in Europe). General Marshall remained in his post as Army Chief of Staff until 1945.

On 18 December the President had a second meeting with Secretary Knox, at which Chester Nimitz was approved as the new CINCPAC. Roosevelt wanted Nimitz 'to get the hell out to Pearl, and stay there till the war was won'.[8] Under Nimitz the carriers and cruisers that had been at sea on 7 December now sallied forth to contest control of the Pacific. Leaving aside battleship strength, the Japanese and American forces were reasonably balanced. Especially important was carrier air power, where the Americans also had the advantage of radar. In addition US Navy signals intelligence, which had been at an advanced state of development even before Pearl Harbor, now became a vital part of the war-winning system.

The shadow-boxing ended in early June 1942, when Admiral Yamamoto took Combined Fleet to sea, with Admiral Nagumo's Mobile Detachment again acting as the vanguard. This time the objective was Midway Atoll, which had narrowly missed attack in December 1941. The run of Japanese luck now ended, along with the element of surprise. All four carriers, veterans of 7 December, were sunk by US Navy dive bombers. The Imperial Navy lost command of the Pacific after only six months.

## The Führer Takes Charge

By 13 December Joseph Stalin was even more confident that the tide had turned. He ordered his two army-group commanders in the Moscow battle to deal ruthlessly with encircled enemy forces. Zhukov and Konev were told that they should 'trap the enemy . . . give the Germans a chance to surrender and promise to spare their lives, and if they do not accept destroy them to the last man'.[9]

Hitler was still in Berlin on the 13th. That day Field Marshal von Brauchitsch arrived at the HQ of Army Group Centre in Smolensk to confer with Bock and to get a better view of the crisis that was developing. It would essentially be the last action of his long military career. Bock was in a state of near despair. 'The Führer has to decide whether the army group [AG Centre] has to fight where it stands, at the risk of being wrecked in the process, or whether it should withdraw, which entails the same risk. If he decides for withdrawal, he must realise that it is doubtful whether sufficient forces will reach the rear to hold a new, unprepared and significantly shorter position.' Brauchitsch, according to Bock, was now in agreement. Both generals were in their early sixties, and neither was in good health. Brauchitsch had suffered a heart attack in the previous month; Bock felt his physical state (he had stomach trouble) had worsened and asked the Army C-in-C to think 'about finding a replacement for me, as I don't know how long I can hold out after my serious illness of the previous year.'[10]

On 15 and 16 December the Russians reached major objectives north of Moscow, taking back the towns of Klin and Kalinin, both on the Moscow-Leningrad railway. The Germans were able to extract most of their troops, although much equipment was abandoned. On 20 December the advancing Soviet forces would finally reach the lines of the Ruza and Lama Rivers, seventy-five miles west of the 6 December starting point, where the Germans had prepared some defensive positions. It was not at all clear that the Russian tide could be dammed there.

To the south of the Soviet capital Guderian's 2nd Panzer Army had now abandoned most of the southern (Stalinogorsk) bulge. Stubborn German resistance and slow movement in the heavy snow by the poorly-trained Russian replacement divisions of Golikov's 10th Army enabled the Germans to hold the Tula-Orel highway, and along this route Guderian was able to extract his forces to the west. It was only on the 17th that the Soviet forces completed their ninety-mile advance from the 7 December starting line. The situation of German 2nd Army (south of Guderian) was not as critical as had been feared, although von Bock had to divert strength from the sectors of Army Group Centre closer to Moscow. Many of the German troops trapped between Elets and Livny were able to escape, but losses were high; the Russians captured 150 guns and 700 vehicles.

The German population was gradually made aware that something grave was happening in Russia. Local Soviet attacks were reported in the Wehrmacht news bulletins over the weekend of 13–14 December and early in the following week. (These were always accompanied by accounts of heavy Soviet losses at the hands of the German Army and the Luftwaffe.) Slipped into the public report of 17 December were some ominous words: 'In the course of the transition from offensive operations to wintertime positional warfare, necessary improvements and shortening of the front are being made in a planned way in various sectors of the Eastern Front.' On the 19th the bulletin mentioned, for the first time, that the defence against enemy attacks had involved 'hard fighting', and on the 20th it reported that 'heavy fighting' was continuing in the Army Group Centre area. On 20 December Goebbels released over the radio an extraordinary statement by Hitler on the *Wintersachensammlung*, the collection of winter clothes for the front. This was not, to be sure, depicted as the bankruptcy of Army supply policy or of Hitler's strategic planning. Rather it was to be an expression of the unity between front-line soldiers and the homeland in the Nazi 'People's Community' (*Volksgemeinschaft*).

Even more remarkable was the new description of the war which was included in the statement: 'Millions of our soldiers stand at the front after a year of the heaviest battles against an enemy far superior in terms of manpower and materiel.' A great victory would in the end be achieved, but for the moment German soldiers were shivering along 'the longest front of all time' stretching from the Arctic to the Black Sea.[11] The Wehrmacht, too, was fighting a 'new war'.

* * *

Late on the morning of Tuesday, 16 December, Hitler's train brought him from Berlin back to his WOLFSSCHANZE headquarters in East Prussia to face the consequences of Zhukov's offensive. A new phase of the command history of the war was about to begin.[12] The German dictator had had only limited contact with his Army commanders since he left East Prussia on the evening of the 8th. In the intervening days, the military crisis in the Moscow area had become acute. Since 1938 Hitler had been C-in-C of the entire Wehrmacht. He now took over, as well, command of the German Army from Field Marshal von Brauchitsch. A confrontation with Brauchitsch at the first daily 'situation meeting' (on the 16th) marked the final breakdown of the relationship between the Führer and his Army C-in-C.

Hitler was, at least, decisive. By midnight of 16–17 December he had confirmed that Army Group Centre was to 'stand fast'. On Thursday, the 18th, he issued his famous order calling for 'fanatical resistance':

> Large-scale retreats cannot be carried out. They will lead to the complete loss of heavy weapons and equipment. Under the personal leadership of the commanders-in-chief, commanders, and officers, the troops are to be compelled to put up fanatical resistance in the positions they occupy,

> without being distracted by enemy breakthroughs on the flanks or in the rear. Only by fighting the battle in this way will time be gained to bring reinforcements from the homeland and the West. Only if reserve troops have occupied the fall-back position can any thought be given to a re-deployment there.[13]

Hitler also made radical personnel changes across the Eastern Front. What mattered to him were willpower and morale. On the afternoon of the 18th (Thursday) General Kluge, former commander of 4th Army, arrived at Smolensk to replace von Bock as C-in-C of Army Group Centre. Bock had a cordial meeting with Hitler at WOLFSSCHANZE on his drive back to Berlin. German propaganda stressed the point that the Field Marshal was not in disfavour.[14] A number of other commanders at army-group and field-army level were relieved in December and January, including Leeb from Army Group North, Guderian from 2nd Panzer Army, Hoepner from Panzer Group 4, and Strauss from 9th Army.

On Monday, 22 December, the sensational news was publicly announced that the Führer was taking over direct command of the German Army. The official statement (dated 19 December) proclaimed that Hitler had taken this step 'while fully appreciating the services of the former C-in-C of the German Army'. Brauchitsch himself was allowed to issue a formal farewell. He explained – truthfully – that he had asked to be relieved some time earlier, because of a heart condition. He expressed confidence that Hitler would lead Germany to victory, and he urged forward the soldiers of 'the greatest army in the world'.[15] The more thoughtful reader of the Nazi press might have wondered why the main announcement had made no reference to the illness of the Field Marshal, and why his removal was not accompanied by any decoration or other recognition.

Although Brauchitsch was never publicly criticised, he was the single person Hitler and the Nazi leadership felt was most responsible for the defeats in Russia in November and December 1941, because of his failure to take account of the supply problems, his short-sighted obsession with the 'prestige' objective of Moscow, and (paradoxically) for his last-minute defeatism proving him to be a 'weakling'.[16]

More interesting, however, was the explanation, which also appeared in the German press on 22 December, of why the Führer had 'decided to unite in his own hands the leadership of the Wehrmacht as a whole [*Gesamtwehrmacht*] with the High Command of the Army'. This official press statement recalled the Führer's decision to become head of the Wehrmacht in February 1938. At that time, based on an 'inner calling and sense of responsibility . . . the state leader [*Staatsmann*] Adolf Hitler decided to be his own supreme military leader.'[17] The course of the war in the east had now given the struggle 'dimensions that have never been seen before' and required further central control. 'The great extent of the theatres of war, the close interconnection of the operations of the ground war and the political and war-economic objectives, as well as the numerical size of the army in comparison with the other branches of the Wehrmacht, compels the Führer to influence to the utmost the operations and supply of the Army and, following his intuitions, to reserve for himself all essential decisions in this field.'[18]

The German newspapers of 22 December also printed Hitler's appeal, 'To the Soldiers of the Army and the Waffen-SS', also dated 19 December. The struggle of the German *Volk*, he declared to his troops, forced on it by 'Jewish capitalist interests', was nearing its climax. Japan had entered the war, which meant that 'decisions of global significance' had to be made. At the same time, in Russia the 'sudden onset of winter' meant that the German armies in the east had to change from a war of movement to a static war of position (*Stellungsfront*). Until the spring the task of the troops would be to hold and defend positions just as fanatically and stubbornly as they had in the earlier battles fought to capture them.

The front now involved the entire continent, from Kirkenes in Norway to the Spanish border. Meanwhile a new offensive had to be prepared for the spring of 1942, which would lead to 'the final destruction of the enemy in the East'. 'These tasks,' Hitler concluded, 'require that the Wehrmacht and the homeland [*Heimat*] be brought to the highest degree of performance in one common effort. The *Army*, however, is the main fighting element of the Wehrmacht. Under these circumstances I have therefore resolved, today, as Supreme C-in-C of the German Wehrmacht, *to take over myself the leadership of the Army*.' Hitler promised that he would bring to this new command structure his own experience as a foot soldier: 'Nothing that is tormenting and troubling you is unknown to me.'[19]

## East versus West

On 15 December Winston Churchill, at sea aboard *Duke of York*, wrote to Stalin to congratulate him: 'It is impossible to describe the relief with which I have heard each successive day of the wonderful victories on the Russian front. I have never felt so sure of the outcome of the war.'[20] But in reality 'Russia victorious' (Churchill's words to Charles Wilson on the following day) created problems for the new Western allies, as well as for the Germans.

After their arrival in the Kola Inlet on 12 December, and a long train journey by way of Vologda, Foreign Secretary Eden's party would arrive in Moscow very early on the 16th. They were greeted at the station by a party including Foreign Commissar Molotov and General Vasilevskii from the General Staff. Four meetings were held in the Kremlin between 16 and 20 December.[21] Eden's visit to Soviet Russia would be revealed to the world in a brief joint communiqué on 29 December, the day he and his party returned safely to Scotland. The conversations were reported to have shown an 'identity of views . . . on all questions relating to the conduct of the war and especially with regard to the necessity for the utter defeat of Hitlerite Germany and the adoption thereafter of measures to render completely impossible any repetition of German aggression'. As for 'the post-war organisation of peace and security', the exchange of views had provided material for 'future elaboration of concrete proposals'.[22] The public communiqué did not tell the whole story. It was, indeed, the *only* outcome of the meeting.

Toward the end of his time in Moscow, on the 19th, Eden was taken with Ambassador Maiskii and a number of British officers and journalists for a four-hour drive to the northwest, to inspect the battlefield around Klin. The town had been the main objective of the Soviet counterattacks in the north, and had been liberated by the forces of 30th Army and 1st Shock Army only a few days earlier. The signs of fighting were everywhere; the Foreign Secretary was even given the chance to speak to German prisoners.[23]

But the main business of the visit was done in the Kremlin. Eden and Stalin devoted some time in their four days of talks to the 'conduct of the war'. The British Chiefs of Staff Committee (COS) had prepared a confidential briefing paper, which Eden used, on 16 December, to outline Britain's military position. He stressed the great improvement since 1940, especially in North Africa and the Mediterranean. Unfortunately, Eden also had to explain that the Japanese attack had 'brought in an absolutely new element into the general situation'. When he left Britain he had had ten RAF squadrons 'in his pocket' to offer to Russia, but now he had been told that these planes were to go to Singapore. As for sending British ground troops, this could not happen until the end of the Libyan campaign, and even then shipping would be limited by the need to move Lend-Lease supplies.

Stalin, for his part, outlined the situation on his front. The turning point had now been reached. The Germans were tired and had not prepared for winter fighting. The USSR had readied large reinforcements and thrown them into action. It would be at least two months before the enemy could bring up his own reinforcements. 'In the final analysis,' Stalin declared, 'the German army is not that strong. Its reputation is highly exaggerated.'[24]

On the last day of the talks (20 December), in response to prompts from London, Eden raised the question of Russian participation in the Far Eastern war. Stalin replied that Soviet entry in the war against Japan would need to be more than a token gesture. Part of the Siberian garrison had been moved to Europe, and four months would be needed to build it up again. In any event it would be better, psychologically, if Japan declared war on USSR, rather than vice versa. There the matter was left. Eden himself thought Russia would do best by concentrating the Red Army against Germany; he did not press the issue.[25]

Stalin made two contributions which showed that he shared in the British-American underestimation of Japan. In the opinion of the Soviet command, Stalin asserted, the Germans had transferred a large air strength (up to 1,500 aircraft) to Japan. It was, they believed, German rather than Japanese planes that had 'delivered such telling blows to the British Navy in the Far East.' These aircraft had probably been withdrawn from the Russian front, and transferred through South America, or perhaps Spain and Portugal. 'We well know from our own experience what kind of flyers the Japanese are. We got a look at them in China. It can surely be said that the latest events in Malaya are not the work of the Japanese.' Stalin also said that while Japan might have early success 'it must fail within a few months', because the Japanese troops were 'worn out'. The end of Japan would come even sooner if it dared to attack the USSR.[26]

* * *

The more significant part of the Moscow conference concerned war aims and the post-war world. For a leader whose tattered armies had been fighting for their lives at the gates of Moscow two weeks earlier, Stalin showed that he possessed both a long-distance perspective and a large appetite. At the first meeting on 16 December the Soviet dictator was remarkably concrete. Eden had put forward a draft agreement couched in general terms and based on the Atlantic Charter. Stalin complained that Eden's proposal was a 'declaration' [*deklaratsiia*] and that the Soviet government wanted a 'treaty' [*dogovor*]; 'A declaration is algebra, while treaties are simple practical arithmetic. We want arithmetic rather than algebra.'[27]

Stalin launched this first meeting with bold arithmetic. The Russians presented two very brief draft treaties of their own, one a 'treaty of alliance and mutual military assistance' and the other a 'treaty on the establishment of mutual agreement . . . in the solution of post-war questions and on . . . joint actions to maintain security in Europe after the termination of the war with Germany'. What was really important, however, was a secret protocol to the second treaty which Stalin tabled and to which he devoted his initial comments: after giving an overview of the European situation, the Soviet dictator laid out a comprehensive territorial deal.

Russia's frontiers, as they had existed on 22 June 1941, would be restored; the USSR would keep all the territories it had annexed in 1939–40. The Third Reich would be broken up, losing East Prussia, the Polish 'corridor' with all territory east of the Oder River, the Rhineland, Austria, and perhaps even Bavaria. Germany would be completely disarmed and would pay reparations in kind, dismantling and distributing industrial plant. The eastern part of East Prussia, including the city of Königsberg, would pass to the USSR for twenty years, as a guarantee of reparations deliveries. Poland would lose territory east of the so-called Curzon line (the eastern ethnic border) but would gain, at the expense of Germany, the western part of East Prussia and the Polish corridor.

Czechoslovakia, Yugoslavia and Greece would be restored. Following known British preferences, Stalin said the USSR would not object to some federations of the smaller European states. Britain would be allowed military bases in France, Belgium, Holland, Norway and Denmark, as well as use of the western German ports. The Red Army would be allowed bases in Romania and Finland. Stalin's diplomatic 'arithmetic' in December 1941 corresponded closely to the eventual reality which lasted from 1945 to 1989; Stalin and Molotov eventually got what they wanted.[28]

Stalin also proposed 'a military union of democratic states in the newly reconstructed Europe; headed by a council or other central organ and having military forces at its disposal.' But implicit in the whole proposal was the notion that it would be *Soviet Russia* that guaranteed the peace of continental Europe. As the draft protocols put it, plans for European organisation, especially in the east, should take into consideration the USSR as 'a power which is waging a great war of liberation in the interests of all the European states subjected to aggression and at present occupied by the forces of Hitlerite Germany, and which is the greatest [*krupneishii*] factor in the cause of making a secure peace in Europe and preventing new acts of aggression by Germany'.

Eden responded to these grand schemes by saying that the British government had not yet seriously discussed the future of Germany or the problems of post-war Europe. 'Here,' he admitted, 'it has fallen behind the Soviet Government.' In the back of the Foreign Secretary's mind, no doubt, was the last-minute message, received via Ambassador Winant, warning against any secret promises to Russia and urging that he adhere to the Atlantic Charter.

Eden did indeed tell Stalin that the US had asked Britain to refrain from making obligations about post-war reconstruction without consultation; he also had to confer with the Dominions. The British government could only give a detailed answer on the concrete territorial questions after discussions in London on his return.

Eden was to be disappointed if he thought that he had defused the situation. The second meeting began in the Kremlin at midnight on 17–18 December, after Stalin had completed a conference with his own senior military commanders. The Soviet leader, evidently still in a bellicose mood, suddenly made the blunt demand that Britain recognise the new western borders, especially regarding Finland, the Baltic States and Romania. This was still arithmetic, but the sum was simpler and cruder. Eden repeated his suggestion that he would refer this question to his government when he returned home, and said that for this reason he had made no effort to contact London. In any event, Eden noted, Prime Minister Churchill was inaccessible on his voyage to America. 'He begged [or so the Soviet minutes put it] not to be asked to do the impossible.' Stalin replied that in this case it would be very difficult to sign the draft treaties.

The argument then became (in the words of Oliver Harvey) 'sticky'. Eden stressed the stipulations in the Atlantic Charter which prohibited border changes without consent. He said that British policy was not to recognise changes that had taken place since the start of the war in September 1939. Stalin's reply was frosty: 'The impression has been created, involuntarily, that the Atlantic Charter was directed not against those people who want to establish world domination, but against the USSR.' Molotov pitched in: 'We are talking about common war aims, about a common struggle, but in one of the most important war aims – our western border – we are unable to obtain the support of Great Britain. Surely this is not right?'

Here was the breaking point. The USSR would not sign any treaties unless Britain secretly accepted the Soviet border changes made between 1939 and 1941. Alec Cadogan, who was present at the second meeting on the 17th, put the matter succinctly when he recalled Stalin's position: 'I thought at first he was simply bluffing. But I was wrong.' 'He [Stalin] feels that he is strong now,' Eden told Harvey, 'and can do what he likes.'[29]

Churchill was not too concerned about the outcome of the Moscow talks. 'Foreign Secretary . . . should not be downhearted if he has to leave Moscow without any flourish of trumpets,' he wrote to Attlee on 20 December. 'The Russians have got to go on fighting for their lives, anyway, and are dependent upon us for very large supplies . . . which we shall faithfully deliver.' However,

Stafford Cripps, the British Ambassador, was not far off the mark in his pessimistic prediction: 'We shall fight two separate wars and we shall suffer as the result.'[30]

* * *

The military situation on the Eastern Front was not in reality as good as Stalin hoped. As Churchill predicted, he would continue to need help from his new allies. Hitler had certainly been very worried. 'The Führer described to me,' Goebbels recalled in March 1942, 'how close we came in the past months to a Napoleonic winter [i.e. 1812]. If for only one moment he had shown weakness, then the front would have slid into collapse, and the ground laid for a catastrophe which would have far overshadowed that of Napoleon.'[31]

But the Red Army's startling advances in front of Moscow in December 1941, and in January and February 1942, would be followed by stalemate. Stalin spread his counteroffensive over a very long front stretching from the Crimea to Leningrad. The raw and ill-equipped new divisions and brigades were not capable of deep operations, and the *Ostheer* did indeed put up 'fanatical resistance'. By mid-January the front had stabilised. The Germans were in roughly the same position they had held in early October 1941, deep in European Russia. Then, in May 1942, a large new German offensive, Operation BLUE, started in southern Russia.

But the Russian victories of November and December 1941 were to be the most important of the whole war. The German war of movement came to a halt in November and December 1941. At Rostov and Leningrad the Germans were stalled, in front of Moscow they suffered a serious defeat. The lines established in front of Moscow and Leningrad in the winter of 1941–42 would be held until the general Soviet counteroffensive began in early 1943. A quick victory had been the only way Germany could win in Russia.[32] Now the Third Reich was to fight a war of attrition against a numerically superior enemy. Because powerful allies were involved, that war would end in defeat, not stalemate. Germany's cause would not be helped by the fact that in the later campaigns a military amateur of fanatical temperament had taken charge of its Army.

## The Special Relationship: Grand Strategy for Victory

Military professionals on both sides were trying to make sense of the new war. General Jodl, Chief of the Operations Staff of the Wehrmacht High Command, had travelled to Berlin with Hitler and Field Marshal Keitel. On 11 December, after the Führer made his Reichstag speech, Jodl telephoned his deputy, Walter

Warlimont, at WOLFSSCHANZE and requested that he draft a paper on likely operations by Germany's new enemy. Warlimont (as he himself later maintained) was very surprised at the turn of events. All the same, at short notice and despite a lack of data, he set to work. 'Overview of the Significance of the Entry of the USA and Japan into the War' was completed on 14 December.[33]

Warlimont was a compact and still youthful-looking man of forty-seven. An artilleryman turned specialist in industrial mobilisation, he spoke good English and had spent a year on secondment to the US Army in 1929–30. He was an intelligent staff officer, but some of his colleagues called him 'the fox' for the caution he took in expressing clear views. His 14 December paper was no exception. He concluded by suggesting that even in the worst case it would take some time for the Allies to build up their forces; Germany would have an opportunity for a further offensive initiative. 'On land it is to be sought only in attacking the Near Eastern position that is important for the British Empire'. Warlimont's words implied that something more decisive, a 'subsequent attack on the British homeland', was now less likely. At sea it was crucial to attack the enemy's shipping to make him give up offensive planning and, eventually, to abandon the struggle.

Most of Warlimont's paper, however, was about defence and the implications of the 'Roosevelt Plan', which had been leaked in the *Chicago Tribune* ten days earlier. What had been disclosed reflected authentic American planning, he believed, as it corresponded with all the steps taken by the United States so far. Warlimont summarised the 'Anglo-Saxon war plans' in four key areas: protection of sea routes, closing the ring around the German-controlled zone, large-scale strategic air attacks, and 'a landing operation aimed at a decisive outcome after the summer of 1943'. He stated that the Japanese surprise attack had made the published 'Roosevelt Plan' meaningless, but much of the subsequent content of his paper suggested he assumed it still had a good deal of validity.

Warlimont thought it was impossible to tell immediately whether 'Anglo-Saxon' forces would concentrate against Germany and Italy, or against Japan, or would be divided evenly between them. He took the 'worst case' of concentration against Germany and Italy, and then examined the options open to the enemy. Preparatory Allied attacks might be made on Morocco and West Africa, 'successes that are very much desired [by the Americans and British] for propaganda purposes'. 'The capture of Algiers and the rest of North Africa would make it possible to tighten the blockade'. The main Allied offensive would include a strategic air offensive directed, especially, at German oil supply. The land invasion of the Continent could only be made in certain locations, where air support could be provided. One likely route was through the Mediterranean. Once in control of North Africa 'a landing can be staged in Italy from Tunis via Sicily. It would confront an Italy that has already been greatly weakened in its capacity to resist'. Most dangerous for Germany would be an offensive in the direction of northern France, Belgium and the Netherlands. Prospects for success depended on 'weakening the German defences along the coast and in the immediate hinterland by gaining complete control of the air from Britain'. The British homeland would provide an excellent base, and for the Allies it could lead to a 'rapid thrust at the heart of the enemy'.

This was a remarkable feat of foresight: Warlimont had anticipated the actual routes of the key operations of the British and Americans in 1942–44: TORCH (North Africa), HUSKY (Sicily), AVALANCHE (Italy) and OVERLORD (northern France).

But, Warlimont continued, all this would take time to organise, as the Anglo-Saxons were operating on exterior lines and their sea routes were vulnerable to attack. American rearmament would not reach its full peak immediately. In the meantime Germany must 'round off the area under our control to make it economically viable and defensible military and politically'. Primarily this involved 'finishing off the campaign in Russia', although this did not mean total victory along the lines of the original BARBAROSSA plan. What mattered was taking the northern ports of Murmansk and Arkhangel'sk to cut off supply from America and Britain and, in the south, taking the oil fields of the Caucasus and surrounding territory.

Warlimont did briefly touch on co-operation with Japan, but only in terms of tying down Soviet troops in eastern Siberia and joint operations against Allied shipping. Overall, the signatory powers of the Tripartite Pact of 11 December 1941 never worked out a global strategy. This was partly because of the near complete physical separation of the European and Asian Axis states, and partly because Japan was unwilling or unable to go to war with the USSR. Hitler did meet Ōshima on 13 December, but, aside from presenting the Ambassador with a medal, he spoke mainly about America and U-boat operations.[34] Ōshima did propose joint operations against India, but for both sides this was quite hypothetical. The Japanese on 15 December submitted the draft of a 'Military Agreement', which was eventually signed by the three Axis powers on 18 January. All this did was to set up zones of operations, the demarcation lines being longitude 70°E (the line ran roughly from the borders of Afghanistan and India south across the Indian Ocean). In practical terms the division of responsibility merely involved operations against Allied shipping. Global strategy was not discussed, except at the most abstract level. Warlimont recalled that he and the professionals of his staff had no involvement in these discussions.[35]

* * *

Little more than a week after Warlimont drafted his speculative paper, the leaders of the western Allies actually met in Washington to ponder grand strategy. On the afternoon of 22 December *Duke of York* arrived in Chesapeake Bay with Churchill and much of the British military leadership on board. The Washington conference was given the codename ARCADIA.

The conference was important at the highest political and diplomatic levels. In his initial proposal to President Roosevelt on 9 December, Churchill had suggested that he might be in Washington for a week. In fact the Prime Minister arrived in Washington on 22 December, taking up residence in the White House, and left over three weeks later, on 14 January. (His travels within that period did include a three-day trip to Canada, and a three-day holiday to Florida.) That Christmas visit did much to tighten his bond with Franklin Roosevelt, a 'friend' whom he had only personally met once before. The visit also did much to cement the 'Special Relationship' in the minds of the American public; the Prime Minister made a powerful speech to Congress on 26 December.

In the secret meetings of the American and British leaders there was no thought of a grand re-ordering of Europe, on the 'arithmetical' lines suggested by Stalin – and evaded by Eden – in Moscow. President Roosevelt did think up the title 'United Nations' for the countries fighting Germany, but politically and diplomatically the ARCADIA conference did not go far beyond the August 1941 Atlantic Charter. The signing of the Declaration of the United Nations began in the White House on the first day of 1942. The first signatories were the President and the Prime Minister, as well as the new Foreign Minister of China, and Ambassador Litvinov from the USSR. There was little to differentiate the technical terms of this declaration from the Tripartite Pact signed in Berlin three weeks earlier; the states involved agreed to employ their 'full resources', to co-operate with other signatories, and not to make a separate peace.[36]

But above all ARCADIA was about military planning and the allocation of resources.[37] The real business took place at twelve broad planning meetings held in the building of the Federal Reserve Board. General Marshall was the most notable figure on the American military side, but Admirals Stark and King, and General Arnold (for the USAAF) were also important. The British military was represented by Admiral Pound and Air Marshal Portal, as well as Field Marshal Dill, the former Chief of the Imperial General Staff.

In terms of grand strategy ARCADIA was important because it confirmed the 'Germany first' priority of the American-British 'ABC' staff talks of the spring of 1941 and of the RAINBOW FIVE American strategy. The planning document entitled 'American-British Grand Strategy' was largely based on a British draft, and it confirmed that 'the Atlantic and the European area was considered to be the decisive theatre'. 'Much has happened since February last,' the Allied planners continued, 'but notwithstanding the entry of Japan into the War, our view remains that Germany is still the prime enemy and her defeat is the key to victory. Once Germany is defeated, the collapse of Italy and the defeat of Japan must follow.' '[I]t should be a cardinal principle of A-B [American-British] strategy,' they continued, 'that only the minimum of force necessary for the safeguarding of vital interests in other theatres should be diverted from operations against Germany.'

That said, there were distinct reminders here of the lack of global realism that had characterised British and American strategic thinking throughout 1941. The strategy against Japan could hardly be limited, as the tasks specified included the defence of Singapore, the Dutch East Indies, the Philippines, and Rangoon in Burma, as well as the 'maritime provinces' of Siberia. These were hardly missions that could be achieved with 'the minimum of force', especially after the losses of Allied ships and aircraft in the first days of the Pacific War.

Arms production was to be increased and shipping lanes secured; the next step would be the 'wearing down' of Germany, and the strengthening and closing of the 'ring' around German-occupied territory. The year 1942, the document suggested, would probably not allow an Allied land offensive except on the Russian front, but in 1943 there would be a 'return to the Continent' by American and British armies from one of several possible directions.[38]

No practical high-level decisions were made at ARCADIA. The emphasis was on building up and defending supply lines in the Pacific and sending some US ground troops to Northern Ireland. The great 1942 debate about the cross-Channel invasion had yet to begin. Churchill's proposal (Operation SUPER-GYMNAST – possibly the worst Allied codename of the war) to invade northwest Africa as soon as possible was rejected. It was only eleven months later that the idea would be realised as Operation TORCH.

* * *

In military terms the 'new war' was, in 1942, much less dramatic for both sides in Western Europe and in Atlantic waters than it would be in the Far East or the Pacific; it was also much less costly than the fighting on the Russian front. In the short term German and American forces could not easily engage one another. Seven weeks would pass before the war against American shipping began. The first cruiser U-boats sent to operate directly against the US coast, in Operation PAUKENSCHLAG (DRUMBEAT), left French ports on 18 December; there were initially just five of them. Only on 18 January did *U 66* sink the tanker SS *Allan Jackson* sixty miles off the North Carolina coast. After that, however, the pace of German success rapidly mounted. The five PAUKENSCHLAG boats would account for twenty-five merchant ships before the last one headed home on 6 February. Later waves of U-boats would have massive successes against merchant ships sailing independently off the East Coast, before the US Navy belatedly introduced a coastal convoy system in May 1942.

The first elements of the American 34th Division, a National Guard formation from the Great Plains, landed in Northern Ireland on 26 January in what was codenamed Operation MAGNET. This was part of the RAINBOW FIVE war plan, worked out months before 7 December. Nearly a year would pass, however, before American soldiers engaged German ones, and this would happen in Algeria and Tunisia.

The first American bomber raid on Europe was not mounted until 12 June 1942, when a dozen B-24 Liberators from Egypt made a one-off long-range strike against the oil refineries at Ploesti in Romania. The vaunted B-17 entered US service over France only on 17 August 1942, and in very small numbers; the first 'Flying Fortress' attack on a target in Germany would come only on 27 January 1943. USAAF pilots first shot down a German plane on 14 August 1942, off Iceland.

As for the British, the 'new war' derailed existing strategy in Europe and North Africa for much of the coming year. General Auchinleck had in the end achieved a major success in December 1941. After the delayed success of Operation CRUSADER Rommel had to pull back 600 miles, giving up all of eastern Libya. On 24 December the Germans abandoned the forward port at Benghazi, and by early January the British had reached El Agheila. Meanwhile Rommel was forced to abandon 8,000 troops – including 2,000 Germans – who were still dug in on the Egyptian border.

The British threw inexperienced troops into the pursuit, and these proved incapable of either overrunning all of Libya or of constructing a sturdy forward line of defence there. The Royal Navy suffered devastating losses in Alexandria harbour when Italian frogmen crippled two battleships with limpet mines. With this, and the arrival of Luftwaffe reinforcements, the British lost control of the Mediterranean supply routes. They had to send ground, sea and air units to the Far East, while the flow of weapons from across the Atlantic (and around the Cape of Good Hope) slowed, as the United States temporarily gave preference to its own forces. In another extraordinary turn of fortune General Rommel mounted a new attack on 21 January 1942, six weeks after his crisis in December. By the beginning of February the 'Desert Fox' had thrown the British back to the Gazala line, just west of Tobruk, and from May 1942 he would launch repeated attacks towards Egypt. In June he finally took Tobruk, along with 30,000 prisoners and a large number of vehicles and supplies. As a military disaster the fall of Tobruk was second only to Singapore. General Auchinleck was replaced.

The tide would eventually turn – and along the general lines that Churchill had conceived for Operation CRUSADER in November 1941. During the summer of 1942 the British were able to reinforce their armies in the Middle East, where American equipment was now arriving in quantity. General Montgomery defeated Rommel in Egypt (at El Alamein in November 1942) and in Libya. Simultaneously the British and Americans mounted an invasion of French North Africa – Operation TORCH – and eight months later an invasion of Sicily forced the Italians out of the war. It had all, however, taken a year longer than Churchill had hoped in November 1941.

From 1943 to 1945 the military and political implications of the new war became apparent. The Allies now held the initiative in most theatres of the global war.

The important exception was Southeast Asia. With all the other fronts to maintain the British had few forces to send, and the US had no great interest in the region. A counteroffensive was mounted in Burma in 1943–45, fought valiantly and effectively by Indian ground troops. But when the war in Europe ended in 1945, Hong Kong and most of Southeast Asia, including Malaya, Indochina, most of the Dutch East Indies and part of Burma were still in Japanese hands. The Japanese thrust to the south in 1941 had had a permanent effect. European colonial power was never effectively restored.

Elsewhere events did not follow the simple outline envisaged at the end of 1941. It took the Red Army much longer than Stalin expected to drive the Wehrmacht out of Russia, and the Third Reich never suffered the internal collapse he anticipated. Nevertheless, the end of the Blitzkrieg in front of Moscow in December 1941 and the swallowing up of the German Army and Luftwaffe in the depths of Russia, created the preconditions for successful operations in the south and west of Europe. The British and Americans did not fully follow the ABC war plan agreed in the spring of 1941 and confirmed at ARCADIA. The United States, rather than simply 'safeguarding vital interests', decided after the outrage of Pearl Harbor to wage an active offensive war against the Japanese in the Pacific. Up to at least November 1942 more American forces were deployed there than in Europe.

The British and Americans disagreed over how best to take down the Third Reich and in the end opted for a 1943 campaign in the Mediterranean – knocking out Fascist Italy – rather than a crossing of the English Channel. The full-scale attack on Normandy would not come until the summer of 1944, by which time the back of the German Army had been broken in Russia. The Axis leaders had hoped the United States would have to divide its resources, but those resources proved to be vast, as was the American will for victory and world power. They also underestimated the potential of the Soviet war economy.

* * *

What I have been arguing in this book is not only that the events of the twelve days from 1 to 12 December 1941 were pivotal, but that they make sense only when taken together. The Germans, Italians and Japanese had created what they hoped would be a global structure – to defeat Britain and to deter the US from entering the war – when they signed the Tripartite Pact in September 1940. If the United States intervened in the war, either in Europe or in Asia, it would face war everywhere. The Tripartite Pact, in turn, was a major source of Japanese-American tension in the months that followed, and ultimately, in December 1941, the pact meant that a Japanese attack on the US was followed by German and Italian declarations of war.

British grand strategy, meanwhile, was above all concerned with bringing the United States into the war as an ally; also important was keeping the Red Army in the field as long as possible. Hitler's own grand strategy led to the attack on the USSR in June 1941. The British Empire was still regarded as the main enemy of the Third Reich, but the Wehrmacht was not able to mount an invasion of the United Kingdom. The Germans hoped to make the British see reason by defeating Russia and removing from the equation Churchill's last possible European ally.

When war did come in the Far East, Japan's leaders attacked the United States in the Philippines and raided the eastern Pacific, because they wanted to invade the British and Dutch colonies in Southeast Asia. Tokyo felt able to attack the British and Dutch colonies, because – 7,000 miles away – Germany had occupied the home territory of two colonial powers (the Netherlands and France), because British forces were committed to other theatres (particularly home defence and North Africa), and because the Red Army's desperate defence of European Russia in Siberia meant that it no longer presented an immediate threat to Japan and its colony in Manchuria. The British, while aware of the threat to their Asian colonies, were afraid to pre-empt the Japanese movement south, because they did not know whether Washington would support such action. But at the same time Churchill thought an attack on British colonies in the Far East was unlikely, because Japan would not also dare to go to war with America.

Hitler declared war on the United States with genuine enthusiasm on 11 December. He certainly did not do so just because of formal treaty obligations under the Tripartite Pact. He also probably made his decision before the full extent of the sudden Japanese victories became clear. He believed that President Roosevelt had been trying to provoke Germany for the last eighteen months by his one-sided support for the Allies, and he probably believed war with America was now inevitable. War with Japan (now fighting alongside Germany) would prevent America from deploying its full strength into Europe. But also important was the stalemate of the Russian campaign, which had become evident by that December. The war in the Pacific would hide German setbacks and allow the Axis to regain the initiative in what had become a global struggle.

President Roosevelt and his advisers underestimated (before 7 December) the military danger to America in the Pacific. Their attention, as far as it was concerned with Japan, was focused on Southeast Asia. Like Churchill they also thought it was unlikely Tokyo would risk war with both Britain and the US. These false assumptions, more than anything else, explain why Washington and London were caught by surprise and failed to exploit the extraordinary intelligence available about Japanese movements and general intentions. Above all, however, the national priority of the Roosevelt administration was still to get to grips with Hitler's Germany rather than become involved in a Far Eastern sideshow.

The Russians were victorious at Moscow and elsewhere in December 1941 because the Wehrmacht was exhausted and because the Red Army had much greater recuperative powers than Hitler and his generals expected. One contributing factor, however, was Stalin's ability to transfer fresh troops from Siberia to Europe, and another was the movement of Luftwaffe units from the Russian front to buttress Mussolini against a British threat in the Mediterranean.

Hitler and the Nazis made their final decisions about the Holocaust in part because of the 'world war' which began on 7 December. This meant that the Jews, especially those of western Europe, no longer served as hostages against American intervention, and because German setbacks in Russia meant a 'territorial' version of the Final Solution – deporting the Jews to Russian territory – was no longer practical.

In hindsight, this global web of events marked the dawn of a 'new world' as well as a 'new war'. Actions set in train in these twelve days would lead to the defeat and transformation of Germany and Italy. December 1941 foreshadowed the collapse of the British Empire in Asia and steepened the descent of Britain from world pre-eminence. In this period began the coming of age of America and Russia as superpowers. The Battle of Moscow marked the rebirth of the Red Army and restored Stalin's confidence; he would end the war in control of half of Europe. And the attack on American territory unleashed the military and industrial might of the United States, with a mission that was self-consciously global.

# List of Participants

## Americans

Bloch, Adm. Claude. Commander of 14th Naval District (HQ: Oahu)
Brereton, Gen. Lewis. Commander of USAAF in the Philippines (HQ: Manila)
Grew, Joseph. Ambassador to Japan
Hart, Adm. Thomas. C-in-C of US Asiatic Fleet (HQ: Manila)
Hopkins, Harry. Adviser to President Roosevelt
Hull, Cordell. Secretary of State
Kimmel, Adm. Husband. C-in-C of Pacific Fleet (HQ: Oahu)
King, Adm. Ernest. C-in-C of Atlantic Fleet; C-in-C, US Fleet, from 20 Dec. 1941
Knox, Frank. Secretary of the Navy
MacArthur, Gen. Douglas. C-in-C of US Army Forces in Far East (HQ: Manila)
Marshall, Gen. George. Chief of Staff (C-in-C) of US Army
Roosevelt, Frankin Delano. President, C-in-C of US armed forces
Safford, Cmdr Laurance. Chief of US Navy codebreaking organisation OP-20-G (HQ: Washington)
Short, Gen. Walter. C-in-C of US Army forces in Hawaii (HQ: Oahu)
Stark, Adm. Harold. Chief of Naval Operations (C-in-C of US Navy)
Stimson, Henry. Secretary of War (Army)
Welles, Sumner. Under Secretary of State
Winant, Gilbert. Ambassador to Britain

## British

Auchinleck, Gen. Claude. C-in-C of British Army in Middle East (HQ: Cairo)
Brooke, Gen. Alan. Chief of Imperial General Staff (C-in-C of British Army) from Dec. 1941
Brooke-Popham, Air Marshal Robert. C-in-C, Far East (for Army and RAF) (HQ: Singapore)
Cadogan, Alexander. Permanent Secretary at the Foreign Office, Chief Adviser to Eden
Cavendish-Bentinck, Victor. Chairman of Joint Intelligence Committee
Churchill, Winston. Prime Minister, Minister of Defence
Craigie, Robert. Ambassador to Japan
Cripps, Stafford. Labour MP, Ambassador to Russia (Kuibyshev)
Cunningham, Gen. Alan. Commander of British 8th Army to Nov. 1941 (under Auchinleck)
Dill, Gen. John. Chief of Imperial General Staff (C-in-C, British Army), to end of Nov. 1941
Eden, Anthony. Foreign Secretary
Halifax, Viscount (E.F.L. Wood). Ambassador to the US

Harvey, Oliver. Private Secretary to Eden
Heath, Gen. Lewis. Commander of III Indian Corps, northern Malaya (under Percival)
Layton, Adm. Geoffrey. C-in-C, China Station, to 8 Dec. 1941 (HQ: Singapore), resumed command after death of Adm. Phillips
Maltby, Gen. Christopher. Commander of Hong Kong garrison
Maltby, Air Marshal Paul. Deputy to Pulford (Singapore)
Martin, John. Private Secretary to Churchill
Murray-Lyon, Gen. David. Commander of 11th Indian Division, northern Malaya (under Heath)
Percival, Gen. Arthur. Commander of British Army forces in Malaya (GOC, Malaya Command) (under Brooke-Popham) (HQ: Singapore)
Phillips, Adm. Tom. C-in-C of British Eastern Fleet (HQ: Singapore)
Portal, Air Marshal Charles. Chief of the Air Staff (C-in-C of RAF)
Pound, Adm. Dudley, 1st Sea Lord (C-in-C of Royal Navy)
Pulford, Air Marshal C.W.H. Commander of RAF forces in Malaya (AOC, RAF Far East) (HQ: Singapore)
Ritchie, Gen. Neil. Commander of British 8th Army in Libya from Nov. 1941 (under Auchinleck)

## Germans

Bock, Field Marshal Fedor von. C-in-C of Army Group Centre (HQ: Smolensk)
Brauchitsch, Field Marshal Walther von. C-in-C of German Army (HQ: MAUERWALD, E. Prussia)
Dietrich, *Obergruppenführer* Sepp. Commander of Waffen-SS *Leibstandarte* Div.
Engel, Maj. Gerhard. Army adjutant to Hitler, 1938–43 (WOLFSSCHANZE, E. Prussia)
Goebbels, Joseph. Propaganda Minister
Guderian, Gen. Heinz. Commander of 2nd Panzer Army (under Bock)
Halder, Gen. Franz. Chief of Army General Staff (HQ: MAUERWALD, E. Prussia)
Hitler, Adolf. Führer and Reich Chancellor, C-in-C of German Armed Forces (Wehrmacht) (HQ: WOLFSSCHANZE, E. Prussia)
Hoepner, Gen. Erich. Commander of Panzer Group 4 (under Bock)
Jodl, Gen. Alfred. Chief of Operations Staff at Wehrmacht High Command (*OKW*) (WOLFSSCHANZE, E. Prussia)
Keitel, Field Marshal Wilhelm. Chief of Staff of Wehrmacht High Command (*OKW*) (HQ: WOLFSSCHANZE, E. Prussia)
Kleist, Gen. Ewald von. Commander of 1st Panzer Army (under AG South)
Kluge, Field Marshal Hans-Günther von. Commander of 4th Army (under Bock)
Kretschmer, Col. Alfred. Military Attaché in Japan
Leeb, Field Marshal Wilhelm von. C-in-C of Army Group North (HQ: Pskov)
Mackensen, Gen. Eberherd von. Commander of III Panzer Corps (under Kleist)
Mackensen, Hans Georg von. Ambassador to Italy
Ott, Gen. Eugen. Ambassador to Japan
Reichenau, Gen. Walter von. C-in-C of Army Group South from 1 Dec. 1941 (replacing Rundstedt) (HQ: Poltava)
Reinhardt, Gen. Hans-Georg. Commander of Panzer Group 3 (under Bock)
Ribbentrop, Joachim von. Reich Foreign Minister
Rommel, Gen. Erwin. Commander of Panzer Group *Afrika*
Rundstedt, Field Marshal Gerd von. C-in-C of Army Group South (HQ: Poltava)
Schmidt, Gen. Rudolf. Acting commander of 2nd Army (under Bock)
Schmundt, Col. Rudolf. Wehrmacht aide-de-camp to Hitler (WOLFSSCHANZE, E. Prussia)
Sodenstern, Gen. Georg von. Chief of Staff of Army Group South
Warlimont, Gen. Walter. Deputy Chief of Operations Section of Wehrmacht High Command (under Jodl) (WOLFSSCHANZE, E. Prussia)
Weizsäcker, Ernst von. State Secretary at Foreign Ministry

### Italians

Ciano, Galeazzo. Foreign Minister
Mussolini, Benito. *Duce* of Fascist Italy, Prime Minister

### Japanese

Fuchida Mitsuo, Commander. Leader of Pearl Harbor air strike force
Homma Masaharu, Gen. Commander of 14th Army (Philippines) (under Terauchi)
Horikiri Zenbei. Ambassador to Italy
Kamimura Shinichi. Chargé d'Affaires in London
Kondō Nobutake, Adm. C-in-C of Southern Force (under Yamamoto)
Kurusu Saburō. Special Envoy to the US
Nagano Osami, Adm. Chief of Naval General Staff (HQ: Tokyo)
Nagumo Chūichi, Adm. C-in-C of Mobile Force (under Yamamoto)
Nomura Kichisaburō. Retired Admiral, Ambassador to the US
Ōshima Hiroshi, Gen. Ambassador to Germany
Ozawa Jisaburō, Adm. Commander of Malaya Force (under Kondō)
Sugiyama Hajime, Gen. Chief of Staff of Japanese Army
Terauchi Hisaichi, Gen. C-in-C of Southern Army (HQ: Saigon)
Tōgō Shigenori. Foreign Minister from Oct. 1941
Tōjō Hideki, Gen. Prime Minister from Oct. 1941
Yamamoto Isoroku, Adm. C-in-C of Combined Fleet
Yamashita Tomoyuki, Gen. Commander of 25th Army (Malaya) (under Terauchi)

### Poles

Anders, Władysław. Commander of Polish Army in Russia
Kot, Stanisław. Ambassador to the USSR
Sikorski, Władysław. Head of Polish government in exile, C-in-C of Polish Army (HQ: London)

### Russians

Golikov, Gen. Fedor. Commander of 10th Army (under Zhukov)
Konev, Gen. Ivan. C-in-C of Kalinin Army Group (HQ: Kushalino)
Leliushenko, Gen. Dmitrii. Commander of 30th Army (under Zhukov)
Litvinov, Maksim. Ambassador to the US
Maiskii, Ivan. Ambassador to Britain
Molotov, Viacheslav. People's Commissar of Foreign Affairs
Rokossovskii, Gen. Konstantin. Commander of 16th Army (under Zhukov)
Shaposhnikov, Marshal Boris. Chief of General Staff (HQ: Arzamas/Moscow)
Sokolovskii, Gen. Vasilii. Chief of Staff of Western Army Group (under Zhukov)
Stalin, Joseph. General Secretary of All-Union Communist Party, Chairman of *Sovnarkom* (Prime Minister), Chairman of the State Defence Committee (*GKO*), Supreme C-in-C of the Red Army (HQ: Moscow)
Vasilevskii, Gen. Aleksandr. Deputy Chief of General Staff (HQ: Moscow)
Vlasov, Gen. Andrei. Commander of 20th Army (under Zhukov)
Zhukov, Gen. Georgii. C-in-C of Western Army Group (HQ: Vlasikha)

# Notes

The following abbreviations for frequently cited sources and publications are used in the Notes and Select Bibliography.

*ADAP*: *Akten zur deutschen auswärtigen Politik, 1918–1945*
ADM: Admiralty records at TNA
BA-MA: Bundesarchiv-Militärarchiv, Freiburg im Breisgau, Gemany
BI: Borthwick Institute for Archives, University of York
*BPM*: *Bitva pod Moskvoi* (ed. Zhilin *et al*)
*C&R*: *Churchill and Roosevelt: The Complete Correspondence* (ed. Kimball)
CAB: Cabinet Office records at TNA
CAC: Churchill Archive Centre, Churchill College, Cambridge
CUOHC: Columbia University Oral History Collection
*CWP*: *Churchill War Papers* (ed. Gilbert)
*DPSR*: *Documents on Polish-Soviet Relations, 1939–1945*
*DRZW*: *Das Deutsche Reich und der Zweite Weltkrieg*
FO: Foreign Office records at TNA
FRPL: Franklin D. Roosevelt Presidential Library, Hyde Park, New York
*FRUS*: *Foreign Relations of the United States*
*Hitler Monologe*: *Adolf Hitler: Monologe im Führer-Hauptquartier 1941–1944* (ed. Jochmann)
*Hitler RP*: *Hitler: Reden und Proklamationen* (ed. Domarus)
*Hitlers Weisungen*: *Hitlers Weisungen für die Kriegführung* (ed. Hubatsch)
HW: Records of Government Communications Headquarters at TNA
IWM: Imperial War Museum, London
IWMD: Imperial War Museum, Duxford
*JC Report*: *Investigation of the Pearl Harbor Attack: Report of the Joint Committee*
*JDW*: *Japan's Decision for War: Records of the 1941 Policy Conference* (ed. Ike)
JM: Japanese Monograph
*KTB*: *Kriegstagebuch*
*KTB OKW*: *Kriegstagebuch des Oberkommandos der Wehrmacht* (eds Greiner and Schramm)
LHCMA: Liddell Hart Centre for Military Archives, King's College, London
*MBPH*: *The 'Magic' Background to Pearl Harbor*
LOC: Library of Congress
NAII: National Archives II, College Park, Maryland
NOA: Naval Operational Archives, Washington, DC
*PHA*: *Hearings before the Joint Committee on the Investigation of the Pearl Harbor Attack*
*PHP*: *Pearl Harbor Papers* (ed. Goldstein and Dillon)
PREM: Prime Minister's Office records at TNA

PSF: President's Secretary's File (FRPL)
*PWTM*: *Principal War Telegrams and Memoranda, 1940–1943*
*RA/VO*: *Russikii Arkhiv: Velikaia Otechestvennaia*
RG: Record Group at NAII
*RGM*: *Reports of General MacArthur*
*RNVM*: *Razgrom nemetskikh voisk pod Moskvoi* (ed. Shaposhnikov)
*SAmO*: *Sovetsko-amerikanskie otnoshenie vo vremia Velikoi Otechestvennoi voiny* (ed. Arbatov)
*SAO*: *Sovetsko-angliiskie otnosheniia vo vremia Velikoi Otechestvennoi voiny*
*TBJG*: *Die Tagebücher von Joseph Goebbels* (ed. Frölich)
TNA: The National Archives, Kew (formerly Public Record Office)
*VB*: *Völkischer Beobachter*
*ViD*: *Voina i diplomatiia* (ed. Rzheshevskii)
*VIZh*: *Voenno-istoricheskii zhurnal*
*VOV/VIO*: *Velikaia Otechestvennaia voina, 1941–1945: Voenno-istoricheskie ocherki* (ed. Zolotarev *et al*)
*Wehrmachtbericht*: *Das Oberkommando der Wehrmacht gibt bekannt* (ed. Wegmann)
WO: War Office records at TNA

## Introduction

1. Martin Gilbert, ed., *The Churchill War Papers*, vol. 3 (London, 2000), p. 1631 (hereafter *CWP*).
2. Winston S. Churchill, *The Second World War*, vol. 3 (London, 1950), p. 540 (hereafter *SWW*).
3. Chapters 1 to 4, which all deal with 1 December, are slightly different, but the order of the chapters – Asia, Russia, Britain, America – is based on the same 'east to west' global scheme.
4. *Nautical Almanac, 1943* (London, 1941), pp. 288–92. In December 1941 Britain and Germany were, as a wartime economy measure, still on 'Summer Time', which was an hour ahead of Standard Time. The European part of the USSR had been permanently an hour ahead of Standard Time since 1930. Because the US did not go over to Daylight Saving Time until February 1942, London was six (not five) hours ahead of Washington, Berlin was seven hours ahead, and Moscow eight hours ahead.

## Chapter 1: Japan, Germany and the Coming World War

1. Ike Nobutaka, ed., *Japan's Decision for War: Records of the 1941 Policy Conferences* (Stanford, 1967), pp. 263–83 (hereafter *JDW*); Sugiyama diary, cited in Herbert P. Bix, *Hirohito and the Making of Modern Japan* (London, 2000), p. 433.
2. *Akten zur deutschen auswärtigen Politik, 1918–1945*, ser. D, vol. XI.1, pp. 175–6 (27 Sept. 1940) (hereafter *ADAP*).
3. *JDW*, pp. 78–9.
4. *JDW*, p. 209.
5. *Foreign Relations of the United States, Japan 1931–1941*, vol. 2, pp. 764–70 (hereafter *FRUS*); *JDW*, p. 253.
6. IWMD Japanese Monograph (hereafter JM) no. 45, 'Imperial General Headquarters Army High Command Record', pp. 38–9; Bix, *Hirohito*, p. 425.
7. On Japanese planning: IWMD, JM no. 45; JM no. 105, 'General Summary of Naval Operations, Southern Force'; JM no. 152, 'Political Strategy prior to Outbreak of War', part 5 (1953); *Reports of General MacArthur* (Tokyo, 1950), vol. II.1, pp. 59–78 (hereafter *RGM*); Hayashi Saburo and Alvin D. Coox, *Kōgun: The Japanese Army in the Pacific War* (Westport, CN, 1978), pp. 29–40; S. Woodburn Kirby *et al.*, *The War Against Japan*, vol. 1 (London, 1957), pp. 89–96 (hereafter Kirby, *WAJ*); Tsuji Masanobu, *Singapore: The Japanese Version of the Malayan Campaign of World War II* (Singapore, 1988), pp. 1–71.

8. IWMD, AL 8/5008, Tanaka Shinichi and Hattori Tahushiro, 'Statement re Southern Area invasion plans' (1949), p. 2; David C. Evans and Mark R. Peattie, *Kaigun: Strategy, Tactics, and Technology in the Imperial Japanese Navy, 1887–1941* (Annapolis, 1997), p. 468.
9. *RGM*, p. 70. The Ryukyu Islands are southwest of Kyushu and include Okinawa.
10. In the pre-war Japanese system the Minister of the Navy was also a serving officer, but the last two incumbents had little direct involvement in operational planning.
11. The pre-war Combined Fleet was divided into numbered fleets. The ten battleships were in 1st Fleet. The eighteen fast heavy cruisers formed 2nd Fleet (under Adm. Kondō Nobutake); this was the scouting force. Three detachments guarded approaches to the homeland: 3rd Fleet, the southwest; 4th Fleet, the southeast; 5th Fleet, the north. The submarines were mostly concentrated in 6th Fleet. Adm. Yamamoto had set up two new organisations within Combined Fleet in 1941: 1st Air Fleet under Adm. Nagumo controlled the Navy's nine aircraft carriers (six large, three small), while 11th Air Fleet was in charge of its long-range, land-based aviation.
12. *Hearings before the Joint Committee on the Investigation of the Pearl Harbor Attack* (Washington, 1946), part 13, pp. 431–84 (hereafter *PHA*).
13. The designation of Kondō's command is sometimes translated as 'Southern Area Force'. American intelligence, based on radio traffic analysis, referred to it as a 'task force'; the British used the term 'special force'.
14. Bix, *Hirohito*, p. 421; *RGM*, pp. 2, 4.
15. Batavia, now Jakarta, was the administrative centre of the Dutch East Indies.
16. *The 'Magic' Background to Pearl Harbor* (Washington, 1977) (hereafter *MBPH*), vol. IV, p. A-321, no. 2443 to London (sent 1 Dec., trans. 5 Dec.); p. A-122, no. 2444 to Washington (sent 1 Dec., trans. 1 Dec.); TNA, HW 12/271, BJ 098509, no. 2443 (decrypt. 4 Dec.), BJ 098563, no. 2444 (decrypt. 5 Dec.).
17. Sources for the November messages from Tokyo to Washington are given on p. 298, nn. 13 and 14.
18. Sources for Japanese messages regarding the 'winds' and 'stop' codes are given on p. 298, n. 15 and p. 302, n. 26.
19. Further details of British and American codebreaking, and the uses to which decrypted messages were put, are given in chs 3 and 4.
20. Carl Boyd, *Hitler's Japanese Confidant: General Ōshima Hiroshi and MAGIC Intelligence, 1941–1945* (Lawrence, KS, 1993).
21. *ADAP*, ser. D, vol. XI.1, pp. 175–6 (27 Sept. 1940), my italics. In German the key phrase is '*von einer Macht angegriffen*'.
22. *MBPH*, vol. IV, p. A-387f, no. 1405 to Tokyo (sent 2 Dec., trans. 10 Dec.). There is no decrypt of no. 1405 in the relevant British file, TNA, HW 12/271.
23. The practice of holding Liaison Conferences had begun after the outbreak of the Sino-Japanese War in 1937. 'Liaison' meant liaison between the civilian Cabinet and the armed-forces' high command; the Emperor was not present. The Liaison Conference was a high-level meeting, second in importance only to an Imperial Conference; the latter ratified the most important decisions of the former. Liaison Conferences met much more frequently than Imperial Conferences; the meeting on 29 Nov. 1941 was the 74th Liaison Conference.
24. *JDW*, pp. 260–1; TNA, HW 12/271, BJ 098442, no. 985 to Berlin (sent 30 Nov., decrypt. 2 Dec.). The wording of the sentence about the extreme danger of war, with the phrase 'sooner than is expected', is the British translation of the decrypt. The wording of the American translation was: 'Say very secretly to them that there is extreme danger that war may suddenly break out between the Anglo-Saxon nations and Japan through some clash of arms and add that the time of the breaking out of this war may come *quicker than anyone dreams* [my italics].' *MBPH*, vol. IV, pp. A-384 to A-385 (trans. 1 Dec.). The Japanese historian Komatsu suggests that the wording of the British version is more

correct. See Komatsu Keiichiro, *Origins of the Pacific War and the Importance of 'Magic'* (Richmond, Surrey, 1999), pp. 322–3, 407.

25. The German account of the 28 Nov. Ōshima-Ribbentrop interview is in *ADAP*, ser. D, vol. XIII.2, pp. 708–10. The contemporary American and British translations of Ōshima's report of the same meeting, from decrypts, are: *MBPH*, vol. IV, p. A-382 to p. A-384, no. 1393 to Tokyo (sent 29 Nov., trans. 1 Dec.); TNA, HW 12/271, BJ 098541 (decrypt. 4 Dec.).
26. This message was read in Washington on 1 Dec. and in London on 4 Dec. The final part of the conversation, with Ribbentrop's promise, is authentic, but was not available in the incomplete post-war German archives; see *ADAP*, ser. D, vol. XIII.2, p. 710, n. 5.
27. *ADAP*, ser. D, vol. XIII.2, pp. 733–5.
28. Hitler's comments on the Russian front will be discussed more fully in the following chapter.
29. *ADAP*, ser. D, vol. XIII.2, pp. 736–7.
30. A fifth scenario would be that Japan would attack Britain, the United States and the USSR simultaneously. Given Japan's resources that did not seem a likely option.
31. Michael Bloch, *Ribbentrop* (London, 1992), p. 345; Ernst von Weizsäcker, *Erinnerungen* (Munich, 1950), p. 324; Joseph Goebbels, *Die Tagebücher von Joseph Goebbels*, part II, vol. 2, (Munich, 1996) p. 339 (22 Nov.) (hereafter Goebbels, *TBJG*).
32. Walter Warlimont, *Im Hauptquartier des deutschen Wehrmacht, 1939–1945* (3rd edn, Munich, 1978), p. 160.
33. Goebbels, *TBJG*, part II, vol. 2, p. 339 (22 Nov.). Goebbels was less optimistic than Hitler; he thought that the Japanese would either make a deal with the Americans or postpone their decision indefinitely. Hitler later gave Ribbentrop credit for seeing the value of the 'pact' with Japan (presumably that of Sept. 1940). See Werner Jochmann, ed., *Adolf Hitler: Monologe im Führer-Hauptquartier 1941–1944: Die Aufzeichnungen Heinrich Heims* (Hamburg, 1980), p. 177 (4–5 Jan. 1942) (hereafter *Hitler Monologe*).
34. Bloch, *Ribbentrop*, p. 345; Weizsäcker, *Erinnerungen*, p. 328.
35. *Kriegstagebuch der Seekriegsleitung 1939–1945*, part A, vol. 26, 28 Oct. 1941 (Bonn, 1991), p. 242 (hereafter *KTB SKL*).
36. *ADAP*, ser. D, vol. XIII.2, pp. 497–500, no. 1974 to Ribbentrop, 4 Oct.; *KTB SKL*, part A, vol. 27 pp. 58–9.
37. *ADAP*, ser. D, vol. XIII.2, pp. 652–4, no. 2472 to Ribbentrop (18 Nov.); pp. 658–9, no. 2491 to Ribbentrop (22 Nov.). Ott and Kretschmer relayed 'rumours' that accurately gave the command structure of the Southern Operation, identifying Terauchi as overall commander and Gen. Tsukada as his Chief of Staff. Four Japanese generals were correctly named as Terauchi's principal field commanders. Yamashita was correctly placed on the island of Hainan (his 25th Army would in fact move from there to Thailand and Malaya), and Iida was correctly placed in northern Indochina (from where his 15th Army would move into Burma). Imamura was placed in Canton, China, but was actually still in Tokyo, and in reality his 16th Army was scheduled for the 'Part Two' attack on the Dutch East Indies. Homma was placed in southern Indochina but would actually operate against the Philippines, with 14th Army. As for the Imperial Navy, the two Germans reported that the 'bulk of the fleet [*Masse Flotte*]' would be committed to the operation in the south; they did not suggest anything about fleet operations elsewhere, for example in the direction of Hawaii. This German message of 22 Nov. was evidently not intercepted by either the British or the Americans.

## Chapter 2: The Fight to the Death in Russia

1. *ADAP*, ser. D, vol. XIII.2, pp. 733–5.
2. Franz Halder, *Kriegstagebuch: Tägliche Aufzeichnungen des Chefs des Generalstabes des Heeres, 1939–1942* (Stuttgart, 1965), vol. 3, p. 322 (hereafter Halder, *KTB*).

3. Ibid.
4. W. Hubatsch, ed., *Hitlers Weisungen für de Kriegführung 1939–1945: Dokumente des Oberkommandos der Wehrmacht* (Frankfurt, 1962) (hereafter *Hitlers Weisungen*), p. 84.
5. Max Domarus, ed., *Hitler: Reden und Proklamationen 1932–1945* (Leonberg, 1988), vol. II.2, p. 1775 (hereafter *Hitler RP*).
6. Fedor von Bock, *Generalfeldmarschall Fedor von Bock: Zwischen Pflicht und Verweigerung – Das Kriegstagebuch* (Munich, 1995), p. 336 (2 Dec.) (hereafter Bock, *KTB*).
7. Bock, *KTB*, p. 336 (1 Dec.).
8. On the Marne analogy see: *Das Deutsche Reich und der Zweite Weltkrieg* (Stuttgart, 1990), vol. 4 (hereafter *DRZW*), pp. 595–6; Heinz Magenheimer, *Moskau 1941: Entscheidungsschlacht im Osten* (Selent, 2009), pp. 185–7.
9. Halder, *KTB*, vol. 3, p. 322 (1 Dec.).
10. The operational details of the fighting around Moscow, here and in later chapters, are based mainly on: *DRZW*; Klaus Reinhardt, *Moscow: The Turning Point* (Oxford, 1992); V.D. Sokolovskii, ed., *Razgrom nemetsko-fashistskikh voisk pod Moskvoi* (Moscow, 1964).
11. Guderian's command had, since early October, been designated a *Panzerarmee* (as was Kleist's in Army Group South). Hoepner and Reinhardt each commanded a *Panzergruppe*. The distinction was temporary and not very meaningful. All four big Panzer formations were similar independent commands, each made up of several corps, and by the New Year they were all designated as Panzer armies.
12. Bock, *KTB*, p. 329.
13. The German term is *Vernichtungsschlacht*; in English 'annihilation' has a stronger meaning, suggesting the killing of the entire opposing force.
14. In particular, Panzer Group 4 had been pulled out of the attack on Leningrad and inserted in the front line between Panzer Group 3 and 4th Army. The aircraft of Richthofen's 8th *Fliegerkorps* were transferred from the Army Group North sector to support Panzer Groups 3 and 4.
15. '*Heeresgruppe Timoschenko*' did not exist as such when Operation TAIFUN began. Marshal Semen Timoshenko (sic) had left the 'Western Theatre' command two weeks before the Battle of Viaz'ma-Briansk began, to take over the unsuccessful defence of Kiev.
16. *Hitlers Weisungen*, pp. 150–1 (6 Sept.); *Hitler RP*, vol. II.2, pp. 1757–8 (2 Oct.). The preliminary attacks of Operation TAIFUN actually began on 30 Sept.
17. Halder, *KTB*, vol. 3, p. 267 (4 Oct.); V.A. Zolotarev *et al.*, eds, *Velikaia Otechestvennaia voina, 1941–1945: Voenno-istoricheskie ocherki* (Moscow, 1998), vol. 1, pp. 225–6 (hereafter *VOV/VIO*).
18. *Hitler RP*, vol. II.2, p. 1767; *Völkischer Beobachter*, 10 Oct. 1941 (hereafter *VB*). For Otto Dietrich's comments on this incident see his *12 Jahre mit Hitler* (Munich, 1955), pp. 101–3. The Reich Press Chief maintained that he relayed, accurately and precisely, a briefing by Hitler, and that General Jodl, Chief of Hitler's Wehrmacht Operations Staff, had approved the press statement.
19. On this often forgotten development see *DRZW*, vol. 4, pp. 680–4, 696–7. The establishment strength of 2nd *Fliegerkorps* was probably around 350–400 aircraft. The British got wind of this planned air transfer quite early, through decrypts of Luftwaffe radio traffic (ULTRA). See F.H. Hinsley *et al.*, *British Intelligence in the Second World War*, vol. II (London, 1981), pp. 77–8. The British assessment at this time, based on the reading of Luftwaffe radio messages, was that 600–800 German aircraft had been transferred west, but this referred to the entire Russian front. See TNA, CAB 81, JIC(41) 452 (Final), 2 Dec.
20. *Hitler RP*, vol. II.2, p. 1775; Goebbels, *TBJG*, II.2, pp. 262–3 (10 Nov.). Goebbels's comments about Volga River crossings may have come from his shaky knowledge of Russian geography. The central and lower Volga – among the initial objectives of BARBAROSSA – were still far away. On the other hand the briefing may have concerned the upper Volga. On that western stretch of the great river Kalinin was already in German hands and Iarsolavl', also on the Volga, was not a wholly unrealistic objective.

21. Earl F. Ziemke, 'Franz Halder at Orsha: The German General Staff Seeks a Consensus', *Military Affairs*, 39:1 (1975), pp. 173–6; *DRZW*, vol. 4, pp. 589–92.
22. Gerhard Engel, *Heeresadjutant bei Hitler, 1938–1943* (Stuttgart, 1974), p. 116. The West German historian Ernst Klink, in *DRZW*, vol. 4, p. 591, argued that von Bock hoped actually to capture Moscow, not just encircle it.
23. Hitler had replaced Field Marshal Werner von Blomberg as head of the *OKW* in February 1938.
24. Goebbels, *TBJG*, part II, vol. 3, p. 144 (20 Jan. 1942).
25. Warlimont, *Im Hauptquartier*, p. 76.
26. BA-MA, RHD 7, 11/4. The handbook was presumably prepared in the second half of Nov., but its estimates were formally dated as of 1 Dec. There is a reference (p. 3) to November offensive operations 'on an operational scale' against the southern wing of German Army Group South; this may refer to the beginnings of the Soviet Rostov counteroffensive in the last days of Nov. Other clues to the dating included some mid-Nov. changes. 50th Army and 30th Army were correctly placed in Western AG, rather than in Southwestern AG or Kalinin AG; 50th had been transferred to Western AG on 10 Nov., the 30th on 17 Nov.
27. Ibid., p. 29. The remainder of Red Army formations were judged to be on the Finnish front, in the Caucasus, in the Far East, and in Central Asia.
28. Ibid., p. 30.
29. Ibid. The formations around Rostov were 37th, 9th and 56th Armies of Soviet Southern AG. The *nominal* strength of these three armies was given as thirteen rifle divisions, two rifle brigades, seven cavalry divisions and three tank brigades.
30. Ibid., p. 4.
31. The *Stavka*, formed in July 1941, was on paper a committee of generals, but they never met as a collective group; Stalin consulted them one by one. *VGK* is the abbreviation of a very long Russian word, *Verkhovnoglavnokomandiushchii*, which means Supreme Commander-in-Chief. The institution of the *Stavka* had also existed in the First World War.

    In addition to his pre-war posts of General Secretary of the Communist Party and Chairman of *Sovnarkom* (Prime Minister), Stalin was also Chairman of the State Defence Committee (*GKO*).
32. *Stavka VGK: Dokumenty i materialy. Russikii Arkhiv: Velikaia Otechestvennaia* (hereafter *RA/VO*), vol. 5(1) (Moscow, 1996), p. 316. In Russian, Konev's command was the *Kalininskii front*, and Zhukov's command was the *Zapadnyi* [Western] *front*; these were large formations made up of several armies. To avoid confusion with the more general meaning of the English word 'front' (e.g. 'Eastern Front'), the translation 'army group' (AG) is used here.
33. Ibid., pp. 316–18; A.M. Vasilevskii, *Delo vsei zhizni* (Moscow, 1989), vol. 1, pp. 163–4.
34. Perkhushkovo is sometimes given as the location of the Zhukov's HQ, but it was actually just the nearest place on the Mozhaisk Highway. Vlasikha was three miles north of the highway, up a forest road.
35. G.K. Zhukov, *Vospominaniia i razmyshleniia*, vol. 2 (Moscow, 1990), pp. 233–4 (hereafter Zhukov, *ViR*).
36. *RA/VO*, vol. 5(1), pp. 312, 313, 320.
37. B.M. Shaposhnikov *et al.*, eds, *Razgrom nemetskikh voisk pod Moskvoi: Moskovskaia operatsiia Zapadnogo front 16 noiabria 1941 g. – 31 ianvaria 1942 g.* (Moscow, 2006), pp. 30–2 (hereafter *RNVM*). The General Staff history put the situation as follows: 'With the taking of the decision to transfer reserve armies to new areas of concentration the decision had been made, in effect, for a counter-blow in the Moscow area, and not just a passive defence of the capital.'
38. The 'old' 19th and 20th Armies were destroyed in the Battle of Viaz'ma-Briansk.
39. One of the mysteries of the Battle of Moscow is why this formation was designated a 'shock army' (*udarnaia armiia*). This suggested, in the terminology of the day, an especially powerful force (which it was not), with an offensive task. The most famous

formation of this type was 3rd Shock Army, which stormed the centre of Berlin in 1945.

40. *RNVM*, pp. 30–2.
41. *RNVM*, p. 7. Zhukov's message to Stalin is printed in A.V. Zhavoronikov's introduction to the 2006 edition of *RNVM*. Despite Zhukov's condemnation, Ermakov went on to hold a number of senior commands later in the war, although mostly at corps level.
42. K.K. Rokossovskii, *Soldatskii dolg* (Moscow, 1997), p. 132. The two generals were old comrades. In the early 1930s Zhukov had been a brigade commander in Rokossovskii's 7th Cavalry division.
43. Zhukov, *ViR*, pp. 244–5. In an early 1960s discussion of the counteroffensive plan, Zhukov stressed that it was the German armoured spearheads on the flanks that were exhausted, not all of Army Group Centre. He also gave the General Staff much of the credit for determining the crucial moment of enemy weakness. See N.G. Pavlenko, 'Polkovodets za "kruglym stolom"', in A.D. Mirkina and V.S. Iarovikov, eds, *Marshal Zhukov: Polkovodets i chelovek* (Moscow, 1988), vol. 2, pp. 150–1, 153.
44. Commander of a mechanised corps when the war began, Vlasov had shown himself to be one of the Red Army's better generals in the battles of the summer and autumn of 1941. This was why he was given a major command in the Battle of Moscow. He was captured outside Leningrad in 1942, when his army was surrounded. In 1945, after being used by the Germans as a figurehead of the anti-Soviet movement, Vlasov fell into Soviet hands and was returned to Moscow and executed. Many detailed Soviet-era accounts of the Battle of Moscow left him out completely.
45. *RA/VO*, vol. 5(1), pp. 312, 313, 320.
46. *RA/VO*, vol. 4(1), pp. 160–1. Vasilevskii, although a close friend of Zhukov, argued that Sokolovskii deserved much of the credit for the counteroffensive plan (*Delo*, vol. 1, pp. 162–3). In the Khrushchev period, Marshal Sokolovskii would be the author of a classic work of Soviet military thought, *Voennaia strategiia* (1962).
47. Uzlovaia was seven miles south of Stalinogorsk, and Bogoroditsk was fourteen miles south of Uzlovaia.
48. A facsimile of Stalin's handwritten response was reproduced in Mirkina and Iarovikov, *Marshal Zhukov*, vol. 1, pp. 216–17. For a version of the map see Sokolovskii, *Razgrom*, p. 176 (fig. 12).

## Chapter 3: London, Libya and the Dangers of the Far East

1. Barrington-Ward papers, printed in *CWP*, p. 1538. Robert Barrington-Ward was editor of *The Times* from 1941 to 1948.
2. For details of Operation CRUSADER see *DRZW*, vol. 3, pp. 658–82; Ken Ford, *Operation Crusader 1941: Rommel in Retreat* (Oxford, 2010); I.S.O. Playfair, *The Mediterranean and the Middle East* (London, 1956), vol. 3, pp. 1–133.
3. CAC, CHAR 20/46/8, Auchinleck to Churchill.
4. CAC, CHAR 20/45/22, Churchill to Auchinleck, 15 Nov.
5. Warren F. Kimball, ed., *Churchill and Roosevelt: The Complete Correspondence* (Princeton, 1984), vol. 1, pp. 252–7 (20 Oct.) (hereafter *C&R*). TNA, CAB 65/24, War Cab. Confidential Annex, WM(41)114th Conclusions, 17 Nov.
6. Soviet tank strength on the Moscow front in early December was about 670 tanks: P.A. Rotmistrov, *Vremia i tanki* (Moscow, 1972), pp. 107–18. Russian historians credit German Army Group Centre with 1,100 tanks, a figure which exaggerates the number of operational vehicles. Guderian, whose tank strength was theoretically about a quarter of that which was available to Army Group Centre, reported at the *start* of the second phase of Operation TAIFUN, on 18 Nov., that he had only 150 tanks available: *DRZW*, vol. 4, p. 985.
7. TNA, WO 106/2509, no. 14782 to WO, 28 Nov. For a comprehensive discussion of strategy in Malaya see Ong Chit Chung, *Operation Matador: Britain's War Plans against the Japanese 1918–1941* (Singapore, 1997).

8. Richard Aldrich, *The Key to the South: Britain, the United States and Thailand during the Approach of the Pacific War, 1929–42* (Oxford, 1993), pp. 342–50.
9. TNA, CAB 65/24, War Cab. Confidential Annex, WM(41)122nd Conclusions, 1 Dec., pp. 50–1; Oliver Harvey, *The War Diaries of Oliver Harvey* (London, 1978), p. 68 (2 Dec.).
10. TNA, CAB 65/24, War Cab. Confidential Annex, WM(41)122nd Conclusions, 1 Dec., pp. 49–61.
11. There is a large literature on the subject of cryptography. I will deal with the subject here with a minimum of technical detail or jargon. For a fuller background to PURPLE and other codes see Steven Budiansky, *Battle of Wits: The Complete Story of Codebreaking in World War II* (New York, 2002), pp. 5–6, 88, 164–9, 176, 351–5; and Robert J. Hanyok and David P. Mowry, *West Wind Clear: Cryptology and the Winds Message Controversy – A Documentary History* (Ft. George Meade, MD, 2008). Although 'codes' and 'ciphers' (or 'cyphers') are technically different things I will use the words 'code' and 'codebreakers' in relation to both.
12. 'BJs' were translated decrypts of intercepted foreign diplomatic messages. They were also known as 'oranges', apparently from the colour of the folder in which they were kept. At the British National Archive (TNA) in Kew they are held in record division HW 12; those sent to the Prime Minister are in the HW 1 division. There is no agreement as to what 'BJ' stood for; the possibilities include 'Black Jumbo', 'Blue Jacket', even 'Bloody Japanese'. Contents of the intercepts and other top level intelligence was summarised in the Admiralty 'Special Intelligence' bulletins, which could be produced several times a day.

    The British and Americans did not decrypt exactly the same Japanese messages, and when they did the translation could differ. The American side of this exchange of information is in the following chapter.

    For a full discussion see Antony Best, *Britain, Japan and Pearl Harbor: Avoiding War in East Asia, 1936–41* (London, 1995) and David Stafford, *Churchill and Secret Service* (London, 1997).
13. *MBPH*, vol. IV, pp. A-12 to A-16, nos 725–7 to Washington (sent 4 Nov., trans. 4 Nov.), p. A-22, no. 736 to Washington (sent 5 Nov., trans 5 Nov.), p. A-89, no. 812 to Washington (sent 22 Nov., trans 22 Nov.), p. A-118, no. 844 to Washington (sent 28 Nov., trans 28 Nov.). There were evidently no British BJs for these messages. However, they are so important that it seems very likely that their contents were made available to the British, either in Washington or in London.
14. TNA, HW 12/270, BJ 098151, circular no. 2364 (sent 20 Nov., decrypt. 25 Nov.). This citation, and those in n. 13, refer to messages intercepted by the Americans or the British. A critical consideration is the date that intercepted messages became available as intelligence. Determining this date is relatively simple for the British 'intercepts' or 'decrypts', as they were dated, following decryption and translation; this is given here as the 'decrypt.' date. The American sources (in *MBPH*) give a date of 'translation' not 'decryption'; this is given here as the 'trans.' date. As the original messages were usually short, it is probably a safe assumption that the 'translation' date is also the date that the text became available for analysis.
15. TNA, ADM 223/321, Special Intelligence no. 429 (25 Nov.); TNA, HW 12/270, BJ 098127 (sent 19 Nov., decrypt 25 Nov.).
16. *C&R*, pp. 277–8 (26 Nov.).
17. TNA, FO 371/27767, no. 266 to FO, 26 Nov. (Hanoi); NAII, RG 59, no. 157 to SS, 26 Nov. (Saigon).
18. *MBPH*, vol. IV, p. A-106, no. 260110 to OPNAV (sent and circulated on 26 Nov.); p. A-106, no. 261331 to OPNAV (sent 26 Nov, issued as circular by OPNAV on 27 Nov.). Station HYPO was the Communications Intelligence Unit (CIU) of the 14th Naval District (Hawaii). The designation HYPO ('H' in the US phonetic alphabet) stood for 'Hawaii'. Station CAST was the CIU of the 16th Naval District (Philippines). The designation CAST ('C') stood for 'Cavite', the naval base outside Manila.

The term 'task force' used by American translators in these reports is somewhat misleading. Later in the war the term came to mean a specific group of ships operating in a particular place. What was created in November 1941 was an *ad hoc* but very large Japanese operational *command* (distinct from the peacetime 1st to 6th Fleets), under Adm. Kondō, which was in turn subordinate to Combined Fleet HQ. One British document described this – more clearly – as a 'special force' (TNA, WO 193/322, no. 1753 to London, 3 Dec.). Neither report mentioned Adm. Kondō by name.

London was certainly informed, at the latest within seven days, of one assessment from the Philippines. This was received from the US Chief of Naval Operations (OPNAV) and forwarded by the British Admiralty Delegation (BAD) in Washington on 3 Dec. However, what was sent by BAD and described as 'Manila appreciation sent . . . 27 November' differs in a number of respects from message no. 261331 (above); in particular it estimated that the southern 'task force' included four aircraft carriers. BAD also remarked that the Manila report 'is confirmed from British sources' (TNA, WO 193/322, no. 1753 to London). According to the post-war notes of Cpt. Alan Hillgarth RN, there was a Naval Intelligence Division report of 1 Dec. to the effect that the special force under C-in-C, 2nd Fleet (Kondō), included four carriers, four battleships, eight heavy cruisers, and numerous smaller ships (TNA, ADM 233/494).

London had also received intelligence on Japanese naval movements indirectly via the C-in-C, Far East, on 28 Nov. (see below). FECB in Singapore had close relations with Station CAST in Manila.

19. *MBPH*, vol. IV, p. A-123.
20. *PHA*, part 14, p. 1405, no. 242005.
21. *PHA*, part 14, p. 1406, no. 272335; TNA, FO 371/27913, F13066, Lockwood to Pound, 28 Nov. In 1940–41 Britain and the United States, as part of the pre-war military co-operation, had exchanged high-level representatives from the various armed services. Among other functions they acted as a channel for the exchange of intelligence. The Special Naval Observer (SPENAVO) in London was Adm. Robert Ghormley.
22. The cruisers were the 7th Squadron (*Sentai*), four 'Mogami' class ships. The Hawaii report of 26 Nov. (no. 260110) had described these as an 'advance unit' (see n. 18). Brooke-Popham did not actually refer to the fact that (according to the decrypts) 30 Nov. 1941 was the end of Tokyo's negotiation period, but he may well have been aware of this. He had certainly seen the Reed report from Hanoi, warning of an attack on the Kra Isthmus on 1 Dec. (see n. 17).
23. TNA, WO 106/2509, no. 14782 to WO, 28 Nov. There were some errors of detail in Brooke-Popham's assessment. The Japanese Army's 5th Division had moved to a forward base at Hainan Island not to southern Indochina. The movement of Japanese troops would be carried out by large transport ships rather than 'motorised landing craft' (MLC); the latter term presumably referred to local coastal craft (motor junks, etc.) commandeered by the Japanese.
24. TNA WO 106/2509, no. 14782 to WO, 28 Nov.
25. TNA, CAB 81/105, JIC(41)439 (18 Nov.); FRPL, Hopkins Papers, box 193, London Military Attaché report, 21 Nov.
26. TNA, CAB 81/105, JIC(41)449 (28 Nov.).
27. This was stressed in the post-mortem prepared on 3 Jan. 1942 by the British Army's Directorate of Military Intelligence (DMI) on the failure to anticipate the general war in the Far East: TNA, WO 208/871.
28. BBC Written Archives Centre, printed in *CWP*, p. 1427.
29. *C&R*, p. 278.
30. See Eden's memorandum of 30 Sept., cited in *The Reckoning* (London, 1965), p. 313; and his letter to Ambassador Craigie of 8 Nov. (TNA, FO 371/35957, pp. 64–5, no. 1479).
31. TNA, FO 371/35957, p. 63, no. 2186 to FO, 1 Nov.

### Chapter 4: Washington, MAGIC and the Japanese Peril

1. Samuel E. Morison, *The Battle of the Atlantic, September 1939–May 1943. History of the United States Naval Operations in World War II*, vol. 1 (London, 1947), pp. 109–13; Jürgen Rohwer, *Chronology of the War at Sea 1939–1945: The Naval History of World War Two* (3rd edn, London, 2005), p. 114. The convoy was also called WS.12X. The regular convoy WS.12, consisting of twenty-four ships, had left Britain for the Middle East on 29 September.
2. Rohwer, *Chronology*, p. 117.
3. *PHA*, part 14, pp. 1060–1, Memo. for the President.
4. Fireside Chat no. 16, 29 Dec. 1940: http://millercenter.org/scripps/archive/speeches/detail/3318.
5. *PHA*, part 15, p. 1491, US-British Staff Conversation Report, 27 Mar. 1941.
6. *C&R*, pp. 102–9.
7. Fireside Chat no. 18, 11 Sep. 1941: http://millercenter.org/scripps/archive/speeches/detail/3323.
8. This comment was supposedly made by Hitler to Ribbentrop at the very end of Nov. It was cited by David Irving, who gave no source: *Hitler's War* (London, 1977), vol. 1, p. 346.
9. Morison, *History*, vol. 1, p. 82; Rohwer, *Chronology*, p. 112. *Admiral Scheer* was a 12,000-ton ship mounting six 12-inch guns. *Tirpitz* was much larger; it displaced 43,000 tons and was armed with eight 15-inch guns. *Mississippi* and *Idaho*, commissioned in 1917 and 1919, were 32,000-ton ships, each armed with twelve 14-inch guns.
10. *FRUS, Japan, 1931–1941*, vol. 2, pp. 772–7. Apparently Tōjō had actually not made such a speech (Komatsu, *Origins*, p. 229).
11. Borthwick Institute, Hickleton Papers, HALIFAX/A.7.8.9, Halifax Diary, 6 Dec. (hereafter Lord Halifax, Family Diary).
12. Britain was still on Summer Time (an hour ahead of GMT) as a wartime expedient. The US did not adopt Daylight Saving Time until Feb. 1942. As a result the time difference was not five hours, but six.
13. *C&R*, pp. 278–9.
14. TNA, FO 371/27913, F13114/86/23, Halifax to Eden, 1 Dec.
15. FRPL, PSF, cont. 22, no. 1736 to Hull; paraphrased in *FRUS, Japan 1931–1941*, vol. 2, pp. 701–4.
16. FRPL, PSF, cont. 22, no. 1814 to Hull, 17 Nov.
17. See p. 298, n. 13.
18. On factors underlying the President's decision not to seek a compromise, see Waldo Heinrichs, *Threshold of War: Franklin D. Roosevelt and American Entry into World War II* (New York, 1988), pp. 206–14.
19. *MBPH*, vol. IV, pp. A-382 to A-384, no. 1393 to Tokyo (trans. 29 Nov.); TNA, HW 12/271, BJ 098541 (4 Dec.).
20. *MBPH*, vol. IV, pp. A-384 to A-385, no. 985 to Berlin (trans. 30 Nov.). The British version of the decrypt was available by 5 p.m. on 2 Dec.: TNA, HW 12/271, BJ 098452; TNA, ADM 223/321, Special Intelligence no. 446.
21. *MBPH*, vol. IV, p. A-122, no. 2444 to Washington (sent 1 Dec. trans. 1 Dec.). This telegram about code machines became available in London only on 5 Dec.: TNA, HW 12/271, BJ 098563.
22. *MBPH*, vol. IV, p. A-120, no. 865 to Washington (sent 1 Dec., trans 1 Dec.). The British files apparently do not contain a BJ of this message.
23. OP-20-G was part of the machinery of the Chief of Naval Operations, in the 20th Division of the Office of Naval Communications; the 'G' section was in charge of communications security. The AN-Code, a general purpose system, is better known as JN-25, the name it was given by the Americans after July 1942.
24. For the assessments of 26 Nov. see p. 298, n. 18.
25. *PHA*, part 17, p. 2636, 14th Naval District [Hawaii], Communication Intelligence Summary, 1 Dec.

26. The 'Mandates' were the former German islands in the Central Pacific – including the Mariana, Caroline, Marshall and Palau groups – which the 1919 Peace Conference had assigned to Japan.
27. *PHA*, part 15, p. 1783, ONI, 'Fortnightly Summary of Current National Situations', 1 Dec. The Japanese had ten battleships (capital ships), organised in the three squadrons (divisions). Two of the fast battleships of the 3rd Squadron had, in reality, been assigned to the Southern Force, and two to the Mobile Force. There were nine Japanese aircraft carriers, but six had been assigned to the Mobile Force and were not in 'home waters'; they had left their normal bases in central Japan on 17–18 November. See ch. 10.
28. *PHA*, part 14, p. 1407, no. 012356 to Hart, 1 Dec.
29. The phrase comes from the subtitle of the book by Kemp Tolley, *The Cruise of the Lanikai: Incitement to War* (Annapolis, 1973). *Lanikai*, an island schooner commanded by Lt. Tolley, was one of the three vessels selected for the 'information patrol'. She had not left Manila Bay before the war began.
30. *PHA*, part 14, p. 1405, no. 242005 (Circular), 24 Nov.; p. 1406, no. 272337 to CINCAF and CINCPAC, 27 Nov. This 'war warning' was discussed in connection with British intelligence in the previous chapter. See ch. 3, nn. 20–1.
31. The President was the Commander-in-Chief of the American armed forces, with Stark and Marshall under him as Chief of Naval Operations and Chief of Staff (for the Army), respectively.
32. *PHA*, part 14, pp. 1328–9, Marshall to MacArthur and Short, 27 Nov.
33. FRPL, PSL, Memorandum for the President.
34. NAII, RG 38, box 147F, appendix 1, 'The Joint Army and Navy Basic War Plan – RAINBOW No. 5', p. 7.

## Chapter 5: Two Doomed Battleships in Singapore

1. *Parliamentary Debates: House of Commons*, ser. 5, vol. 376, col. 1360. For the decision to send *Prince of Wales* and *Repulse* to Singapore, see Arthur J. Marder, *Old Friends, New Enemies: The Royal Navy and the Imperial Japanese Navy* (Oxford, 1981), vol. 1, pp. 213–41, 365–93.
2. In August 1941 the Royal Navy comprised eleven capital ships from the First World War era (nine battleships and two battlecruisers), two early post-war battleships, and two new battleships (with a third nearing operational readiness).
3. TNA, ADM 199/1934, PM Personal Minute, 25 Aug. 1941.
4. BBC Written Archives Centre, printed in *CWP*, p. 1426.
5. TNA, HW 12/2170, BJ 098017 (sent 19 Nov., decrypt. 22 Nov.), 098314 (sent 26 Nov., decrypt. 29 Nov.), 098529 (sent 29 Nov., decrypt 4 Dec.).
6. Marder, *Friends*, pp. 365–71.
7. Ibid., p. 365.
8. Robert Butow, *Tojo and the Coming of War* (Princeton, 1961), p. 370.
9. Ugaki Matome, *Fading Victory: The Diary of Admiral Matome Ugaki, 1941–1943* (Pittsburgh, 1991), p. 34 (2 Dec.).
10. IWMD, AL 8/5007, p. 16.
11. *MBPH*, vol. IV, p. A-214, circ. no. 2445 (sent 2 Dec., trans. 8 Dec.), p. A-216, circ. no. 2447 (sent 2 Dec., trans. 6 Dec.); TNA, HW 12/271, BJ 098603 (decrypt. 6 Dec.).
12. *MBPH*, vol. IV, pp. A-122, no. 867 to Washington (sent 2 Dec., trans. 3 Dec.); TNA, HW 12/271, BJ 098540 (decrypt. 4 Dec.).
13. For accounts of Hitler's flight to southern Russia: Hans Baur, *Mit Mächtigen zwischen Himmel und Erde* (Oldendorf, 1971), pp. 211–13; *Hitler RP*, vol. II.2, pp. 1787–9. There is also a reference to a brief account by Hitler's orderly, Heinz Linge, about the unplanned extension of Hitler's trip, in Eberhard Jäckel, 'Die deutsche Kriegserklärung an die Vereinigten Staaten von 1941', in *Im Dienste Deutschlands und des Rechts*, ed. F.J. Kroneck and T. Oppermann (Baden-Baden, 1981), pp. 130–1. See also C.G. Sweeting,

*Hitler's Squadron: The Fuehrer's Personal Aircraft and Transport Unit, 1933–1945* (Dulles, VA, 2001).

14. For events at Poltava, quoting the recollections of Gen. von Sodenstern, Chief of Staff of AG South: Günther Blumentritt, *Von Rundstedt: The Soldier and the Man* (London, 1952), p. 114. See also *DRZW*, vol. 4, p. 535.
15. Bock, *KTB*, p. 336 (2 Dec.).
16. Robert Forczyk, *Moscow 1941: Hitler's First Defeat* (Botley, UK, 2006), p. 82; Paul Carell, *Unternehmen Barbarossa: Der Marsch nach Russland* (Frankfurt, 1967), p. 156. The reconnaissance detachment came from Pionier-Bataillon 62, which was directly subordinate to Panzer Group 4. On the Khimki probe as a symbol see Karl-Heinz Janssen, 'Bis Chimki: Warum der deutsche Musketier nicht bis zum Kreml kam', *Die Zeit*, no. 51 (13 Dec. 1991).
17. *RA/VO*, vol. 4(1), pp. 164–5 (2 Dec.). Zhukov's plan of 30 Nov. had laid down a 3 Dec. start. Sokolovskii issued a second directive at 2.00 a.m. on Tuesday, 2 Dec. (half an hour after the directive to 1st Shock Army), ordering its neighbour, 20th Army, to begin its attack at dawn on Wednesday, 3 Dec.; this was consistent with Zhukov's general directive. Zhukov did not sign these important directives; probably he was absent in the early hours of 2 Dec., visiting other headquarters.
18. Pavlenko, 'Polkovodets', pp. 155–6. Zhukov recalled that the incident occurred on 2 or 3 Dec. See also *RNVM*, pp. 84–7; Sokolovskii, *Razgrom*, pp. 140, 149; V.A. Zhilin *et al.*, eds, *Bitva pod Moskvoi: Khronika, fakty, liudi*, 2 vols (Moscow, 2002), vol. 1, pp. 854–5, 868, GSh Situation Report, 3, 4 Dec. (hereafter *BPM*). According to the history of the battle edited by Sokolovskii, the Western AG HQ was at one point within 3–4km of the front line (p. 149, n. 1).
19. Heinz Guderian, *Erinnerungen eines Soldaten* (Heidelberg, 1951), p. 233.
20. BA-MA, RH 2/2671, *Lagebericht Ost* no. 170; Halder, *KTB*, vol. 3, p. 323 (2 Dec.).
21. TNA, CAB 81/105, JIC(41) 452 (Final), 'The Russian Campaign'. The timing of this paper was probably influenced both by events in Russia and by Foreign Secretary Eden's imminent trip to Moscow.
22. *ADAP*, ser. D, vol. XIII.2, p. 738, no. 2597 to Foreign Ministry.
23. TNA, CAB 69/2 (2 Dec.). Churchill did not mention an attack on Malaya as one of the likely threats. It was presumably taken as a given that Britain would always defend its own territory.
24. TNA, HW 12/271, BJ 098442, no. 985 to Berlin (sent 30 Nov., decrypt. 2 Dec.); ADM 223/321 Special Intell. no. 447. See ch. 1.
25. See ch. 1.
26. *MBPH*, vol. V, pp. 55–6, no. 2409 to Washington (sent 27 Nov., trans. 2 Dec.). The 'stop' code set-up message was sent to Japanese embassies and consulates worldwide; it was not specifically intended for Washington.
27. *FRUS, Japan 1931–1941*, vol. 2, pp. 778–81.
28. Yale University Library, Stimson Diary, 2 Dec.

## Chapter 6: The President's Secret Promise

1. William H. Bartsch, *December 8, 1941: MacArthur's Pearl Harbor* (College Station, TX, 2003), p. 231; IWMD, AL 7/1336, 'Malay Invasion Plan', 1951, p. 2; Ugaki, *Diary*, pp. 35–6 (4 Dec.); Agawa Hiroyuki, *The Reluctant Admiral: Yamamoto and the Imperial Navy* (Tokyo, 1979), pp. 246–7; Donald J. Goldstein and Katherine V. Dillon, eds, *The Pearl Harbor Papers: Inside the Japanese Plans* (Washington, DC, 1993), p. 89 (hereafter *PHP*). The Emperor had received an earlier briefing on all aspects of naval planning from Admirals Shimada and Nagano, the Navy Minister and the Chief of the Naval General Staff, on 30 November: Kawamura Noriko, 'Emperor Hirohito and Japan's Decision to Go to War with the United States: Reexamined', *Diplomatic History* 31:1 (2007), p. 78.
2. *RA/VO*, vol. 4(1), pp. 165–6 (3 Dec.).

3. Bock, *KTB*, pp. 337–8 (3 Dec.); Halder, *KTB*, vol. 3, p. 325 (3 Dec.).
4. For the Stalin-Sikorski meeting see *Documents on Polish-Soviet Relations, 1939–1945* (London, 1961), vol. 1, pp. 231–43 (hereafter *DPSR*).
5. Gabriel Gorodetsky, ed., *Stafford Cripps in Moscow 1940–1942: Diaries and Papers* (London, 2007), p. 217 (5 Dec.). Eden's planned visit to Moscow is discussed in ch. 7.
6. Harry Hopkins, President Roosevelt's close adviser, visited Moscow in July 1941, and Lord Beaverbook and the American 'Special Envoy' Averell Harriman followed in September. Those discussions, however, had been mainly concerned with the practicalities of Allied supply for Russia.
7. W. Anders, *An Army in Exile: The Story of the Second Polish Corps* (London, 1949), pp. 83–91.
8. *DPSR*, vol. 1, pp. 244–6.
9. Stanislaw Kot, *Conversations with the Kremlin and Dispatches from Russia* (London, 1963), p. xii.
10. CAC, ACAD 1/10, Cadogan Diary, 17 Dec.
11. There is an interesting account by Gen. P.A. Belov, the commander of one of Zhukov's cavalry corps, about a meeting with Stalin and Zhukov in the Kremlin in mid-Nov.; the aim of the meeting was to discuss counterattack plans. Aside from noting that Stalin had aged excessively since he last saw him (in 1933), Belov thought that in many respects Zhukov was the more dominant individual, and certainly the more self-possessed. P.A. Belov, *Za nami Moskva* (Moscow, 1963), p. 43.
12. Pavlenko, 'Polkovodets', p. 153. Much of Zhukov's original comment was later restored. See G. Zhukov, 'Kontrnastuplenie pod Moskvoi', *Voenno-istoricheskii zhurnal*, 1966, no. 10, p. 85.
13. *I Documenti Diplomatici Italiani*, ser. 9, vol. 7 (Rome, 1987), pp. 825–7; Galeazzo Ciano, *Diary, 1937–1943* (London, 2002), pp. 470–1.
14. *MBPH*, vol. IV, pp. A-388 to A-389, no. 1407 to Foreign Ministry (sent 3 Dec., trans. 6 Dec.). No German account of the meeting between Ōshima and Ribbentrop survives; see *ADAP*, ser. D, vol. XIII.2, p. 767, n. 6.
15. *MBPH*, vol. IV, p. A-388, no. 1408 to Foreign Ministry (sent 3 Dec., trans. 6 Dec.).
16. CAC, CHAR 20/36/12, Churchill to Ismay, 3 Dec.
17. TNA, CAB 81/88, JIC(41) 36th meeting; TNA, HW 12/271, no. 2443 to London, BJ 098509; ADM 223/321, Special Intelligence no. 452.
18. Lord Alanbrooke, *War Diaries, 1939–1945* (London, 2001), p. 206 (3 Dec.); Harvey, *Diaries*, pp. 68–9 (3 Dec.); TNA, CAB 69/2, Defence Committee (Ops), 3 Dec.
19. TNA, FO 371/27913, pp. 41–2, no. 6672 to Halifax, 3 Dec.
20. FRPL, Pare Lorentz Chronology; *PHA*, part 2, pp. 492–4 (Welles testimony).
21. TNA, PREM 3/156/5, Halifax to Eden, 3 Dec.
22. TNA, FO 371/27913, pp. 41–2, no. 6672 to Halifax, 3 Dec.
23. BI, Lord Halifax, Family Diary (3 Dec.).
24. *PHA*, part 8, p. 3667 (Safford testimony), part 14, no. 031855 to CINCAF, CINCPAC. For the original intercept see ch. 1, n. 16. On the non-response of CINCPAC, see *PHA*, part 6, p. 2764 (Kimmel testimony).

## Chapter 7: Hitler and Japan's War of Conquest

1. Tagaya Osamu, *Mitsubishi Type 1 Rikko 'Betty' Units of World War 2* (Botley, Oxford, 2001), p. 21.
2. *Enterprise* was west of the International Date Line, so the launch time for the Marine fighters destined for Wake, the morning of 4 December, corresponded to 3 December in Hawaii. *Lexington* departed Pearl Harbor on the morning of the 5th, Hawaiian time.
3. On Kimmel see Gordon Prange, *At Dawn We Slept: The Untold Story of Pearl Harbor* (Harmondsworth, 1991), pp. 49–52, and his testimony at the Joint House hearings in *PHA*, part 6, pp. 2497–920 (15–21 Jan. 1946).

4. Richardson had fallen out with Washington in the autumn of 1940, over the long-term stationing of the fleet in Hawaii, 2,400 miles from its usual main base at San Diego. This created major administrative, logistic and personnel problems, and the Admiral had made his case, intemperately, to the highest powers in the land. Richardson's concerns were about these problems, rather than the vulnerability of the fleet in Hawaii. See James O. Richardson, *On the Treadmill to Pearl Harbor* (Washington, DC, 1973).
5. 'Betty' Stark's peculiar nickname came from his Naval Academy days, and referred to Elizabeth Stark, the wife of a hero of the American Revolution. Stark used a similar nickname for Kimmel, whom he called 'Mustafa', after Kemal Atatürk.
6. *PHA*, part 16, p. 2237, letter to Stark, 26 May 1941.
7. NAII, RG 38, box 147F. On naval war plans see Edward S. Miller, *War Plan Orange: The U.S. Strategy to Defeat Japan, 1897–1945* (Annapolis, 1991).
8. The Caroline Islands lay to the west of the Marshalls and were at the centre of the Japanese Mandates. The Imperial Navy had constructed a forward fleet base in the vast atoll at Truk.
9. *PHA*, part 16, p. 2252.
10. *PHA*, part 14, p. 1406 (no. 272337 to CINCPAC, CINCAF), p. 1407 (no. 290110 to CINCPAC), part 16, p. 2255, letter to Stark, 2 Dec.
11. NAII, RG 38, box 147F. See also Kimmel's description of the implementation of WPPAc-46 in *PHA*, part 6, pp. 2529–31 (Joint Committee testimony). His contingency plan for immediate operations, dated at noon on 5 Dec., is printed in *PHA*, part 17, p. 2714.
12. *PHA*, part 17, pp. 2721–2 (Bellinger statement, 19 Dec. 1941). Some of the older PBY-3 flying boats urgently required repair and upkeep. The fifty-four new PBY-5s had arrived very recently (in Nov.) and had serious 'shake-down' problems.
13. In his excellent book on Pacific war-planning, Edward Miller speculated that Kimmel and his Chief of Staff, Capt. Charles McMorris, were attempting, unbeknownst to Adm. Stark, to lure the Japanese into a major fleet engagement (*War Plan Orange*, ch. 25). This speculation is not, in my view, supported by the evidence. Kimmel was following the general directive, which required some action and which would keep the Japanese from devoting their full force to operations against the Malay barrier. He did not have reliable information about Japanese bases in the Marshalls, so a preliminary probing phase was essential.
14. IWMD, AL 8/5007, p. 16; JM no. 107, p. 17; Tsuji, *Singapore*, pp. 72–6. There are minor discrepancies in the sources about the size of the main Hainan convoy. In JM no. 107 it is stated that there were nineteen transport ships in all, but the vessels are not named.
15. Ike, *JDW*, pp. 284–5. The brief minutes of the Liaison Conference deal with relations with the United States, and there is a reference to a document 'On Dealing with the Netherlands'. There is no recorded mention of Britain, either in the form of a breaking of relations or a declaration of war.
16. The German historian Peter Herde suggests that Ribbentrop probably obtained Hitler's approval by telephone on the evening of the 4th: 'Italien, Deutschland und der Weg in den Krieg im Pazifik 1941', *Sitzungberichte* XXI: 1 (1983), p. 86. Hitler's flight schedule is not known, but if he left after sunrise in Poltava, and had a three to four hour flight, he probably would not have reached the WOLFSSCHANZE compound until the early afternoon. He would certainly have been exhausted when he got there. If Hitler was then allowed to sleep before reaching an important decision, this would not be a unique case; he was also left undisturbed during the critical morning of 6 June 1944, which delayed the deployment of Panzer reserves after the Normandy landings.
17. *RA/VO*, vol. 4(1), pp. 166–7 (4 Dec.).
18. *RA/VO*, vol. 4(1), p. 167 (4 Dec.). On the key importance of German exhaustion see Zhukov's 1965 recollections in Pavlenko, 'Polkovodets', pp. 150–1.
19. BA-MA, RH 19 II/127 (FHO); RH 19 II/122, p. 28, emphasis in original.
20. Halder, *KTB*, vol. 3, p. 327 (4 Dec.).

21. *Sovetsko-angliiskie otnosheniia vo vremia Velikoi Otechestvennoi voiny, 1941–1945: Dokumenty i materialy* (Moscow, 1983), vol. 1, p. 180, Maiskii to NKID, 1 Dec. (hereafter *SAO*). Eden recalled in his diary that 'Stalin had been told I was bringing armies' (Birmingham UL, Lord Avon Papers, AP 2/1/21, Eden Personal Diary, 4 Dec.).
22. Gen. Alan Brooke had replaced Gen. Dill three days earlier as C-in-C of the British Army (Chief of the Imperial General Staff, CIGS).
23. TNA, CAB 65/24, WM(41) 124th, Confidential Annex; CAC, ACAD 1/10, Cagodan Diary, 4 Dec.
24. Alanbrooke, *Diaries*, p. 207 (4 Dec.).
25. *FRUS, 1941*, vol. 1, pp. 193–4, Eden memo.
26. Despite the danger to the Soviet capital, Stalin decided to mark the twenty-fourth anniversary of the Bolshevik Revolution (7 Nov. 1941) with the traditional military parade. Like Stalin's decision to remain in the Kremlin after the partial evacuation of Moscow in mid-Oct., his decision to hold the Red Square parade as normal was a gesture of self-confidence which gave an important boost to Soviet morale.
27. *SAO*, vol. 1, pp. 171–2, Stalin to Churchill, 8 Nov.
28. *FRUS, 1941*, vol. 1, p. 192, Eden memo (4 Dec.); TNA, PREM 3/402, Churchill to Stalin, 21 Nov.; *SAO*, vol. 1, pp. 178–9, Stalin to Churchill, 23 Nov.
29. *FRUS, 1941*, vol. 1, pp. 193–4, Eden memo.
30. TNA, CAB 65/24, WM(41) 124th, Confidential Annex.
31. CAC, ACAD 1/10, Cadogan Diary, 4 Dec. There is no archival record of a 'telegram from Roosevelt', and Cadogan was presumably referring to Halifax's account of the 3 Dec. meeting. In the printed edition of Cadogan's diary the incorrect reverse meaning of the text ('we could *now* guarantee the Dutch') is given: '[Churchill] said we could *not* guarantee Dutch [my italics]': David Dilkes, ed., *The Diaries of Sir Alexander Cadogan, O.M., 1938–1945* (London, 1971), p. 416 (4 Dec.).

    Eden also noted a 'good message' from Roosevelt (Birmingham UL, Lord Avon Papers, AP 2/1/21, Eden Personal Diary, 4 Dec.).
32. TNA, WO 106/2509.
33. John Chapman argues that this signal was sent because '[t]he "Winds" messages indicating war with the United States and Britain were intercepted and correctly interpreted by the central agencies on 4 December.' See John W.M. Chapman, ed., *The Price of Admiralty: The War Diary of the German Naval Attaché in Japan, 1939–1943*, vol. 4 (Ripe, Sussex, 1989), p. xxiii, n. 47. For the transmission (or non-transmission) of the 'winds execute' message see the following sub-section of this chapter. Chapman is a judicious and thorough historian, but he produces no evidence to support this assertion.
34. TNA, HW 12/271, BJ 098540, no. 867 to Washington; TNA, ADM 223/321, SI no. 456. The American version is in *MBPH*, vol. IV, p. A-122.
35. TNA, WO 208/87. *Gaimushō* telegram no. 867 to Washington included an order to destroy the codes of other ministries, which presumably included the codes used by the Army and Navy attachés. Davidson argued that earlier Japanese messages about codes (such as the one sent on 1 Dec.) might have been issued by Tokyo from a fear that those codes had been compromised. The intercepted message sent on 2 Dec. was different: '[Japanese] addressees were told on December 2nd to destroy certain ciphers having a military implication, from which it was almost certain that war was intended.'
36. TNA, HW 12/271, BJ 098541, no. 1393 to Tokyo. The Americans had translated this three days earlier; the text is in *MBPH*, vol. IV, pp. A-382 to A-384 (sent 29 Nov., trans. 1 Dec.).
37. *Chicago Tribune*, 4 Dec., pp. 1, 10–11. The *Tribune* article did not actually attach the name 'Victory Program' to the 'war plans' or the 'confidential document', and indeed that name was only used informally among the planners and by later historians. The name had been published elsewhere in the press that autumn, but in connection with economic mobilisation rather than general strategy. The document which Manly was

shown was the 'Joint Board Estimate of United States Over-All Production Requirements', dated 11 Sept. 1941; see Steven T. Ross, ed., *American War Plans: 1919–1941* (New York, 1992), vol. 5, pp. 143–298. For background see Mark S. Watson, *Chief of Staff: Prewar Plans and Preparations* (Washington, 1950). pp. 331–66.

38. In the end the US only deployed 90 divisions, not 215. The decisive American attack did not begin until a year later than predicted, in June 1944. The planners assumed that Germany would occupy Russia to the White Sea-Moscow-Volga River line, inclusive, by July 1942 and that 'militarily Russia will be impotent subsequent to that date'. (The estimate was drafted back in September 1941, when the Red Army was in headlong retreat.) Finally, of course, the men who drew up the document did not anticipate that Japan would plunge the United States into war.
39. *ADAP*, vol. XII.2, pp. 773–4, no. 4250 to Foreign Ministry (4 Dec.); Goebbels, *TBJG*, part II, vol. 1, p. 433 (5 Dec.).
40. For the initial FBI report, prepared on 5 Dec.: FRPL, PSF, box 82.
41. This is the claim in William Stevenson, *A Man Called Intrepid: The Secret War* (New York, 1976), pp. 298–301. According to this account the documents were planted on Senator Wheeler by agents of the Political Warfare Division of an organisation called British Security Coordination, which was based in New York. The credibility of this claim is not strengthened by the statement that the Victory Program was a 'plant' that had been 'concocted' by BSC staff. It was, of course, a real document.
42. Thomas Fleming, 'The Big Leak', *American Heritage* 38:8 (1987), pp. 64–71.
43. Burton K. Wheeler, *Yankee from the West: The Candid, Turbulent Life Story of the Yankee-born U.S. Senator from Montana* (New York, 1977), pp. 21–36; Douglas M. Charles, *J. Edgar Hoover and the Anti-Interventionists: FBI Political Surveillance and the Rise of the Domestic Security State, 1939–1945* (Columbus, OH, 2007), pp. 115–37.
44. *New York Times*, 10 Dec., p. 8.
45. As set up on 19 November, the code phrase 'east wind rain' was supposed to mean that Japanese relations with the United States were in danger of breaking down; 'west wind clear' applied the same warning regarding the British Empire.
46. Safford seems to have been motivated by a sense that Adm. Kimmel had been unfairly treated after the outbreak of war with Japan. On Safford and his claims regarding the 'winds execute' telegram see Hanyok, *West Wind*. Safford made the clearest presentation of his case in a typescript statement dated 1 Feb. 1946, a facsimile of which is printed in Hanyok, pp. 231–54. For Safford's later testimony see *PHA*, part 8, pp. 3593–893 (Joint Committee, 2–6 Feb. 1946), part 26, pp. 387–94 (Hart Inquiry, 29 Apr. 1944).
47. The Burma Road was China's last supply route to the outside world, running through difficult territory from the port of Rangoon in British Burma to Kunming in China. The American government had recently allowed the recruitment of US pilots for an American Volunteer Group (the famous 'Flying Tigers') to protect this area.
48. TNA, FO 371/27914, F13314/86/23, Halifax to FO, 6 Dec.
49. BI, Lord Halifax, Family Diary, 19 Nov.; BI, Hickleton Papers, HALIFAX/A.7.8.19, Lord Halifax Secret Diary, 4 Dec. (hereafter Lord Halifax, Secret Diary).

### Chapter 8: The Lull Before Two Storms

1. A second element of the invasion force departed around dusk – at 6.20 p.m. – from near Cape St Jacques, off Saigon.
2. Tolley, *Lanikai*, pp. 268–70. USS *Isabel* returned to Manila Bay on the morning of the 8th. Neither of the other two picket boats (chartered civilian vessels) had put to sea by that time.
3. According to the Eastern Fleet war diary, Phillips departed Singapore on the 4th. Since he arrived in Manila on the afternoon of the 5th he probably made an intermediate stop, perhaps in North Borneo.

4. NOA, Hart Papers, Hart Private Diary, 5 Dec.
5. TNA, ADM 199/1185, C-in-C, Eastern Fleet, War Diary.
6. *ADAP*, vol. XII.2, pp. 779–80 (no. 3295 to Rome), 781–2 (Memo. by Mackensen).
7. TNA, HWD 12/271, BJ 098693, no. 1416 to Foreign Ministry (sent 5 Dec., decrypt. 8 Dec.).
8. The extraordinary night-time diplomacy was almost certainly not the result of an awareness in Berlin that war was only hours away. It is most likely that Ribbentrop was making up for time lost during Hitler's unexpected delay in Russia.
9. *RA/VO*, vol. 4(1), pp. 170–1; *BPM*, vol. 1, p. 24.
10. BA-MA, R19 II/122, p. 31 (5 Dec.); Guderian, *Erinnerungen*, p. 235; Halder, *KTB*, vol. 3, pp. 327–8 (5 Dec.).
11. Halder, *KTB*, vol. 3, p. 328 (5 Dec.).
12. TNA, CAB 81/105, JIC(41) 460. In a book published in 1977 the Irish-based author Constantine FitzGibbon told a sensational story about the JIC meeting on 5 Dec., based on a private letter from Cavendish-Bentinck; see *Secret Intelligence in the Twentieth Century* (London, 1977), p. 255n. 'We knew that they changed course,' Cavendish-Bentinck wrote; 'I remember presiding over a JIC meeting and being told that a Japanese fleet was sailing in the direction of Hawaii, asking "Have we informed our trans-atlantic brethren?" and receiving an affirmative reply.' FitzGibbon thought that it was 'bureaucratic inefficiency' that prevented the Americans from acting on this, rather than anything more sinister on Roosevelt's part. This quote has, however, sometimes been used as evidence of British foreknowledge of the Pearl Harbor attack, e.g. George Victor, *The Pearl Harbor Myth: Rethinking the Unthinkable* (Washington, DC, 2007), pp. 42–3.

    However, this is not a reliable source. The Pearl Harbor force did not, as we will see, 'change course'. Cavendish-Bentinck surely had in mind the movement of the convoy off Indochina, although that occurred on the following day, 6 Dec. (when there was no JIC meeting). It is also worth recalling that he wrote the letter to FitzGibbon many years after the event, when he was in his eighties.
13. TNA, CAB 69/1 (5 Dec.); Llewellyn Woodward, *British Foreign Policy in the Second World War*, vol. 2 (London, 1971), p. 180; Herman Bussemaker, 'Paradise in Peril: The Netherlands, Great Britain, and the Defence of the Netherlands East Indies', *Journal of Southeast Asian Studies* 31:1 (2000), p. 135.
14. *SAO*, vol. 1, pp. 181–3, Maiskii to NKID, 5 Dec.
15. *FRUS, 1941*, vol. 1, pp. 194–5, Hull to Winant (for Eden), 5 Dec.
16. *FRUS, Japan, 1931–1941*, vol. 2, pp. 781–4.
17. *PHA*, part 14, pp. 1373–84.
18. Assuming Perkins's account is accurate, what Secretary Knox 'revealed' was probably based on the Navy intelligence assessments of 26 Nov., which had been further developed in the ONI Bulletin of 1 Dec. These had reported the 'task force' set up to operate in the South China Sea and the Mandates. Few of the members of the Cabinet had been cleared for MAGIC, so they could not be told about the details (or existence) of intelligence sources.
19. Columbia Oral History Collection (hereafter CUOHC), Frances Perkins, 'Reminiscences', pp. 35–45.

## Chapter 9: General Zhukov Throws in his Armies

1. Morison, *History*, vol. 3, p. 151; LHCMA, Pownall Diary, 30 Jan. 1942.
2. NOA, Hart Papers, Hart Private Diary, 5, 6 Dec.
3. NOA, Hart Papers, box 3, 'Report of a Conference [6 Dec.]' pp. 1–5. At a conference on 27 Nov. with Hart and Francis Sayre, the US High Commissioner, MacArthur reportedly stated that he did not expect war before the coming spring; Hart was more pessimistic (Francis B. Sayre, *Glad Adventure* [New York, 1957], p. 221). At a press

conference on 6 Dec. the General said that he thought war would not come before Jan. 1942 (Clark G. Lee, *They Call it Pacific: An Eye-Witness Story of Our War against Japan from Bataan to the Solomons* [New York, 1943], p. 24).

4. NOA, Hart Papers, box 3, 'Report of a Conference [6 Dec.]' pp. 8–10; NAII, RG 165, box 260, MacArthur to Marshall, 7 Dec.
5. NAII, RG 80, box 45, no. 070327 to CNO; NOA, Hart Papers, Hart Private Diary, 7 Dec.; TNA, ADM 234/330, 'Loss of H.M. Ships *Prince of Wales* and *Repulse*' (1955), p. 30. According to the war diary of the RAF command in Singapore, Admiral Phillips was expected back in Singapore at 8.15 a.m. on the 7th. Assuming a ten or eleven hour direct non-stop flight from Manila, he must have departed in the late evening (TNA, AIR 23/3577).
6. NAII, RG 80, box 260, Report to OPNAV, no. 070327. The probable meaning of the last point about the release of the cruisers was that this could be effected once the American attack on Truk had blocked any further Japanese advance (or raids) south towards Australia.
7. *PHA*, part 14, p. 1405, no. 242005 to CINCAF, CINCPAC, etc. The addressees were instructed to inform senior Army officers in their area.
8. *PHA*, part 14, p. 1329, Marshall to MacArthur, 27 Nov.; no. 1004 to Marshall, 28 Nov.
9. NOA, Hart Papers, Hart Private Diary, 26 Nov.
10. *PHA*, part 14, p. 1406, no. 272337 to Stark; NOA, Hart Papers, Hart Private Diary, 29 Nov.
11. NOA, Hart Papers, Hart Private Diary, 28 Nov. The Japanese message setting up the three possible variants of the 'winds' warning' was sent on 19 Nov. and translated in Washington on 27 Nov. (28 Nov. in Manila). This was not, of course, the 'winds execute' message.
12. NOA, Hart Papers, Hart Private Diary, 3 Dec.
13. For US strategy in the Philippines: Louis Morton, *Fall of the Philippines. The United States Army in World War II* (Washington, 1953), pp. 14–50, 61–73; Morison, *History*, pp. 149–63; Russell F. Weigley, 'The Role of the War Department and the Army', in *Pearl Harbor as History*, ed. Dorothy Borg and Okamoto Shumpei (New York, 1973), pp. 165–88.
14. NAII, RG 38, box 147F, 'The Joint Army and Navy Basic War Plan – RAINBOW No. 5', appendix I to WPL 46. The May 1941 RAINBOW FIVE plan, still in force in Nov., listed the Philippines as a joint task, although the implication was that, as far as the Army was concerned, the islands would be defended by forces already in place. The Navy's role was limited, despite the fact that the plan noted '[t]he responsibility of the Commander-in-Chief, United States Asiatic Fleet, for supporting the defense of the Philippines remains so long as that defense continues' (section VII, para. 37–40). There was no reference to any role for the Pacific Fleet.
15. NOA, Hart Papers, Memo. of Conversation between Hart and MacArthur, 22 Sept. 1941.
16. On the bomber strategy see Bartsch, *December 8*, and E. Kathleen Williams, 'Deployment of the AAF on the Eve of Hostilities', in Wesley F. Craven and James L. Cate, eds, *Plans and Early Operations: January 1939 to August 1942. The Army Air Forces in World War II* (Chicago, 1948), vol. 1, pp. 175–93.

    The bomber advocates also had their own objectives, which were to carve out an independent and decisive role for the new Army Air Force, and to prevent any more B-17s being drained away to the British under Lend-Lease. The closest parallel to the USAAF's proposal, I would argue, was Nikita Khrushchev's scheme to deploy missiles into Cuba in 1962.
17. On air operations over the Gulf of Siam on 6 December, see TNA, WO 172/15, GHQ Far East, War Diary; ADM 199/1185, C-in-C, Eastern Fleet, War Diary; Paul Maltby, 'Report on the Air Operations during the Campaigns in Malaya and the Netherlands East Indies from 8th December 1941 to 12th March 1942', *Supplement to The London*

*Gazette*, no. 38216, 26 Feb. 1948, pp. 1363–4; Christopher Shores and Brian Cull, *Bloody Shambles*, vol. 1 (London, 1992), pp. 74–5.

The two fast battleships and the heavy cruisers of Adm. Kondō's Southern Force were some distance to the southeast, so Ramshaw could not have spotted a battleship. The warships he saw were either the close escort (light cruiser *Sendai* and destroyers) or Ozawa's heavy cruisers. The fast merchant ships of the main convoy had been joined by the two slow transports that left Hainan earlier, and by the group of seven ships that left the mouth of the Mekong near Saigon on the 5th.

18. TNA, WO 172/17, GOC, Malaya, War Diary; A.E. Percival, 'Operations of Malaya Command, from 8th December, 1941, to 15th February, 1942', *Supplement to The London Gazette*, no. 38215, 20 Feb. 1948, p. 1267. The HQ of Heath's second division, 9th Indian, was in Kuala Lumpur, but its two brigades were stationed on the east coast, one at Kota Bharu and the other at Kuantan. The III Corps reserve, another brigade, was on the west side of Malaya at Ipoh, halfway between the Thai border and Kuala Lumpur.
19. CAC, ACAD 1/10, Cadogan Diary, 6 Dec.; Brooke, *Diaries*, p. 208 (6 Dec.).
20. Alanbrooke, *Diaries*, p. 208 (6 Dec.); CAC, ACAD 1/10, Cadogan Diary, 6 Dec.
21. TNA, CAB 79/55, COS(41) 44th Meeting (6 Dec.); Marder, *Old Friends*, p. 404.
22. TNA, HW 12/271, BJ 098603 (sent 2 Dec., decrypt. 6 Dec.); ADM 223/321, Special Intelligence no. 460, 6 Dec.; HW 12/271, BJ 098602 (sent 27 Nov., decrypt. 6 Dec.); ADM 223/321, Special Intelligence no. 461, 6 Dec.
23. Robert Brooke-Popham, 'Operations in the Far East from 17th October 1940 to 27th December 1941', *Supplement to The London Gazette*, no. 38183, 22 Jan. 1948, p. 555.
24. Marder, *Old Friends*, p. 505; CAC, DUFC 3/7, Letter to Churchill, 18 Dec. The view of the historian Louis Allen on Brooke-Popham was that he was by no means incompetent but did suffer, at this moment, from a fatal indecision; see Louis Allen, *Singapore: 1941–1942* (London, 1993), pp. 53–4, 112–13). Brian Farrell's interpretation was that Brooke-Popham had been appointed as C-in-C, Far East, because he had a reputation for being 'patient and conciliatory' and was unlikely to 'rock the boat'; that he acted cautiously in Dec. was therefore not surprising; see Brian P. Farrell, *The Defence and Fall of Singapore* (Stroud, UK, 2005) pp. 70–1, 140–1.
25. A.E. Percival, *The War in Malaya* (London, 1949), pp. 106, 108.
26. As mentioned in ch. 3, it is quite possible that attempting to implement Operation MATADOR would have led even sooner to a British military catastrophe. The Japanese troops were well-led veterans. At Kota Bharu on 8–9 Dec., even with the aid of some beach defences and significant air strength, the local (Indian) brigade was quickly overwhelmed by the invading Japanese. Taking the hypothetical case a step further, the successful Japanese landing at Kota Bharu would have threatened the rear of any MATADOR force. On the other hand the commander of the spearhead force (Gen. Murray-Lyon) had prepared his 11th Division for an advance rather than a defensive battle, and his 11th Indian Division was demoralised by the decision not to move into Thailand.
27. *MBPH*, vol. IV, p. A-127. The text of this very long message was broken up into fourteen batches of text for purposes of transmission. The transmission instalments did not correspond directly to the content of the message, i.e. a long preamble and seven substantive points.
28. *FRUS*, *Japan, 1931–1941*, vol. 2, pp. 787–92; *MBPH*, vol. IV, pp. A-130 to A-133.
29. *ADAP*, vol. XII.2, pp. 777–8, no. 2657 to Ribbentrop; p. 786, no. 2282 to Ott. According to the published details, Ott's message took nearly forty-one hours to reach Berlin. The time of despatch was 1.00 a.m. on 5 Dec., which would correspond to 5.00 p.m. on 4 Dec. in Berlin.
30. *PHA*, part 14, pp. 1246–7, no. 5918 to Hull; no. 5921 to Hull. Given the position of the sighting, the convoy was certainly much more than fourteen hours from the Kra Isthmus at 12.46 a.m. The distance was about 340 nautical miles, at least twenty-eight hours for a transport steaming at twelve knots.

31. *PHA*, part 15, p. 1680, no. 061255 to Stark; p. 1680, Schuirmann to State Department, 6 Dec.; NOA, Stark Papers, box 4, Diary 1941–42. 'Kontron' was probably a mistaken version of 'Koh Trang' or 'Koh Kong', the anchorage on the Cambodian coast. It is not clear what 'scouting force' Admiral Hart was referring to. USS *Isabel* had arrived in the area on the previous morning, on President Roosevelt's personal orders, but her crew probably could not have seen inside the anchorage. It is possible that there were covert US Navy PBY flights near Camranh Bay.
32. *FRUS, Japan 1931–1941*, vol. 2, pp. 785–6.
33. *PHA*, part 10, pp. 4662–3 (JC Hearings, 15 Feb. 1946).
34. Bock, *KTB*, p. 240 (6 Dec.).
35. Engel, *Heeresadjutant*, p. 117 (6 Dec.).
36. Helmuth Greiner and Percy Ernst Schramm, eds, *Kriegstagebuch des Oberkommandos der Wehrmacht (Wehrmachtführungsstab) 1940–1945*, vol. 1 (Frankfurt, 1961) (hereafter *KTB OKW)*, pp. 796–7, *OKH Tagesmeldung*, 6 Dec.; Halder, *KTB*, vol. 3, p. 330.
37. Halder, *KTB*, vol. 3, p. 329 (6 Dec.).
38. *Hitler RP*, vol. II.2, p. 1775 (8 Nov.).
39. BA-MA, RHD 7, 11/4, *Kriegswehrmacht*, pp. 30–33, 100, 103. The low *Kampfwert* was evidently based on the calculation that these divisions were under-strength in terms of men and equipment; it was not simply based on a German assumption of inherent Russian inferiority.
40. For detailed 'order of battle' information see A.N. Grylev, ed., *Boevoi sostav Sovetskoi armii*, part 1 (Moscow, 1963). Not publicly available until after 1991, this invaluable source was prepared by the Military-Historical Section (*VIO*) of the Soviet General Staff.
41. The 'ski battalion' [*lyzhnyi batal'on*] was a unit of 500–1,000 men. The Russians had by Dec. organised a considerable number of these units in 1st Shock Army and some other formations. For a post-battle Soviet assessment of their limited tactical value see Michael Parrish, ed., *Battle for Moscow: The 1942 Soviet General Staff Study* (Washington, DC, 1989),. pp. 36–43.
42. RNVM, pp. 150–1; Pavlenko, 'Polkovodets', pp. 156–7. See also F.I. Golikov, *V Moskovskoi bitve: Zapiski komandarma* (Moscow, 1967). As of 24 Nov. five of Golikov's divisions had no weapons at all (p. 26).
43. This assumes that a Soviet brigade is counted as equivalent to about a third of a division.
44. I am here following the argument of Walter S. Dunn, *Stalin's Keys to Victory: The Rebirth of the Red Army* (Westport, CN, 2006), pp. 78–80. For important new documentary material on the emergency reconstruction of the Red Army in the summer and autumn of 1941 see Sergei Kudriashov, ed., *Voina: 1941–1945* (Moscow, 2010).
45. A pre-war 'rifle division' (i.e. infantry division) had consisted of nine rifle battalions (each of about a thousand men) organised in three regiments; the newly-formed rifle brigades were made up of three or four rifle battalions. Full-strength pre-war rifle divisions had considerable fire power, with two artillery regiments, plus anti-aircraft and anti-tank battalions (*diviziony*) – a total of 144 artillery pieces. A December 1941 rifle brigade possessed only two or three artillery or mortar battalions. The addition of artillery and support troops – engineers, signals, etc. – gave pre-war rifle divisions an establishment of 14,500 men; wartime rifle brigades numbered only 4,000–6,000 men.
46. A tank brigade typically consisted of two tank battalions and a motor-rifle battalion, with an establishment of only fifty-three tanks.
47. Alexander Hill, 'British "Lend-Lease" Tanks and the Battle for Moscow, November–December 1941 – A Research Note', *Journal of Slavic Military Studies* 12:2 (2006), pp. 289–95; Alexander Hill, 'British "Lend-Lease" Tanks and the Battle for Moscow, November–December 1941 – Revisited', *Journal of Slavic Military Studies* 22:4 (2009), pp. 574–87; *VOV/VIO*, p. 249. The main Soviet-built heavy tank was the KV, and the main medium tanks the T-28 and the new T-34.

48. The thirteen 'Siberian' divisions in the Battle of Moscow in late Nov. and early Dec. included the following: two tank divisions and three rifle divisions from Far Eastern Army Group, one Guards rifle division and three normal rifle divisions from the Transbaikal Military District, and four rifle divisions from the Siberian Military District. (Other Siberian divisions fought elsewhere in European Russia, notably around Leningrad.)

   The Siberian contribution, however, needs to be compared with the total strength in the Western and Kalinin Army Groups on 1 Dec. 1941. This amounted to three tank divisions, twenty-two tank brigades, one motorised rifle division, sixty-five rifle divisions, seventeen rifle brigades, and seventeen cavalry divisions.
49. Pavlenko, 'Polkovodets', p. 154.
50. The normal Russian chronology of the Battle of Moscow has a defensive phase running from 30 Sept. until 5 Dec., and an offensive phase running from 6 Dec. until 20 Apr. 1942. The parts of the battle fought north of Moscow are known as the 'Klin-Solnechnogorsk offensive operation' (6–25 Dec.) and the 'Kalinin offensive operation' (5 Dec.–7 Jan.). Zhukov's southern attack is called the 'Tula offensive operation' (6–16 Dec.), while Timoshenko's advance against German 2nd Army is the 'Elets offensive operation' (6–16 Dec.).

## Chapter 10: Date of Infamy

1. For the air operations over the South China Sea and the Gulf of Siam on 7 Dec. see TNA, AIR 23/3577; Shores and Cull, *Shambles*, pp. 75–80; Kirby, *WAJ*, pp. 181–3; Maltby, 'Air Operations', pp. 1364–5.
2. Allen, *Singapore*, p. 105. Bedell was an Australian pilot assigned to a British (RAF) squadron, No. 205. The Catalina was probably not shot down because it discovered the main invasion force, as that was a hundred miles to the southwest. It may have been near an escort ship and three transports that departed Phu Quoc Island at 3.30 a.m. and headed for a rendezvous with the main force (see map in IWMD, JM no. 107, p. 18).
3. *C&R*, p. 280. There was evidently no intention to send this 'declaration' to Japan on 7 Dec. In the event it was a dead letter.
4. *Principal War Telegrams and Memoranda, 1940–1943* (Nendeln, Liechtenstein, 1976), vol. 4, *Far East*, sect. 1, doc. 14 (hereafter *PWTM*).
5. NOA, Hart Papers, Hart Private Diary, 7 Dec.
6. *PHA*, part 10, pp. 5082–3 (Creighton testimony). As mentioned in ch. 8, the War Office telegram was FE 50, sent from Whitehall very early on Friday (5 Dec.) and received in Singapore that afternoon (local time). Captain Creighton's report was sent over twenty-four hours later, at 10.56 p.m. on the 6th. Creighton did not have any official contact with Brooke-Popham (he was attached to Admiral Layton RN). He probably learned about FE 50 informally from Francis G. Brink, the US Army Colonel who was attached to Brooke-Popham's HQ, and with whom he shared a house. Neither American officer, however, would admit to this at the post-war Congressional hearings. See *PHA*, part 10, pp. 5084, 5086–7 (Creighton testimony); part 11, pp. 5514–15 (Brink testimony).
7. NAII, RG 80, box 45, no. 070645 to Stark, 7 Dec. Presumably it had taken some time before Hart read Creighton's cable. Hart copied his no. 070645 to Admiral Kimmel in Hawaii. As it was transmitted from Manila at 8.15 p.m. on 6 Dec. (Hawaii time) it is unlikely that Kimmel read it before the following fateful morning.
8. NOA, Hart Papers, Hart Private Diary, 7 Dec.
9. Percival, *War in Malaya*, p. 110; *PWTM*, vol. 4, *Far East*, sect. 1, doc. 8, no. 16052/7 to War Office; TNA WO 172/17, Malaya Command War Diary, 7 Dec.
10. *MBPH*, vol. IV, pp. A-130 to A-133 (sent 6 Dec., trans. 7 Dec.).
11. *MBPH*, vol. IV, p. A-129 (sent 6 Dec., trans. 7 Dec.).
12. TNA, HW 12/271, BJ 098694, circ. no. 2494 (decrypt. 8 Dec.). The 'stop' code or 'hidden text' code, it will be recalled, listed code words which Tokyo would insert into messages

that had been ended with the word 'stop'; these code words would give Japanese diplomats secret warnings of changes in Japan's relations with other countries; see ch. 1.

The words 'are extremely critical' is a translation of the Japanese 'plain text' produced by the British codebreakers. There was a significant difference between the American and British translations of the meaning of a key codeword (the Japanese proper name '*hattori*') in the 'stop' code. The Americans understood *hattori* to signify that relations with certain countries were 'not in accordance with expectation' (*MBPH*, vol. V, p. 56), while the British understood *hattori* to signify that relations were 'extremely critical'. The British version was evidently more accurate; see the discussion in Komatsu, *Origins*, pp. 268–9, where the translation 'facing a crisis' (not necessarily an 'extreme' one) is suggested.

13. Butow, *Tojo*, pp. 387–91. According to Komatsu, Col. Tomura Morio of the General Staff delayed Roosevelt's message, as he knew an aeroplane had already been shot down by Japanese forces 'near Malaya', presumably a reference to the incident with F.O. Bedell's Catalina (*Origins*, p. 325).
14. For Kostenko's plan see *RA/VO*, vol. 4(1), pp. 168–9 (4 Dec.).
15. Günter Wegmann, ed., *'Das Oberkommando der Wermacht gibt bekannt. . .': Der deutsche Wehrmachtbericht*, vol. 1 (Osnabrück, 1982), p. 742 (8 Dec.) (hereafter *Wehrmachtbericht*); *KTB OKW*, p. 798 (7 Dec.); Halder, *KTB*, vol. 3, p. 332 (7 Dec.).
16. Bock, *KTB*, pp. 341–2 (7 Dec.).
17. *DRZW*, vol. 4, p. 558; Halder, *KTB*, vol. 3, p. 332 (7 Dec.).
18. Halder, *KTB*, vol. 3, p. 332 (7 Dec.). By 'High Command' (*die Oberste Führung*) Halder presumably meant Hitler and the officers around him at the Armed Forces HQ (*OKW*), as well as von Brauchitsch at the German Army HQ (*OKH*). The town of Ruza was 55 miles west of Moscow and not far from the current anchor point of German 4th Army; Ostashkov, however, lay 105 miles west of Kalinin, so the proposed German 'reserve line' would have run diagonally from northwest to southeast, roughly parallel to the Moscow-Leningrad railway. All the German gains to the north and northwest of the Soviet capital would have to be given up.
19. Engel, *Heeresdjutant*, pp. 117–18 (7 Dec.). Engel, the Army adjutant at WOLFSSCHANZE, professed to be alarmed by the suggestion of Hitler replacing Brauchitsch when Schmundt told him about it.
20. Alanbrooke, *Diaries*, p. 208 (7 Dec.).
21. TNA, ADM 234/330, p. 29.
22. The Japanese note was not included in the BJs for 7 Dec. (TNA, HW 12/271), nor did it appear in any of the Admiralty Special Intelligence summaries (TNA, ADM 223/321) prepared on that day.
23. *CWP*, p. 1574.
24. Winant, *Letter*, pp. 197–8.
25. CAC, CHAR 20/46/37, Churchill to Auchinleck, 7 Dec.
26. *New York Times*, 7 Dec., p. 54, 8 Dec., p. 9.
27. See n. 12 above. Yale UL, Stimson Diary, 7 Dec.; Prange, *Dawn*, p. 489; Hanyok and Mowry, *West Wind*, pp. 45–6; *PHA*, part 9, pp. 3969–72 (Kramer testimony to JC); *MBPH*, vol. V, p. 57, circ. no. 2494 (sent 7 Dec., trans. 7 Dec.). This was not translated by the British codebreakers until after the war began; see TNA, HW 12/271, BJ 098694, circ. no. 2494 (sent 7 Dec., decrypt. 8 Dec.).
28. This important timing is based on *PHA*, part 5, pp. 2185–6 (Stark testimony to JC), and part 8, p. 3392 (McCollum testimony to JC).
29. *PHA*, part 14, p. 1334; Prange, *Dawn*, pp. 494–6, 567–8. The 'one o' clock message' was actually more a declaration than an 'ultimatum'. The information General Marshall introduced about the Japanese destruction of cipher machines was not based on any of the three messages that had become available that morning. Marshall's message also made no reference to the large Japanese convoy that had been sighted on Saturday afternoon in the southern part of the South China Sea.

30. For the Kota Bharu landings see Kirby, *WAJ*, pp. 188–91, 526–7; Farrell, *Singapore*, pp. 103, 141–4; IWMD, AL 17/5182, 'Outlines of Malayan Campaign by 18th Division' (1946); Tsuji, *Singapore*, pp. 93–6; IWMD, JM no. 107, 'Malaya Invasion Operations', pp. 20–1; K.D. Bhargava and K.N.V. Sastri, *Campaigns in South-East Asia, 1941–42. Official History of the Indian Armed Forces in the Second World War* (n.p., 1960), pp. 118–38.
31. In this book I have tried to deal with the events of one day in a specific chapter; despite the global complexities, this is usually possible. There is, however, no neat way to deal with the Kota Bharu landings, which began on 8 Dec. but before the attack on Pearl Harbor on 7 Dec. The landings that occured a couple of hours later (on 8 Dec.) on the Kra Isthmus are dealt with in ch. 11.

    For the timing of the Kota Bharu landing I have relied on General Percival's post-war despatch, which specified 12.25 a.m. See Percival, 'Operations of Malaya Command', p. 1268. This is also the time used in the revised British outline of Naval operations, ADM 234/330, p. 7. Brooke-Popham's post-war despatch, however, gave the time of the first Japanese landing as 1.30 a.m. (p. 555), and that time was also used by a Japanese post-war source (IWMD, JM no, 107, p. 20). The original war diary of [British] GHQ, Far East, cited the report 'three small ships' off Kota Bahru at 11.00 p.m. on 7 Dec., logged at 11.20, but these could have been part of the screening force. At 1.20 a.m. this war diary had the entry 'Japanese attempted landing' and a call for air strikes (TNA, WO 172/15). In Japanese plans the landing time was set for midnight (IWMD, AL 7/1336, p. 4).
32. The fact that some of the British sighting reports mentioned Japanese ships 'north of Kota Bharu' did not necessarily mean that a landing was expected there. Kota Bharu was the air base from which the search planes were operating; the ships sighted were in the middle of the Gulf of Siam, and they could just as likely have been heading for the Kra Isthmus.
33. According to two summaries prepared for the Allies after the war, evidently by former Japanese naval officers, it was Adm. Ozawa (who was subordinate to Adm. Kondō) who insisted on taking Kota Bharu. See IWMD, JM no. 107, 'Malaya Invasion Naval Operations [Revised Edition]', p. 10; IWMD, AL 7/1335, 'Summary of Malay Landing Operational Plan'.

    Another post-war account, possibly prepared by Japanese Army officers, maintained that it was the Army which demanded simultaneous landings at Singora, Patani and Kota Bharu, against initial opposition from the Japanese Navy; see IWMD, AL 8/5007, 'Malaya Landing Operation'. In view of the fact that it was in the interests of the Navy to neutralise Kota Bharu aerodrome, it would seem more likely that the initiative came from Admiral Ozawa.
34. The 3/17th Dogras were the third battalion of the 17th Dogra Regiment.
35. On the Singapore air raid see Kirby, *WAJ*, p. 183; Shores and Cull, *Shambles*, pp. 85–7; Maltby, 'Air Operations', pp. 1365–6. An earlier attack by the Genzan Wing, scheduled to hit Singapore just after midnight, had been abandoned due to adverse weather conditions.
36. John Prados, *Combined Fleet Decoded: The Secret History of American Intelligence and the Japanese Navy in World War II* (Annapolis, 1995), pp. 158–77. A number of revisionist books have argued that the Japanese did send radio messages. The best-known of these is Robert B. Stinnett, *Day of Deceit: The Truth about FDR and Pearl Harbor* (New York, 2001). For a critical review by Philip Jacobsen see *Cryptologia*, 24:2 (2000), pp. 110–18.
37. *PHP*, p. 121, Yamamoto to Takahashi, 19 Dec. 1941.
38. *PHA*, part 39, p. 321. Adm. Stark learned that the Japanese were attaching particular importance to the precise time of 1.00 p.m. in Washington. In Stark's defence, the fact that 1.00 p.m. corresponded to 7.30 a.m. in Hawaii was not self-evidently significant. That hour (7.30 a.m.) was not even the time of sunrise. The sun rose in Honolulu at 6.27 a.m. and the 'morning twilight' was ninety minutes before that; see *Investigation of the Pearl*

*Harbor Attack: Report of the Joint Committee on the Investigation of the Pearl Harbor Attack, Congress of the United States* (Washington, DC, 1946), pp. 489–90 (hereafter *JC Report*).

39. For the attack on Oahu see Prange, *Dawn*, pp. 483–540 *passim*; Fukudome Shigeru, 'Hawaii Operation' and Fuchida Mitsuo, 'The Attack on Pearl Harbor', in *The Japanese Navy in World War II*, ed. Raymond O'Connor (Annapolis, 1972), pp. 2–27.
40. Prange, *Dawn*, pp. 499–501. The IC was modelled on the sector stations (or 'filter rooms') of the RAF in the Battle of Britain, in which information about aircraft movements was plotted onto a large map display. Not only was the Opana sighting ignored before the morning strike, it was also not taken into consideration, later in the day, when the American command on Hawaii was attempting to work out the direction in which the Japanese fleet could be found.
41. The attack force was made up of three different types of aircraft. The Nakajima B5N (later known to the Allies by the codename KATE) was a three-seater which was used as a torpedo bomber or a high-altitude 'level' or horizontal bomber. The Aichi D3A (VAL) was a two-seat dive bomber. The fighters were all of the famous Mitsubishi A6M Zero (ZEKE) type.
42. *PHA*, part 17, pp. 2867–8, Tinker report of 22 Dec. 1941. Early morning was the most dangerous time of day, because the attacking aircraft carriers could dash forward some 250 miles under cover of darkness.
43. The strike force over Oahu was 4,300 miles from Adm. Yamamoto's flagship, back in Japan. In view of this it is quite surprising that the messages transmitted using the aircraft radios of Fuchida and some of his crews were received there. Nevertheless, that claim is made in the accounts of Fuchida and Adm. Ugaki (Yamamoto's Chief of Staff). See Prange, *Dawn*, p. 504; Ugaki, *Diary*, p. 43 (8 Dec.); Fuchida, 'Attack', in O'Connor, *Japanese Navy*, p. 24.
44. *PHA*, part 32, p. 344 (Ramsey testimony to Navy COI).
45. The torpedo attack from the north sank the target ship *Utah* (a converted dreadnought) and badly damaged the old light cruiser *Raleigh*. The new light cruiser *Helena*, alongside Dock 1010, was also damaged by a torpedo.
46. The eighth battleship, USS *Pennsylvania*, was in dry dock nearby.
47. Prange, *Dawn*, p. 509.
48. For details of the loss of *Arizona* and *Oklahoma* see Norman Friedman, *U.S. Battleships: An Illustrated Design History* (London, 1986), pp. 415–16. Prange's account is incorrect about the damage to *Arizona* (*Dawn*, p. 507); she was not hit by a torpedo, and Kimmel could not therefore have witnessed this specific event. The wreck of the *Arizona* is now the main Pearl Harbor memorial, dedicated in 1962, as well as a mass war grave.
49. Prange, *Dawn*, p. 516; *PHA*, part 23, p. 898 (Roberts Commission). Kimmel kept the spent bullet as a souvenir.
50. Adm. Nagumo would later be second-guessed for not launching further strikes against Pearl Harbor, targeting harbour installations and vulnerable tanks of fuel oil. The Japanese commander surely did the right thing. His responsibility was to prevent damage to his vital ships. He did not know the location of the American aircraft carriers, nor the full strength of the surviving enemy air squadrons on Oahu. A swift getaway had always been a key part of the orders that he had been given.
51. NAII, RG 457, SRH-406, 'Pre-Pearl Harbor Jap Naval Despatches', pp. 112–13.
52. For the President's activities in the later part of the day see the memorandum dictated by Harry Hopkins on 7 Dec.: Georgetown UL, Hopkins Papers, box 6, folder 19 (hereafter Hopkins memorandum, 7 Dec.).
53. *FRUS, 1931–1941*, vol. 2, pp. 786–7.
54. *PHA*, part 20, pp. 4520–4; NOA, Nimitz Papers, Command Summary, book 1, no. 080450 to OPNAV, 8 Dec.
55. BI, Hickleton Papers, Lord Halifax, Family Diary, A.7.8.9, 9 Dec.
56. Alanbrooke, *Diaries*, p. 209 (7 Dec.).

57. W. Averell Harriman and Elie Abel, *Special Envoy to Churchill and Stalin 1941–1946* (New York, 1975), p. 111.
58. *CWP*, p 1576, n. 1; Churchill, *SWW*, p. 538. The attack on Pearl Harbor began at 7.25 p.m., London time.
59. *CWP*, pp. 1577–8.
60. Churchill, *SWW*, pp. 539–40.
61. CUOHC, Perkins, 'Reminiscences', p. 67; Yale UL, Stimson Diary, 7 Dec.; Hopkins memorandum, 7 Dec. See the stenographic notes in FRPL, FDR Speech Files, cont. 68, no. 1399a. Detailed stenographic notes were highly unusual for any meeting with the wily FDR.
62. Yale UL, Stimson Diary, 7 Dec.
63. Hopkins memorandum, 7 Dec.
64. FRPL, FDR Speech Files, cont. 68, no. 1399a. For classic, and in my view convincing, explanations of the Pearl Harbor attack see Roberta Wohlstetter, *Pearl Harbor: Warning and Decision* (Stanford, 1962), and Prange, *Dawn*. The definitive 'official' statement of the Congressional Investigation is in *JC Report*, pp. 251–65. For the 1942 conclusions of the Roberts Commission see *PHA*, part 39, pp. 1–20.
65. *JC Report*, p. 253. The 'plans that contemplated the precise type of attack' was a reference to Kimmel's Pacific Fleet Confidential Letter No. 2CL-41 of Feb. 1941, the Martin-Bellinger report of Mar. 1941, and a plan for the use of heavy bombers to defend Oahu which was sent to US Army Air Force HQ in Washington in Aug. 1941. All three discussed the danger of a surprise air attack on Oahu.
66. Prange, *Dawn*, provides a balanced view of Kimmel and Short. For more recent polemics see Edward L. Beach, *Scapegoats: A Defense of Kimmel and Short at Pearl Harbor* (Annapolis, 1995), and John Lambert and Norman Polmar, *Defenseless: Command Failures at Pearl Harbor* (St Paul, MN, 2003).

    Adm. Claude Bloch, who was in charge of the naval installations (and naval defences) on Hawaii, was not officially criticised at all in later investigations. His command, the 14th Naval District, was essentially a pre-retirement post. Bloch had been C-in-C, United States Fleet – in effect commander of the Pacific Fleet – from 1938 to Jan. 1940. For a critical judgement of Adm. Bloch see Prange, *Dawn*, pp. 731–3.
67. *PHA*, part 39, p. 21; *JC Report*, p. 252.
68. For reasons of space, one thread of evidence has not been followed: messages between Tokyo and the Japanese spy network in Hawaii. On 24 Sept. 1941, the Japanese Foreign Ministry requested the Honolulu consulate to provide more detailed information. It asked about the location of US warships in five specific areas of Pearl Harbor, and it requested such details as whether the ships were tied up alongside one another. See *MBPH*, vol. III, pp. A-189 to A-190, no. 83 to Honolulu (trans. 9 Oct. 1941). The zones of the harbour were later known in American discussion as the 'bomb plots'.

    The American intelligence officials in Washington who decrypted and distributed these messages made two important mistakes. First, they assumed that because Pearl Harbor was the major American fleet base it was of *general* interest to the Japanese, rather than a target for attack. And second, they believed (incorrectly) that Adm. Kimmel was aware of these decrypts. For details see Prange, *Dawn*.
69. For a good recent introduction to this debate see Richard Aldrich, *Intelligence and the War against Japan: Britain, America and the Politics of Secret Service* (Cambridge, 2000), pp. 68–91. Relatively recent examples of the conspiracy genre are: Victor, *Pearl Harbor Myth*; Stinnett, *Day*; James Rusbridger and Eric Nave, *Betrayal at Pearl Harbor: How Churchill Lured Roosevelt into War* (London, 1991).

    David Irving has a chapter entitled 'Day of Perfidy' in his venomous but heavily-researched biography of Churchill, but even he does not attempt to accuse his subject of advanced knowledge of the Pearl Harbor attack; see *Churchill's War*, vol. 2, pp. 203–40.

70. The argument needs to get beyond the question of whether the destruction of the careers of Kimmel and Short was 'fair' or not. This was war, not an employment tribunal; the United States suffered very heavy losses and the two commanders could have done much to mitigate those losses.

It is not relevant to the issue of the individual responsibility of Kimmel and Short that other American commanders made mistakes. Gen. Marshall and Adm. Stark, and a number of their subordinates (notably Adm. R.K. Turner, Stark's head of War Plans), bore at least a degree of responsibility. Adm. Bloch, responsible for the security of Pearl Harbor, was not reprimanded. Gen. MacArthur and Gen. Brereton in the Philippines might equally well have been found in 'dereliction of duty' had their actions undergone similar investigation; they certainly made serious errors of judgement.

One might also argue that in the real world of Dec. 1941 Kimmel and Short were 'necessary' scapegoats. The alternative would have been a purge of the American high command, a wartime overturn of the military administrative system, and a self-destructive political crisis.

71. *JC Report*, p. 262; *PHA*, part 6, p. 2521 (JCH), my italics.

72. The fullest source on Japanese naval planning, based partly on interviews with surviving senior naval officers, is Prange, *Dawn*. See also IWMD, JM no. 152, pp. 43–69; Sadao Asada, 'The Japanese Navy and the United States', in Borg and Okamoto, *Pearl Harbor*, pp. 250–60; Evans and Peattie, *Kaigun*, pp. 471–9.

73. The fullest biography of Yamamoto in English is still Agawa, *Yamamoto*.

74. Remarkable as Yamamoto was, I do not share a common opinion of him as an original strategist, an infallible military commander, or a man of peace. The Admiral's conception of war with the United States mimicked that of the war with Russia in 1904–5. His tactical model came from the British torpedo-plane strike against the Italian Fleet at Taranto in Nov. 1940. His limitations as a fleet commander became evident in his conduct of the Battle of Midway in 1942. And as for his being a man of peace or a 'reluctant admiral', Yamamoto was the advocate of an unprovoked attack in violation of international law, and of operations in support of a campaign of aggression on the largest scale in Southeast Asia. (*Reluctant Admiral* was the title of the English translation of *Yamamoto Isoruku*, published in Japanese in 1969.) The Admiral took as a given Japan's 1930s ideology of national aggression and expansion. Although, like a number of other elite Japanese, he had experience of life in the USA, he completely misjudged the impact that the Pearl Harbor attack would have on American public opinion.

75. *Kido Butai* is often translated as 'Strike Force', and Nagumo's command is indeed most famous for conducting the eventual strike against Oahu. However, it could more correctly be seen as a 'mobile force' or a 'flying squadron' (in the old-fashioned naval sense), comparable to the American pre-war 'Scouting Force, Pacific Fleet'.

76. Japanese espionage activities in Hawaii were organised by the Naval General Staff, not by Combined Fleet. They were presumably intended to gather information about the main operating base of the US Pacific Fleet, rather than to support a surprise air attack; this changed in late Sept. 1941 (see n. 68 above).

77. See IWMD, JM no. 102, pp. 15–20. Japanese submarine operations have been neglected in histories of the Pearl Harbor attack because, unlike the air attack, they were unsuccessful. The large submarine force achieved nothing at all during the period of the raid, although *I-6* would damage carrier *Saratoga* with a torpedo off Oahu on 11 Jan.

There were disagreements about the plans for the Hawaiian Operation between the Naval General Staff (under Adm. Nagano) and the staff of Combined Fleet. According to Adm. Fukudome (Nagano's chief planner), it was the NGS that insisted on the deployment of a large force of submarines in Hawaiian waters, as it was not confident that the air strike would succeed; see O'Connor, *Japanese Navy*, pp. 11–12. This conflicts with Prange's version (*Dawn*, p. 202), where the use of submarines is described as Yamamoto's idea; Prange's account was based on a 1948 interview with Adm. Shimizu Mitsumi, commander of the Navy's submarine force.

78. The 46-ton 'A' type submarines were a pre-war secret weapon; approximately 50 were built in 1938–42. Armed with two torpedoes, they were electric-powered and capable of bursts of high speed. The pre-war operational concept was that they would operate in the open seas, launched (and recovered) by purpose-built surface ships. Their use at Pearl Harbor was essentially a suicide mission; it was also tactically foolhardy, as it risked giving up the element of surprise for the air attack, and it nearly did so. All five midget submarines were sunk, and only one crew member survived. There has been recent speculation that some of the 'midgets' were able to fire torpedoes during the air attack; the evidence is unconvincing (PBS NOVA, 'Killer Subs in Pearl Harbor', first aired 5 Jan. 2010).

    Ironically, more primitive 'midgets' would achieve success twelve days after Pearl Harbor. Three much smaller craft, manned by Italians, crippled two British battleships in Alexandria harbour.
79. *PHP*, pp. 138–9 (Kusaka memoir).
80. Oikawa Koshirō was minister of the navy (in the second and third Konoe cabinets) from Sept. 1940 to Oct. 1941; Shimada Shigetarō (an Academy classmate and friend of Yamamoto) was minister from Oct. 1941 to July 1944, in the Tōjō cabinet.
81. O'Connor, *Japanese Navy*, p. 11.
82. *PHP*, pp. 118–19. The battles were Ichinotani (1184), Okehazama (1560) and Kawakanakajima (1561). Yamamoto had made similar arguments in his 7 Jan. 1941 letter to Navy Minister Oikawa: 'The most important thing we have to do first of all in a war with the U.S., is to fiercely attack and destroy the U.S. main fleet at the outset of the war, so that the morale of the U.S. Navy and her people goes down to such an extent that it can never be recovered.' *PHP*, p. 116.
83. Donald Detwiler, ed., *War in Asia and the Pacific* (New York, 1980), vol. 2, doc. 6, Tōjō interrogation 28 Feb. 1948. Tōjō was in American custody at this time, under threat of death for war crimes, so his testimony must be read with caution. It is impossible to believe that Tōjō was not aware of the complex Army-Navy plan to occupy the Philippines as a necessary part of the operations against Malaya, Burma, Borneo and the Dutch East Indies.
84. The fact remains, however, that planning of both the US Army and Navy in 1941 took in detailed discussion of a carrier raid on Hawaii, under political and military conditions very close to those of 7 Dec. 1941. It was certainly not thought that such an operation was technically impossible. See *JC Report*, pp. 75–87.
85. Irving, *Hitler's War*, p. 353; Keitel, *Mein Leben*, p. 343; Warlimont, *Hauptquartier*, p. 221. No primary source is given for Irving's account, but it was possibly Hewel. See also Ian Kershaw, *Hitler 1936–45: Nemesis* (London, 2000), p. 953, n. 287. Midnight does seem late for the news to have reached East Prussia, as the BBC broadcast the news at around 10.00 p.m. German time, and Ambassador Ōshima heard the news on the radio in Berlin at 11.00 p.m.
86. Goebbels, *TBJG*, part II, vol. 2, pp. 339 (22 Nov.), 452–3 (8 Dec.). From Goebbels's diary it would appear that Hitler called him during the night of 7–8 Dec., and that this was when a decision was made to summon the Reichstag. However, the Propaganda Minister dictated his diary on the 8th, and he also reported later developments (from the morning of 8 Dec.) in the diary, including President Roosevelt's decision to summon Congress, and news at 6.00 a.m. (German time) that war had been declared (presumably by Japan).
87. TNA, HW 12/271, BJ 098722, no. 1432 to Tokyo (sent 8 Dec., decrypt. 9 Dec.); TNA, ADM 223/321, SI no. 469. The American translation is in *MBPH*, vol. IV, pp. A-391 to A-392 (sent 8 Dec.); the date of translation is given as 5 Dec., which is clearly incorrect.
88. Ciano, *Diary*, p. 472.
89. Goebbels, *TBJG*, part II, vol. 2, p. 339 (22 Nov.). Goebbels then mentioned that direct US involvement would cause the war as a whole to be further prolonged, but that this

had to be accepted. It is not clear whether this was his own view or also Hitler's. The Propaganda Minister did say that this development showed that he (Goebbels) had been right to prepare the German *Volk* for a hard struggle. For a rather similar judgement, made a few weeks later, by Hitler himself, see *Hitler Monologe*, p. 193 (10 Jan. 1942): 'America is for us just a question of holding out with a will of iron' (*Amerika ist für uns nur eine Frage des eisernen Durchhaltens*).

90. *Hitler Monologe*, p. 184 (7 Jan. 1942).
91. Goebbels, *TBJG*, part II, vol. 2, p. 453 (8 Dec.).

## Chapter 11: The Beginning of the End of the British Empire

1. For events on Wake see: R.D. Heinl, *The Defense of Wake* (Washington, DC, 1947); Frank O. Hough *et al.*, *History of US Marine Corps Operations in World War II*, vol. 1 (Washington, DC, 1958), pp. 95–110; Morison, *History*, vol. 3, pp. 229–35.
2. For Guam see Hough, *History of USMC*, pp. 75–6.
3. For the Philippines on 8 Dec. see Bartsch, *December 8*, pp. 257–407; Morton, *Fall*, pp. 77–90; Richard L. Watson, 'Pearl Harbor and Clark Field', in Craven and Cate, eds, *Army Air Forces*, pp. 201–13.
4. Lewis H. Brereton, *The Brereton Diaries: The War in the Air in the Pacific, in the Middle East and Europe, 3 October 1941–8 May 1945* (New York, 1946), pp. 38–9.
5. NOA, Hart Papers, 'Report of a Conference', p. 5 (6 Dec.).
6. For FEAF strength and losses on 8 Dec. see Watson in Craven and Cate, eds, *AAF*, pp. 201, 203, 213.
7. For these developments see: Mark R. Peattie, *Sunburst: The Rise of the Japanese Naval Air Power, 1909–1941* (London, 2002); Tagaya, *'Betty' Units*, pp. 6–15. The two Mitsubishi bombers (G3M and G4M) were also known, respectively, as the Type 96 and Type 1, after the Japanese calendar years in which they entered service (1936, 1941). Later, in 1942, the Allies assigned code names to these aircraft: 'Nell' and 'Betty'. The Zero was the Mitsubishi A6M (or Type 0); fighters of this type flew from carriers during the Pearl Harbor raid.
8. On the mishandling of the air defences see Bartsch, *December 8*, p. 420. Bartsch laid particular blame on Maj. Orrin Grover, commander of 24th Pursuit Group at Clark Field.
9. John Costello wrote a book arguing that there were sinister reasons for MacArthur's hesitation to launch an immediate strike from Philippine territory; he was, Costello argued, financially dependent on President Manuel Quezon, who hoped to keep his territory out of the war. John Costello, *Days of Infamy: MacArthur, Roosevelt, Churchill, the Shocking Truth Revealed* (New York, 1995), pp. 267–72.

   The General certainly received lavish payments, but there is little other evidence to support this speculation, and in any event MacArthur agreed to the air strike after about five hours' delay. Other historians have argued that MacArthur suffered some sort of nervous breakdown during the morning: see, for example, William Manchester, *American Caesar: Douglas MacArthur, 1880–1964* (Boston, 1978), p. 156. This also seems unlikely. Until the midday attack on Clark Field there was not a great deal to have a nervous breakdown about, and while MacArthur was a pompous windbag, he was not incompetent.
10. Some historians maintain that American aircraft – Army or Navy – carried out secret spy flights over Formosa. There were formal Japanese complaints about over-flights (on 27 Nov.), and some American participants later claimed to have taken part in such flights. Neither assertion, however, was backed up by documentary evidence. The most fully-researched American account, by William Bartsch, suggests that there were no US Army flights over Formosa in the weeks before 8 Dec. Bartsch considered it possible that the navy might have mounted PBY flights earlier (*December 8*, pp. 201; 230; 470, n. 12; 474–5, n. 3).

11. Waldo H. Heinrichs, *American Ambassador: Joseph C. Grew and the Development of the United States Diplomatic Tradition* (New York, 1986), p. 358; TNA, FO 371/35957, Craigie to Eden, 4 Feb. 1943, pp. 24–6.
12. *ADAP*, ser. D, vol. XIII.2, pp. 805–7. The Japanese did not, in the end, block the Vladivostok route. It became an extremely important channel for Lend-Lease supplies throughout the period 1942–45.
13. An English text of the 'Rescript' (i.e. edict) is printed in *RGM*, vol. I.1, plate no. 1. The content of the document is discussed in Bix, *Hirohito*, pp. 433–6.
14. Ugaki, *Diary*, p. 44. The six slower battleships did put to sea during the Midway operation in June 1942, but in a support role only. The four fast battleships, converted battlecruisers, saw much more action. Two new super-battleships were commissioned in 1942.
15. For the landing in the Kra Isthmus see TNA, CAB 120/518; IWMD, AL 17/5181, Kawamura Saburō, 'Summary of the Malayan Operation of the 5th Division'; Farrell, *Singapore*, pp. 107–9, 141–2, 150–4; Kirby, *WAJ*, pp. 177–88, 191–2, 521–3; Tsuji, *Singapore*, pp. 79–82. Kawamura was commander of the 9th Bde (5th Div.) and commanded the two regiments landed at Singora.
16. Nakhorn, Bandon, Jumbhorn and Prachuab were occupied by 143rd Rgt of 55th Div. (15th Army). The ships carrying this regiment started from Saigon rather than Hainan, but operated in co-ordination with the main 25th Army convoy.
17. LHCMA, Brooke-Popham Papers, 6/8/37. This was part of a 1947 internal discussion about the despatches that were about to be published. For the unsuccessful British air attacks on 8 Dec. see Kirby, *WAJ*, p. 184; Maltby, 'Air Operations', pp. 1365–7; Shores and Cull, *Shambles*, pp. 80–5, 87–97.
18. The fourth regiment of 5th Div. (21st Rgt) was intended to arrive as a reinforcement in Singora on 27 Dec. Rear-echelon elements of 5th Div. were scheduled to arrive in Singora in two convoys on 16 and 27 Dec. Of the elements of 18th Div., 56th Rgt landed at Kota Bharu on 8 Dec. 124th Rgt would occupy the oil-rich colony of British Borneo in mid-Dec., and two regiments (55th and 114th) were scheduled to arrive as reinforcements in early Jan.
19. *JDW*, pp. 225, 280–1; Kirby, *WAJ*, pp. 162–3.
20. Yoji Akashi, 'General Yamashita Tomoyuki: Commander of the 25th Army', in Brian P. Farrell, ed., *Sixty Years On: The Fall of Singapore Revisited* (Singapore, 2002), pp. 185–207; Farrell, *Singapore*, pp. 108–9; Tachikawa Kyoichi, 'General Yamashita and his Style of Leadership: The Malaya/Singapore Campaign', in Brian Bond and Tachikawa Kyoichi, eds, *British and Japanese Military Leadership in the Far Eastern War, 1941–45* (London, 2004), pp. 75–87.
21. Kirby, *WAJ*, pp. 183–4, 525. The 'stab in the back' was a reference to the Italian declaration of war against an embattled France, in June 1940, rather than to Pearl Harbor.
22. British and Indian units were basically organised as regiments, which were deployed operationally as battalions. To take an example, 3/16th Punjabis were the 3rd Battalion of the 16th Punjab (Infantry) Regiment. Battalion personnel strength was around 800 men, typically organised in three companies.
23. TNA, ADM 234/330, p. 30.
24. Derek Howse, *Radar at Sea: The Royal Navy in World War 2* (Basingstoke, 1993), pp. 123–4. Admiral Phillips took a strong interest in his flagship's electronics, and had inspected them as soon as he came aboard in Scotland.
25. On the lack of accurate information on Japanese air strength in Indochina, especially torpedo bombers, see Marder, *Old Friends*, vol. 1, pp. 413–14, 433–4.
26. TNA, ADM 234/330.
27. For the defence of Hong Kong see: Kirby, *WAJ*, pp. 107–51; C.M. Maltby, 'Operations in Hong Kong from 8th to 25th December, 1941', *Supplement to The London Gazette*, no. 38190, 27 Jan. 1948; Philip Snow, *The Fall of Hong Kong: Britain, China, and the Japanese Occupation* (New Haven and London, 2003).

28. *Wehrmachbericht*, p. 743 (9 Dec.).
29. *KTB OKW*, p. 801 (8 Dec.).
30. Guderian, *Erinnerungen*, p. 237; Bock, *KTB*, p. 343 (8 Dec.).
31. Bock, *KTB*, pp. 343–4 (8 Dec.).
32. *Wehrmachtbericht*, p. 742 (8 Dec.); *Hitler's Weisungen*, pp. 171–4 (8 Dec.). As we have seen, winter preparations and strategy had been taken up by Hitler on the 6th (Halder, *KTB*, vol. 3, p. 328). This was probably a result of his flight to the Rostov front on 2–4 Dec. and of his talks with front-line commanders.
33. No. 1693 (8 Dec.), printed in *KTB OKW*, pp. 1076–82.
34. Engel, *Heeresadjutant*, p. 118 (8 Dec.).
35. *DRZW*, vol. 4, p. 558.
36. TNA, HWD 12/271, no. 1437 to Tōgō, BJ 098748 (sent 8 Dec., decrypt. 9 Dec.).
37. *ADAP*, vol. XIII.2, pp. 799–800, no. 2294 to Ott; TNA, HW 12/271, BJ 098760, no. 1440, 1441 to Tōgō (decrypt. 10 Dec.).
38. On Chełmno see Christopher R. Browning, *The Origins of the Final Solution: The Evolution of Nazi Jewish Policy, September 1939–March 1942* (London, 2005), pp. 416–19.
39. Absolute certainty should not be attached to the date of 8 Dec. as the start of the killing operation in Chełmno, although this was used in the post-war trial (Browning, *Origins*, p. 542, n. 146); the date of 5 Dec. was also given in trial documentation. In addition, the gas van had been used in Nov. for a number of small killing 'actions', as it travelled from Posen to Chełmno. More broadly, it should be said that Chełmno was the implementation of general Nazi mass-murder policies decided some weeks earlier, in Oct. 1941.
40. On the Wannsee meeting: Browning, *Origins*, pp. 407, 410; Christian Gerlach, 'The Wannsee Conference, the Fate of German Jews, and Hitler's Decision in Principle to Exterminate all European Jews', *Journal of Modern History*, 70:4 (1998), pp. 759–812.
41. Reinhardt to M. Luther, 8 Jan. 1942, printed in Johannes Tuchel, *Am Grossen Wannsee 56–58: Von der Villa Minoux zum Haus der Wannsee-Konferenz* (Berlin, 1992), p. 115. See the discussion of this question in Browning, *Origins*, p. 540, n. 112, and Gerlach, 'Wannsee', p. 793. Hans Safrian, in *Die Eichmann-Männer* (Vienna, 1993), p. 169, argued that the setback at Moscow was of special importance. Browning (pp. 407–8) disagreed with this, evidently on the grounds that an extermination policy (rather than a policy of deportation and death beyond the Urals) had already been decided upon in Oct. 1941. My own view would be that on 7 or 8 Dec., when the postponement of the Wannsee meeting had been decided upon, it was not evident that the military situation had changed so much for worse since 29 Nov., when the meeting was first arranged.

    Martin Gilbert in *The Holocaust: The Jewish Tragedy* (London, 1986), p. 279, stated that the Wannsee meeting was postponed 'because of America's entry into the war'. Gilbert produced no supporting evidence, but Hitler's return to Berlin and the proposed Reichstag meeting – both following Pearl Harbor – are indeed likely factors. This will be discussed further in ch. 15, in connection with the Reich Chancellery meeting of Nazi leaders on 12 Dec.
42. CAC, CHAR 20/20/65–67, Churchill to King George VI, 8 Dec.
43. Harvey, *Diaries*, pp. 70–2 (8 Dec.); CAC, ACAD 1/10, Cadogan Diary, 8 Dec.
44. *C&R*, p. 282; *CWP*, p. 1582; Churchill, *SWW*, pp. 542–3. Article 1 of the Third Hague Convention (1907) read as follows: 'The Contracting Powers recognize that hostilities between themselves must not commence without previous and explicit warning, in the form either of a reasoned declaration of war or of an ultimatum with conditional declaration of war' (http://avalon.law.yale.edu/20th_century/hague03.asp, accessed 4 Jan. 2010).
45. *Parl. Debates: HC*, ser. 5, vol. 376, col. 1358–61.
46. Robert Rhodes James, *Chips: The Diaries of Sir Henry Channon* (London, 1996), pp. 313–14 (8 Dec.) (hereafter Channon, *Diaries*); Harold Nicholson, *Diaries and Letters*, (London, 1967) vol. 2, p. 194 (8 Dec.).

47. CAC, HARV 1, Harvie-Watt to Churchill, 12 Dec.
48. *Congressional Record*, vol. 87, part 9, pp. 9504–6, 9519–37, 8 Dec. The most famous phrase in the speech no doubt owed something to Secretary Hull, who concluded a press statement with the following words: 'Japan in its recent professions of a desire for peace has been infamously false and fraudulent' (*FRUS, Japan, 1931–1941*, vol. 2, p. 793).
49. *C&R*, p. 283 (8 Dec.).
50. CUOHC, Perkins, 'Reminiscences', pp. 97–8.
51. *ADAP*, ser. D, vol. XIII.2, pp. 796–8.
52. Yale UL, Stimson Diary, 7 Dec. (sic).
53. FRPL, Pres. Safe Files, box 128, Donovan to Roosevelt, 13 Nov. 1941.
54. *MBPH*, vol. IV, pp. A-382 to A-384 (no. 1393 to Foreign Ministry); CAC, CHAR 20/20/67, Churchill to King George VI, 8 Dec.
55. Weizsäcker, *Erinnerungen*, p. 328.
56. *FRUS, 1941*, vol. 1, pp. 661–3, G.A. Arbatov *et al.*, eds, *Sovetsko-amerikanskie otnoshenie vo vremia Velikoi Otechestvennoi voiny 1941–1945: Dokumenty i materialy*, vol. 1 (Moscow, 1984), pp. 143–4 (hereafter *SAmO*).
57. NOA, Nimitz Papers, 'CINCPAC Greybook', 8 Dec., 081700 to CINCLANT.
58. Ibid., 8 Dec., 090139 to CINCPAC.

## Chapter 12: FDR Begins the American Century

1. For the air battles of 9 Dec. see: TNA, CAB 120/518, Brooke-Popham, 'Operations in the Far East', p. 556; Maltby, 'Air Operations', pp. 1367–8; Shores and Cull, *Shambles*, pp. 99–107; TNA, AIR 23/3577.
2. *Japan Times and Advertiser*, 14 Dec. 1941, p. 1.
3. For naval operations off Malaya on 9 Dec. see: TNA, ADM 234/330; Marder, *Old Friends*, pp. 420–521.
4. *ADAP*, ser. D, vol. XIII.1, pp. 807–8, no. 2699 to Ribbentrop, 9 Dec. The timing of the Ott-Tōgō meeting is based on the hour of Ott's despatch to Berlin, i.e. 8.20 a.m., 9 Dec. Tokyo time.
5. *RA/VO*, vol. 4(1), pp. 176–7.
6. Bock, *KTB*, p. 344.
7. Goebbels, *TBJG*, part II, vol. 2, pp. 463–9 (10 Dec.).
8. Goebbels, *TBJG*, part II, vol. 2, p. 468 (10 Dec.). Goebbels dictated his diary notes on the 10th, but he was describing a meeting which occurred at midday on the 9th. It would therefore seem likely that Hitler had made the decision to postpone the Reichstag session at about the time of his arrival in Berlin on the 9th.
9. TNA, PREM 3/290/1, no. 1644 to Churchill; CAC, CHAR 20/46/51, Churchill to Smuts, 9 Dec.
10. TNA, HW 12/271, no. 1432 to Tōgō, BJ 698722 (decrypt. 9 Dec.); no. 1437 to Tōgō, BJ 698748 (decrypt. 9 Dec.).
11. *C&R*, p. 283, Churchill to Roosevelt, 9 Dec.
12. BI, Lord Halifax, Family Diary, 9 Dec. The American version of Ōshima's no. 1432 is in *MBPH*, vol. IV, pp. A-391 to A-392, with an incorrect translation date of 5 Dec.; the translation of no. 1437 is on p. A-392 and – unusually – is marked as 'Not dated'. Another message sent by Ōshima on the 8th (nos 1440/1/2) transmitted the German proposed terms for the new Tripartite Pact (received by Ōshima after 5.00 p.m. on 8 Dec.) and was available as an American translation on the 9th (*MBPH*, vol. IV, pp. A-392 to A-393). It was not decrypted by the British until 10 Dec. (as BJ 098760).
13. CAC, CHAR 20/46/68, Halifax to Churchill, 9 Dec. (12.50 a.m.).
14. NOA, Nimitz Papers, 'CINCPAC Greybook', 9 Dec., 091812 to CINCPAC. The Hawaiian Islands are an archipelago including, among the larger islands, Oahu, Maui, Hawaii ('The Big Island'), Kauai and Molokai. Oahu was by a large margin the most

heavily populated and had a developed defensive system. In theory the Japanese could have occupied one of the undefended islands and developed bases to neutralise or blockade Oahu. Midway was also part of the archipelago, although it was 1,300 miles from Oahu, to the northwest,

15. NAII, RG 165, Box 1.
16. Fireside Chat no. 19, 9 Dec. 1941: http://millercenter.org/scripps/archive/speeches/detail/3325, accessed 23 Dec. 2010. These radio addresses, direct to the American people (by their 'firesides'), were a powerful presidential tool. The first was delivered on 12 Mar. 1933; it dealt with the great banking crisis.
17. FRPL, Berle Diary, 9 Dec.
18. BI, Lord Halifax, Family Diary, 9 Dec.

## Chapter 13: Force 'Z' and the Malayan Tragedy

1. For details of the occupation of Guam see Hough, *History of USMC*, vol. 1, pp. 75–8.
2. Morton, *Fall*, pp. 102–3.
3. NOA, Hart Papers, Hart Private Diary, 7 Dec.
4. On operations in Thailand and Malaya see Farrell, *Singapore*, pp. 153, 155; Kirby, *WAJ*, pp. 186–7, 204–5; Tsuji, *Singapore*, pp. 72–92.
5. Howse, *Radar at Sea* p. 281.
6. The account of the attack on Force 'Z' is based mainly on two semi-official sources: TNA, ADM 234/330 and IWMD, JM no. 107, 'Malaya Invasion Naval Operations'. The best English-language account is that of Arthur J. Marder, which incorporates Japanese sources: *Old Friends*, pp. 462–90. British and Japanese sources give slightly different times for events; the former are used here.
7. William H. Garzke *et al.*, 'Death of a Battleship' (2009): http://www.rina.org.uk/c2/uploads/death%20of%20a%20battleship.pdf accessed 20 Dec. 2010. This account, by three experts, is based on examinations of the wreck of *Prince of Wales* in 2007–8.

   The aerial torpedoes which sank *Prince of Wales* and *Repulse* were Type 91. Contrary to Correlli Barnett (*Engage the Enemy More Closely: The Royal Navy in the Second World War* [London, 1991], p. 421), the Japanese aircraft which attacked Force 'Z' did not carry the famous Type 93 'Long Lance' torpedo. The Type 93 was a much heavier weapon with a warhead of 490kg (1,080lb), three times the size of that of the Type 91 (as well as having much longer range and much higher speed). It could be carried only by cruisers and destroyers. The Type 91 was a small torpedo which entered service in 1931 and differed little from aerial torpedoes used by other countries. It had a relatively small warhead weighing 150kg (331 lb) or 205kg (452lb), depending on the version.
8. Tom Phillips was not the only senior Allied naval officer killed in these first days of the war. Rear Admiral Isaac Kidd (born in 1884), commander of BatDiv One, was killed in the explosion of *Arizona* at Pearl Harbor.
9. TNA, ADM 116/5553, Draft despatch, Mar. 1942, p. 17.
10. Account of Captain Miwa, cited in Marder, *Old Friends*, p. 510–11.
11. *Wehrmachtbericht*, p. 743 (11 Dec.); *BPM*, vol. 2, p. 67.
12. Bock, *KTB*, p. 345 (10 Dec.).
13. Ibid., p. 346 (10 Dec.); BA-MA, RH 19II/122, *Heeresgruppe Mitte*, KTB Nr. 6 (10 Dec.).
14. Goebbels, *TBJG*, part II, vol. 2, pp. 475–6 (11 Dec.).
15. Ibid., p. 476 (11 Dec.).
16. *ADAP*, ser. D, vol. XIII.2, pp. 811–12. Ribbentrop's message was probably drafted before the decision to put off Hitler's speech from Wednesday to Thursday was made known.
17. Ibid., pp. 817–20.
18. Weizsäcker, *Erinnerungen*, p. 328; *ADAP*, ser. D, vol. XIII.2, pp. 812–13 (to Washington), 817–20 (to Rome).

19. CAC, CHAR 20/49, Churchill to Eden, 10 Dec. This message was despatched at 5.35 a.m.; it may well have been drafted by Churchill late on the 9th.
20. Churchill, *SWW*, p. 551; *CWP*, p. 1594 (Hill). In his memoirs Churchill added to events by suggesting he was alone in the room. It also seems unlikely that at this hour Pound could have reported with certainty that Phillips had drowned. All the same, the drama of the story was genuine.
21. *Parl. Debates: HC*, 5th ser., vol. 376, col. 1501; Channon, *Diary*, p. 314 (10 Dec.); CAC, CHAR 20/20/68, King George VI to Churchill, 10 Dec.
22. *FRUS, The Conferences at Washington, 1941–1942, and Casablanca, 1943* (Washington, 1968), p. 7; *C&R*, p. 284.
23. CAC, CHAR 20/46/64, Auchinleck to Churchill, 10 Dec.
24. Yale UL, Stimson Diary, 10 Dec. The changed decision of the *Pensacola* convoy was confirmed by the Joint Board later in the afternoon (NAII, RG 165, box 1).
25. *C&R*, p. 286.
26. NOA, Nimitz Papers, 'CINCPAC Greybook', no. 102042 to OPNAV. Kimmel could not have anticipated the collapse of the Malay barrier or Japanese naval raids into the Indian Ocean. In reality the US Pacific Fleet would have an even better opportunity than Kimmel expected to develop a raiding strategy of its own.
27. Goebbels, *TBJG*, part II, vol. 2, pp. 471, 475 (11 Dec.).

### Chapter 14: Hitler's War on America

1. R.D. Heinl, *The Defense of Wake* (Washington, 1947); Morison, *History*, vol. 3, pp. 229–35.
2. For the approaches to Jitra on the 11 Dec. see: TNA, CAB 106/53, 'The 11th Indian Division in Malaya'; LHCMA, Heath Diary; Bhargava and Sastri, *South-East Asia*, pp. 139–52, 159–66; Farrell, *Singapore*, pp. 156–8; Kirby, *WAJ*, pp. 207–13; Tsuji, *Singapore*, pp. 107–27.
3. Bock, *KTB*, p. 347.
4. *Parl. Debates: HC*, ser. 5, vol. 376, cols 1686–97.
5. Channon, *Diary*, pp. 314–15 (11 Dec.); Nicolson, *Diaries*, p. 196 (11 Dec.).
6. *Hitler RP*, p. 1809–10.
7. *ADAP*, ser. D, vol. XIII.2, pp. 812–13, 817.
8. Ibid., pp. 817–20.
9. Benito Mussolini, *Opera omnia di Benito Mussolini*, ed. Eduardo Susmel and Duilio Susmel (Florence, 1959, 1960), vol. 29, pp. 403–5 (10 June 1940), vol. 30, pp. 140–2 (11 Dec. 1941).
10. Goebbels, *TBJG*, part II, vol. 2, pp. 468 (10 Dec.), 476 (11 Dec.). For the text of the speech see *Hitler RP*, pp. 1793–811.
11. Goebbels, *TBJG*, part II, vol. 2, p. 485 (12 Dec.).
12. The note Ribbentrop handed to Leland Morris made no reference to the US Victory Program or the *Chicago Tribune* leak.
13. *ADAP*, ser. D, vol. XIII.2, pp. 616–17.
14. *FRUS, 1941*, vol. 1, pp. 590–1; *Congressional Record*, vol. 87, part 9, pp. 9652–3, 9665–7 (11 Dec.).
15. *SAmO*, pp. 144–5 for texts of Molotov's instructions and Litvinov's report. Hull referred to this meeting between FDR and Litvinov in his account of his own meeting with Litvinov in the afternoon. As Hull put it, Litvinov 'came in contact with the President' during his visit to Hopkins, but the Soviet Ambassador 'did not go into detail' with him (Hull) about what had been said (*FRUS, 1941*, vol. 4, p. 742). Meetings with Hull and Litvinov are not listed in the Pare Lorentz Chronology (FRPL) of the President's activities on this day.
16. *FRUS, 1941*, vol. 4, pp. 742–4; *Department of State Bulletin*, vol. V, no. 129, p. 506, 13 Dec. 1941.

17. Stark and Turner may have overstated their concerns in order to make sure that Army reinforcements were sent to the Hawaiian Islands rather than dispersed over the Pacific (especially to the Philippines) – or even sent to Europe. Nevertheless, inaccurate alarmist views are evident in other assessments and statements made during this period.

## Chapter 15: World War and the Destruction of the Jews

1. NOA, Hart Papers, Hart Private Diary, 12 Dec.
2. Farrell, *Singapore*, p. 160. For the Battle of Jitra on the 12 Dec. see: TNA, CAB 106/53, 'The 11th Indian Division in Malaya'; Bhargava and Sastri, eds, *South-East Asia*, pp. 159–66; Farrell, *Singapore*, pp. 158–61; Kirby, *WAJ*, pp. 206–13; Tsuji, *Singapore*, pp. 107–27.
3. Kedah was a relatively large 'state' in northwestern Malay, extending a hundred miles south from near the Thai border to near Penang. Formally, it was a British protectorate. The administrative centre was Alor Star (now Alor Setar).
4. Kirby, *WAJ*, p. 210.
5. CAC, CHAR 20/46/125, WSC to Governor of Hong Kong, 12 Dec.
6. *Wehrmachtbericht*, p. 745 (12, 13 Dec.).
7. BA-MA, RH 19II/122, KTB HGM, 12 Dec.
8. *RA/VO*, vol. 4(1), pp. 178–9; A.V. Korotkov *et al.*, eds, 'Posetiteli kremlevskogo kabineta I.V. Stalina: Zhurnaly (tetradi) zapisi lits, priniatykh pervym gensekom 1924–1953 gg', *Istoricheskii arkhiv* 2 (1996), p. 71.
9. *Soobshcheniia Sovetskogo Informbiuro*, vol. 1 (Moscow, 1944), pp. 407–9 (12 Dec.).
10. *Pravda*, 13, 17 Dec.
11. *CWP*, p. 1617.
12. CAC, CHAR 20/49, Churchill to Eden, 12 Dec.
13. *C&R*, pp. 287, 289.
14. CAC, JACB 1/11, Jacob diary, 12 Dec.
15. Goebbels, *TBJG*, part II, vol. 2, p. 493 (13 Dec.)
16. Ibid., pp. 494–5 (13 Dec.). I follow closely here the interpretation of the German historian Christian Gerlach, 'Wannsee', pp. 759–812.
17. Goebbels, *TBJG*, part II, vol. 2, pp. 498–9 (13 Dec.).
18. *Hitler RP*, vol II.1, p. 1058 (30 Jan. 1939).
19. The treatment of the Polish Jews after Sept. 1939 had reached a new stage of barbarity, although there was not yet a policy of systematic mass execution.
20. It is impossible to argue that the killings of Jews on Soviet territory was *not* the beginning of genocide. However, it was not actually the same as the comprehensive murder of *all* of Europe's Jews, including those of Greater Germany.
21. Gerlach, 'Wannsee', p. 790.

## Chapter 16: The New War and a New World

1. *CWP*, p. 1631.
2. Of the 433 US servicemen captured in Wake only 17 or so would die in captivity. Most of the civilians survived, but 98 contractors who had the misfortune still to be on Wake in Oct. 1943 were murdered by the occupiers.
3. CAC, CSCT 2/30, W. Churchill to Clementine Churchill, 21 Dec.
4. *FRUS, Conferences*, p. 27, Memorandum of 17 Dec.
5. Allen, *Singapore*, pp. 260–1; Fujiwara Iwaichi, *F. Kikan: Japanese Army Intelligence Operations in Southeast Asia During World War II* (Hong Kong, 1983), pp. xiii–xx, 77–188; Shahnawaz Khan, *Memories of INA and its Netaji* (Delhi, 1946), pp. 14–23.
6. Goebbels, *TBJG*, part II, vol. 2, p. 495 (13 Dec.); *Hitler Monologe*, p. 156 (18 Dec.).
7. FRPL, PSF, box 59, Report by the Secretary of the Navy to the President.
8. CUOHC, 'Reminiscences of Admiral Chester W. Nimitz', p. 58.

9. *RA/VO*, vol. 5(1), pp. 333–4.
10. Bock, *KTB*, p. 349.
11. *Wehrmachtbericht*, pp. 748–50; *Hitler RP*, vol. II.2, p. 1815.
12. For the events in East Prussia following Hitler's return see especially Geoffrey P. Megargee, *Inside Hitler's High Command* (Lawrence, KS, 2000), pp. 142–69.
13. *KTB OKW*, pp. 1084–5, no. 1738 to HGM, 18 Dec.
14. The unexpected death of Field Marshal Reichenau in January, after a stroke, meant that Bock would be recalled from his 'medical leave' after only three weeks and installed as C-in-C of Army Group South. This command was still, in Hitler's eyes, the most important in the German Army.
15. *VB*, 23 Dec., reprinted in *Hitler RP*, vol. II.2, p. 1813. The text of Brauchitsch's statement is printed in *Hitler RP*, vol. II.2, p. 1815, n. 561.
16. *Hitler Monologe*, pp. 183 (6–7 Jan. 1942), 210 (17–18 Jan. 1942); Goebbels, *TBJG*, part II, vol. 3, pp. 144–5 (20 Jan. 1942), 510–11 (20 Mar. 1942).
17. The German word, translated here as 'supreme military leader', is *Feldherr*. A more direct translation of *Feldherr*, 'warlord', sounds antiquated, extreme or even comic in English, but it might not have seemed that way to a German reader in 1941.
18. *Hitler RP*, vol. II.2, pp. 1814–15 (19 Dec.).
19. *VB*, 23 Dec.
20. CAC, CHAR 20/50, Telegram to Stalin, 15 Dec.
21. O.A. Rzheshevskii, ed., *Voina i diplomatiia. Dokumenty, kommentarii 1941–1942* (Moscow, 1997), pp. 11–62 (hereafter *ViD*); for the British version see TNA, CAB 66/20/39, WP(42)8, N109/5/38, Eden memo.
22. *The Times*, 29 Dec., p. 4.
23. Birmingham UL, Avon Papers, 20/3/3, Desk Diary, 19 Dec.; *Moskva prifrontovaia, 1941–1942: Arkhivnye dokumenty i materialy* (Moscow, 2001), pp. 391–2.
24. *ViD*, pp. 24–5.
25. Ibid., pp. 58–9; Harvey, *War Diaries*, p. 77.
26. *ViD*, pp. 23–4.
27. Ibid., pp. 15–30.
28. Ibid., pp. 15–18, 26–8. The similarities between Stalin's 1941 territorial proposal and the 1945 settlement are remarkable. Stalin was proposing in Dec. 1941 a Polish-German border (the Oder-Neisse line) which was the same as what would be agreed upon at the Yalta Conference in Feb. 1945. The draft Soviet treaty presented to Eden on 16 Dec. 1941 referred to Poland receiving 'the western part of East Prussia'. In discussion with the British Foreign Secretary, Stalin said that 'Poland should be given all lands up to the Oder, and rest will be Prussia or, more accurately, not Prussia but the state of Berlin'.

    There were some differences. The 1945 territorial settlement included the *permanent* cession of the Königsberg (now Kaliningrad) region to the USSR, and the grant of *all* of Silesia (including the area between the Oder and Western Neisse rivers) to Poland. Britain did indeed use bases in France, Belgium, Netherlands, Denmark and Norway, after 1945, but within the context of NATO.
29. CAC, ACAD 1/10, Cadogan Diary, 17 Dec.; Harvey, *Diaries*, p. 76 (18 Dec.). A twenty-year alliance treaty between Russia and Britain was eventually signed in May 1942, during a trip by Molotov to Britain. Molotov did not demand British recognition of the 1941 borders. By then the situation on the German-Russian front was worse, and it was becoming clear to Stalin that the defeat of Nazi Germany would be a long haul.
30. CAC, CHAR 20/50, Churchill to Attlee, 20 Dec.; Gorodetsky, *Cripps*, p. 224 (19 Dec.).
31. Goebbels, *TBJG*, part II, vol. 3, p. 510 (20 Mar. 1942). Hitler made similar comments in an evening discussion with his intimate circle at WOLFSSCHANZE at the end of February, expressing his relief at the end of winter. *Hitler Monologe*, p. 300 (26–27 Feb. 1942).
32. On the importance of Moscow see Reinhardt, *Moscow*; Robert M. Citino, *The German Way of War* (Lawrence, KS, 2005), pp. 290–305.
33. BA-MA, RH2/1521; Warlimont, *Hauptquartier*, pp. 222–3.

34. *ADAP*, ser. E, vol. I, pp. 17–21. The Führer and Ambassador Ōshima had a second meeting on 3 Jan. 1942 (*ADAP*, ser. E, vol. I, pp. 157–64). For Hitler's positive view of Ōshima see *Hitler Monologe*, p. 177 (4–5 Jan. 1942).
35. *ADAP*, ser. E, vol. I, pp. 260–2; *DRZW*, vol. 6, pp. 140–3; Warlimont, *Hauptquartier*, pp. 223–4.
36. *FRUS, 1942*, vol. 1, pp. 25–6.
37. On the ARCADIA conference see *FRUS, Conferences*, pp. 1–415; David J. Bercuson and Holger H. Herwig, *One Christmas in Washington: Roosevelt and Churchill Forge the Grand Alliance* (New York, 2006); J.M.A. Gwyer, *Grand Strategy*, vol. III, part 1 (London, 1964), pp. 349–401; Maurice Matloff and Edwin M. Snell, *Strategic Planning for Coalition Warfare, 1941–1942* (Washington, DC, 1980), pp. 97–122.
38. *FRUS, Conferences*, pp. 214–17, 'American-British Grand Strategy', 31 Dec.

# Select Bibliography


### ***Archives***

*British Archives*

Special Collections, Cadbury Research Library, University of Birmingham
Avon Papers: Anthony Eden Diaries

Borthwick Institute for Archives, University of York [BI]
Hickleton Papers: Lord Halifax Diaries

Churchill Archive Centre, Churchill College, Cambridge [CAC]
Alexander Cadogan Papers [ACAD]
Winston Churchill Papers [CHAR]
Ian Jacob Papers [JACB]
John Martin Papers [MART 1]
Lord Norwich (Duff Cooper) Papers [DUFC]
Stephen Roskill Papers [ROSK]

Imperial War Museum, London [IWM]
Lewis Heath Papers
Arthur Percival Papers

Imperial War Museum, Duxford [IWMD]
*Japanese AL Documents ('Japanese Archivist and Librarian Series')*
AL 7/1335 'Summary of Malay Landing Operational Plan by Japanese Navy'
AL 7/1336 'Malay Invasion Plan'
AL 8/5007 'Malaya Landing Operation'
AL 8/5008 'Statement re Southern Area invasion plans'
AL 17/5181 'The Summary of the Malayan Operations of the 5th Division'
AL 17/5182 'Outlines of Malayan Campaign by 18th Division'

*Japanese Monographs*
JM 11 'Philippines Air Operations Record: Phase One'
JM 24 'Southern Army Operations Record, Dec–41 to Aug–45'
JM 45 'Imperial General Headquarters Army High Command Record'
JM 97 'Pearl Harbor Operations: General Outline of Orders and Plans'
JM 102 'Submarine Operations Dec 41–Apr 42'
JM 105 'General Summary of Naval Operations, Southern Force'

JM 107 'Malaya Invasion Operations'
JM 147 'Political Strategy prior to the Outbreak of War', part III
JM 150 'Political Strategy prior to the Outbreak of War', part IV
JM 152 'Political Strategy prior to the Outbreak of War', part V
JM 177 'Thailand Operations Record (1941–1945)'

Liddell Hart Centre for Military Archives, Kings College, London [LHCMA]
Robert Brooke-Popham Papers
Henry Pownall Diary

The National Archives, Kew [TNA]
ADM 199 War of 1939–45, War History Cases
ADM 223 Naval Intelligence Division
ADM 234 Naval Staff History: Narratives and Battle Summaries
AIR 20 Air Ministry Unregistered Papers
AIR 23 Overseas Commands Papers
CAB 65 War Cabinet Minutes: Confidential Annexes
CAB 66 War Cabinet Papers
CAB 69 War Cabinet Defence Committee (Operations)
CAB 79 Chiefs of Staff Committee (Wartime) Minutes
CAB 80 Chiefs of Staff Committee (Wartime) Memoranda
CAB 81 Joint Intelligence Sub-Committee (Wartime) Minutes and Memoranda
CAB 84/3 Joint Planning Committee
CAB 106 Cabinet Office Historical Section Files
CAB 163/2 No. 30 Military Mission
FO 371 Foreign Office General Correspondence
HW 1 Intelligence for Prime Minister
HW 12 GCCS: BJ Series
PREM 3 Prime Minister's Office: Operational Correspondence and Papers
WO 106 DMO and Intelligence Papers
WO 172 War of 1939–45, Command War Diaries
WO 193 Wartime Directorate of Military Operations
WO 208 Wartime Directorate of Military Intelligence

### *German Archives*

Bundesarchiv-Militärarchiv, Freiburg im Breisgau [BA-MA]
RH 2 *Oberkommandos des Heeres*
RH 19 I *Heeresgruppe Süd*
RH 19 II *Heeresgruppe Mitte*
RH 21-2 *2 Panzerarmee*
RHD 7 *Amtdrucksachen*
RW 5 *Oberkommando der Wehrmacht*

### *United States Archives*

Columbia University Oral History Collection [CUOHC]
H. Kent Hewitt
Chester Nimitz
Frances Perkins

Franklin D. Roosevelt Presidential Library, Hyde Park, NY [FRPL]
President's Personal File
President's Secretary's File

Adolf Berle Papers
Harry Hopkins Papers
Henry Morgenthau Diaries
Pare Lorentz Chronology

Georgetown University Archive, Washington, DC
Harry Hopkins Papers

Library of Congress, Washington, DC
Frank Knox Papers

National Archives II, College Park, MD [NAII]
RG 38 Office of the Chief of Naval Operations
RG 59 Department of State
RG 80 Department of the Navy
RG 107 Office of the Secretary of War
RG 165 War Department General and Special Staffs
RG 225 Records of Joint Army and Navy Boards and Committees
RG 457 National Security Agency

Naval Operational Archive, Washington, DC [NAO]
Thomas Hart Papers
Chester Nimitz Papers

Yale University Library
Henry Stimson Diary

### Newspapers

*Japan Times and Advertiser* (Tokyo)
*New York Times*
*Pravda*
*Straits Times* (Singapore)
*The Times* (London)
*Völkischer Beobachter*

### Published primary sources: documents, diaries

#### General

Kimball, Warren F., ed., *Churchill and Roosevelt: The Complete Correspondence*, vol. 1 (Princeton, 1984) [*C&R*]

#### Britain

Alanbrooke, Lord, *War Diaries, 1939–1945*, ed. Alex Danchev and Daniel Todman (London, 2001)
Despatches (*Supplements to The London Gazette*)
Auchinleck, Sir Claude J.E., 'Operations in the Middle East from 1st November 1941 to 15th August 1942', no. 38177, 13 Jan. 1948, pp. 309–400
Brooke-Popham, Robert. 'Operations in the Far East from 17th October 1940 to 27th December 1941', no. 38183, 22 Jan. 1948, pp. 535–76
Maltby, C.M., 'Operations in Hong Kong from 8th to 25th December, 1941', no. 38190, 27 Jan. 1948, pp. 699–726
Maltby, Paul, 'Report on the Air Operations during the Campaigns in Malaya and the

Netherlands East Indies from 8th December 1941 to 12th March 1942', no. 38216, 26 Feb. 1948, pp. 1347–415
Percival, A.E., 'Operations of Malaya Command, from 8th December 1941 to 15th February 1942', no. 38215, 20 Feb. 1948, pp. 1245–346
Gilbert, Martin, ed., *The Churchill War Papers*, vol. 3 (London, 2000) [*CWP*]
Gorodetsky, Gabriel, ed., *Stafford Cripps in Moscow, 1940–1942: Diaries and Papers* (London, 2007)
Harvey, Oliver, *The War Diaries of Oliver Harvey* (London, 1978)
James, Robert Rhodes, *Chips: The Diaries of Sir Henry Channon* (London, 1996) [Channon, *Diaries*]
Nicholson, Harold, *Diaries and Letters*, vol. 2 (London, 1967)
*Principal War Telegrams and Memoranda, 1940–1943*, 7 vols, Cabinet Office, Cabinet History Series (Nendeln, Liechtenstein, 1976)
*Parliamentary Debates: House of Commons*

### Germany

*Akten zur deutschen auswärtigen Politik, 1918–1945*, series D, vols XI.1, XIII.2; series E, vol. I (Bonn, 1964, 1970; Göttingen, 1969) [*ADAP*]
Below, Nicolaus von, *Als Hitlers Adjutant 1937–45* (Mainz, 1980)
Bock, Fedor von, *Generalfeldmarschall Fedor von Bock: Zwischen Pflicht und Verweigerung – Das Kriegstagebuch* (Munich, 1995) [Bock, *KTB*]
Chapman, John W.M., ed., *The Price of Admiralty: The War Diary of the German Naval Attaché in Japan, 1939–1943*, vol. 4 (Ripe, Sussex, 1989)
Domarus, Max, ed., *Hitler: Reden und Proklamationen 1932–1945*, vol. II.2 (Leonberg, 1988) [*Hitler RP*]
Engel, Gerhard, *Heeresadjutant bei Hitler 1938–1943: Aufzeichnungen des Majors Engel* (Stuttgart, 1974)
Goebbels, Joseph, *Die Tagebücher von Joseph Goebbels*, ed. Elke Frölich, part II, vols 1, 2 and 3 (Munich, 1996) [*TBJG*]
Greiner, Helmuth, and Percy Ernst Schramm, eds, *Kriegstagebuch des Oberkommandos der Wehrmacht (Wehrmachtführungsstab) 1940–1945*, vol. 1 (Frankfurt, 1961) [*KTB OKW*]
Halder, Franz, *Kriegstagebuch: Tägliche Aufzeichnungen des Chefs des Generalstabes des Heeres, 1939–1942*, vol. 3 (Stuttgart, 1965) [Halder, *KTB*]
Hillgruber, Andreas, ed., *Staatsmänner und Diplomaten bei Hitler: Vertrauliche Aufzeichnungen über Unterredungen mit Vertretern des Auslandes 1939–1941*, vol. 1 (Frankfurt, 1967)
Hubatsch, W., ed., *Hitlers Weisungen für die Kriegführung 1939–1945: Dokumente des Oberkommandos der Wehrmacht* (Frankfurt, 1962) [*Hitlers Weisungen*]
Jochmann, Werner, ed., *Adolf Hitler: Monologe im Führer-Hauptquartier 1941–1944: Die Aufzeichnungen Heinrich Heims* (Hamburg, 1980) [*Hitler Monologe*]
*Kriegstagebuch der Seekriegsleitung 1939–1945*, part A, vols 27–8 (Bonn, 1991) [*KTB SKL*]
Wegmann, Günter, ed., '*Das Oberkommando der Wehrmacht gibt bekannt . . .': Der deutsche Wehrmachtbericht*, vol. 1 (Osnabrück, 1982) [*Wehrmachtbericht*]

### Italy

Ciano, Galeazzo, *Diary, 1937–1943* (London, 2002)
*I Documenti Diplomatici Italiani*, series 9, vol. 7 (Rome, 1987)
Mussolini, Benito, *Opera omnia di Benito Mussolini*, ed. Eduardo Susmel and Duilio Susmel, vols. 29–30 (Florence, 1959, 1960)

### Japan

Goldstein, Donald J., and Katherine V. Dillon, eds, *The Pearl Harbor Papers: Inside the Japanese Plans* (Washington, DC, 1993) [*PHP*]
Ike Nobutaka, ed., *Japan's Decision for War: Records of the 1941 Policy Conferences*, (Stanford, 1967) [*JDW*]
*Reports of General MacArthur*, vol. II, part I, *Japanese Operations in the Southwest Pacific Area* (Tokyo, 1950) [*RGM*]
Ugaki Matome, *Fading Victory: The Diary of Admiral Matome Ugaki, 1941–1943* (Pittsburgh, 1991)

### Poland

*Documents on Polish-Soviet Relations, 1939–1945* (London, 1961) [*DPSR*]

### Russia

Arbatov, G.A. *et al.*, ed., *Sovetsko-amerikanskie otnoshenie vo vremia Velikoi Otechestvennoi voiny 1941–1945: Dokumenty i materialy*, vol. 1 (Moscow, 1984) [*SAmO*]
Grylev, A.N. ed., *Boevoi sostav Sovetskoi armii*, part 1 (Moscow, 1963)
Gurov, A.A. *et al.*, eds, *G.K. Zhukov v bitve pod Moskvoi: Sbornik dokumentov* (Moscow, 1994)
Korotkov, A.V. *et al.*, eds, 'Posetiteli kremlevskogo kabineta I.V. Stalina: Zhurnaly (tetradi) zapisi lits, priniatykh pervym gensekom 1924–1953 gg.', *Istoricheskii arkhiv*, 2 (1996), pp. 3–72.
Kudriashov, S., ed., *Voina: 1941–1945* (Moscow, 2010)
*Moskva prifrontovaia, 1941–1942: Arkhivnye dokumenty i materialy* (Moscow, 2001)
*Moskva voennaia, 1941–1945. Memuary i arkhivnye dokumenty* (Moscow, 1995)
Parrish, Michael, ed., *Battle for Moscow: The 1942 Soviet General Staff Study* (Washington, DC, 1989)
*Russikii Arkhiv: Velikaia Otechestvennaia* [*RA/VO*]
vol. 2(1) *Prikazy Narodnogo Komissara Oborony SSSR* (Moscow, 1997)
vol. 4(1) *Bitva pod Moskvoi: Sbornik dokumentov* (Moscow, 1997)
vol. 5(1) *Stavka VGK: Dokumenty i materialy* (Moscow, 1996)
vol. 12(1) *General'nyi shtab v gody Velikoi Otechestvennoi voiny: Dokumenty i materialy 1941 god* (Moscow, 1997)
Rzheshevskii, O.A., ed., *Voina i diplomatiia: Dokumenty, kommentarii 1941–1942* (Moscow, 1997) [*ViD*]
Shaposhnikov, B.M. *et al.*, eds, *Razgrom nemetskikh voisk pod Moskvoi: Moskovskaia operatsiia Zapadnogo front 16 noiabria 1941 g.–31 ianvaria 1942 g.* (Moscow, 2006)
*Soobshcheniia Sovetskogo Informbiuro*, vol. 1 (Moscow, 1944)
*Sovetsko-angliiskie otnosheniia vo vremia Velikoi Otechestvennoi voiny, 1941–1945: dokumenty i materialy*, 2 vols (Moscow, 1983) [*SAO*]
Zhilin, V.A. *et al.*, eds, *Bitva pod Moskvoi: Khronika, fakty, liudi*, 2 vols (Moscow, 2002) [*BPM*]

### United States

*Congressional Record*
*Department of State Bulletin*
*Foreign Relations of the United States* [*FRUS*]
*1941*, vol. 1 *General, The Soviet Union* (Washington, DC, 1958)
*1941*, vol. 4 *The Far East* (Washington, DC, 1956)
*1941*, vol. 5 *The Far East* (Washington, DC, 1956)

*1942*, vol. 1 *General, The British Commonwealth, the Far East* (Washington, DC, 1960)
*The Conferences at Washington, 1941–1942, and Casablanca, 1943* (Washington, DC, 1968)
*Japan, 1931–1941*, vol. 1 (Washington, DC, 1943)
*Japan, 1931–1941*, vol. 2 (Washington, DC, 1943)
*Hearings before the Joint Committee on the Investigation of the Pearl Harbor Attack*, 39 parts (Washington, DC, 1946) [*PHA*]
*Investigation of the Pearl Harbor Attack: Report of the Joint Committee on the Investigation of the Pearl Harbor Attack, Congress of the United States* (Washington, DC, 1946) [*JC Report*]
*The 'Magic' Background to Pearl Harbor* (Washington, DC, 1977), vols III, IV and V [*MBPH*]
Ross, Steven T., ed., *American War Plans: 1919–1941*, vols 4–5 (New York, 1992)

## BOOKS AND ARTICLES

Agawa Hiroyuki, *The Reluctant Admiral: Yamamoto and the Imperial Navy* (Tokyo, 1979)
Aldrich, Richard J., *Intelligence and the War against Japan: Britain, America and the Politics of Secret Service* (Cambridge, 2000)
——*The Key to the South: Britain, the United States and Thailand during the Approach of the Pacific War, 1929–42* (Oxford, 1993)
Allen, Louis, *Singapore: 1941–1942* (London, 1993)
Anders, W., *An Army in Exile: The Story of the Second Polish Corps* (London, 1949)
Anfilov, V.A., *Krushenie pokhoda Gitlera na Moskvu 1941* (Moscow, 1989)
Barnett, Correlli, *Engage the Enemy More Closely: The Royal Navy in the Second World War* (London, 1991)
Bartsch, William H., *December 8, 1941: MacArthur's Pearl Harbor* (College Station, TX, 2003)
Bell, Christopher M., 'The "Singapore Strategy" and the Deterrence of Japan: Winston Churchill, the Admiralty, and the Dispatch of Force Z', *English Historical Review* 116 (2001), pp. 604–34.
Best, Antony, *Britain, Japan and Pearl Harbor: Avoiding War in East Asia, 1936–41* (London, 1995)
——*British Intelligence and the Japanese Challenge in Asia, 1914–41* (Basingstoke, 2002)
Bhargava, K.D., and K.N.V. Sastri, *Campaigns in South-East Asia, 1941–42. Official History of the Indian Armed Forces in the Second World War* (New Delhi, 1960)
Bix, Herbert P., *Hirohito and the Making of Modern Japan* (London, 2000)
Blair, Clay, *Silent Victory: The U.S. Submarine War against Japan* (Philadelphia, 1975)
Bloch, Michael, *Ribbentrop* (London, 1992)
Blumentritt, Günther, 'Moscow', in W. Kreipe, ed, *The Fatal Decisions* (London, 1956), pp. 29–74
Bond, Brian, and Kyoichi Tachikawa, eds, *British and Japanese Military Leadership in the Far Eastern War, 1941–45* (London, 2004)
Borg, Dorothy, and Okamoto Shumpei, eds, *Pearl Harbor as History: Japanese-American Relations, 1931–1941* (New York, 1973)
Boyd, Carl, *Hitler's Japanese Confidant: General Ōshima Hiroshi and MAGIC Intelligence, 1941–1945* (Lawrence, KS, 1993)
Braithwaite, Rodric, *Moscow 1941: A City and its People at War* (London, 2006)
Browning, Christopher R., *The Origins of the Final Solution: The Evolution of Nazi Jewish Policy, September 1939–March 1942* (London, 2005)
Budiansky, Steven, *Battle of Wits: The Complete Story of Codebreaking in World War II* (New York, 2002)
Bussemaker, Herman Theodore, 'Paradise, in Peril: The Netherlands, Great Britain, and the Defence of the Netherlands ,ast Indies', *Journal of Southeast Asian Studies* 31:1 (2000), pp. 115–36.

Butow, Robert, *Tojo and the Coming of War* (Princeton, 1961)
Chung, Ong Chit, *Operation Matador: Britain's War Plans against the Japanese 1918–1941* (Singapore, 1997)
Churchill, Winston S., *The Second World War*, vol. 3 (London, 1950) [*SWW*]
Compton, James, *The Swastika and the Eagle: Hitler, the United States, and the Origins of the Second World War* (London, 1967)
Costello, John, *Days of Infamy: MacArthur, Roosevelt, Churchill – the Shocking Truth Revealed* (New York, 1995)
Cowman, Ian, *Dominion or Decline: Anglo-American Naval Relations in the Pacific, 1937–1941* (Oxford, 1996)
Craven, Wesley F., and James L. Cate, eds, *Plans and Early Operations: January 1939 to August 1942. The Army Air Forces in World War II*, vol. 1 (Chicago, 1948)
*Das Deutsche Reich und der Zweite Weltkrieg*, vols 4 and 6 (Stuttgart, 1983, 1990) [*DRZW*]
Dunn, Walter S., *Stalin's Keys to Victory: The Rebirth of the Red Army* (Westport, CN, 2006)
Eden, Anthony, *The Eden Memoirs*, vol. 3 (London, 1965)
Erickson, John, *The Road to Stalingrad* (New York, 1975)
Evans, David C., and Mark R. Peattie, *Kaigun: Strategy, Tactics, and Technology in the Imperial Japanese Navy, 1887–1941* (Annapolis, 1997)
Farrell, Brian P., ed., *The Defence and Fall of Singapore* (Stroud, UK, 2005)
——*Sixty Years On: The Fall of Singapore Revisited* (Singapore, 2002)
Ferris, John. '"Worthy of Some Better Enemy?": The British Estimate of the Imperial Japanese Army 1919–41 and the Fall of Singapore', *Canadian Journal of History* 28:2 (1993), pp. 223–56
Fleming, Thomas. 'The Big Leak', *American Heritage* 38:8 (December 1987), pp. 64–71
Förster, Jürgen, *Die Wehrmacht im NS-Staat: Eine strukturgeschichtliche Analyse* (Munich, 2007)
Gerlach, Christian. 'The Wannsee Conference, the Fate of German Jews, and Hitler's Decision in Principle to Exterminate All European Jews', *Journal of Modern History* 70:4 (1998), pp. 759–812
Gilbert, Martin, *Winston S. Churchill*, vol. 6 (London, 1986)
Glantz, David, *Colossus Reborn: The Red Army at War 1941–1943* (Lawrence, KS, 2005)
Guderian, Heinz, *Erinnerungen eines Soldaten* (Heidelberg, 1951)
Gwyer, J.M.A., *Grand Strategy*, vol. 3, part 1 (London, 1964)
Haggie, Paul, *Britannia at Bay: The Defence of the British Empire against Japan, 1931–1941* (Oxford, 1981)
Hanyok, Robert J., and David P. Mowry, *West Wind Clear: Cryptology and the Winds Message Controversy – A Documentary History* (Fort George Meade, MD, 2008)
Hayashi Saburo, and Alvin D. Coox, *Kōgun: The Japanese Army in the Pacific War* (Westport, CN, 1978)
Hayes, Grace Person, *The History of the Joint Chiefs of Staff in World War II: The War against Japan* (Annapolis, 1982)
Heinrichs, Waldo H., *American Ambassador: Joseph C. Grew and the Development of the United States Diplomatic Tradition* (New York, 1986)
——*Threshold of War: Franklin D. Roosevelt and American Entry into World War II* (New York, 1988)
Henderson, Nicholas. 'Hitler's Biggest Blunder', *History Today* 43 (April 1993), pp. 35–43
Herde, Peter, 'Italien, Deutschland und der Weg in den Krieg im Pazifik 1941', in *Sitzungberichte der wissenschaftlichen Gesellschaft an der Johann Wolfgang Goethe Universität Frankfurt am Main* XX:1 (1983)
Herwig, Holger H., *Politics of Frustration: The United States in German Naval Planning, 1889–1941* (Boston, 1976)
Hillgruber, Andreas, *Hitlers Strategie: Politik und Kriegsführung, 1940–1941* (Frankfurt, 1965)

Hinsley, F.H. *et al.*, *British Intelligence in the Second World War: its Influence on Strategy and Operations*, vol. II (London, 1981)
Hoehling, A.A., *The Week before Pearl Harbor* (New York, 1963)
Hofmann, Rudolf. 'Die Schlacht von Moskau', in *Entscheidungsschlachten des Zweiten Weltkrieges*, ed. H.-A. Jacobsen and J. Rohwer (Frankfurt, 1960), pp. 139–84
Hough, Frank O. *et al.*, *History of U.S. Marine Corps Operations in World War II*, vol. 1 (Washington, 1958)
Ickes, Harold L., *The Secret Diary of Harold L. Ickes*, vol. 3 (London, 1955)
Irving, David, *Churchill's War*, vol. 2 (London, 2001)
——*Hitler's War*, vol. 1, *1939–1942* (London, 1977)
Jäckel, Eberhard, 'Die deutsche Kriegserklärung an die Vereinigten Staaten von 1941', in *Im Dienste Deutschlands und des Rechts: Festschrift für Wilhelm G. Grewe etc.*, ed. F.J. Kroneck and T. Oppermann (Baden-Baden, 1981), pp. 117–37
James, D. Clayton, *The Years of MacArthur*, vols 1 and 2 (Boston, 1970, 1975)
Kawamura Noriko, 'Emperor Hirohito and Japan's Decision to Go to War with the United States: Reexamined', *Diplomatic History* 31:1 (2007), pp. 51–80
Keitel, Wilhelm, *Mein Leben: Pflichterfüllung bis zum Untergang*, ed. Werner Maser (Berlin, 1998)
Kirby, S. Woodburn *et al.*, *The War Against Japan*, vol. 1 (London, 1957)
Kirkpatrick, Charles E., *An Unknown Future and a Doubtful Present: Writing the Victory Plan of 1941* (Washington, DC, 1990)
Komatsu Keiichiro, *Origins of the Pacific War and the Importance of 'Magic'* (Richmond, Surrey, 1999)
Kot, Stanislaw, *Conversations with the Kremlin and Dispatches from Russia* (London, 1963)
Krebs, Gerhard, *Japans Deutschlandpolitik 1935–1941: Eine Studie zur Vorgeschichte des Pazifischen Kieges*, 2 vols (Hamburg, 1984)
Lambert, John W., and Norman Polmar, *Defenseless: Command Failures at Pearl Harbor* (St Paul, MN, 2003)
Langer, William L., and S. Everett Gleason, *The Undeclared War, 1940–1941* (New York, 1953)
Large, Stephen S., *Emperor Hirohito and Shōwa Japan: A Political Biography* (London, 1992)
Layton, Edwin T., *And I Was There: Pearl Harbor and Midway – Breaking the Secrets* (New York, 1985)
Leutze, James, *A Different Kind of Victory: A Biography of Admiral Thomas C. Hart* (Annapolis, 1971)
Löffler, Jürgen, *Walther von Brauchitsch (1881–1948): Eine politische Biographie* (Frankfurt, 2001)
Lundstrom, John B., *The First South Pacific Campaign: Pacific Fleet Strategy, December 1941–June 1942* (Annapolis, 1976)
Magenheimer, Heinz, *Moskau 1941: Entscheidungsschlacht im Osten* (Selent, 2009)
Marder, Arthur J., *Old Friends, New Enemies: The Royal Navy and the Imperial Japanese Navy*, vol. 1 (Oxford, 1981)
Marston, Daniel, ed., *The Pacific War Companion: From Pearl Harbor to Hiroshima* (Oxford, 2005)
Matloff, Maurice, and Edwin M. Snell, *Strategic Planning for Coalition Warfare, 1941–1942* (Washington, DC, 1980)
Mawdsley, Evan, *Thunder in the East: The Nazi-Soviet War* (London, 2005)
Megargee, Geoffrey P., *Inside Hitler's High Command* (Lawrence, KS, 2000)
Miller, Edward S., *War Plan Orange: The U.S. Strategy to Defeat Japan, 1897–1945* (Annapolis, 1991)
Mirkina, A.D. and V.S. Iarovikov, eds, *Marshal Zhukov: Polkovodets i chelovek*, 2 vols (Moscow, 1988)
Morison, Samuel Eliot, *History of the United States Naval Operations in World War II*, vols 1 and 3 (London, 1947, 1948)

Morley, James W., ed., *The Fateful Choice: Japan's Advance into Southeast Asia, 1939–1941* (New York, 1980)
Morton, Louis, *Fall of the Philippines. The U.S. Army in World War II* (Washington, 1953)
——*Strategy and Command: The First Two Years. The U.S. Army in World War II* (Washington, 1961)
O'Connor, Raymond, ed., *The Japanese Navy in World War II* (Annapolis, 1972)
Offner, Arnold A., *The Origins of the Second World War: American Foreign Policy and World Politics, 1917–1941* (Malabar, FL, 1986)
Pavlenko, N.D., 'Polkovodets za "kruglym stolom"', in A.D. Mirkina and V.S. Iarovikov, eds, *Marshal Zhukov* (Moscow, 1988), vol. 2, pp. 146–62.
Percival, A.E., *The War in Malaya* (London, 1949)
Playfair, I.S.O., *The Mediterranean and the Middle East*, vol. 3 (London, 1960)
Pogue, Forrest, *George C. Marshall: Ordeal and Hope, 1939–1942* (London, 1968)
Prados, John, *Combined Fleet Decoded: The Secret History of American Intelligence and the Japanese Navy in World War II* (Annapolis, 1995)
Prange, Gordon, *At Dawn We Slept: The Untold Story of Pearl Harbor* (Harmondsworth, 1991)
Reinhardt, Klaus, *Moscow: The Turning Point* (Oxford, 1992)
Reynolds, David, *The Creation of the Anglo-American Alliance, 1937–1941: A Study in Competitive Co-operation* (London, 1981)
Rich, Norman, *Hitler's War Aims*, vol. 1 (New York, 1973)
Roberts, Geoffrey, *Stalin's Wars: From World War to Cold War, 1939–1953* (New Haven and London, 2006)
Rohwer, Jürgen, *Chronology of the War at Sea 1939–1945: The Naval History of World War Two* (3rd edn, London, 2005)
Rohwer, Jürgen and Eberhard Jäcker, eds, *Kriegswende Dezember 1941* (Koblenz, 1984)
Rokossovskii, K.K., *Soldatskii dolg* (Moscow, 1997)
Samsonov, A.M., *Porazhenie Vermakhta pod Moskvoi* (Moscow, 1981)
Seaton, Albert, *The Battle for Moscow, 1941–1942* (London, 1971)
——*Stalin as Warlord* (London, 1976)
Shores, Christopher, and Brian Cull, *Bloody Shambles*, vol. 1 (London, 1992)
Snow, Philip, *The Fall of Hong Kong: Britain, China, and the Japanese Occupation* (New Haven and London, 2003)
Sokolovskii, V.D., ed., *Razgrom nemetsko-fashistskikh voisk pod Moskvoi* (Moscow, 1964)
Stafford, David, *Churchill and Secret Service* (London, 1997)
Stinnett, Robert B., *Day of Deceit: The Truth about FDR and Pearl Harbor* (New York, 2001)
Svetlishin, N.A., *Krutye stupeni sud'by: Zhizn' i ratnye podvigi marshala G.K. Zhukova* (Khabarovsk, 1992)
Tagaya, Osamu, *Mitsubishi Type 1 Rikko 'Betty' Units of World War 2* (Botley, Oxford, 2001)
Thomas, David, 'Foreign Armies East and Germany Military Intelligence in Russia, 1941–1945', *Journal of Contemporary History* 22 (1987), pp. 261–302
Tolley, Kemp, *The Cruise of the Lanikai: Incitement to War* (Annapolis, 1973)
Tsuji Masanobu, *Singapore: The Japanese Version of the Malayan Campaign of World War II* (Singapore, 1988)
Utley, Jonathan G., *Going to War with Japan, 1937–1941* (Knoxville, TN, 1985)
Vasilevskii, A.M., *Delo vsei zhizni*, vol. 1 (6th edn, Moscow, 1989)
*Velikaia Otechestvennaia voina 1941–1945: Entsiklopediia* (Moscow, 1985)
Warlimont, Walter, *Im Hauptquartier des deutschen Wehrmacht 1939–1945* (3rd edn, Munich, 1978)
Watson, Mark S., *Chief of Staff: Prewar Plans and Preparations* (Washington, DC, 1950)
Weinberg, Gerhard L., 'Pearl Harbor: The German Perspective', in *Germany, Hitler, and World War II: Essays in Modern German and World History* (Cambridge, 1995), pp. 18–23
——*World in the Balance: Behind the Scenes of World War II* (Hanover, NH, 1981)

Weizsäcker, Ernst von, *Erinnerungen* (Munich, 1950)
Wetzler, Peter, *Hirohito and War: Imperial Tradition and Military Decision Making in Prewar Japan* (Honolulu, 1998)
Willmott, H.P., *Empires in the Balance: Japanese and Allied Pacific Strategies to April 1942* (Annapolis, 1982)
Wohlstetter, Roberta, *Pearl Harbor: Warning and Decision* (Stanford, 1962)
Woodward, Llewellyn, *British Foreign Policy in the Second World War*, vol. 2 (London, 1971)
Zhukov, G.K., *Vospominaniia i razmyshleniia*, vol. 2 (10th edn, Moscow, 1990) [*ViR*]
Ziemke, Earl F., and Magna Bauer, *Moscow to Stalingrad: Decisions in the East* (Washington, DC, 1987)
Zimmerman, J.C., 'Pearl Harbor Revisionism: Robert Stinnett's *Day of Deceit*', *Intelligence and National Security* 17:2 (2002), pp. 127–46
Zolotarev, V.A. *et al.*, eds, *Velikaia Otechestvennaia voina, 1941–1945: Voenno-istoricheskie ocherki*, vol. 1 (Moscow, 1998) [*VOV/VIO*]

# Index